A DIGEST

OF THE

LAW OF AGENCY.

BY

WILLIAM BOWSTEAD,

OF THE MIDDLE TEMPLE, BARRISTER-AT-LAW;

Formerly Holder of Studentship and First Certificate of Honour of the Council of Legal Education;

Constitutional Law and Legal History Prizeman;

Senior Real Property Scholar of the Middle Temple.

THE LAWBOOK EXCHANGE, LTD.

Clark, New Jersey

2007

ISBN-13: 978-1-58477-700-7
ISBN-10: 1-58477-700-1

The quality of this reprint is equivalent to the quality of the original work.

THE LAWBOOK EXCHANGE, LTD.
33 Terminal Avenue
Clark, New Jersey 07066-1321

Please see our website for a selection of our other publications and fine facsimile reprints of classic works of legal history:
www.lawbookexchange.com

Library of Congress Cataloging-in-Publication Data

Bowstead, William, d. 1935.
A digest of the law of agency / William Bowstead.
p. cm.
Originally published: London : Sweet & Maxwell, 1896.
Includes bibliographical references and index.
ISBN-13: 978-1-58477-700-7 (alk. paper)
ISBN-10: 1-58477-700-1 (alk. paper)
1. Agency (Law)--Great Britain. I. Title.
KD2020.B69 2006
346.4102'9--dc22

2006002537

Printed in the United States of America on acid-free paper

A DIGEST

OF THE

LAW OF AGENCY.

BY

WILLIAM BOWSTEAD,

OF THE MIDDLE TEMPLE, BARRISTER-AT-LAW;

Formerly Holder of Studentship and First Certificate of Honour of the Council of Legal Education;

Constitutional Law and Legal History Prizeman;

Senior Real Property Scholar of the Middle Temple.

LONDON:

SWEET & MAXWELL, LTD., 3, CHANCERY LANE,

Law Publishers.

MANCHESTER: MEREDITH, RAY & LITTLER;

DUBLIN: HODGES, FIGGIS & CO., LTD., AND E. PONSONBY;

MELBOURNE AND SYDNEY: C. F. MAXWELL.

1896

LONDON:
PRINTED BY C. F. ROWORTH, GREAT NEW STREET, FETTER LANE, E.C.

PREFACE.

My object in writing this Digest has been to reduce the English Law of Agency to a concise statement of definite rules and principles, illustrated by decided cases. While I have thus attempted by the form of the Work to facilitate the study of the law, I have at the same time endeavoured, by referring to practically all the reported cases bearing on the subject, and by appending a full and comprehensive Index, to render the Work useful to practitioners for purposes of reference.

W. BOWSTEAD.

Temple,

January, 1896.

TABLE OF CONTENTS.

PAGE

Preface - - - - - - - iii
Table of Cases - - - - - - - xv

CHAP.

I.—Preliminary - - - - - - 1
II.—Implied Agency of Married Women, &c. - - 13
III.—Appointment of Agents - - - - 29
IV.—The Doctrine of Ratification - - - - 34
V.—Authority of Agents - - - - 50
VI.—Duties of Agents - - - - - - 88
VII.—Liabilities of Agents to their Principals - 126
VIII.—Rights of Agents against their Principals - - 149
IX.—Relations between the Principal and Third Persons - - - - - - 205
X.—Relations between Agents and Third Persons - 270
XI.—Determination of Agency - - - - 319

Appendix.—Factors Act, 1889 - - - - - 335

CHAPTER I.

Preliminary.

ART.

1. Definitions - - - - - - - 1
2. *Del credere* agency - - - - - - 2
3. Capacity to act as principal - - - - 4
4. Capacity to act as agent - - - - - 5
5. For what purposes an agent may be appointed - - 7
6. Co-agents - - - - - - - - 8
7. How the relation of agency arises - - - - 10
8. Doctrine of holding out - - - - - 12

CHAPTER II.

Implied Agency of Married Women, &c.

ART. PAGE

9. Presumption of authority from cohabitation - - 14
10. Implied authority as housekeeper - - - - - 16
11. *Primâ facie*, no authority where separated - - 17
12. Where separated by mutual consent - - - - 18
13. Where living apart without the husband's consent - 21
14. Where living apart in consequence of husband's misconduct, &c. - - - - - - 21
15. Effect of adultery by the wife - - - - - - 24
16. Implied authority to acknowledge debts for necessaries - 26
17. Husband not liable unless credit given to him - - 26
18. Authority implied from cohabitation as man and wife - 27
19. Child no implied authority to pledge parents' credit - 28

CHAPTER III.

Appointment of Agents.

20. Authority to execute a deed - - - - 29
21. Appointment in other cases - - - - - 29
22. Appointment by corporations - - - - 31

CHAPTER IV.

The Doctrine of Ratification.

23. Ratification equivalent to previous authority - - 34
24. What acts may be ratified - - - - - 35
25. Who may ratify - - - - - - 37
26. Circumstances under which, and within what time, an act may be ratified - - - - - - 39
27. Conditions necessary for ratification - - - 41
28. How an act may be ratified - - - - - 43
Ratification by companies - - - - 44
29. Effect of ratification - - - - - - 46

CHAPTER V.

AUTHORITY OF AGENTS.

ART. PAGE

30. Authority cannot exceed powers of principal - - 50
31. Construction of authority given in general terms - - 51
32. Authority conferred in ambiguous terms - - - 53
33. Construction of powers of attorney - - - - 54
34. Construction of authority not given under seal - - 56

IMPLIED AUTHORITY.

35. To do what is necessary for or incidental to effective execution of express authority - - - - - 57
36. Implied authority of general agents - - - 59
37. Implied authority where employed in course of business as agent - - - - - - - 62
38. Authority implied from special customs - - - 65

Implied Authority of particular classes of Agents as incidental to their employment.

(1) Factors - - - - - - 68
(2) Brokers - - - - - - - 69
(3) Auctioneers - - - - - 71
(4) Counsel - - - - - - 72
(5) Solicitors - - - - - - 73
(6) Shipmasters - - - - - - 74

39. Delegation of authority - - - - - 80
40. Principal and sub-agent - - - - - 83

CHAPTER VI.

DUTIES OF AGENT.

41. Duty to perform his undertaking - - - - 88
42. Duty to obey instructions, or act according to usage and for principal's benefit - - - - - - 88
43. Duty to keep principal's property separate, and to preserve correct accounts - - - - - 91

CHAPTER VI.—DUTIES OF AGENT—*continued.*

ART. PAGE

44. Duty to exercise due skill, care and diligence - - - 93
45. Duty to pay over money received to use of principal - 96
46. Estopped from denying principal's title - - - 99

Duties arising from the Fiduciary Character of the Relationship.

47. Duty to make full disclosure where any personal interest 102
48. Agent who purchases property, as such, in own name, is a trustee - - - - - - - - 106
49. Duty to make full disclosure where he deals with the principal - - - - - - - 107
50. Duty to account in equity - - - - - 111
51. Duty to account for all secret profits - - - 114

Special Duties of Particular Classes of Agents.

(1) Factors - - - - - - - 120
(2) Brokers - - - - - - - 121
(3) Shipmasters - - - - - 122
(4) Auctioneers - - - - - - - 122
(5) Solicitors - - - - - - 123

CHAPTER VII.

LIABILITIES OF AGENTS TO THEIR PRINCIPALS.

52. In respect of contracts entered into on behalf of the principal - - - - - - - 126
53. Liability on bills of exchange signed without qualification 127
54. Liability for negligence and other breaches of duty - 128
55. Measure of damages for negligence or other breach of duty 137
56. Liability of agents accepting bribes - - - 139
57. Where liable to pay interest - - - - - 141
58. Liability to attachment - - - - - 142
59. Liability for acts of sub-agents - - - - 143
60. Rights of principal on agent's bankruptcy - - 144

CHAPTER VIII.

RIGHTS OF AGENTS AGAINST THEIR PRINCIPALS.

Section 1.

RIGHT OF REMUNERATION.

ART. PAGE

61. Founded on an express or implied contract - - - 149
62. Commission only on transactions directly resulting from the agency - - - - - - - 152
63. Remuneration may be payable though the principal acquires no benefit - - - - - - - 156
64. Principal liable in damages if he wrongfully prevents agent from earning remuneration - - - - 159
65. No remuneration in respect of illegal or wagering transactions - - - - - - - 164
66. No remuneration in cases of misconduct or breach of duty 166

Section 2.

RIGHTS OF REIMBURSEMENT AND INDEMNITY.

67. Indemnity from all liabilities, and reimbursement of all expenses, incurred in course of agency - - - 169
68. Liabilities incurred under rules or usages of particular markets - - - - - - - 172
69. No indemnity or reimbursement in respect of illegal, wagering, or unauthorized transactions, or of liabilities or expenses incurred in consequence of own default - 175

Section 3.

RIGHT OF LIEN.

70. Definitions of particular and general possessory liens - 180
71. Possessory lien of agents - - - - - 180
72. Confined to rights of principal, except in the case of money or negotiable securities - - - - - - 188
73. Lien of sub-agents - - - - - - 191

    Solicitor's charging lien on property recovered or preserved through his instrumentality - - - - 193

    Shipmaster's lien - - - - - - 197
74. How lien extinguished - - - - - 198

Section 4.

RIGHTS OF STOPPAGE IN TRANSITU, *INTERPLEADER, AND ACCOUNT.*

ART.		PAGE
75.	Right of stoppage *in transitu* - - - -	200
76.	Right to interplead - - - - - -	201
77.	Right to an account - - - - -	203
78.	No right to sue principal on contracts entered into on his behalf - - - - - -	204

CHAPTER IX.

RELATIONS BETWEEN THE PRINCIPAL AND THIRD PERSONS.

Section 1.

WHAT ACTS OF AGENTS BIND THEIR PRINCIPALS.

79.	Acts within scope of apparent authority - - -	205
80.	Not bound by acts beyond scope of authority, or not done in course of employment - - - -	208
81.	Dealings with money and negotiable securities - -	212
82.	Dealings protected by the Factors Act, 1889 - -	213
83.	Lien of consignee for advances to apparent owner of goods	217
84.	No unauthorized act binding with respect to persons with notice - - - - - - -	218
85.	Holding out another as agent - - - -	219

Section 2.

RIGHTS AND LIABILITIES OF THE PRINCIPAL ON CONTRACTS MADE BY AGENT.

86.	May sue or be sued in own name - - - -	222
87.	Foreign principals - - - - -	224
88.	Deeds - - - - - - -	225
89.	Bills, notes and cheques - - - - -	226
90.	Broker's bought and sold notes - - - -	228
91.	Effect of particular customs or usages - - -	229
92.	Effect on right to sue the principal of giving credit to or obtaining judgment against the agent - - -	230

CHAP. XI.—*continued.*

ART. PAGE

93. How far right of recourse to principal affected by a settlement between principal and agent - - - 233
94. Right of undisclosed principal to sue in own name - - 235
95. Fraud, misrepresentations, or knowledge of agent may be set up in an action by the principal - - - 236
96. How far principal bound by payment to, or settlement with, or set-off against agent - - - - 238

Section 3.

LIABILITY OF THE PRINCIPAL FOR TORTS OF AGENT.

97. Principal liable for all agent's torts in course of employment on his behalf - - - - - 245
98. Money, &c., misappropriated by agent - - - 250
99. Principal not liable for wrongs outside course of employment on his behalf - - - - - 251
100. How far liable for intentional wrongs by agent - - 255
101. How far liable for misrepresentations believed by agent to be true - - - - - - 258
102. Not liable for misrepresentations by agent as to credit, &c., of third persons - - - - - 260

Section 4.

ADMISSIONS BY AND NOTICE TO AGENT.

103. How far agent's admissions evidence against the principal - - - - - - - 260
104. Doctrine of constructive notice - - - - 264
Constructive Notice to Purchasers for Value. - 267
105. Rights of principal where agent bribed - - - 268

CHAPTER X.

Relations between Agents and Third Persons.

Section 1.

LIABILITIES OF AGENTS IN RESPECT OF CONTRACTS MADE BY THEM.

ART.		PAGE
106.	Public agents not liable on contracts made as such	270
107.	Agent liable if he contracts personally, but not if he contracts merely as an agent	272
108.	Liability on contracts under seal	277
109.	Liability on bills of exchange, promissory notes and cheques	278
110.	Other written contracts	281
111.	Admissibility of parol evidence of intention	285
112.	Verbal contracts	287
113.	Liable if shown to be the real principal	288
114.	Liability when no principal in existence	289
115.	Implied warranty of authority	289
116.	Measure of damages for breach of warranty of authority	293

Section 2.

LIABILITIES OF AGENTS IN RESPECT OF MONEYS RECEIVED BY THEM.

117.	Money paid by third persons	297
118.	Money received to use of third persons	301

Section 3.

RIGHTS OF AGENTS AGAINST THIRD PERSONS.

119.	Right of agent to sue in own name on contracts made by him	303
120.	Effect of intervention of or settlement with the principal	307
121.	Defences available where agent sues in own name	310
122.	Right of agent to sue for money paid by mistake, &c.	310
123.	No right of action for promised bribes	311

CHAP. X.—*continued.*

Section 4.

LIABILITIES OF AGENTS IN RESPECT OF TORTS COMMITTED ON PRINCIPAL'S BEHALF.

ART.		PAGE
124.	Agent personally liable for all wrongs committed by him	311
125.	Conversion by innocent agent - - - -	314
126.	Agents not liable for torts of co-agents or sub-agents -	318

CHAPTER XI.

DETERMINATION OF AGENCY.

127.	Determination by effluxion of time, &c. - - -	319
128.	How agent's authority may be determined - - -	320
129.	When authority irrevocable - - - -	320
130.	Powers of attorney irrevocable in favour of purchasers for value - - - - - - -	324
131.	Revocation of authority by death or insanity - -	326
132.	Revocation of authority by bankruptcy of principal - -	327
133.	Determination of authority by notice of revocation or renunciation - - - - - -	329
134.	When notice of revocation to third persons necessary -	332
135.	Protection of agent acting under power of attorney without notice of revocation - - - - -	333

TABLE OF CASES.

Abbott, Ex parte, 263.
Abel *v.* Sutton, 51, 211.
Aberdeen Rail. Co. *v.* Blakie, 103.
Abraham *v.* Deakin, 253.
Acey *v.* Fernie, 60, 209.
Adams, Ex parte, 195.
——— *v.* Hall, 288.
Adamson *v.* Jarvis, 177.
Adansonia Fibre Co., Re, 228.
Addison *v.* Gandassequi, 231.
Aggs *v.* Nicholson, 228, 281.
Alder *v.* Boyle, 159.
Alexander *v.* Gibson, 58.
——— *v.* Mackenzie, 218.
——— *v.* Sizer, 281.
——— *v.* Southey, 318.
Alfred, The, 76.
Allan *v.* Miller, 280.
Allen *v.* Denstone, 261.
——— *v.* L. & S. W. Rail. Co., 62, 253.
Alley *v.* Hotson, 321.
Allkins *v.* Jupe, 165, 176.
Alson *v.* Sylvester, 126.
Ancona *v.* Marks, 36.
Anderson *v.* Sanderson, 262.
——— *v.* Watson, 48, 313.
Anglo-Maltese Hydraulic Dock Co., Re, 189.
Angus *v.* Maclachlan, 199.
Antrobus *v.* Wickens, 156.
Appleton *v.* Binks, 277.
Archer's case, 114, 118.
Armstrong *v.* Stokes, 234.
Arnold *v.* Mayor of Poole, 32.
Arnot *v.* Biscoe, 313.
Arthur *v.* Barton, 75, 76.
Ashbury Carriage Co. *v.* Riche, 36.
Aste *v.* Montague, 333.
Atkins *v.* Carwood, 15.
Atkyns *v.* Amber, 308.
——— *v.* Pearce, 25.
Atlantic Marine Ins. Co. *v.* Huth, 79.
Attenborough *v.* L. & St. Kath. Docks, 201.
Att.-Gen. *v.* Chesterfield, 85.
——— *v.* Corp. of Leicester, 313.
——— *v.* ——— London, 100.
——— *v.* Jackson, 209.
——— *v.* Riddle, 245.
——— *v.* Siddon, 245.
——— *v.* Trueman, 188.
——— *v.* Walmsley, 188.
Attwood *v.* Mannings, 55, 209, 218.
August, The, 74.
Austin *v.* Chambers, 106.
——— *v.* Guardians of Bethnal Green, 32.
Australia, The, 36, 44, 78.
Australian Steam Nav. Co. *v.* Morse, 79.
Auty *v.* Hutchinson, 272.

Badman, Ex parte, 41.
Baemeister *v.* Fenton, 287.
Bagnall *v.* Carlton, 117.
Bailey *v.* Chadwick, 152.
Baines *v.* Ewing, 211.
Baker *v.* Keen, 28.
——— *v.* Langhorn, 126, 127.
——— *v.* Sampson, 22, 24.
Balch *v.* Symes, 185.
Baldry *v.* Bates, 58.
Balfe *v.* West, 88.
Bamford *v.* Shuttleworth, 299.
Bank of Bengal *v.* Fagan, 56.
——— ——— *v.* M'Leod, 56.
——— New South Wales *v.* Owston, 61, 254.
——— Scotland *v.* Watson, 58.
Banque Jacques Cartier *v.* Banque D'Epargne, 35, 41.
Barber *v.* Taylor, 89.
Barford *v.* Stuckey, 225.
Baring *v.* Corrie, 2, 68, 70, 121, 181, 240, 241.
——— *v.* Stanton, 119, 150.
Barker *v.* Furlong, 315, 316, 317.
——— *v.* Greenwood, 52, 244.
——— *v.* Harrison, 116.
Barlow *v.* Browne, 303.
Barnett *v.* Crystal Palace Co., 247.
——— *v.* South London Tram Co., 211, 263.
Baron *v.* Husband, 303.
Barrett *v.* Deere, 222.
Barron *v.* Fitzgerald, 178.
Barrow *v.* Dyster, 287.
Barry *v.* Stevens, 112.
Bartlett *v.* Pentland, 53, 245.
——— *v.* Pickersgill, 31, 106.
Barton's Hill Coal Co. *v.* M'Guire, 246.
Barton's Hill Coal Co. *v.* Reid, 246.
Barwick *v.* English Joint Stock Bank, 258.
Bateman *v.* Mid-Wales Rail. Co., 4.
Bates *v.* Pilling, 248.
Battams *v.* Tompkins, 149.
Bauerman *v.* Radenius, 310.
Bawden *v.* London, Edin. & Glas. Ins. Co., 237, 264.
Bayley *v.* M. S. & L. Rail. Co., 249.
——— *v.* Wilkins, 57, 173.
Bayliffe *v.* Butterworth, 173.
Baylis *v.* Watkins, 23, 124.
Bayntun *v.* Cattle, 97.
Bazeley *v.* Forder, 22.
Beal *v.* South Devon Rail. Co., 93, 129.
Beale, Re, 154.
——— *v.* Arabin, 19.
Beall, Ex parte, 189, 190.
Bear *v.* Stevenson, 318.
Beattie *v.* Ebury, 291.
Beauchamp *v.* Poley, 134.
Beaufort *v.* Neeld, 57, 206.
——— *v.* Taylor, 57, 206.
Beaumont *v.* Boultbee, 112, 166.
Beldon *v.* Campbell, 75, 76.
Bell *v.* Auldjo, 70.
—— *v.* Nixan, 9.
Benham *v.* Batty, 43.
Bennett *v.* Bayes, 312.
Benson *v.* Duncan, 77, 79.
——— *v.* Heathorn, 105, 142.
Bentley *v.* Craven, 104.
——— *v.* Griffin, 26, 231.
Berkeley *v.* Hardy, 29, 91, 226.
Berrie (or Berry) *v.* Howitt, 196.
Bertram *v.* Godfray, 54, 88, 89, 137.
Best *v.* Heys, 202.
Betham *v.* Benson, 261.
Betteley *v.* Reed, 101.
Betts *v.* Gibbins, 177.
—— *v.* De Vitre, 246.
Bexwell *v.* Christie, 89, 90, 123, 131.

Beyer v. Adams, 98.
Bickerton v. Burrell, 304.
Biddle v. Bond, 100, 102.
Biffin v. Bignell, 19.
Bigg v. Strong, 43.
Biggs v. Bree, 123.
—— v. Gordon, 149.
—— v. Head, 124.
—— v. Lawrence, 238, 262.
Bilbee v. Hasse, 156.
Bingham v. Allport, 207.
Bird, Ex parte, 274.
—— v. Boulter, 6, 11.
—— v. Brown, 34, 39, 40, 46, 48.
—— v. Jones, 18.
Birmingham Banking Co., Ex parte, 82.
Bishop, Ex parte, Re Fox, 171.
Blackburn v. Haslam, 237.
—— v. Mason, 52, 68, 85, 172, 245.
—— v. Scholes, 238, 319.
—— v. Vigors, 267.
Blackstone v. Wilson, 263.
Blades v. Free, 326, 333.
Blain, Ex parte, 212.
Blore v. Sutton, 81, 84.
Bloye's Trust, Re, 104.
Blyth v. Fladgate, 136.
—— v. Whiffin, 112, 201, 203.
Bock v. Gorrisson, 181.
Boden, Ex parte, 146.
—— v. French, 53.
Bold Buccleugh, The, 197.
Bolton Partners v. Lambert, 41.
Bone v. Ekless, 97.
Bonita, The v. The Charlotte, 41, 45, 78.
Bonzi v. Stewart, 99.
Boorman v. Brown, 70, 122, 131.
Borries v. Imp. Ottoman Bank, 240.
Bosanquet, Ex parte, 41.
Bostock v. Jardine, 67, 70, 105, 121.
Boston Deep Sea, &c. Co. v. Ansell, 140, 142.
Bottomley v. Fisher, 281.
Bousfield v. Cresswell, 95.
—— v. Wilson, 98.
Bowen v. European Bank, 202.
—— v. Morris, 307.
Bower v. Jones, 151.
Bowes, Re, 185.
Bowker v. Austin, 188.
Bowlby v. Bell, 178.
Bowles, Re, 55.
—— v. Orr, 113.
—— v. Stewart, 255.
Boyle v. Atty, 76.
Brace v. Calder, 161.
Bracey v. Carter, 168.
Braddick v. Smith, 203.
Bradley v. Riches, 265.
Brady v. Todd, 1, 2, 58.
Bramble v. Spiller, 305.
Brandeo v. Barnett, 181, 185, 186, 190.
Bray v. Chandler, 152.
Brazier v. Kemp, 220.
Breming v. Mackie, 51, 244.
Brewer v. Sparrow, 45, 48.
Bridger v. Savage, 98.
Bridges v. Garrett, 51, 244.
Bright, Ex parte, 4, 147, 333.
Briscoe v. Briscoe, 195.
Bristow v. Taylor, 330.
—— v. Whitmore, 44, 197.
British Mutual Banking Co. v. Charnwood Forest Rail. Co., 255.
Broad v. Thomas, 150, 152, 159, 161.
Broadbent v. Barlow, 148.
Brocklesby v. Permanent Temperance Bldg. Society, 207.

Bromley *v.* Holland, 329, 330.
Brook *v.* Hook (*or* Hoop), 36.
Brookman *v.* Rothschild, 103, 104, 122.
Brooks *v.* Hassell, 58.
Broomhead, Re, 181, 185, 199.
Brown *v.* Ackroyd, 23, 24.
——— *v.* Andrew, 8, 9.
——— *v.* Byers, 56.
——— *v.* Kennedy, 111, 150.
——— *v.* Powell Duffryn Steam Coal Co., 80.
——— *v.* Southouse, 142.
——— *v.* Staton, 72, 123.
Browning *v.* Prov. Ins. Co. of Canada, 222.
Brunswick *v.* Crowl, 164.
Bryans *v.* Nix, 183.
Bryant *v.* Flight, 150.
——— *v.* La Banque du Peuple, 54, 55.
——— *v.* Quebec Bank, 54.
Buchanan *v.* Findlay, 187.
Buck, Ex parte, 145, 182.
Buckley, Ex parte, 228, 279.
Bulkeley *v.* Dunbar, 312.
———— *v.* Wilford, 137.
Bull *v.* Price, 159.
Buller *v.* Harrison, 300.
Burdett *v.* Willett, 146.
Burdick *v.* Garrick, 92, 114, 142.
Burgoine *v.* Taylor, 137.
Burgon *v.* Sharpe, 79.
Burmester v. Norris, 61.
Burn *v.* Brown, 187.
Burnes *v.* Pennell, 253.
Burnett *v.* Bouch, 150.
Buron *v.* Denman, 35, 47, 312.
Burrough *v.* Skinner, 123, 299.
Burt *v.* Palmer, 262, 263.
Butler *v.* Knight, 63, 73, 74, 123, 130, 206, 319.
Caine *v.* Horsefall, 149.
Calder *v.* Dobell, 223, 232.
Callan, Ex parte, 31.
Callen, Re, 187.
Calvert, Ex parte, 199.
Cammell *v.* Sewell, 78.
Campanari *v.* Woodburn, 167, 326, 331.
Campbell *v.* Hassell, 66, 70, 239.
———— *v.* Larkworthy, 169.
Cape Breton Co., Re, 105, 119.
Capel *v.* Thornton, 57.
Capital Fire Ins. Asson., Re, 189, 190.
Capp *v.* Topham, 179.
Cargill *v.* Bower, 318.
Cargo *v.* Galam, 197.
——- *v.* The Sultan, 77.
Carlow, Ex parte, 146.
Carr *v.* Hinchcliffe, 240.
—— *v.* Jackson, 288.
Carriage Co-op. Supply Asson., Re, 118.
Carter *v.* Palmer, 115.
Cartwright *v.* Hateley, 85.
Caruthers *v.* Graham, 158.
Cary *v.* Webster, 297, 298.
Cass *v.* Rudele, 277.
—— *v.* Spurr, 223.
Cassaboglou *v.* Gibbs, 93, 137.
Castlegate, The, 197.
Castrique *v.* Buttigieg, 128.
Catlin *v.* Bell, 82.
Catterall *v.* Hindle, 244.
Cave *v.* Cave, 265.
—— *v.* Mackenzie, 31.
Cavendish-Bentinck *v.* Fenn, 105, 120.
Cella, The, 198.
Chadburn *v.* Moore, 65, 91, 210.
Chapleo, *v.* Brunswick Building Society, 251, 292.
Chapman, Re, Ex parte Edwards, 300.

Chapman *v.* Shepherd, 174.
——— *v.* Van Toll, 135.
Charles Amelia, The, 197.
Charleston *v.* London Tram. Co., 253.
Charter *v.* Trevelyan, 107.
Chartered Bank of Australia *v.* White, 181, 185.
Chedworth *v.* Edwards, 141.
Cherry *v.* Colonial Bank of Australasia, 290, 291.
Chesterfield and Mid Silkstone Colliery Co. *v.* Hawkins, 225.
Chinnock *v.* Sainsbury, 321.
Cholmondeley *v.* Clinton, 124.
Christofferson *v.* Hansen, 277.
Church *v.* Imp. Gaslight Co., 32.
City Bank *v.* Barrow, 64.
Clack *v.* Wood, 158.
Clarke *v.* Perrier, 43, 48.
——— *v.* Tipping, 89, 91, 92, 112, 120.
Clifford *v.* Laton, 15, 18, 21.
Clutterbuck *v.* Coffin, 271.
Coaks *v.* Boswell, 110.
Coates *v.* Lewes, 240.
——— *v.* Pacey, 175, 176.
Cobb *v.* Becke, 87.
Cobequid Marine Ins. Co. *v.* Barteaux, 78.
Cochran *v.* Irlam, 69, 71, 82, 120.
Cochrane *v.* Rymill, 315, 317.
Cockburn *v.* Edwards, 110, 125.
Coe *v.* Wise, 247.
Coggs *v.* Bernard, 88, 121.
Cohen *v.* Kittell, 134.
——— *v.* Paget, 150.
Cole *v.* North Western Bank, 214.
Coleman *v.* Riches, 256.
Coles *v.* Bristow, 67.
——— *v.* Trecothick, 30, 81, 82, 83, 122.
Collen *v.* Gardner, 60, 218.
——— *v.* Wright, 290, 296.
Collins *v.* Griffin, 143.
Collyer *v.* Dudley, 92.
Colmer *v.* Ede, 188.
Combe's case, 81, 91.
Comber *v.* Anderson, 89, 129, 133.
Commonwealth Land, &c., Co., Re, 73.
Connelly *v.* Lawson, 21.
Consolidated Co. *v.* Curtis, 316.
Cooke, Ex parte, 146.
——— *v.* Eshelby, 241.
——— *v.* Wilson, 282, 305.
Coombe's case, 4.
Cooper *v.* De Tastet, 99, 201.
——— *v.* Lloyd, 25.
Cope *v.* Rowlands, 164.
——— *v.* Thames Haven Dock, &c., Co., 32.
Copeland *v.* Stein, 189.
Coppin *v.* Craig, 309.
——— *v.* Walker, 309.
Cormack *v.* Digby, 254.
Cornfoot *v.* Fowke, 237, 258, 259.
Cornwall *v.* Wilson, 45, 48.
Cortis *v.* Kent Waterworks Co., 9.
Cotton *v.* James, 212.
Cousin's Trusts, Re, 267.
Coutourier *v.* Hastie, 3.
Cowdry *v.* Day, 109.
Cowell *v.* Betteley, 196.
——— *v.* Simpson, 181, 198.
Cowley *v.* Sunderland, 247.
Cox *v.* Leech, 168.
——— *v.* Midland Counties Rail. Co., 59, 61.
——— *v.* Prentice, 300.
Craddock *v.* Rogers, 110.
Cranch *v.* White, 313.
Crantz *v.* Gill, 28.
Crawley's claim, 170, 174.

Crawshay v. Thornton, 201.
Croft v. Alison, 256.
Cropper v. Cook, 67, 171.
Crosskeys v. Mills, 123.
Crossley v. Magniac, 243.
Crowe v. Ballard, 109.
Crowfoot v. Gurney, 302, 322, 324.
Crowl, Re, 164.
Crowther v. Elgood, 123, 143.
Cullen v. Queensberry, 220.
——— v. Thompson, 7, 312.
Cunningham, Re, 210.
——— v. Collier, 271.
Curlewis v. Birkbeck, 205, 238, 332.
Curling v. Shuttleworth, 299.
Curtis v. Barclay, 58, 171.
——— v. Nixon, 154.
——— v. Williamson, 233.
Cutter v. Powell, 152.

Dadswell v. Jacobs, 92.
Dale and Plant, Re, 38.
——— v. Humfrey, 287.
Dallow v. Garrold, 195.
Dalton v. Irwin, 168.
Danby v. Coutts, 55.
Daniel v. Adams, 64, 72.
Dantra v. Stiebel, 139.
Dartnall v. Howard, 135.
Daubigny v. Duval, 218.
Daun v. Simmons, 63, 210.
Davies, Ex parte, Re Sadler, 100, 102, 201.
——— v. Clough, 124.
——— v. Jenkins, 313, 314.
——— v. Lowndes, 194.
Davis v. Artingstall, 317.
——— v. Howard, 175.
Davison v. Donaldson, 234, 235.
Dean and Gilbert's claim, 162.
Deare v. Soutten, 22.
Debenham v. Mellon, 14, 15, 16.
De Bouchout v. Goldsmid, 56.
De Bussche v. Alt, 80, 81, 83, 84, 106, 110, 116.
De Comas v. Prost, 323.
De la Chaumette v. Bank of England, 191.
De Mattos v. Benjamin, 98.
Denew v. Deverell, 168.
Dennys v. Sargeant, 18.
Dent v. Dunn, 234.
Derry v. Peek, 258, 259.
Deslandes v. Gregory, 284.
Devala Prov. Gold Mining Co., Re, 263.
Deverell v. Bolton, 30.
Dicas v. Stockley, 193, 199.
Dickinson v. Lilwall, 320.
——— v. Naul, 304, 307.
——— v. Valpy, 61.
Die Elbinger Actien Gesellschaft v. Claye, 224, 273.
Diggle v. Higgs, 331.
Dingle v. Hare, 57, 66, 69.
Dinwiddie v. Bailey, 203.
Dixon, Ex parte, Re Henley, 68, 205, 238, 240.
——— v. Broomfield, 12.
——— v. Ewart, 328.
——— v. Hammond, 97, 99.
——— v. Hurrell, 21.
——— v. Stansfield, 184.
Dodsley v. Varley, 221, 333.
Doe d. Lyster v. Goldwin, 40.
——— Mann v. Warlters, 40.
——— Willis v. Martin, 255.
——— v. Robinson, 82, 84.
Donelly v. Popham, 49.
Dooby v. Watson, 135.
Doorman v. Jenkins, 134.
Douglas, Re, 327, 329.
——— v. Ewing, 215.
Dowman v. Williams, 283.

Dramburg v. Pollitzer, 224, 273.
Dresser v. Norwood, 241, 265.
Drew v. Nunn, 4, 326, 333.
Drinkwater v. Goodwin, 69, 183, 243, 308, 324.
Druce v. Levy, 175.
Drum Slate Quarry Co., Re, 119, 142.
Ducarrey v. Gill, 228.
Dudley, Re, 143.
Duero, The, 248.
Dufresne v. Hutchinson, 131.
Dumas, Ex parte, 146.
Duncan v. Beeson, 179.
——— v. Benson, 77, 79.
——— v. Hill, 179.
——— v. Skipwith, 134.
Dunn v. Newton, 231.
Dunne v. English, 105.
Durrant, Ex parte, 154.
Durrell v. Evans, 6, 57.
Dutton v. Marsh, 280, 282.
Dyas v. Cruise, 89, 205.
Dyer v. Munday, 250.
—— v. Pearson, 220.
Dyster, Ex parte, 121, 204.

Eaglesfield v. Londonderry, 291, 312.
East India Co. v. Henchman, 89, 103, 139, 268.
——— v. Hensley, 209.
——— v. Tritton, 299.
Eastern Counties Rail. Co. v. Broom, 36, 47, 250.
Eastland v. Burchell, 18, 20.
Eccossaise SS. Co. v. Lloyd, 143.
Eden v. Ridsdale Lamp, &c. Co., 118.
Edgar v. Fowler, 331.
Edge, Re, 143.
Edgell v. Day, 92, 125.
Edmunds v. Bushell, 60, 206.
Edwards, Ex parte, Re Chapman, 300.
——— Johnson, 86, 87, 193.
——— v. Havill, 76.
——— v. Hodding, 299.
——— v. L. & N. W. Ry. Co., 41, 62, 254.
——— v. Mid. Rail. Co., 247.
——— v. Towels, 18.
Eliza Cornish, The, 78.
Elkington v. Hurter, 292.
Elliott v. Turquand, 329.
Ellis v. Goulton, 299.
—— v. Turner, 256.
Elsee v. Gatward, 88, 134.
Emery v. Emery, 24.
Emma Silver Mining Co. v. Grant, 117.
Emma Silver Mining Co. v. Lewis, 117.
Emmens v. Elderton, 161.
Emmerson v. Heelis, 6, 11, 71.
Emmett v. Norton, 16, 17, 20, 25.
Empress Engineering Co., Re, 38.
English and Scottish Marine Ins. Co., 163.
Entwistle v. Dent, 57.
Erlanger v. New Sombrero Phosphate Co., 117.
Esdaile v. La Nauze, 55.
Espin v. Pemberton, 266.
Essery v. Cobb, 276.
Etna Ins. Co., 166.
Evans v. Nichol, 101.
——— v. Smallcombe, 45.

Fairlie v. Fenton, 304, 306, 307.
——— v. Hastings, 261.
Falk v. Fletcher, 200.
Fanny, The, 75, 79.
Farebrother v. Ansley, 169.
——— v. Simmons, 5.
Farley v. Turner, 146.

Farmer *v.* Robinson, 330.
——— *v.* Russell, 98.
Farrer *v.* Lacy, 90.
Farrow *v.* Wilson, 326.
Favenc *v.* Bennett, 238.
Faviell *v.* Eastern Counties Rail. Co., 33, 63, 73.
Fawcett *v.* Whitehouse, 116.
Fawcus, Re, 145, 182.
Fawkes *v.* Lamb, 307.
Feise *v.* Wray, 200.
Fell *v.* Brown, 128.
—— *v.* Parkin, 234.
Fenn *v.* Harrison, 58, 209.
Ferguson *v.* Carrington, 44, 46.
Feronia, The, 198.
Ferrars *v.* Robins, 90, 122, 131.
Fiddey, Re, 194.
Fielding *v.* Kymer, 69, 121.
Filmer *v.* Lynn, 221.
Firbank *v.* Humphreys, 290, 291, 294.
Fish *v.* Kempton, 241.
Fisher *v.* Drewitt, 157, 158.
——— *v.* Marsh, 303.
——— *v.* Miller, 321.
——— *v.* Smith, 186, 192.
——— *v.* Val de Travers Co., 137.
Fitzgerald *v.* Dressler, 209.
Fitzmaurice *v.* Bayley, 43.
Fitzroy Bessemer Steel Co., Re, 265.
Flanagan *v.* G. W. Rail. Co., 109.
Fleet *v.* Murton, 287.
Flemyng *v.* Hector, 220.
Flint *v.* Woodin, 104.
Fluker *v.* Taylor, 113.
Foley *v.* Hill, 113.
Foreman *v.* G. W. Rail,, 6, 207.
Forristall *v.* Lawson, 21.
Foster *v.* Bates, 38, 326.
——— *v.* Pearson, 89.
Fox, Re, Ex parte Bishop, 171.
Fox *v.* Frith, 281.
Foxcroft *v.* Wood, 182.
Franklyn *v.* Lamond, 122, 275.
Fray *v.* Voules, 90, 123, 130.
Freeman *v.* Appleyard, 213.
——— *v.* Fairlie, 330.
——— *v.* Rosher, 42, 246.
Freestone *v.* Butcher, 15, 16.
Frith *v.* Cartland, 148.
—— *v.* Forbes, 187.
Frixione *v.* Tagliafferro, 44, 49, 171, 176.
Frontin *v.* Small, 91.
Frost *v.* Oliver, 76.
Fry *v.* Fry, 141.
Fuentes *v.* Montis, 206.
Fuller *v.* Bennett, 266.
——— *v.* Eames, 158.
——— *v.* Wilson, 259.
Fullwood *v.* Akerman, 149.
Furlong *v.* South London Tram. Co., 249.
Furnival *v.* Bogle, 72.

Gaby *v.* Driver, 299.
Gadd *v.* Houghton, 282, 284.
Gaetano and Maria, The, 74, 75.
Galland, Re, 184.
Gardner *v.* Baillie, 56.
——— *v.* McCutcheon, 103, 122.
Garth *v.* Howard, 261.
Gaskell *v.* Chambers, 117.
Gatty *v.* Field, 331.
Gauntlett *v.* King, 42, 246.
Gaussen *v.* Morton, 322.
General Exchange Bank *v.* Horner, 89, 118.
George *v.* Clagett, 240.
Georges *v.* Georges, 185.
Gibbs *v.* Daniel, 109.
Giblin *v.* McMullen, 134.
Gibson *v.* Crick, 153.
——— *v.* Jeyes, 110.

Gibson v. Minet, 301, 331.
——— v. Winter, 310.
Gidley v. Palmerston, 270, 271.
Gill v. Kymer, 69, 121.
Gillard v. Wise, 98.
Gillett v. Peppercorne, 103.
Gillow v. Aberdare, 57, 166, 320.
Gilman v. Robinson, 205, 208, 221.
Glasgow, The, 78.
Glover v. Langford, 282.
Gobind Chunder Sind v. Ryan, 215.
Godefroy v. Dalton, 123, 136.
——— v. Jay, 136.
Godfrey v. Furze, 146.
Godin v. London Assurance Co., 181, 190.
Godwin v. Francis, 297.
Goff v. G. N. Rail., 249.
Gomme v. Franklin, 27.
Goodland v. Blewitt, 207.
Goodman v. Harvey, 212.
Goodson v. Brooke, 64.
Goodtitle v. Woodward, 40.
Goodwin v. Robarts, 213.
Goom v. Aflalo, 229.
Gordon v. Rolt, 255.
Gosling's case, 264.
Gosling v. Birnie, 101.
Goupy v. Harden, 128.
Govier v. Hancock, 25.
Graham v. Ackroyd, 169.
——— v. Musson, 12, 30.
Grant v. Fletcher, 121, 228.
——— v. Norway, 75, 79.
——— v. United Kingdom Switchback Rail. Co., 45.
Gratitudine, The, 77, 79.
Graves v. Legg, 264.
——— v. Masters, 60, 209.
Gray v. Gutteridge, 123, 299.
—— v. Haig, 89, 91, 92, 166.
—— v. Kirby, 87.
Great Luxembourg Rail. Co. v. Magnay, 105.
Great Western Ins. Co. of New York v. Cunliffe, 113, 119.
G. W. Rail. v. Willis, 262.
Green v. Bartlett, 155.
——— v. Elgie, 314.
——— v. Hopke, 282.
——— v. London Gen. Omnibus Co., 256.
——— v. Lucas, 157.
——— v. Maitland, 101.
——— v. Mules, 151.
Greenwood, Ex parte, 147.
Gregory, Ex parte, 147.
——— v. Parker, 26.
——— v. Piper, 249.
Grice v. Kenrick, 309.
Griffin v. Weatherby, 301, 321.
Griffiths v. Williams, 83.
Grindley v. Barker, 9.
Grogan v. Smith, 158.
Groom v. Cheesewright, 194.
Grove v. Dubois, 3, 127.
Guerreiro v. Peile, 69, 91, 120.
Guichard v. Morgan, 69.
Gunn v. Roberts, 41, 76.
Gunnis v. Erhart, 71, 211.
Gurney v. Gibb, 133.
——— v. Womersley, 298.
Guthrie v. Armstrong, 9.
Guy v. Churchill, 195.
Gwatkin v. Campbell, 89, 108.

Hadley v. Baxendale, 137.
Hagedorn v. Oliverson, 38.
Hahn v. North German Pitwood Co., 282.
Haines v. Busk, 165.
Hall v. Fuller, 179.
Hallett's Estate, Re, 146.
Hamburgh, The, 77.
Hamer v. Sharp, 65, 91, 210.

Hamilton v. Baker, 197.
——— v. Young, 68, 106.
Hammond v. Barclay, 183.
——— v. Thorpe, 293.
Hamond v. Holiday, 168.
Hampden v. Walsh, 331.
Hancock v. Hudson, 278.
Hanson v. Roberdeau, 275.
Hardacre v. Stewart, 313.
Hardie v. Grant, 25.
Hardwicke v. Vernon, 140, 142.
Hargreaves v. Rothwell, 266.
Harington v. Hoggart, 142.
Harker v. Edwards, 66, 67, 172.
Harmer v. Bell, 197.
——— v. Cornelius, 93.
Harper v. Godsell, 55.
Harrington v. Churchward, 203.
——— v. Victoria Graving Dock Co., 311.
Harris v. Morris, 22, 25.
——— v. Nickerson, 275.
——— v. Osborn, 125.
——— v. Petherick, 149.
——— v. Truman, 148.
Harrison v. Grady, 14, 15, 21.
——— v. Jackson, 29.
———, ——— v., 332.
Harsant v. Blaine, 92, 93, 141.
Hart v. Frame, 136.
Hartas v. Ribbons, 179.
Hartop, Ex parte, 271, 288.
Harvey v. Norton, 19, 27.
Haselar v. Lemoyne, 42, 246.
Hastings v. Pearson, 217.
Hatch v. Hale, 63, 246.
Hatsall v. Griffith, 98.
Hawkes v. Dunn, 200.
Hawkins v. Kemp, 7.
Hawley v. Sentance, 43.
Hawtayne v. Bourne, 61.
Hay's case, 119.
Hay v. Goldsmidt, 55.
Hayes v. Tindall, 94.
Haynes v. Foster, 71.
Hazard v. Treadwell, 208.
Heald v. Kenworthy, 234.
Healey v. Storey, 281.
Heard v. Pilley, 30, 31.
Heath v. Chilton, 301.
Heinrich, The, 195.
——— v. Sutton, 194.
Heisch v. Carrington, 244.
Helgear v. Hawke, 51.
Hemmings v. Pugh, 112.
Henchman v. E. I. Co., 89, 103, 139, 268.
Henderson v. Australian Steam Navign. Co., 31, 32, 33.
——— v. Barnewell, 71, 82.
Henley, Re, 68, 205, 238.
Herald v. Connah, 278.
Hern v. Nichols, 246.
Hersey, The, 77.
Heugh v. Abergavenny, 7.
Heyman v. Neale, 228.
Heyworth v. Knight, 205.
Hibbert v. Bayley, 122, 132.
Hick v. Tweedy, 282.
Hiern v. Mill, 266.
Higgins v. Senior, 285.
Hilberry v. Hatton, 35, 43, 47.
Hill v. Kitching, 158.
Hinde v. Whitehouse, 6.
Hindley v. Westmeath, 21.
Hine v. SS. Ins. Syndicate, 245.
Hobhouse v. Hamilton, 273.
Hobler, Re, 72.
Hoby v. Built, 125, 132.
Hockin v. Cooke, 29.
Hodgkinson v. Fletcher, 20, 21.
——— v. Kelly, 67, 174, 229.
Hodgson v. Anderson, 301, 321.
Hogg v. Snaith, 55.
Hoggard v. Mackenzie, 184.
Holder v. Cope, 20.

Holding *v.* Elliott, 285, 288.
Holl *v.* Griffin, 101.
Holland *v.* Russell, 299.
Hollington, Ex parte, 73.
Hollins v. Fowler, 316.
Hollis *v.* Claridge, 189.
Hollman *v.* Pullin, 289, 304.
Holmes *v.* Tutton, 310.
Holt *v.* Brien, 17.
—— *v.* Ely, 311.
Hood *v.* Reeve, 263.
Hooper, Re, 124.
——— *v.* Treffrey, 169.
Hope, The, 198.
Hopkinson *v.* Smith, 123, 167.
Horford *v.* Wilson, 158.
Hornby *v.* Lacy, 3, 126, 236, 241.
Horsfall *v.* Fauntleroy, 233.
Horwood *v.* Heffer, 24.
Hough *v.* Manzanos, 282.
Houghton *v.* Matthews, 69, 184, 273.
Houliston v. Smyth, 21, 24.
Hovil *v.* Pack, 44.
Howard's case, 82.
Howard *v.* Baillie, 55, 56.
——— *v.* Braithwaite, 74, 218.
——— *v.* Chapman, 60.
——— *v.* Patent Ivory Co., 38.
——— *v.* Sheward, 58, 64, 206.
——— *v.* Tucker, 261.
Howell, Ex parte, 57, 59.
——— *v.* Batt, 302.
Hubbard *v.* Phillips, 293.
Hubbersty *v.* Ward, 79.
Hudson *v.* Granger, 243, 324.
Hugh *v.* Abergavenny, 7, 312.
Hughes *v.* Greame, 292, 296.
Hull *v.* Pickersgill, 35, 48, 313.
Humble *v.* Hunter, 224.
Humphrey *v.* Lucas, 229.
Hunt *v.* De Blaquiere, 15.
—— *v.* Maniere, 100.
Hunter *v.* Atkins, 111.
——— *v*, Belcher, 112.
——— *v.* Caldwell, 136.
——— *v.* Parker, 45, 78.
Huntley *v.* Bulwer, 168.
Hurry *v.* Rickman, 246.
Hurst *v.* Holding, 166.
Hussie *v.* Christie, 77.
Hutcheson *v.* Eaton, 282.
Hutchins *v.* Hutchins, 124.
Hutchinson *v.* Tatham, 286.
Huth, Ex parte, 104, 122, 269.
Hutton *v.* Bullock, 65, 224, 273.
Hyde *v.* Johnson, 8.
—— *v.* Price, 20.

Ida, The, 261.
Imperial Bank *v.* L. & St. Kath. Docks Co., 200, 287.
——— Mercantile Credit Co. *v.* Coleman, 108, 114.
——— Wine Co., Re, 163.
Inchbald *v.* Western Neilgherry, &c. Co., 162.
Ingram *v.* Little, 26.
Ireland *v.* Livingstone, 53, 54.
——— *v.* Thomson, 78.
Ireson *v.* Pearman, 135.
Irvine *v.* Union Bank of Australia, 36, 47.
——— *v.* Watson, 234, 235.
Iveson *v.* Conington, 272.

Jacob *v.* Magnay, 143.
James, Ex parte, 104, 144, 251.
——— *v.* Ricknell, 64, 74.
——— *v.* Smith, 30, 31, 106.
Jarmain *v.* Hooper, 73, 248.
Jeffrey *v.* Crawford, 152.
Jenkins *v.* Betham, 95.
——— *v.* Hutchinson, 276, 288.
——— *v.* Morris, 227.
Jenner *v.* Morris, 22.
Jenny Lind, The, 198.

Jessel *v.* Bath, 80.
Jetley *v.* Hill, 221.
Jewesbury *v.* Newbold, 15, 27.
Johns *v.* Simons, 76.
Johnson, Re, Ex parte Edwards, 86, 87, 193.
——— *v.* Ogilby, 274, 288.
Johnston's claim, 133, 137.
Johnston *v.* Kershaw, 53.
——— *v.* Usborne, 176.
Johnstone *v.* Sumner, 18, 19, 21, 22.
Jolly *v.* Rees, 14, 16.
Jones *v.* Bird, 247.
—— *v.* Jackson, 279.
—— *v.* Littledale, 285, 288.
—— *v.* Peppercorne, 181, 186, 190.
—— *v.* Phipps, 59.
Jonmenjoy Coondoo *v.* Watson, 54, 56.
Jordan *v.* Norton, 219.
Joseph *v.* Nox, 79.
Josephs *v.* Pebrer, 164, 176.
Jourdaine *v.* Le Fevre, 181.

Kahl *v.* Jahnsen, 261.
Kaltenbach *v.* Lewis, 242.
Karnak, The, 74.
Kaye *v.* Brett, 239.
Keay *v.* Fenwick, 43, 44, 48, 166.
Kell *v.* Nainby, 223.
Kelner *v.* Baxter, 38, 289.
Kemeys *v.* Proctor, 71.
Kennedy *v.* Gouveia, 284.
Kidson *v.* Dilworth, 286.
Kilgour *v.* Finlyson, 51, 211.
Kimber *v.* Barber, 116, 120.
King *v.* Anderson, 108.
—— *v.* Rossett, 112.
—— The *v.* Beeston, 9.
——— *v.* Longnor, 4, 29.
Kinloch *v.* Craig, 183.
——— *v.* Sec. of State for India, 85, 271.
Kirchner *v.* Venus, 172, 197.
Kirkham *v.* Peel, 117.
Kirkstall Brewery *v.* Furness Rail., 262.
Kirton *v.* Braithwaite, 207.
Kleinwort *v.* Cassa Marittima de Genoa, 77.
Knatchbull *v.* Hallett, 146.
Knight *v.* Faith, 78.
——— *v.* Fitch, 165.
——— *v.* Lee, 177.
Knox *v.* Bushell, 14.
Kruger *v.* Wilcox, 199.
Kymer *v.* Suwercropp, 235.
Kynaston *v.* Crouch, 328.

Lacey *v.* Hill, Crawley's claim, 170, 174.
——— *v.* ——, Scrimgeour's claim, 174.
Ladywell Mining Co. *v.* Brooks, 120.
Laidler *v.* Elliott, 135.
Lambert *v.* Heath, 89, 95, 129.
Lands Allotments Co., Re, 114.
Lane *v.* Cotton, 270.
—— *v.* Ironmonger, 15.
Langan *v.* G. W. Rail. Co., 59, 61.
Langhorn *v.* Allnutt, 264.
Langton *v.* Waite, 229.
Law *v.* Wilkins, 28.
Lawrance, Re, 188.
Lawrence *v.* Fletcher, 193.
Leadbitter *v.* Farrow, 280.
Learoyd *v.* Bracken, 165.
Lee *v.* Bayes and Robinson, 318.
—— *v.* Bullen, 126, 127, 171, 304.

Lee v. Everest, 276.
—— v. Munn, 299.
—— v. Walker, 95.
Lees v. Nuttall, 106.
Le Feuvre v. Lloyd, 128.
Le Neve v. Le Neve, 265.
Lennard v. Robinson, 285.
Levi v. Abbott, 73.
Levy v. Barnard, 200.
—— v. Richardson, 209.
Lewis v. Nicholson, 276.
—— v. Ramsdale, 55, 215.
—— v. Read, 42.
—— v. Samuel, 179.
Lickorish, Ex parte, 110.
Lidlow v. Wilmot, 20.
Lilley v. Doubleday, 130.
Limpus v. L. G. O. Co., 257.
Lindus v. Bradwell, 227.
Linford v. Prov. Horse, &c. Ins. Co., 59, 61, 210.
Lissett v. Reave, 229.
Lister v. Stubbs, 141.
Litchfield v. Jones, 143.
Litt v. Martindale, 219.
Little v. Kingswood Colly. Co., 124.
—— v. Newton, 82.
Llewellyn v. Winckworth, 221.
Lloyd v. Guibert, 75.
—— v. Sigourney, 219.
Lockwood v. Abdy, 85.
—— v. Levick, 158.
Logan, Ex parte, 163.
London Chartered Bank of Australia v. White, 185.
London and Scottish Bank, Re, 163.
London Financial Association v. Kelk, 45.
Long v. Millar, 288.
Lord v. Hall, 82.
—— v. Kellett, 30.
Loring v. Davis, 53.
Lovegrove v. White, 64, 74.
Lowe v. G. N. Rail. Co., 62, 250.
Lowry v. Guildford, 135.
Lowther v. Lowther, 104.
Lucas v. Dorrein, 187.
Lucey v. Ingram, 254.
Luckie v. Bushby, 242.
Luddy's Trustees v. Peard, 108, 125.
Ludgater v. Love, 237, 259.
Ludlow, Mayor of, v. Charlton, 32.
Lumley v. Nicholson, 155.
Lupton v. White, 92.
Lyell v. Kennedy, 38, 46, 100.
Lynch v. Coel, 72.
Lyons v. Martin, 255.
Lyster v. Goldwin, 40.

Maanss v. Henderson, 192, 193.
Macbeath v. Ellis, 319.
—— v. Haldimund, 271.
MacCall v. Australian Meat Co., 320.
McCaull v. Strauss, 229.
McClure v. Schemeil, 232, 235.
McCollin v. Gilpin, 283.
M'Combie v. Davies, 218.
MacDonnell, Ex parte, 329.
Mace v. Cadell, 146.
McEntire v. Potter, 317, 328.
Macfarlane v. Giannacopulo, 233.
—— v. Lister, 194, 197.
M'Gillivray v. Simpson, 180.
McGowan v. Dyer, 209.
McKay's case, 117.
McKay v. Commercial Bank of New Brunswick, 257.
Mackenzie v. Johnston, 113.
—— v. Pooley, 75.
Mackersy v. Ramsays, 144.
Maclean v. Dunn, 34, 44.
McLean v. Fleming, 75, 80, 261.

Macleod v. Artola, 151.
——— v. Jones, 109.
Maclure, Ex parte, 163.
M'Manus v. Crickett, 255.
McPherson v. Watt, 109.
Madden v. Kempster, 184.
Maester v. Atkins, 158.
Magdalena Steam Navigation Co., Re, 45.
Magee v. Atkinson, 274, 288.
Mahony v. East Holyford Mining Co., 222.
——— v. Kekule, 282.
Mainprice v. Westley, 276.
Mainwaring v. Brandon, 138.
——— v. Leslie, 18.
Makepeace v. Rogers, 112.
Malcolm v. Scott, 302.
Mallough v. Barber, 94, 132.
Maltby v. Christie, 94.
Man v. Shiffner, 193.
Mann v. Forrester, 181, 192, 239.
——— v. Warlters, 40.
Mansell v. Clements, 155.
Manser v. Back, 330.
Manson v. Baillie, 151.
Mare v. Charles, 279.
Margaret Mitchell, The, 78, 330.
Maria, The, 254.
Markwick v. Hardingham, 10, 327.
Marsh v. Jelf, 64, 72, 167.
Marshall v. Cliff, 263.
——— v. Parsons, 149.
Marten v. Roche, 213.
Martin v. Gibbon, 172.
Martini v. Coles, 69, 121.
Martinius v. Helmuth, 202.
Mary Ann, The, 198.
Mason v. Clifton, 49, 86.
——— v. Hamilton, 202.
——— v. Joseph, 81.
Massey's case, 146.
Massey v. Banner, 93, 94, 130.
——— & Carey, Re, 168.
——— v. Davies, 104.
Mather, Ex parte, 89, 176, 177.
Matilda, The, 75, 79.
Matthews v. Haydon, 143.
Maund v. Monmouth Canal Co., 247.
Maunder v. Conyers, 221.
Maw v. Pearson, 85.
May v. Skey, 22.
Maydew v. Forrester, 132, 138.
Mayhew v. Eames, 238.
Meek v. Wendt, 295.
Megaw v. Molloy, 71.
Melhado v. Porto Alegre, &c. Rail. Co., 38.
Melville v. Doidge, 251.
Mercer v. Graves, 195.
Merryweather v. Nixan, 312.
Mersey Docks Trustees v. Gibbs, 247.
Messenger, Re, 199.
Metcalfe v. Clough, 321.
——— v. Shaw, 26, 231.
Metropolitan Asylum Board v. Kingham, 40.
——— Bank v. Herron, 140.
Meux's Executors' case, 261.
Mews v. Carr, 11.
Meyer v. Dresser, 80.
Middleditch v. Sharland, 112.
Middleton v. Welles, 111.
Mildred v. Maspons, 242.
Miles' Claim, 228.
Miles v. Bernard, 129.
——— v. McIlwraith, 245.
Miller v. Beale, 151.
Milvan v. Perez, 277.
Misa v. Currie, 181, 185, 190.
Mitchell, Re, 143.
——— v. Crassweller, 254.

Mitchell *v.* Hayne, 202.
——— *v.* Kahl, 295.
Mitcheson *v.* Oliver, 75.
Mizen *v.* Pick, 20.
Moffatt *v.* Bateman, 93, 134.
——— *v.* Parsons, 207.
Mole *v.* Smith, 72.
Molony *v.* Kernan, 107.
Monet, Ex parte, 143.
Monro *v.* De Chemant, 27.
Montagu *v.* Benedict, 15.
——— *v.* Forwood, 85, 192, 242.
Montaignac *v.* Shitta, 207.
Montesquieu *v.* Sandys, 110.
Montreal Ass. Co. *v.* M'Gillivray, 4, 49.
Moody *v.* Spencer, 193.
Moore *v.* Maxwell, 149.
——— *v.* Metropolitan Ry. Co., 249.
——— *v.* Mourgue, 89, 95, 129, 133.
——— *v.* Usher, 203.
Morgan *v.* Blyth, 136.
——— *v.* Chetwynd, 15.
——— *v.* Couchman, 233.
——— *v.* Elford, 139.
——— *v.* Minett, 111.
Morris *v.* Cleasby, 3, 126.
——— *v.* Salberg, 73, 248.
——— *v.* Wilson, 223.
Morrison, Ex parte, 196.
——— *v.* Thompson, 114, 116.
Mortimer *v.* Wright, 28.
Mortlock *v.* Buller, 30.
Mostyn *v.* Mostyn, 74.
Moxon *v.* Sheppard, 194.
Muir *v.* Fleming, 185.
Mullens *v.* Miller, 58, 237.
Mulligan *v.* M'Donough, 128.
Murphy *v.* Boese, 12.
——— *v.* O'Shea, 109.
Murray *v.* East India Co., 56.
——— *v.* Mann, 99.
Mutual Aid Permanent Building Society, Re, 144, 251.
Mynn *v.* Joliffe, 59.

National Bolivian Navigation Co. *v.* Wilson, 206.
——— Coffee Palace Co., Re, 295.
——— Exchange Co. of Glasgow *v.* Drew, 257.
——— Mercantile Bank *v.* Rymill, 317.
Navulshaw *v.* Brownrigg, 112, 215.
Nayler *v.* Yearsley, 156.
Naylor *v.* Mangles, 181.
Negus *v.* Forster, 18, 19.
Neilson *v.* James, 121, 138.
Nelson *v.* Aldridge, 71.
——— *v.* Powell, 234.
Neptune, The, 197.
Nevill *v.* Fine Arts and General Ins. Co., 247.
New Zealand and Australian Land Co. *v.* Watson, 84, 85, 192, 243.
Newall *v.* Tomlinson, 300.
Newlands *v.* Natnl. Employers' Accident Association, 252.
Newson *v.* Thornton, 69.
Nicholls *v.* Wilson, 125, 167.
Nichols *v.* Diamond, 279.
Nicholson, Re, 199.
Nickalls *v.* Merry, 229.
Nickolson *v.* Knowles, 96, 201.
Nickson *v.* Brohan, 205, 332.
Nobel's Explosives Co. *v.* Jones, 312.
Norfolk *v.* Worthy, 224.
North's case, 143.
North Australian Territory Co., Re, 114, 118.

N. Eastern Rail. *v.* Jackson, 118.
Northumberland Avenue Hotel Co., Re, 38.
Norton *v.* Fazan, 26.
——— *v.* Herron, 283.
Nurse *v.* Durnford, 293.

Oates *v.* Hudson, 301.
O'Brien *v.* Lewis, 111, 125.
Odessa Tramways Co. *v.* Mendel, 268.
Ogden *v.* Hall, 282, 284.
Oglesby *v.* Yglesias, 277.
O'Grady *v.* Cardwell, 271.
Okell *v.* Charles, 227, 279.
Olding *v.* Smith, 209, 261.
Oliver *v.* Court, 104, 123.
Onward, The, 77.
Oom *v.* Bruce, 304.
Ormerod *v.* Tate, 194, 196.
Osborn *v.* Gillett, 246.
O'Sullivan *v.* Thomas, 331.
Ottaway *v.* Hamilton, 22, 23.
Ottleif *v.* Gilby, 124.
Oursell, Ex parte, 146.
Overend, Gurney & Co. *v.* Gibb, 133.
Owen *v.* Cronk, 298.
—— *v.* Gooch, 274, 288.
Owens, Re, 166.
Oxenham *v.* Smythe, 290.
Oxford *v.* Crow, 44.

Padwick *v.* Hurst, 114, 203.
——— *v.* Stanley, 113, 203.
Page *v.* Defries, 249.
Paice *v.* Walker, 282, 284.
Palethorp *v.* Furnish, 262.
Palk *v.* Force, 164.
Palmer *v.* Day, 329.
——— *v.* Goodwin, 166.
——— *v.* Hutchinson, 270.
Panama Telegraph Co. *v.* India Rubber, &c., Co., 268.
Panmure, Ex parte, 295.
Panthea, The, 198.
Papè *v.* Westacott, 52, 90, 131, 244.
Papillon *v.* Brunton, 59.
Pappa *v.* Rose, 96.
Pariente *v.* Lubbock, 57, 88, 89, 129.
Park *v.* Hammond, 132.
Parker *v.* M'Kenna, 103, 114, 115.
——— *v.* Winlow, 283.
Parkins *v.* Hawkshaw, 263.
Parsons *v.* Thompson, 165.
Partington, Re, Partington *v.* Allen, 136.
——— *v.* Hawthorne, 232.
Parton *v.* Crofts, 6, 69.
Patent Floor Cloth Co., Re, 162.
Paterson *v.* Gandassequi, 224, 231.
——— *v.* Tash, 69.
Patten *v.* Rea, 254.
Pauli, Ex parte, Re Trye, 147.
Pavy's Patent Felted Fabric Co., Re, 183.
Paxton *v.* Courtnay, 172.
Payne *v.* Leconfield, 71.
Pearce *v.* Rogers, 211.
Pearse *v.* Boulter, 60.
——— *v.* Green, 92, 141.
Pearson's case, 118.
Pearson *v.* Cardon, 202.
——— *v.* Graham, 317, 328.
——— *v.* Scott, 52, 68, 70, 229, 245.
Pease, Ex parte, 147.
Peers *v.* Sneyd, 59.
Pelham *v.* Hilder, 66.
Pemberton, Ex parte, 188.
———, Re, 104, 122, 269.
Penkivil *v.* Connell, 280.
Peppercorne *v.* Clench, 173.
Perkins *v.* Smith, 313.
Perry *v.* Barnett, 175.
—— *v.* Holl, 54.

Petch v. Lyon, 263.
Peterson v. Ayre, 273.
Peto v. Hague, 261.
Petty v. Anderson, 223.
Phelps v. Prothero, 236.
Phillips v. Phillips, 112.
Phillipson v. Hayter, 13, 15, 16, 17.
Phosphate Sewage Co. v. Hartmont, 139.
Pickering's claim, Re, 225.
Pickering v. Busk, 220.
Pickernell v. Jauberry, 79.
Pigott v. Thompson, 307.
Pike v. Ongley, 286.
Pilot v. Craze, 220.
Pinto v. Santos, 85.
Pisani v. Gibraltar, 110, 125.
Pitman v. Francis, 135.
Pitt v. Zalden, 135.
Platt v. Depree, 158.
Pole v. Leask, 10, 12, 50, 57, 332.
Polhill v. Walter, 226, 228, 278, 292.
Pollock v. Stables, 66, 173.
Portalis v. Tetley, 217.
Portuguese Consolidated Copper Mines, Re, 41.
Pott v. Bevan, 44.
Poulton v. L. & S. W. Rail. Co., 4, 50, 253.
Pourier v. Morris, 63, 65.
Pow v. Davis, 296.
Power v. Butcher, 204.
——— v. Power, 92, 114.
Powles v. Page, 266.
Precious v. Abel, 221.
Prescott v. Flynn, 221.
Price v. Taylor, 280.
Prickett v. Badger, 160.
Priestley v. Fernie, 232.
Prince v. Clark, 44.
Pristwick v. Poley, 73.
Pritchard v. Roberts, 194.
Prosperino Palasso, The, 261.
Prosser v. Allen, 270.
Provincial Ins. Co. of Canada v. Leduc, 304.
Pulteney v. Keymer, 180.
Purves v. Landell, 135.

Quebec and Richmond Rail. Co. v. Quinn, 81.
Queen of Spain v. Parr, 116, 169.
Quinn, Ex parte, 199.

Rabone v. Williams, 240.
Railton v. Hodgson, 288.
Rainbow, The, 199.
Raleigh v. Atkinson, 322, 323.
Ramozotti v. Bowring, 240.
Randell v. Trimen, 290, 296.
Ranger v. G. W. Rail., 247.
Rawlyns v. Vandyke, 19.
Rayner, Ex parte, 226.
——— v. Grote, 306.
——— v. Mitchell, 254.
——— v. Pearson, 261.
Read v. Anderson, 64, 177, 321, 324.
—— v. Rann, 152, 159, 161.
Readdy v. Prendergast, 110.
Reece v. Rigby, 136.
Reed v. Moore, 18.
—— v. Norris, 115.
Reeve v. Conyngham, 20, 27.
—— v. Palmer, 94.
—— v. Reeve, 151.
Reg. v. Cumberland, 33.
—— v. Stephens, 245.
Reid v. Dreaper, 272.
—— v. Teakle, 15.
Reneaux v. Teakle, 14.
Renpor, The, 76.
Reuter v. Electric Telegraph Co., 44.

Reynolds v. Peapes, 273, 282.
——— v. Smith, 172.
Rhodes v. Forwood, 161, 319.
——— v. Sugden, 195.
Rhosina, The, 247.
Rice v. Chute, 271.
——— v. Shepherd, 23.
Rich v. Coe, 221.
Richards v. W. Middlesex Waterworks Co., 252.
Richardson v. Anderson, 64.
——— v. Cartwright, 60.
——— v. Du Bois, 15.
——— v. Williamson, 291, 295.
Rimell v. Sampayo, 221.
Rimmer v. Knowles, 159.
Ringdove, The, 198.
Rinquist v. Ditchell, 75.
Risbourg v. Bruckner, 48.
Robbins v. Fennell, 84, 86, 87.
Roberts, Re, 110.
——— v. Barnard, 160.
——— v. Ogilby, 10, 98, 99.
——— v. Smith, 151.
Robertson v. Fauntleroy, 302, 321.
Robins v. Bridge, 276.
Robinson v. Gleadow, 44.
——— v. Mollett, 66, 67, 80, 106, 170.
——— v. Rutter, 309.
Robson v. Kemp, 190, 324.
Rocher v. Busher, 76.
Roe v. Birkenhead, &c. Rail. Co., 254.
— d. Rochester v. Pierce, 34, 40, 46.
Rogers, Ex parte, Re Rogers, 170.
——— v. Boehm, 141.
Rolfe v. Abbott, 28.
Rolland v. Hart, 265.
Rosewarne v. Billing, 178.
Ross v. Buxton, 194, 196.
Rossiter v. Trafalgar Life Ass. Co., 81.
Rotherham Alum and Chemical Co., Re, 38.
Rothschild v. Brookman, 103, 104, 122.
Rowe v. London Pianoforte Co., 254.
Rowles v. Senior, 314.
Royal British Bank v. Turquand, 205.
Royle v. Busby, 276.
Rucker v. Lunt, 150.
Ruddock v. Marsh, 17.
Ruddy v. Mid G. W. Rail. Co., 262.
Rumball v. Metropolitan Bank, 213.
Rusby v. Scarlett, 211.
Russell v. Hankey, 93, 129, 131.
——— v. Palmer, 136.
Ryan v. Sams, 27, 332.

Sadler, Re, Ex parte Davies, 100, 102, 201.
——— v. Leigh, 223, 307.
Sainsbury v. Jones, 297.
Salacia, The, 276.
Salford (Mayor of) v. Lever, 139, 269.
Salisbury v. Metropolitan Rail. Co., 313.
Salomans v. Pender, 105, 167.
Samuel v. Rowe, 70.
Sanderson v. Griffith, 37.
Sargent v. Morris, 305.
Saunderson v. Glass, 111.
Savery v. King, 107, 110, 125.
Sawers, Re, 212.
Saxon v. Blake, 273.
Scarf v. Jardine, 332.
Schack v. Anthony, 225.

Schjott v. Schjott, 293.
Schmaling v. Tomlinson, 84, 85.
Schumack v. Lock, 261.
Scott v. Dunbar, 109.
—— v. Ebury, 38.
—— v. Franklin, 181, 185.
—— v. Manchester, 247.
—— v. Surman, 69, 146.
Scrimgeour's Claim, 174.
Seaber v. Hawkes, 274, 288.
Seaton v. Benedict, 14.
Sec. of State for India v. Kamachee Boye Sahaba, 35, 47.
Segrave v. Kirwan, 125.
Segreda, The, 78.
Selsey v. Rhoades, 108.
Semenza v. Brinsley, 241.
Sentance v. Hawley, 172.
Seroka v. Kattenberg, 246.
Service v. Bain, 176, 178.
Seton v. Slade, 72, 320.
Seymour v. Bridge, 175.
—— v. Greenwood, 250.
—— v. Pychlau, 204.
Shallcross v. Oldham, 117.
Shand v. Grant, 299.
Sharland v. Mildow, 7, 300, 312.
Sharman v. Brandt, 5, 306.
Sharpe v. Foy, 265.
Shaw v. Arden, 168.
—— v. Port Philip Gold Mining Co., 256.
—— v. Woodcock, 3.
Shee v. Clarkson, 6, 99.
Shelton v. Livius, 71, 211.
—— v. Springett, 28.
Shenstone v. Hilton, 315.
Shepard v. Brown, 204.
Shepherd v. Mackoul, 23.
Sheridan v. New Quay Co., 102.
Shiells v. Blackburne, 96, 134.
Shipman v. Thompson, 326.
Shippey v. Gray, 195.
Shirreff's Claim, 163.
Shoolbred, Ex parte, 255.
Short v. Spackman, 305.
Sigourney v. Lloyd, 219.
Simmons v. L. J. S. Bank, 213.
Simons v. Patchett, 295.
Simpson's Claim, 210.
Simpson v. Lamb, 160, 163.
—— v. Swan, 176.
Sims v. Brittain, 85.
Sivewright v. Archibold, 228.
Skinner v. Stocks, 223.
—— v. Weguelin, 144.
Smallpiece v. Dawes, 223.
Smally v. Smally, 6.
Smalz v. Avery, 306.
Smart v. Sandars, 68, 88, 321, 323.
Smethurst v. Mitchell, 230, 234.
Smith, Ex parte, 146.
——, Re, Ex parte Bright, 147.
—— v. Barton, 94.
—— v. Birmingham Gas Co., 247.
—— v. Blyth, 136.
—— v. Cologan, 43, 48.
—— v. Gould, 77.
—— v. Hammond, 202.
—— v. Keal, 74, 248, 252.
—— v. Lascelles, 89, 121, 130.
—— v. Levaux, 203.
—— v. Lindo, 170.
—— v. Lyon, 310.
—— v. M'Guire, 1, 2, 206, 218.
—— v. North Met. Tram Co., 250.
—— v. Plummer, 197.
—— v. Price, 138.
—— v. Reynolds, 172.
—— v. Sleap, 301.
—— v. Sorby, 269.
—— v. Troup, 63, 73, 206.
—— v. Webster, 63, 65, 74.

Smout *v.* Ilbery, 290, 293.
Smyth *v.* Anderson, 224, 231.
Snee *v.* Prescott, 231, 303.
Snelgrove *v.* Ellringham Collry. Co., 161.
Snell, Re, 74.
Snook *v.* Davidson, 181, 193.
Snowball, Ex parte, 327, 329.
Snowdon *v.* Davis, 300.
Soames *v.* Spencer, 34, 40, 44.
Société Générale de Paris *v.* Tramways Union Co., 266.
Solly *v.* Rathbone, 69, 86, 192.
Solomon *v.* Barker, 89, 90, 93, 121, 131.
Solomons *v.* Bank of England, 191, 219.
Solway, The, 261.
Somerset, Re, 5.
South of Ireland Collry. Co. *v.* Waddle, 31, 32, 33.
Southampton *v.* Brown, 225.
Southwell *v.* Bowditch, 283.
Sowerby *v.* Butcher, 280.
Spackman *v.* Evans, 35, 42, 44.
Spain, Queen of *v.* Parr, 116, 169.
Spears *v.* Hartley, 181, 199.
Spedding *v.* Nevell, 297.
Speight *v.* Gaunt, 7.
Spencer *v.* Topham, 110.
Spiller *v.* Paris Skating Rink Co., 38.
Spittle *v.* Lavender, 48, 281, 282.
Spurr *v.* Cass, 223.
Stackpole *v.* Erle, 165.
Stafford *v.* Clark, 146.
Stagg *v.* Elliott, 218.
Stainton *v.* Carron Co., 114.
Standage *v.* Creighton, 261.
Staveley *v.* Uzielli, 333.
Stearine Co. *v.* Heintzmann, 139.
Stein *v.* Cope, 64.
Stephens *v.* Badcock, 85.
Stevens *v.* Biller, 2, 186.
——— *v.* Elwall, 313.
——— *v.* Hill, 302.
——— *v.* Hinshelwood, 57, 61, 254.
——— *v.* Midland Counties Rail. Co., 247, 312.
——— *v.* Woodward, 254.
Stevenson *v.* Mortimer, 224, 311.
Stewart *v.* Aberdein, 53, 245.
——— *v.* Fry, 303.
Stocken *v.* Pattrick, 23.
Stokes *v.* Trumper, 168.
Stone *v.* Cartwright, 318.
Stonehouse *v.* Grant, 76.
Storey *v.* Ashton, 254.
Strachan, Re, 146.
Strathmore *v.* Vane, 185.
Strauss *v.* Francis, 63, 72, 205, 218.
Stuart *v.* Haigh, 290.
——— *v.* Welch, 202.
Stubbing *v.* Heintz, 211.
Sullivan *v.* Pearson, 196.
Summers *v.* Solomon, 251.
Sunderland Marine Ins. Co. *v.* Kearney, 304.
Sutton, Ex parte, 82.
——— *v.* Gray, 3.
——— *v.* Spectacle Makers' Co., 32.
——— *v.* Tatham, 63, 66, 172.
Sweet *v.* Pym, 200.
Sweeting *v.* Pearce, 52, 53, 68, 229, 245.
Swift *v.* Jewesbury, 8, 260, 312.
Swinfen *v.* Swinfen, 72, 90.
Swire *v.* Francis, 144, 251, 258.
Sydney and Wigpool Iron Ore Co. *v.* Bird, 117.
Sykes *v.* Giles, 52, 71, 122, 244.
—— *v.* Howarth, 246.
Symons *v.* Blake, 196.

Taff Vale Rail. Co. v. Giles, 247.
Tagart v. Marcus, 308.
Tanner v. Christian, 283.
——— v. European Bank, 202.
Taplin v. Barrett, 155.
——— v. Florence, 323.
Tardrew v. Howell, 197.
Tasker v. Shepherd, 162, 326.
Tate v. Hyslop, 267.
Taylor, Re, 199.
——— v. Blacklow, 124, 132.
——— v. Brewer, 151.
——— v. Green, 257.
——— v. Lendey, 331.
——— v. Plumer, 147.
——— v. Robinson, 182.
——— v. Salmon, 106.
——— v. Sheppard, 233.
——— v. Stray, 173.
Teed v. Beere, 114.
Tenant v. Elliott, 98.
Tetley v. Shand, 122, 204.
Thacker v. Hardy, 169, 176, 177, 321.
——— v. Moates, 76.
Thames, The, 248.
Thickbroom, Re, 147.
Thomas v. Bishop, 278.
——— v. Finlayson, 293.
Thompson v. Bell, 250.
——— v. Cartwright, 265.
——— v. Davenport, 231.
——— v. Gardiner, 6, 70, 228.
——— v. Havelock, 122.
——— v. Meade, 116.
Thorne v. Heard, 256.
Thornton v. Meux, 230.
Thynne v. St. Maur, 5.
Tickel v. Short, 138.
Tigress, The, 200.
Todd v. Emly, 220.
—— v. Reid, 53, 245.
—— v. Robinson, 205, 221.
Tomson v. Judge, 111.
Topham v. Braddick, 121.
Toplis v. Grane, 169, 176.
Toppin v. Healey, 166, 167.
Tottenham v. Green, 207.
Touche v. Metropolitan Warehousing Co., 38.
Toulmin v. Millar, 153, 156.
Townend v. Drakeford, 229.
Townsend v. Inglis, 208.
Townson v. Wilson, 298.
Tribe v. Taylor, 154.
Trickett v. Tomlinson, 206.
Trimble v. Hill, 331.
Trueman v. Loder, 221, 332.
Truettell v. Barandon, 219.
Trye, Re, 147.
Turnbull v. Garden, 116.
Turner v. Burkinshaw, 92, 142.
——— v. Goldsmith, 161.
——— v. Hockey, 315.
——— v. Rooks, 23.
——— v. Thomas, 242.
Turpin v. Bilton, 88, 94, 132.
Turrell v. Collet, 272.
Twycross v. Dreyfus, 270.
Twynam v. Porter, 194.
Tyars v. Alsop, 111.
Tyrrell v. Bank of London, 104, 142.

Udell v. Atherton, 257.
Underwood v. Lewis, 125, 167.
——— v. Nicholls, 52, 245.
United Service Co., Re, 133, 137.
Unwin v. Wolseley, 271.

Van Omeron v. Dowick, 79.
Van Sandau v. Browne, 125, 167.
Van Toll v. Chapman, 135.
Varden v. Parker, 126.
Venning v. Bray, 330.
Victor, The, 78.
Viney v. Chaplin, 74.

Wadsworth, Re, 195.
——— *v.* Marshall, 125.
Waithman *v.* Wakefield, 46.
Wake *v.* Harrop, 286.
Waldo *v.* Martin, 165.
Walker *v.* Birch, 181, 185.
——— *v.* G. W. Rail. Co., 60.
——— *v.* Rostron, 302, 324.
——— *v.* S. E. Rail. Co., 254.
Wallace *v.* Woodgate, 199.
Waller *v.* Drakeford, 205.
——— *v.* Holmes, 86, 193.
Wallis, Re, 110.
Walsh *v.* Whitcomb, 321.
Walsham *v.* Stainton, 140.
Walshe *v.* Provan, 184.
Ward *v.* G. O. Co., 256.
——— *v.* Sharp, 107, 125.
——— *v.* Stuart, 149.
Waring *v.* Favenck, 231.
Warlow *v.* Harrison, 123, 170, 275, 330.
Warner *v.* M'Kay, 243.
Warr *v.* Jones, 297.
Wart *v.* Wolley, 134.
Warwick *v.* Noakes, 129.
——— *v.* Slade, 178, 331.
Waters *v.* Shaftesbury, 107, 204.
Watson *v.* King, 322.
——— *v.* Murrell, 272.
——— *v.* Swann, 37, 38.
——— *v.* Threlkeld, 27.
Watteau *v.* Fenwick, 60, 208, 210.
Waud, Re, 226.
Weary *v.* Alderson, 73, 83.
Webb *v.* Smith, 301.
Webster *v.* De Tastet, 134.
——— *v.* Seekamp, 76.
Weeks *v.* Propert, 292, 294.
Weir *v.* Barnett, 255, 258, 318.
Wellfield *v.* Adamson, 76.
Welstead *v.* Levy, 310.
Wenham, Ex parte, 72, 73.
Wentworth *v.* Lloyd, 110.
West London Commercial Bank *v.* Kitson, 291, 293.
Westacott *v.* Bevan, 196.
Western Bank of Scotland *v.* Addie, 236, 247, 255, 257.
Westwood *v.* Bell, 181, 192.
Whaley Bridge Calico Co. *v.* Green, 117.
Whatman *v.* Pearson, 248.
Whitcomb *v.* Minchin, 104.
White, Ex parte, Re Nevill, 3.
——— *v.* Baxter, 152.
——— *v.* Bayley, 100.
——— *v.* Benckendorff, 204.
——— *v.* Chapman, 166.
——— *v.* Cuyler, 91.
——— *v.* Lincoln, 167.
——— *v.* Proctor, 6, 11, 71, 83.
Whitecombe *v.* Jacob, 146.
Whitehead *v.* Greetham, 96, 135.
——— *v.* Lord, 125, 167, 326.
——— *v.* Taylor, 36, 41, 48.
——— *v.* Tuckett, 220.
Whitehouse *v.* Abberly, 261.
Whiteley *v.* Pepper, 248.
Whiteman *v.* Hawkins, 138.
Whitfield *v.* Brand, 146, 147.
——— *v.* Despencer, 270.
Whitley, Re, 31.
Wickham *v.* Wickham, 3.
Wilde *v.* Gibson, 258.
Wilkins *v.* Carmichael, 197.
Wilkinson *v.* Alston, 152.
——— *v.* Coverdale, 134.
——— *v.* Martin, 153, 156.
Wilks *v.* Back, 91.
Williams *v.* Evans, 52, 71, 90, 244.
——— *v.* Everett, 302.
——— *v.* Innes, 263.
——— *v.* Gibbs, 136.
——— *v.* Mason, 8, 260.
——— *v.* Millington, 180, 275, 305.

Williams v. North China Ass. Co., 35, 40.
——— v. Potts, 101.
——— v. Preston, 255.
——— v. Stevens, 115.
——— v. Trye, 112.
Williamson v. Babour, 105, 113.
——— v. Barton, 274, 288.
——— v. Page, 77.
Willis v. Martin, 255.
Wilmot v. Smith, 207.
Wilson v. Anderton, 313.
——— v. Barthrop, 278.
——— v. Brett, 93, 96, 135.
——— v. Ford, 21, 22, 23.
——— v. Glossop, 25.
——— v. Hart, 223.
——— v. Millar, 79.
——— v. Poulter, 45, 48.
——— v. Short, 105, 122.
——— v. Tunman, 34, 35, 37, 46.
——— v. Turner, 263.
——— v. West Hartlepool Ry. Co., 44, 222.
Wiltshire v. Sims, 51, 63, 70, 71, 90, 210.
Wing v. Harvey, 208.
Withington v. Herring, 55.
Witt, Re, 182.
Wolfe v. Findlay, 141.
Wolff v. Horncastle, 35, 48.
Wood, Re, Ex parte Boden, 146.
——————Wenham, 72, 73.
——— v. Baxter, 275.
——— v. Rowcliffe, 217.
Woodin v. Burford, 58.
Woodley v. Coventry, 101.
Woolfe v. Horne, 275.
Woollen v. Wright, 37.
Worrall v. Harford, 189.
Wray v. Kemp, 83.
Wren v. Kirton, 130.
Wright v. Bigg, 205.
——— v. Castle, 74.
——— v. Dannah, 5.
——— v. Proud, 111.
Wyatt v. Hertford, 235.
Wylde v. Radford, 187.
Wyllie v. Pollen, 266.

Xenos v. Wickham, 65, 70.

Yarborough v. Bank of England, 247.
Yates v. Farebrother, 123.
——— v. Freckleton, 63, 73.
——— v. Hoppe, 322, 323.
Young v. Cole, 63, 67, 174.
——— v. Grote, 179.
——— v. Schuler, 285.
——— v. White, 239.
——— v. Wright, 263.

Zinck v. Walker, 147.
Zulueta v. Vinent, 101.
Zwilchenbart v. Alexander, 94, 122.

A DIGEST

OF

THE LAW OF AGENCY.

CHAPTER I.

PRELIMINARY.

Article 1.

DEFINITIONS.

AN agent is a person having express or implied authority to represent or act on behalf of another person, who is called his principal.

A general agent is an agent who has authority—

(a) to act for his principal in all matters, or in all matters concerning a particular trade or business, or of a particular nature; or

(b) to do some act in the ordinary course of his trade, profession or business as an agent, on behalf of his principal; *e.g.*, where a solicitor, factor or broker is employed, as such (*a*).

A special agent is an agent who has only authority to do some particular act, or represent his principal in

(*a*) See *Brady* v. *Todd*, 1861, 9 C. B. N. S. 592, 30 L. J. C. P. 223; 7 Jur. N. S. 827; 4 L. T. 212, 9 W. R. 483, *Smith* v. *M'Guire*, 1858, 3 H. & N. 554, 27 L. J. Ex. 465, 1 F. & F. 199. The distinction between general and special agents is only of importance in determining the nature and extent of the authority conferred. See Articles 35 to 38.

some particular transaction, such act or transaction not being in the ordinary course of his trade, profession, or business as an agent (*a*).

A factor is a mercantile agent whose ordinary course of business is to sell or dispose of goods, of which he is intrusted with the possession or control by his principal (*b*).

A broker is an agent whose ordinary course of business is to negotiate and make contracts for the sale and purchase of goods and other property, of which he is not intrusted with the possession or control (*b*).

An auctioneer is an agent whose ordinary course of business is to sell by public auction goods or other property, of which he may or may not be intrusted with the possession or control.

A mercantile agent, within the meaning and for the purposes of the Factors Act, 1889 (*c*), is a mercantile agent having, in the customary course of his business as such agent, authority either to sell goods, or to consign goods for the purpose of sale, or to buy goods, or to raise money on the security of goods (*d*).

Article 2.

DEL CREDERE AGENCY.

A *del credere* agent is a mercantile agent who, in consideration of a higher rate of remuneration than is

(*a*) See note (*a*), *ante*, p. 1.

(*b*) See *Baring* v. *Corrie*, 1818, 2 B. & A. 137; 20 R. R. 383; *Stevens* v. *Biller*, 1883, 25 Ch. Div. 31, 53 L. J. Ch. 249, 50 L. T. 36, 32 W. R. 419, C. A.

(*c*) 52 & 53 Vict. c. 45. (The Act is set out in the Appendix.)

(*d*) *Ibid.* s. 1. The expression goods includes wares and merchandise.

usually paid, guarantees that persons with whom he enters into contracts on behalf of the principal shall duly perform those contracts (*e*). Such an agent is said to act under a *del credere* commission.

In effect, a *del credere* agent is a surety for the due performance by the persons with whom he deals, of contracts made by him with them on his principal's behalf (*e*). But it has been held that an agreement by an agent to sell on a *del credere* commission is not a promise to answer for the debt, default, or miscarriage of another person, within the meaning of the 4th section of the Statute of Frauds (*f*), and it is not necessary that such an agreement should be in writing (*f*). A *del credere* agency may be inferred from a course of conduct between the parties (*g*).

Distinction between del credere agent and vendee.—Where goods were consigned by A. to B. for the purpose of sale, and it was agreed that B. should have the right to sell at such prices and on such terms as he thought fit, and that B. should pay an agreed price for the goods sold by him within a fixed period after the sale thereof, it was held that the relation between A. and B. was that of vendor and purchaser, not that of principal and agent (*h*). But the mere fact that a person employed to sell goods is allowed by way of remuneration all the profit obtained by him over and above an agreed price, and that he guarantees the payment of that agreed price to the person employing him, does not prevent the relation between them

(*e*) See *Morris* v. *Cleasley*, 1816, 4 M. & S. 566, 14 R. R. 531; *Hornby* v. *Lacy*, 1817, 6 M. & S. 166; *Grove* v. *Dubois*, 1 T. R. 112.

(*f*) 29 Car. II. c. 3, *Coutourier* v. *Hastie*, 1852, 8 Ex. 40; 22 L. J. Ex. 97, *Sutton* v. *Gray*, (1894) 1 Q. B. 285; 9 Rep. 106. But see *Wickham* v. *Wickham*, 1855, 2 Kay & J. 487.

(*g*) *Shaw* v. *Woodcock*, 1827, 7 B. & C. 73; 9 D. & R. 889.

(*h*) *Ex p. White, re Nevill*, 1870, L. R. 6 Ch. 397; 40 L. J. Bk. 73; 24 L. T. 45; 19 W. R. 488.

being that of principal and agent, if it appears from the circumstances as a whole that their intention was to establish a *del credere* agency (*i*).

Articlc 3.

CAPACITY TO ACT AS PRINCIPAL.

Capacity to contract or do any other act by means of an agent is co-extensive with the capacity of the principal to himself make the contract or do the act that the agent is authorized to make or do. Provided that, where capacity to do a particular act exists only by virtue of a special custom, the act cannot be done by means of an agent unless the custom warrants its being so done (*j*).

Thus, an infant or lunatic is bound by a contract made by his agent with his authority, where the circumstances are such that he would have been bound if he had himself made the contract (*k*). On the other hand, a corporation or joint stock company has no capacity to appoint an agent for any purpose, or to do any act, beyond the scope of their charter or memorandum of association (*l*).

(*i*) *Ex p. Bright, re Smith*, 1879, 10 Ch. Div. 566, 48 L. J. Bk. 81, 39 L. T. 649, 27 W. R. 385, C. A.

(*j*) *Combe's case*, 9 Co. R. 75, where it was held that an infant had no power to appoint an attorney to make a feoffment on his behalf under the custom of gavelkind, though by virtue of the custom he had power to convey by feoffment himself.

(*k*) See *King* v. *Longnor*, 1833, 4 B. & Ad. 647, 1 N. & M. 576, *Drew* v. *Nunn*, 1879, 4 Q. B. D. 661, 48 L. J. Q. B. 591, 40 L. T. 671, 27 W. R. 810, C. A.

(*l*) *Montreal Assurance Co.* v. *M'Gillivray*, 1859, 13 Moo. P. C. C. 87; 8 W. R. 165, P. C.; *Bateman* v. *Mid Wales Rail. Co.*, 1866, L. R. 1 C. P. 499, 35 L. J. C. P. 205, 1 H. & R. 508, 14 W. R. 672, 12 Jur. N. S. 453, *Poulton* v. *L. & S. W. Rail. Co.*, 1867, L. R. 2 Q. B. 534, 36 L. J. Q. B. 294, 17 L. T. 11, 8 B. & S. 616.

Formerly, a married woman had no power to appoint an attorney, but the 40th section of the Conveyancing Act, 1881 (*m*), provides that a married woman, whether an infant or not, shall have power, as if she were unmarried and of full age, by deed to appoint an attorney on her behalf for the purpose of executing any deed or doing any other act which she might herself execute or do.

Article 4.

CAPACITY TO ACT AS AGENT.

All persons of sound mind, including infants and other persons with limited or no capacity to contract on their own behalf, are competent to act and contract as agents. Provided that—

(a) no married woman is competent to act as the next friend or guardian *ad litem* of an infant plaintiff or defendant (*n*);

(b) no party to a contract is competent to sign the contract as the agent of another party thereto so as to satisfy the provisions of the 4th section of the Statute of Frauds, or (probably) of the 4th section of the Sale of Goods Act, 1893 (*o*);

(c) the personal liability of the agent on the contract of agency, and upon contracts entered into by him with third persons, is

---

(*m*) 44 & 45 Vict. c. 41.

(*n*) *Re Somerset, Thynne* v. *St. Maur*, 1887, 34 Ch. Div. 465; 56 L. J. Ch. 733; 56 L. T. 145.

(*o*) 29 Car. II. c. 3; 56 & 57 Vict. c. 71. See *Sharman* v. *Brandt*, 1871, L. R. 6 Q. B. 720; 40 L. J. Q. B. 312; 19 W. R. 936; *Wright* v. *Dannah*, 1809, 2 Camp. 203; 11 R. R. 693, *Farebrother* v. *Simmons*, 1822, 5 B. & A. 333.

dependent on his capacity to contract on his own behalf (*p*).

An act done by an agent, as such, is deemed to be the act of the principal who authorized it, the agent being looked upon merely as an instrument: hence the rule that a person having no capacity to contract on his own behalf is competent to contract on behalf of, and so as to bind, his principal. So, where an agent, who was unable to read, was authorized to enter into and sign a contract on his principal's behalf, it was held that the principal could not avoid a written contract made by the agent, on the ground of his inability to read it (*q*).

The agent of one party to a contract is not incompetent to act as the agent of the other party thereto, where he can do so consistently with his duty to his principal. Thus, a broker frequently acts for both the buyer and the seller of goods, and an insurance broker for the assured as well as the underwriters (*r*). The signature of a broker employed by both buyer and seller, or of an auctioneer, to a contract of sale, operates as the signature of both parties within the meaning of the 4th or 17th section of the Statute of Frauds, or of the 4th section of the Sale of Goods Act, 1893 (*s*). And it has been held that a clerk or factor of one of the parties to a contract is competent to act as the agent of the other party for the same purpose (*t*).

(*p*) See *Smally* v. *Smally*, 1700, 1 Eq. Ab. 6.

(*q*) *Foreman* v. *G. W. Rail. Co.*, 1878, 38 L. T. 851.

(*r*) See *Shee* v. *Clarkson*, 1810, 12 East, 507; 11 R. R. 473.

(*s*) *Parton* v. *Crofts*, 1864, 16 C. B. N. S. 11, 33 L. J. C. P. 189; 10 L. T. 34, 12 W. R. 553, *Thompson* v *Gardiner*, 1876, 1 C. P. D. 777, *Emmerson* v. *Heelis*, 1809, 2 Taunt. 38, 11 R. R. 520, *White* v. *Procter*, 1811, 4 Taunt. 209, 13 R. R. 580, *Hinde* v. *Whitehouse*, 1806, 7 East, 558; 3 Smith, 528, 8 R. R. 676.

(*t*) *Durrell* v. *Evans*, 1862, 1 H. & C. 174, 31 L. J. Ex. 337, 9 Jur. N. S. 104, 7 L. T. 97, 10 W. R. 665, *Bird* v. *Boulter*, 1833, 1 N. & M. 313; 4 B. & Ad. 443.

Article 5.

FOR WHAT PURPOSES AN AGENT MAY BE APPOINTED.

An agent may be appointed for the purpose of executing any deed, or making any contract, or doing any other act on behalf of the principal, which he might himself execute, make, or do, except where the act is required by statute to be done by the principal in person, or is an act in pursuance of a power or authority conferred, or duty imposed, upon the principal personally, the exercise or performance of which involves personal discretion or skill (*u*). Provided, that the relationship of principal and agent cannot impose upon the agent any obligation to commit a wrongful act, or discharge him from any liability in respect thereof (*v*).

Discretionary powers.—A person who is given a power or authority of a discretionary nature must, as a general rule, exercise it in person. Thus, where the consent of a particular person was required for the execution of a power of appointment, it was held that he had no power to appoint an agent to consent thereto in his place, the authority being one involving personal discretion (*w*). The rules as to delegation of authority by agents are founded upon the same principle (*x*).

(*u*) As to the employment of agents by trustees, see Trustee Act, 1893, s. 17. And see *Speight* v. *Gaunt*, 1883, 9 App. Cas. 1; 53 L. J. Ch. 419; 50 L. T. 330, 32 W. R. 435, H. L.

(*v*) See *Cullen* v. *Thompson*, 1862, 4 Macq. H. L. Cas. 424, 432, H. L.; *Heugh* v. *Abergavenny*, 1874, 23 W. R. 40, *Sharland* v. *Mildow*, 1846, 5 Hare, 469; 15 L. J. (N. S.) Ch. 434, 10 Jur. 771.

(*w*) *Hawkins* v. *Kemp*, 1803, 3 East, 410.

(*x*) See Article 39.

Statutes requiring personal performance.—Lord Tenterden's Act (*y*) requires that certain documents, in order to have legal effect, shall be signed by certain parties. It has been held that, to satisfy the provisions of that statute, the document must be signed by the party himself, and that the signature of an agent is insufficient, even if expressly ratified by the principal (*z*).

Authority to commit a tort.—The relationship of principal and agent is recognized in tort for the purpose of charging the principal, but not for the purpose of discharging the agent. Where an agent commits a tort by the authority of his principal, the rule is that they are both personally responsible, and the agent has no right of indemnity from the principal (*a*).

Article 6.

CO-AGENTS.

An authority given to two or more persons is, in the absence of a provision that they may execute it severally, presumed to be given to them jointly (*b*).

Where a joint authority is of a private nature, all the co-agents must join in its execution, in order to bind the principal, unless it is provided that a specified number shall form a quorum (*b*); but where the authority is of a public nature, it is sufficient, as a general

(*y*) 9 Geo. IV. c. 14, s. 6.

(*z*) *Williams* v. *Mason*, 1873, 28 L. T. 232; 21 W. R. 386; *Swift* v. *Jewesbury*, 1874, L. R. 9 Q. B. 301, 43 L. J. Q. B. 56, 30 L. T. 31; 22 W. R. 319, *Hyde* v. *Johnson*, 1836, 3 Scott, 289, 2 Bing. N. C. 776; 2 Hodges, 94. The Mercantile Law Amendment Act, 1856 (19 & 20 Vict. c. 97), s. 13, renders the decision in this last case unimportant.

(*a*) See Articles 97, 124, and 125.

(*b*) *Brown* v. *Andrew*, 1849, 18 L. J. Q. B. 153, 13 Jur. 938; Illustrations 1 and 3.

rule, if it is executed by a majority of the persons in whom it is vested (*c*).

Where an authority is given to two or more persons severally, any one or more of them may execute it without the concurrence of the other or others (*d*).

Illustrations.

1. A provisional committee appointed eight specified persons to act as a managing committee on their behalf. Six of such persons gave an order within the scope of the authority conferred. Held, that the provisional committee were not bound by the order (*e*).

2. It was provided by statute (9 Geo. I. c. 7), that the churchwardens and overseers of a parish, with the major part of the parishioners, should have authority to enter into contracts for providing for the poor. Held, that the contract of a majority of the churchwardens and overseers bound the others (*f*).

3. Two persons filled the office of clerk to the trustees of a road. Held, that they must contract jointly in order to bind the trustees (*g*).

4. A power of attorney was given to fifteen persons, "jointly or severally to execute such policies as they or any of them should jointly or severally think proper." Held, that a policy executed by four of such persons was binding on the principal (*h*).

(*c*) Illustration 2. And see *Grindley* v. *Barker*, 1798, 1 B. & P. 229; 4 R. R. 787; *Cortis* v. *Kent Waterworks Co.*, 1827, 7 B. & C. 314.

(*d*) Illustration 4.

(*e*) See note (*b*), *ante*, p. 8.

(*f*) *The King* v. *Beeston*, 1789, 3 T. R. 592; 1 R. R. 777.

(*g*) *Bell* v. *Nixan*, 1832, 9 Bing. 393, 2 M. & Scott, 534.

(*h*) *Guthrie* v. *Armstrong*, 1822, 5 B. & A. 628.

Article 7.

HOW THE RELATION OF AGENCY ARISES.

The relation of agency exists, and can only exist, by virtue of the express or implied assent of both principal and agent (*h*).

The assent of the principal is implied whenever another person occupies such a position that, according to the ordinary usages of mankind, he would be understood to have the principal's authority to act on his behalf (*i*).

The assent of the agent is implied whenever he acts or assumes to act on behalf of another person, and after having so acted or assumed to act he is not permitted, in an action by such person, to deny that the agency in fact existed, or that he acted on such person's behalf (*j*).

The relationship of principal and agent may arise—

(a) by express appointment by the principal (*k*);

(b) by implication of law from the situation of the parties (*l*); or

---

(*h*) See *Markwick* v. *Hardingham*, 1880, 15 Ch. Div 349; *Pole* v. *Leask*, 1862, 33 L. J. Ch. 155, 8 L. T. 645, 9 Jur. N. S. 829. There is one exception to this rule, founded on the duty of a husband to provide his wife with necessaries suitable to her station. In certain cases the wife is said to be an agent of necessity, and has authority to pledge his credit, even if he expressly forbids her to do so. See Article 14 (Chapter II.).

(*i*) See the judgment in *Pole* v. *Leask*, 1862, 33 L. J. Ch. 155, 8 L. T. 645, 9 Jur. N. S. 829.

(*j*) See *Roberts* v. *Ogilby*, 1821, 9 Price, 269.

(*k*) See Chapter III.

(*l*) Illustration 1. As to the implied agency of married women, &c., see Chapter II. As to the implied agency of partners, see the Partnership

(c) by subsequent ratification by the principal of acts done on his behalf (*m*).

Where a person assumes to act on behalf of another, the assent of the person on whose behalf the act is done will not be implied from his mere silence or acquiescence, unless the situation of the parties is such as to raise a presumption that the act is done by his authority (*n*).

Illustrations.

1. A. buys property at a sale by auction. Both the auctioneer and his clerk are implied agents of A. for the purpose of signing the contract of sale on his behalf, so as to satisfy the requirements of the 4th section of the Statute of Frauds (*o*), or of the 4th section of the Sale of Goods Act, 1893 (*p*), it being understood that they, in the ordinary course of business, have authority to sign the contract on behalf of the highest bidder (*q*). Subsequently to the sale, B. buys certain unsold lots by private contract with the auctioneer. The auctioneer is not an implied agent of B. for the purpose of signing the contract on his behalf (*r*).

2. A. called at B.'s office and verbally agreed to be responsible for the price of certain goods to be supplied by B. to a third person. B.'s clerk, in A.'s presence, made and signed a memo-

---

Act, 1890 (53 & 54 Vict. c. 39), ss. 5 to 16. Every partner is a general agent of his firm and of his copartners for the purposes of the partnership business.

(*m*) See Chapter IV.

(*n*) Illustrations 2 and 3.

(*o*) 29 Car. II. c. 3.

(*p*) 56 & 57 Vict. c. 71.

(*q*) *Emmerson* v. *Heelis*, 1809, 2 Taunt. 38, 11 R. R. 520; *White* v. *Procter*, 1811, 4 Taunt. 209; 13 R. R. 580; *Bird* v. *Boulter*, 1833, 1 N. & M. 313, 4 B. & Ad. 443.

(*r*) *Mews* v. *Carr*, 1856, 1 H. & N. 484.

randum of the agreement. Held, that the clerk had no implied authority to sign as A.'s agent, and that there was not a sufficient memorandum in writing of the agreement to satisfy the 4th section of the Statute of Frauds (*s*).

3. A.'s traveller sold goods to B., and in B.'s presence wrote out two memoranda of the sale and put B.'s name upon them. One of the memoranda he handed to B., the other he retained. Held, that he had no implied authority to sign a memorandum of the contract as B.'s agent, and that the memorandum was not sufficient to satisfy the 17th section of the Statute of Frauds as against B. (*t*).

Article 8.

DOCTRINE OF HOLDING OUT.

Where a person, by words or conduct, represents or permits it to be represented that another person is his agent, he will not be permitted to deny the agency with respect to any third persons dealing, on the faith of any such representation, with the person so held out as an agent, even if no agency existed in fact (*u*).

(*s*) *Dixon* v. *Broomfield*, 1814, 2 Chit. 205. See also *Graham* v. *Musson*, 1839, 7 Scott, 769, 3 Bing. N. C. 603, 3 M. & G. 368.

(*t*) *Murphy* v. *Boese*, 1875, L. R. 10 Ex. 126, 44 L. J. Ex. 40, 32 L. T. 122, 23 W. R. 474.

(*u*) See illustrations to Article 85. This is an instance of the principle of estoppel *in pais*: *Pole* v. *Leask*, 1862, 33 L. J. Ch. 155, 8 L. T. 645; 9 Jur. N. S. 829.

CHAPTER II.

Implied agency of married women, etc.

The implied authority of a wife to pledge the credit of her husband arises partly from her position as manager of his household, partly from his duty to keep her provided with necessaries suitable to her station in life, or to the style in which he permits her to live (*a*). Formerly, where a wife carried on a separate trade with the permission of her husband, she had implied authority to pledge his credit for goods supplied for the purposes of such trade. But, since the passing of the Married Women's Property Act, 1882 (*b*), the presumption is that contracts made by a wife for the purposes of a separate trade or business carried on by her, are made on her own behalf in respect of her separate property, and her husband is not liable on any such contract, unless it is proved that credit was given to him, and that either he expressly authorized her to pledge his credit, or held her out as having such authority to the person with whom the contract was made. A wife's implied authority to pledge her husband's credit is now restricted to necessaries, either for herself or for the household, and it is not increased by the insanity or lunacy of the husband (*c*). The existence and nature of the authority depend upon whether she lives with her

---

(*a*) See *Phillipson* v. *Hayter*, 1870, L. R. 6 C. P. 38; 40 L. J. C. P. 14; 23 L. T. 556, 19 W. R. 130. As to what are considered necessaries, see *Morgan* v. *Chetwynd*, 1865, 4 F. & F. 451; *Jewesbury* v. *Newbold*, 1857, 26 L. J. Ex. 247; *Hunt* v. *De Blaquiere*, 1829, 5 Bing. 550.

(*b*) 45 & 46 Vict. c. 75.

(*c*) *Richardson* v. *Du Bois*, 1869, L. R. 5 Q. B. 51; 39 L. J. Q. B. 69; 21 L. T. 635, 18 W. R. 62, 10 B. & S. 830.

husband or not; and if not, upon what is the cause of the separation, and whether it is by mutual consent or otherwise.

Article 9.

PRESUMPTION OF AUTHORITY FROM COHABITATION.

Where a husband and wife live together, the mere fact of cohabitation raises a presumption that she has authority to pledge his credit for necessaries suitable to the style in which they live (*d*); but there is no presumption of authority to borrow money in his name, even for the purpose of purchasing necessaries for the price of which he would have been liable if they had been bought on his credit (*e*).

The presumption of authority from the mere fact of cohabitation may be rebutted by proof—

(a) that she had not in fact authority to pledge his credit (*f*); or

(b) that she was already adequately provided with necessaries, or that he had made her a sufficient allowance therefor (*g*).

Authority is confined to suitable necessaries.—The presumption of authority from cohabitation is confined to necessaries suitable

(*d*) *Harrison* v. *Grady*, 1865, 12 Jur. N. S. 140; 13 L. T. 369, 14 W. R. 139, *Jolly* v. *Rees*, 1864, 5 C. B. N. S. 628, 33 L. J. C. P. 177.

(*e*) *Knox* v. *Bushell*, 1857, 3 C. B. N. S. 334.

(*f*) *Jolly* v. *Rees*, 1864, 5 C. B. N. S. 628, 33 L. J. C. P. 177; *Debenham* v. *Mellon*, 1880, 6 App. Cas. 24, 50 L. J. Q. B. 155, 43 L. T. 673, 29 W. R. 141, H. L.

(*g*) *Seaton* v. *Benedict*, 1828, 5 Bing. 28, 2 M. & P. 66; *Debenham* v. *Mellon*, *supra*, *Reneaux* v. *Teakle*, 1853, 8 Ex. 680, 22 L. J. Ex. 241; 17 Jur. 351.

to the style in which the husband chooses to live (*h*). If the wife orders goods that are not suitable to his style of living (*i*), or if the orders are of an extravagant nature (*k*), or are excessive in extent (*k*), there is no presumption of authority, and the husband is not liable, unless he is proved to have expressly authorized her, or held her out as having authority, to purchase the goods, or to have ratified the transactions. The question whether the goods are suitable necessaries is a question of fact for the jury, and the burden of proof lies on the person supplying them (*l*), except in the case of such things as wearing apparel, delivered at the joint residence (*m*), which are presumed to be necessaries until the contrary is shown (*m*).

Effect of forbidding her to pledge his credit.—Even in the case of suitable necessaries, the presumption of authority may be rebutted by proof that she had no authority in fact. The question whether the wife acted as her husband's agent, and with his authority, in any particular transaction, is a question for the jury to decide, upon the evidence given (*n*), and the proper question to leave to them (if the goods were bought on his credit) is whether they were bought with his authority, not merely whether they were suitable necessaries (*o*). If they find that she did not intend to pledge his credit, but contracted

---

(*h*) *Phillipson* v. *Hayter*, 1870, L. R. 6 C. P. 38; 40 L. J. C. P. 14; 23 L. T. 556; 19 W. R. 130.

(*i*) *Harrison* v. *Grady*, 1865, 12 Jur. N. S. 140; 13 L. T. 369; 14 W. R. 139; *Montagu* v. *Benedict*, 1825, 5 D. & R. 532, 3 B. & C. 631; *Atkins* v. *Carwood*, 1837, 7 C. & P. 756.

(*k*) *Debenham* v. *Mellon*, *supra*, note (*f*); *Lane* v. *Ironmonger*, 1844, 13 M. & W. 368; 14 L. J. Ex. 35, Ex. Ch.; *Freestone* v. *Butcher*, 1840, 9 C. & P. 643.

(*l*) *Phillipson* v. *Hayter*, 1870, L. R. 6 C. P. 38; 40 L. J. C. P. 14, 23 L. T. 556; 19 W. R. 130.

(*m*) *Jewesbury* v. *Newbold*, 1857, 26 L. J. Ex. 247; *Clifford* v. *Laton*, 1827, 3 C. & P. 15; M. & M. 101.

(*n*) *Lane* v. *Ironmonger*, 1844, 13 M. & W. 368; 14 L. J. Ex. 35, Ex. Ch.; *Freestone* v. *Butcher*, 1840, 9 C. & P. 643.

(*o*) *Reid* v. *Teakle*, 1853, 13 C. B. 627; 22 L. J. C. P. 161; 17 Jur. 841.

in respect of her separate estate (*p*), or that, though she intended to pledge his credit, he had in fact forbidden her to do so (*q*), he is not liable, even if the person who supplied the goods had no notice that her authority had been revoked (*q*), unless the husband had invested her with an appearance of authority, or had done some act leading the plaintiff to suppose that she had his authority to purchase the goods (*q*). But if a husband, by words or conduct, holds his wife out as having authority, he is liable to any person dealing with her on the faith of such holding out, notwithstanding a revocation of her authority, and though he had expressly forbidden her to pledge his credit, unless such person had actual notice of the revocation or prohibition (*r*).

Article 10.

IMPLIED AUTHORITY AS HOUSEKEEPER.

Where a wife, who is living with her husband, has the management of the household, she is his general agent in all household matters, and has implied authority to pledge his credit for all such things as are necessary in the ordinary course of such management (*s*).

Every act done by a wife within the scope of her implied authority as manager of his household binds the husband, unless she has in fact no authority to do the particular act, and the person dealing with her

(*p*) *Freestone* v. *Butcher*, 1840, 9 C. & P. 643.

(*q*) *Jolly* v. *Rees*, 1864, 5 C. B. N. S. 628, 33 L. J. C. P. 177, Ex. Ch.; *Debenham* v. *Mellon*, 1880, 6 App. Cas. 24, 50 L. J. Q. B. 155, 43 L. T. 673; 29 W. R. 141, H. L.

(*r*) See *Jetley* v. *Hill*, 1884, 1 C. & E. 239, *Filmer* v. *Lynn*, 1835, 4 N. & M. 559, 1 H. & W. 59, *Debenham* v. *Mellon*, *supra*. And see Article 10.

(*s*) *Emmett* v. *Norton*, 1838, 8 C. & P. 506, *Phillipson* v. *Hayter*, 1870, L. R. 6 C. P. 38, 40 L. J. C. P. 14, 23 L. T. 556, 19 W. R. 130.

has, at the time of the transaction, notice that she is exceeding her actual authority (*t*).

Illustrations.

1. The wife of a labourer ordered provisions for the house. The husband was held liable for the price, though he had supplied his wife with sufficient money to keep house, the person supplying the goods having had no notice of that fact (*u*).

2. A husband, during a temporary absence from home, made his wife a sufficient allowance for herself and the family. A tradesman supplied her with goods on credit, knowing that the husband had made her the allowance. Held, that the husband was not liable for the price of the goods (*v*).

Where a wife occupies the position of her husband's housekeeper, he is deemed to hold her out to the world as having the usual authority of a housekeeper, and is bound by all acts within the scope of such apparent authority, unless the persons dealing with her know that her authority is expressly limited, and that she is acting in excess thereof (*x*). Her implied authority as housekeeper is, however, confined to necessaries connected with the domestic department and suitable to the style in which the husband lives, and it does not extend to articles of luxury (*y*). The onus of proof that goods supplied on her orders are suitable necessaries lies on the person supplying them (*y*).

Article 11.

PRIMÂ FACIE, NO AUTHORITY WHERE SEPARATED.

Where a wife is separated from her husband, she has, *primâ facie*, no implied authority to pledge his

(*t*) Illustrations 1 and 2.

(*u*) *Ruddock* v. *Marsh*, 1857, 1 H. & N. 601.

(*v*) *Holt* v. *Brien*, 1821, 4 B. & A. 252.

(*x*) See note (*s*), *ante*, p. 16.

(*y*) *Phillipson* v. *Hayter*, 1870, L. R. 6 C. P. 38; 40 L. J. C. P. 14; 23 L. T. 556, 19 W. R. 130.

credit, and the burden lies upon any person seeking to charge the husband on her contracts of proving that the circumstances of the separation are such as to raise a presumption of authority (*z*).

Where a tradesman gives credit to a wife living apart from her husband, he ought to make inquiries as to the cause of the separation; and if he does not do so, he trusts her at his peril, and is not entitled to charge the husband, unless he proves that she is justified in living apart (*a*). Where the husband was living abroad, and it was sought to charge him for necessaries supplied to his wife in England, it was held that the plaintiff must prove that she was not sufficiently provided for, and that it was necessary for her to pledge her husband's credit (*b*).

Article 12.

WHERE SEPARATED BY MUTUAL CONSENT.

Where husband and wife are separated by mutual consent, and she has agreed to accept a specified allowance, she has no implied authority to pledge his credit so long as that allowance is regularly paid, whether it is adequate or not (*c*); but if the agreed allowance be not regularly paid, then she has implied

---

(*z*) *Edwards* v. *Towels*, 1843, 6 Scott N. R. 641; 5 M. & G. 624; 12 L. J. C. P. 239; *Johnstone* v. *Sumner*, 1858, 3 H. & N. 261, 27 L. J. Ex. 341; 4 Jur. N. S. 462.

(*a*) *Mainwaring* v. *Leslie*, 1826, 2 C. & P. 507, M. & M. 18; *Reed* v. *Moore*, 1832, 5 C. & P. 200, *Clifford* v. *Laton*, 1827, 3 C. & P. 15; M. & M. 101.

(*b*) *Bird* v. *Jones*, 1828, 3 M. & R. 121. See also *Dennys* v. *Sargeant*, 1834, 6 C. & P. 419.

(*c*) *Eastland* v. *Burchell*, 1878, 3 Q. B. D. 432, 47 L. J. Q. B. 500, 38 L. T. 563, 27 W. R. 290, *Negus* v. *Forster*, 1882, 46 L. T. 675, 30 W. R. 671, C. A.

authority to pledge his credit for necessaries suitable to her station in life (*d*).

Where husband and wife are separated by mutual consent, and there has been no agreement by her to accept a specified allowance, she has implied authority to pledge his credit for necessaries suitable to her station in life, unless she has adequate separate means, or is provided with an adequate allowance, either by her husband or some other person (*e*).

Where the wife is permitted to have the custody of the children, necessaries for them are deemed to be necessaries for her (*f*).

Effect of the husband's misconduct, where separated by mutual consent.—In *Biffin* v. *Bignell*, 1862 (*g*), the Exchequer Chamber laid down that, where a husband consents to a separation on condition that his wife shall accept a certain allowance, she has no implied authority to pledge his credit so long as the allowance is duly paid, even if it be inadequate, unless he has been guilty of such misconduct as to justify her in living apart without his consent; because, by not fulfilling the conditions on which his consent was given, she is, in effect, living apart without his consent. But in *Negus* v. *Forster*, 1882 (*h*), where there had been an agreement for a separation with an allowance of 100*l.* a year, and the parties had resumed cohabitation, and then again separated, and the wife had, subsequently, obtained

(*d*) *Beale* v. *Arabin*, 1877, 36 L. T. 249.

(*e*) *Johnstone* v. *Sumner*, 1858, 3 H. & N. 261; 27 L. J. Ex. 341; 4 Jur. N. S. 462; *Harvey* v. *Norton*, 1840, 4 Jur. 42.

(*f*) *Rawlyns* v. *Vandyke*, 1800, 3 Esp. 250.

(*g*) 7 H. & N. 877; 31 L. J. Ex. 189; 8 Jur. N. S. 647; 6 L. T. 248; 10 W. R. 322, Ex. Ch.

(*h*) 46 L. T. 675; 30 W. R. 671, C. A.

a judicial separation with alimony 180*l.* a year, on the ground of the husband's misconduct prior to the second separation, it was held by the Court of Appeal that, the 100*l.* a year having been regularly paid, the original separation deed was a good defence to an action for the price of necessaries supplied to the wife after the second separation but before the decree for judicial separation and alimony. And it would, therefore, seem that misconduct of the husband, combined with inadequacy of the wife's income, does not give her implied authority to pledge his credit, where the amount of such income has been expressly agreed upon, and is duly paid. The true principle seems to be that where, on a separation by mutual consent, the wife expressly agrees to accept a certain allowance, she thereby estops herself from afterwards disputing the sufficiency thereof. It is quite clear, at all events, that where the wife consents to accept a certain income, the inadequacy thereof raises no presumption of authority to pledge her husband's credit (*i*).

Where amount of allowance not fixed.—Where there has been no agreement as to the amount of her allowance, the liability of a husband, who consents to his wife living apart, for the price of necessaries supplied to her on his credit, depends upon whether she is adequately provided for or not. If he pays her an adequate allowance, she has no implied authority to pledge his credit (*k*), and he is not liable for the price of goods supplied to her, even if the person supplying them has no notice of the allowance (*l*). So, he is not liable for goods supplied to her, if he can show that she has adequate separate means (*m*), or that she receives adequate maintenance from some source, whether

---

(*i*) *Eastland* v. *Burchell*, 1878, 3 Q. B. D. 432; 47 L. J. Q. B. 500; 38 L. T. 563, 27 W. R. 290; *Hyde* v. *Price*, 1797, 3 Ves. 445.

(*k*) *Mizen* v. *Pick*, 1838, 3 M. & W. 481, *Holder* v. *Cope*, 1846, 2 C. & K. 437, *Emmett* v. *Norton*, 1838, 8 C. & P. 506, *Hodgkinson* v. *Fletcher*, 1814, 4 Camp. 70; 15 R. R. 725.

(*l*) *Reeve* v. *Conyngham*, 1847, 2 C. & K. 444, *Mizen* v. *Pick*, 1838, 3 M. & W. 481.

(*m*) *Ludlow* v. *Wilmot*, 1817, 2 Stark. 86, 19 R. R. 684.

he supplies it or not (*n*). The question of adequacy is a question of fact for the jury. If they find that the allowance made by him is inadequate, and that she is not otherwise sufficiently provided for according to her station in life, she has implied authority to pledge his credit for suitable necessaries, though she may have acquiesced in the amount of the allowance (*o*).

Article 13.

WHERE LIVING APART WITHOUT THE HUSBAND'S CONSENT.

Where a wife leaves her husband without his consent, or lives apart from him contrary to his wishes, she has no implied authority to pledge his credit, unless he has been guilty of such misconduct as to justify her in so leaving him or living apart (*p*).

Article 14.

WHERE LIVING APART IN CONSEQUENCE OF HUSBAND'S MISCONDUCT, ETC.

Where a wife has been deserted by her husband (*q*), or has been turned away by him without adequate cause (*r*), or has left him in consequence of misconduct on his part justifying her in so leaving him (*s*), and is

---

(*n*) *Clifford* v. *Laton*, 1827, 2 C. & P. 15; M. & M. 101; *Dixon* v. *Hurrell*, 1838, 8 C. & P. 717.

(*o*) *Hodgkinson* v. *Fletcher*, 1814, 4 Camp. 70; 15 R. R. 725.

(*p*) *Hindley* v. *Westmeath*, 1827, 6 B. & C. 200; 9 D. & R. 351; *Johnstone* v. *Sumner*, 1858, 3 H. & N. 261, 27 L. J. Ex. 341; 4 Jur. N. S. 462.

(*q*) *Wilson* v. *Ford*, 1868, L. R. 3 Ex. 63; 37 L. J. Ex. 60; 17 L. T. 605, 16 W. R. 482.

(*r*) *Harrison* v. *Grady*, 1865, 13 Jur. N. S. 140; 13 L. T. 369; 14 W. R. 139; *Forristall* v. *Lawson*, *Connelly* v. *Lawson*, 1876, 34 L. T. 903.

(*s*) *Houliston* v. *Smyth*, 1825, 3 Bing. 127; 10 Moore, 482, 2 C. & P. 22.

living apart from him, it is an irrebuttable presumption of law that she has authority to pledge his credit—

(a) for necessaries suitable to her station in life, unless she is adequately provided for;

(b) for costs reasonably incurred in taking proceedings against him (*t*); and

(c) where she has been given the custody of the children by reason of his misconduct, for their maintenance and education, even if they are living with her contrary to his wishes (*u*).

Where a husband has deserted his wife, he is bound in equity to repay money lent to her for, and expended in, the purchase of necessaries (*x*).

The authority referred to in this article is said to be an authority of necessity (*y*), and the husband is bound to pay for goods ordered by the wife in the exercise thereof, even if he gave the person supplying them express notice not to trust her (*z*). The fact that he makes her an allowance is no defence, if it is found by the jury to be inadequate (*a*).

Costs of legal proceedings.—Where a wife is turned away by her husband, or is compelled to leave him in consequence of his

---

(*t*) *Ottaway* v. *Hamilton*, 1878, 3 C. P. D. 393, 47 L. J. C. P. 725, 38 L. T. 925, 26 W. R. 783, C. A., *Wilson* v. *Ford*, *supra*, note (*q*).

(*u*) *Bazeley* v. *Forder*, 1868, L. R. 3 Q. B. 559, 37 L. J. Q. B. 237, 18 L. T. 756, 9 B. & S. 599.

(*x*) *Jenner* v. *Morris*, 1861, 30 L. J. Ch. 361, 7 Jur. N. S. 375; 3 L. T. 871, 9 W. R. 391, *Deare* v. *Soutten*, 1869, L. R. 9 Eq. 151, 21 L. T. 523; 18 W. R. 203 overruling *May* v. *Skey*, 1849, 16 Sim. 588, 18 L. J. Ch. 306, 13 Jur. 594.

(*y*) See *Johnstone* v. *Sumner*, 1858, 3 H. & N. 261, 27 L. J. Ex. 341; 4 Jur. N. S. 462.

(*z*) *Harris* v. *Morris*, 1801, 4 Esp. 41, 2 R. R. 786, and see Article 15, Illustration 3.

(*a*) *Baker* v. *Sampson*, 1863, 14 C. B. N. S. 383.

violence, and it is necessary to take proceedings to oblige him to keep the peace, he is liable for the costs of such proceedings, as between solicitor and client, even if he allows her an adequate separate maintenance (*b*). So, a wife has implied authority to pledge her husband's credit for costs, as between solicitor and client, reasonably incurred in the institution and prosecution of proceedings for divorce (*c*). And it has been held that he is liable for costs incurred by her in filing a petition for judicial separation, even if it be not proceeded with, provided there are reasonable grounds therefor (*d*). But in such cases the solicitor ought, before commencing proceedings, to make proper investigation and inquiry into all the circumstances; and he is not entitled to recover the costs from the husband in the absence of success unless he can show that there was at least great probability of success (*e*). In *Wilson* v. *Ford* (*f*), where a husband had deserted his wife without cause, and left her without means of subsistence, it was held that she had implied authority to pledge his credit for the costs—(a) of a suit for restitution of conjugal rights; (b) of taking counsel's opinion as to whether a verbal promise of a settlement made by the husband at the time of the marriage could be enforced in equity; and (c) of consultations with her solicitor as to the best means of dealing with tradesmen who had supplied her with necessaries and were pressing her for money, and also with the landlord of a house in which she and her husband had lived, who was threatening to distrain for rent, upon furniture which had been hers before marriage.

(*b*) *Shepherd* v. *Mackoul*, 1813, 3 Camp. 326, 14 R. R. 752; *Turner* v. *Rooks*, 1839, 2 P. & D. 294; 10 A. & E. 47.

(*c*) *Ottaway* v. *Hamilton*, 1878, 3 C. P. D. 393, 47 L. J. C. P. 725; 38 L. T. 925, 26 W. R. 783, C. A.; *Stocken* v. *Pattrick*, 1873, 39 L. T. 507.

(*d*) *Rice* v. *Shepherd*, 1862, 12 C. B. N. S. 332; 6 L. T. 432; *Brown* v. *Ackroyd*, 1856, 5 El. & Bl. 819, 25 L. J. Q. B. 193, 2 Jur. N. S. 283.

(*e*) *Baylis* v. *Watkins*, 1864, 33 L. J. Ch. 300; 10 Jur. N. S. 114; 9 L. T. 741; 12 W. R. 324.

(*f*) 1868, L. R. 3 Ex. 63, 37 L. J. Ex. 60; 17 L. T. 605; 16 W. R. 482.

What degree of misconduct justifies a wife in leaving her husband.—It was decided in *Horwood* v. *Heffer* (1811) (*g*) that no amount of ill-treatment, short of personal violence, or such as to induce a reasonable fear of personal violence, would entitle a wife to pledge her husband's credit after leaving his house without his consent. But in *Houliston* v. *Smyth* (1825) (*h*) it was laid down that such conduct as bringing a prostitute into the house, or threatening to confine the wife in a madhouse, was equivalent to turning her away. It is clear that such cruelty as renders it no longer safe for the wife to remain in the house (*i*), or such violent conduct as causes a reasonable apprehension of personal violence (*k*), justifies her in leaving her husband, and living apart from him.

Article 15.

EFFECT OF ADULTERY BY THE WIFE.

A husband is under no obligation to support his wife, and she has no implied authority to pledge his credit, whether they live together or not, and even if he has himself been guilty of misconduct, after she has committed adultery, unless he connived at or has condoned the offence (*l*). Provided, that if, being aware of her adultery, he continues to hold her out as his agent, he is liable to the same extent as if her authority had continued, with respect to any persons

---

(*g*) 3 Taunt. 421.

(*h*) 3 Bing. 127, 10 Moore, 482; 2 C. & P. 22.

(*i*) *Emery* v. *Emery*, 1827, 1 Y. & J. 501; *Baker* v. *Sampson*, 1863, 14 C. B. N. S. 383.

(*k*) *Brown* v. *Ackroyd*, 1856, 5 El. & Bl. 819, 25 L. J. Q. B. 193; 2 Jur. N. S. 283.

(*l*) Illustrations 1 and 2.

dealing with her on the faith of such holding out, without notice of the determination of her authority (*m*).

Where a husband connives at or has condoned his wife's adultery, her implied authority is not affected thereby (*n*).

Illustrations.

1. A husband committed adultery with a woman whom he brought to the house where he lived with his wife, and, after treating his wife with great cruelty, turned her out of doors. Then the wife committed adultery, after which she offered to return home, but her husband refused to receive her. Held, that the husband was not liable for necessaries supplied to her after her adultery (*o*).

2. A husband turns his wife away without cause. She commits adultery. He is not liable for goods supplied to her after the adultery, even if the person supplying them has no notice of the adultery (*p*), and the goods are absolute necessaries (*q*).

3. A husband connives at his wife's adultery, and then turns her away. She has implied authority to pledge his credit for necessaries, and he is liable for the price thereof, even if he gave express notice to the person supplying them not to trust her (*r*). The same rule applies if a husband condones his wife's adultery, and subsequently turns her away (*s*).

4. A husband, knowing of his wife's adultery, permitted her to continue living in his house with the children. Held, that

---

(*m*) Illustration 4.

(*n*) Illustration 3.

(*o*) *Govier* v. *Hancock*, 1796, 6 T. R. 603; 3 R. R. 271.

(*p*) *Emmett* v. *Norton*, 1838, 8 C. & P. 506; *Atkyns* v. *Pearce*, 1857, 2 C. B. N. S. 763; 26 L. J. C. P. 252; 3 Jur. N. S. 1180.

(*q*) *Hardie* v. *Grant*, 1838, 8 C. & P. 512; *Cooper* v. *Lloyd*, 1859, 6 C. B. N. S. 519.

(*r*) *Wilson* v. *Glossop*, 1888, 20 Q. B. D. 354; 57 L. J. Q. B. 161; 58 L. T. 707; 36 W. R. 296, C. A.

(*s*) *Harris* v. *Morris*, 1801, 4 Esp. 41; 2 R. R. 786.

he was liable for the price of necessaries supplied to her by a tradesman who was ignorant of the circumstances (*t*).

Article 16.

IMPLIED AUTHORITY TO ACKNOWLEDGE DEBTS FOR NECESSARIES.

Whenever a wife has implied authority to pledge her husband's credit, she has also implied authority to acknowledge on his behalf a debt incurred in pursuance thereof, and such an acknowledgment, if it is in writing and signed by her, interrupts the operation of the Statute of Limitations (*u*).

Article 17.

HUSBAND NOT LIABLE UNLESS CREDIT GIVEN TO HIM.

No husband is liable for the price of necessaries supplied to his wife, whether they live together or not, where exclusive credit is given to the wife (*x*), or to some third person, by the person supplying them.

Thus, where a wife, separated from her husband with his consent, lived with her uncle, and ordered necessaries from a tradesman who gave credit to the uncle, and whose former bills for goods supplied to her had been paid by the uncle, it was held that the husband was not liable, though he did not make his

---

(*t*) *Norton* v. *Fazan*, 1798, 1 B. & P. 226; 4 R. R. 785.

(*u*) *Gregory* v. *Parker*, 1808, 1 Camp. 394, 10 R. R. 712, 9 Geo. IV. c. 14, s. 6, 19 & 20 Vict. c. 97, s. 13. But see *Ingram* v. *Little*, 1883, 1 C. & E. 186.

(*x*) *Bently* v. *Griffin*, 1814, 5 Taunt. 356; *Metcalfe* v. *Shaw*, 1811, 3 Camp. 22; 13 R. R. 740.

wife any allowance (*y*). But the mere fact that the goods are booked in the wife's name is not conclusive evidence of an intention to give credit to her alone. The jury must be satisfied that, at the time the contract was made, the person supplying the goods intended to give credit to her to the exclusion of her husband (*z*).

Article 18.

AUTHORITY IMPLIED FROM COHABITATION AS MAN AND WIFE.

Where a man lives with a woman as his wife, she has implied authority to pledge his credit, during the continuance of the cohabitation, to the same extent as if she were legally married to him.

Where there is no cohabitation, the mere fact that a man permits a woman to assume his name is not sufficient to raise a presumption of authority to pledge his credit (*a*). But if they live together as man and wife, he is liable for the price of necessaries supplied to her on his credit, even if the tradesman knew when he supplied the goods that they were not married (*b*). This implied authority determines on a separation, and the mere fact that he had represented her to be his wife does not render him liable for the price of necessaries supplied to her after the separation (*c*). If, however, he held her out to third persons as his agent, they are entitled to deal with her as such, and to charge him accordingly, until they receive notice that the connection has determined (*d*).

(*y*) *Harvey* v. *Norton*, 1840, 4 Jur. 42. See also *Reeve* v. *Conyngham*, 1847, 2 C. & K. 444.

(*z*) *Jewesbury* v. *Newbold*, 1857, 26 L. J. Ex. 247.

(*a*) *Gomme* v. *Franklin*, 1859, 1 F. & F. 465.

(*b*) *Watson* v. *Threlkeld*, 1794, 2 Esp. 637, 5 R. R. 760, *Ryan* v. *Sams*, 1848, 12 Q. B. 460, 17 L. J. Q. B. 271; 12 Jur. 745.

(*c*) *Monro* v. *De Chemant*, 1815, 4 Camp. 215.

(*d*) *Ryan* v. *Sams*, *supra*, note (*b*).

Article 19.

CHILD NO IMPLIED AUTHORITY TO PLEDGE PARENT'S CREDIT.

Children have no implied authority, as such, to pledge the credit of their parents, even for the supply of necessaries.

In the absence of proof of an express or implied contract on his part, a father is no more liable than a stranger for debts incurred by his children without his authority; and the obligation to maintain his children affords no legal inference of a promise to pay for necessaries supplied to them (*e*). To render a parent liable for goods supplied to his child, the person supplying them must give some evidence of his authority or assent (*f*). Where a minor has ordered suitable necessaries, and some evidence of authority has been given, it is a question for the jury whether the circumstances of the case are such as to justify them in inferring that they were ordered with the father's authority (*g*). In such cases, slight evidence of authority is sufficient to establish a case for the jury (*g*).

(*e*) *Shelton* v. *Springett*, 1851, 11 C. B. 452, *Mortimer* v. *Wright*, 1840, 6 M. & W. 482, 4 Jur. 465, *Cranz* v. *Gill*, 1796, 2 Esp. 471; 5 R. R. 746.

(*f*) *Rolfe* v. *Abbott*, 1833, 6 C. & P. 286.

(*g*) *Law* v. *Wilkins*, 1837, 1 N. & P. 697, 6 A. & E. 718; *Baker* v. *Keen*, 1819, 2 Stark. 501.

CHAPTER III.

Appointment of agents.

An agent may be appointed by a power of attorney, a formal instrument under seal; by writing; or merely by word of mouth.

Article 20.

AUTHORITY TO EXECUTE A DEED.

Where an agent is authorized to execute a deed on behalf of his principal, his authority must be given by an instrument under seal (*a*), except where the deed is executed in the name and presence of the principal and the authority is conferred at the time of its execution, in which case it may be given by word of mouth (*b*).

So, a partner cannot bind his firm or the other partners by deed, unless expressly authorized under seal to do so (*c*), except where the deed is executed by the authority and in the presence of all the partners (*d*).

Article 21.

Except as provided in Article 22, an agent may be appointed either by deed, by writing, or merely by

(*a*) *Berkeley* v. *Hardy*, 1826, 8 D. & R. 102; 5 B. & C. 355.
(*b*) *The King* v. *Longnor*, 1833, 4 B. & Ad. 647; 1 N. & M. 576.
(*c*) *Harrison* v. *Jackson*, 1797, 7 T. R. 207; 5 R. R. 422.
(*d*) *Hockin* v. *Cooke*, 1791, 4 T. R. 313.

word of mouth, for any purpose except the execution of a deed.

Provided that, where an agent is verbally authorized to purchase land, and purchases and takes a conveyance of the land in his own name, he becomes a trustee for the principal within the meaning of the 7th section of the Statute of Frauds (*e*), which requires that all trusts of land shall be proved by writing; and the statute may be pleaded by the agent as a defence to an action by the principal to compel him to perform the trust and transfer the land (*f*).

An agent may be appointed by word of mouth, even where he is authorized to enter into a contract required by statute to be in writing, as in the case of contracts within the 4th section of the Statute of Frauds, or the 4th section of the Sale of Goods Act, 1893 (*g*). The first three sections of the Statute of Frauds expressly provided that agents appointed for the purposes of those sections should be authorized in writing, but the 8 & 9 Vict. c. 106, now requires a deed for those purposes, and it is therefore necessary that the agents should be appointed under seal. And those were the only purposes for which a written, as distinct from a verbal, appointment was necessary. So, it has been held that authority to subscribe the name of the principal

---

(*e*) 29 Car. II. c. 3.

(*f*) *James* v. *Smith*, (1891) 1 Ch. Div. 384; 65 L. T. 544. The statute must be specially pleaded, in order that it may be made available by way of defence. It is not necessary to plead the particular section, but where an agent pleaded the wrong section, he was not permitted to amend. *Ibid.*

(*g*) *Mortlock* v. *Buller*, 1804, 10 Ves. 311; 7 R. R. 417; *Coles* v. *Trecothick*, 1804, 9 Ves. 234, 249a; 1 Smith, 233; 7 R. R. 167; *Deverall* v. *Bolton*, 1812, 18 Ves. 509, *Graham* v. *Musson*, 1839, 7 Scott, 769, 778; 5 Bing. N. C. 603, *Heard* v. *Pilley*, 1869, L. R. 4 Ch. 548; 38 L. J. Ch. 718; 17 W. R. 750; 21 L. T. 68. And see *Lord* v. *Kellett*, 1833, 2 Myl. & K. 1.

to the memorandum of association of a joint stock company may be given verbally (*h*).

Agent to purchase land.—A contract for the purchase of land made by an agent, as such, vests the equitable estate in the principal, and the contract may be enforced by the principal as against both the vendor and the agent, even if the agent was appointed orally, provided that the legal estate has not been conveyed to him (*i*). But if the land has been conveyed to the agent, so as to vest the legal estate in him, he is a trustee for the principal, and may take advantage of the 7th section of the Statute of Frauds, if the trust is not evidenced by writing (*k*). This doctrine was criticised in *Heard* v. *Pilley* (1869) (*i*), but was recognised as good law in *James* v. *Smith* (1891) (*l*). The statute provides that all declarations or creations of trusts or confidences of any lands, tenements, or hereditaments (including leaseholds for years), shall be proved by some writing, signed by the party who is by law enabled to declare such trust, or else they shall be wholly void (*m*).

Article 22.

APPOINTMENT BY CORPORATIONS.

The appointment of an agent by a corporation must be under their common seal. Provided, that this rule does not apply to trading corporations (*n*) or joint

(*h*) *Re Whitley, ex p. Callan*, 1886, 32 Ch. Div. 337; 55 L. J. Ch. 540; 54 L. T. 912, 34 W. R. 505.

(*i*) *Heard* v. *Pilley*, 1869, L. R. 4 Ch. 548; 38 L. J. Ch. 718; 17 W. R. 750; 21 L. T. 68; *Cave* v. *Mackenzie*, 1877, 46 L. J. Ch. 564, 37 L. T. 218.

(*k*) *Bartlett* v. *Pickersgill*, 1785, 1 Cox, 15; 4 East, 577, n.; 1 R. R. 1.

(*l*) (1891) 1 Ch. 384; 65 L. T. 544.

(*m*) 29 Car. II. c. 3, s. 7.

(*n*) *South of Ireland Colliery Co.* v. *Waddle*, 1869, L. R. 4 C. P. 617; 38 L. J. C. P. 338. affirming L. R. 3 C. P. 463, Ex. Ch.; *Henderson* v.

stock companies, nor in any case where its application would cause very great inconvenience, or tend to defeat the very purpose for which the corporation was created (*o*). A trading corporation may appoint an agent by parol for any purpose within the scope of the objects of incorporation, except the execution of a deed (*p*).

Thus, it has been held that the engagement, by a board of guardians, of a clerk to the master of a workhouse, must be under seal, to bind the board of guardians (*q*). So, the appointment of a solicitor to a municipal corporation must be under seal, except where there is a local custom to the contrary (*r*). Where an attorney was retained by a municipal corporation to oppose a bill in parliament, it was held that, in the absence of a retainer under seal, he was not entitled to recover his costs (*s*).

Exceptions.—The common law rule was that all contracts by corporations must be under their common seal. But it is now settled that corporations may bind themselves by parol, whenever the acts in question are so frequently recurring, or so insignificant, that the affixing of the seal would be a great inconvenience (*o*). And that trading corporations are bound by their parol contracts, without reference to their frequency, or to the magnitude of the subject matter thereof, whenever the

---

Australian Steam Navigation Co., 1855, 5 El. & Bl. 409, 24 L. J. Q. B. 322; 1 Jur. N. S. 830.

(*o*) *Church* v. *Imperial Gaslight Co.*, 1838, 6 A. & E. 846, 3 N. & P. 35; *Mayor of Ludlow* v. *Charlton*, 6 M. & W. 815, 822.

(*p*) See note (*n*), *ante*, p. 31.

(*q*) *Austin* v. *Guardians of Bethnal Green*, 1874, L. R. 9 C. P. 91; 43 L. J. C. P. 100, 29 L. T. 807, 22 W. R. 406. See also *Cope* v. *Thames Haven Dock, &c. Co.*, 1849, 3 Ex. 841, 18 L. J. Ex. 345; 6 Railw. Cas. 83.

(*r*) *Arnold* v. *Mayor of Poole*, 1842, 5 Scott, N. R. 741, 4 M. & G. 860; 12 L. J. C. P. 97.

(*s*) *Sutton* v. *Spectacle Makers Co.*, 1864, 10 L. T. 411; 12 W. R. 742.

contracts are within the scope of the objects of incorporation (*t*).

Holding out.—Where a corporation hold out or permit a person to appear as their agent, they are bound by his acts as such, with respect to persons dealing with him in good faith and without notice of any informality, though he has not been formally appointed. Thus, where an attorney, who had not been appointed under seal, appeared in an action for a corporation to the knowledge of the directors, it was held that the corporation were bound by his acts as their attorney (*u*).

(*t*) *South of Ireland Colliery Co.* v. *Waddle*, *supra*, note (*n*), *Henderson* v. *Australian Steam Navigation Co.*, *supra*, note (*n*). See also *Reg.* v. *Cumberland*, 1848, 5 Railw. Cas. 332, 5 D. & L. 431, 17 L. J. Q. B. 102; 12 Jur. 1025.

(*u*) *Faviell* v. *Eastern Counties Rail. Co.*, 1848, 2 Ex. 344; 6 D. & L. 54; 17 L. J. Ex. 297. And see Article 85, Illustrations 7 and 8.

CHAPTER IV.

THE DOCTRINE OF RATIFICATION.

Article 23.

RATIFICATION EQUIVALENT TO PREVIOUS AUTHORITY.

WHERE an act is done in the name or on behalf of a person without his authority by another person assuming to act as his agent, the person in whose name or on whose behalf the act is done may, by ratifying the act, make it as valid and effectual, subject to the provisions of this chapter, as if it had been originally done by his authority, whether the person doing the act was an agent exceeding his authority, or was a person having no authority to act for him at all (*a*).

Illustrations.

1. A. enters into and signs a written contract on behalf of B., without authority. B. subsequently ratifies the contract. A. is deemed to have been B.'s duly authorized agent within the meaning of the 4th and 17th sections of the Statute of Frauds, and of the 4th section of the Sale of Goods Act, 1893 (*b*).

(*a*) See *Wilson* v. *Tunman*, 1843, 6 M. & G. 236, 6 Scott, N. R. 894, *Bird* v. *Brown*, 1850, 4 Ex. 786, 19 L. J. Ex. 155, 14 Jur. 132, *Roe*, d. *Rochester* v. *Pierce*, 1809, 2 Camp. 96, 11 R. R. 673.

(*b*) *Maclean* v. *Dunn*, 1828, 1 M. & P. 761, 4 Bing. 722, *Soames* v. *Spencer*, 1822, 1 D. & R. 32.

2. An agent, without authority, insures goods on behalf of his principal. The principal ratifies the policy. The policy is as valid as if the agent had been expressly authorized to insure the goods (*c*).

3. A government agent does an act in excess of his authority. The government ratifies the act. The act is deemed to be an act of state (*d*).

Article 24.

WHAT ACTS MAY BE RATIFIED.

Every act, whether lawful or unlawful (*e*), which is capable of being done by means of an agent, except an act which in its inception is void (*f*), is capable of ratification by the person in whose name or on whose behalf it is done.

Illustrations.

1. A., on B.'s behalf, but without his authority, purchases from C. a chattel which C. has no right to sell, under such circumstances that the purchase of the chattel is a conversion. B. ratifies the purchase. B. is guilty of conversion (*g*).

2. A., an agent of a corporation, assaults B. on their behalf.

(*c*) *Wolff* v. *Horncastle*, 1798, 1 B. & P. 316; 4 R. R. 808, *Williams* v. *North China Ass. Co.*, 1876, 1 C. P. D. 757; 35 L. T. 884, C. A.

(*d*) *Buron* v. *Denman*, 1848, 2 Ex. 167; *Secretary of State for India* v. *Kamachee Boye Sahaba*, 1859, 7 Moo. Ind. App. 476; 13 Moo. P. C. 22, P. C.

(*e*) Illustrations 1, 2, and 5; *Hull* v. *Pickersgill*, 1819, 1 Brod. & B. 282; 3 Moore, 612, 21 R. R. 598; *Wilson* v. *Tunman*, 1843, 6 M. & G. 236, 6 Scott, N. R. 894.

(*f*) See illustrations 6 and 7; *Spackman* v. *Evans*, 1868, L. R. 3 H. L. 171, 244, H. L.; *Banque Jacques Cartier* v. *Banque D'Epargne*, 1887, 13 App. Cas. 111; 57 L. J. P. C. 42, P. C.

(*g*) *Hilberry* v. *Hatton*, 1864, 2 H. & C. 822; 33 L. J. Ex. 190; 10 L. T. 39.

The corporation ratify the assault. The corporation is civilly liable to B. for the assault (*h*).

3. A shipmaster unnecessarily, and without the authority of the owners, sells his ship. The owners may ratify the sale (*i*), which then will become valid and binding (*i*).

4. A., a solicitor, at the request of B., the holder of a bill of exchange, sues on the bill in the name of C. without C.'s knowledge or authority. C. ratifies the action. A. is entitled to recover the amount of the bill (*k*).

5. A. distrains B.'s goods in the name of B.'s landlord, but without the landlord's authority. The landlord may ratify the distraint, and it is then deemed to have been done by his authority (*l*).

6. A. signs an instrument in B.'s name without his authority and with intent to defraud. B. cannot ratify the signature, because it is a forgery and is void in its inception (*m*).

7. The directors of a company enter into a contract which is not within the scope of the memorandum of association. The contract cannot be ratified by the company, even with the assent of every shareholder, because it is *ultra vires*, and therefore void (*n*). But a contract which is *intra vires* entered into on a company's behalf by the directors, without authority, may be ratified by the company (*o*).

(*h*) *Eastern Counties Rail. Co.* v. *Broom*, 1851, 6 Ex. 314, 6 Railw. Cas. 743, 20 L. J. Ex. 196, 15 Jur. 297, Ex. Ch.

(*i*) *The Australia*, 1859, 13 Moo. P. C. C. 132, Swabey, 486.

(*k*) *Ancona* v. *Marks*, 1862, 7 H. & N. 686, 31 L. J. Ex. 163, 8 Jur. N. S. 516, 5 L. T. 753.

(*l*) *Whitehead* v. *Taylor*, 1839, 10 A. & E. 210, 2 P. & D. 367.

(*m*) *Brook* v. *Hook*, 1871, L. R. 6 Ex. 89, 40 L. J. Ex. 50, 24 L. T. 34, 19 W. R. 508.

(*n*) *Ashbury Carriage Co.* v. *Riche*, 1875, L. R. 7 H. L. 653, 44 L. J. Ex. 185, 33 L. T. 450, H. L.

(*o*) *Irvine* v. *Union Bank of Australia*, 1877, 2 App. Cas. 366, 46 L. J. P. C. 87, 37 L. T. 176, P. C.

Article 25.

WHO MAY RATIFY.

The only person who has power to effectively ratify an act is the person in whose name or on whose behalf the act was done (*p*), and it is necessary that he should have been in existence (*q*) and capable of being ascertained (*r*) at the time that the act was done, but it is not necessary that he should be known, either personally or by name, to the person doing the act (*s*).

Illustrations.

1. A sheriff, acting under a valid writ of execution, as an agent of the Court, wrongfully seizes goods which are not the property of the debtor. The execution creditor cannot, by becoming a party to an interpleader issue or otherwise, ratify the act of the sheriff so as to render himself liable for the wrongful seizure, because the act was not done by the sheriff on his behalf, but in performance of a public duty (*t*).

2. A. enters into an agreement professedly on behalf of B.'s wife and C. B. cannot ratify the agreement so as to give him a right to sue upon it jointly with his wife and C. (*u*).

3. The promoters of a prospective company enter into a contract on behalf of the company before its incorporation. The company cannot ratify the contract, because it was not in exist-

(*p*) Illustrations 1 and 2.

(*q*) Illustration 3.

(*r*) *Watson* v. *Swann*, 1862, 11 C. B. N. S. 756, 31 L. J. C. P. 210.

(*s*) Illustration 4.

(*t*) *Wilson* v. *Tunman*, 1843, 6 M. & G. 236, 6 Scott, N. R. 894, *Woollen* v. *Wright*, 1862, 1 H. & C. 554, 31 L. J. Ex. 513, 7 L. T. 73, Ex. Ch.

(*u*) *Sanderson* v. *Griffith*, 1826, 5 B. & C. 909, 8 D. & R. 643.

ence at the time the contract was made (*x*). The company may, of course, make a new contract on the same terms as the old (*y*), and it may incur an equitable liability by reason of the perception of a benefit under the contract (*z*), or on the doctrine of part performance (*a*); but it cannot ratify the contract.

4. A. effects an insurance on goods on behalf, generally, of every person interested. Any person interested in the goods may subsequently ratify the insurance so far as concerns his interest, and the underwriters will then be bound by the policy to that extent (*b*). So, a person may act on behalf of an heir, or an administrator, or the owner of particular property, whoever he may be, though unascertained and unknown to him, and when ascertained, the person on whose behalf the act was done may ratify it (*c*), provided that he was capable of being ascertained, and was contemplated by the person doing the act at the time that it was done (*d*).

(*x*) *Kelner* v. *Baxter*, 1866, L. R. 2 C. P. 174, 36 L. J. C. P. 94, 15 L. T. 213, 15 W. R. 278, *Re Empress Engineering Co.*, 1880, 16 Ch. Div. 125, 43 L. T. 742, C. A. overruling *Spiller* v. *Paris Skating Rink Co.*, 1878, 7 Ch. Div. 368, 36 W. R. 456. See also *Re Northumberland Avenue Hotel Co.*, 1886, 33 Ch. Div. 16, 54 L. T. 777, C. A., *Re Rotherham Alum and Chemical Co.*, 1883, 25 Ch. Div. 103, 53 L. J. Ch. 290, 50 L. T. 219, C. A., *Scott* v. *Ebury*, 1867, L. R. 2 C. P. 255, *Re Dale and Plant*, 1889, 61 L. T. 206, 5 T. L. R. 585, *Melhado* v. *Porto Alegre, &c. Rail. Co.*, 1874, L. R. 9 C. P. 503, 43 L. J. C. P. 253, 31 L. T. 57.

(*y*) *Howard* v. *Patent Ivory Co.*, 1888, 38 Ch. Div. 156, 57 L. J. Ch. 878; 58 L. T. 395, 36 W. R. 801.

(*z*) *Touche* v. *Metropolitan Warehousing Co.*, 1871, L. R. 6 Ch. 671, *Re Dale and Plant*, *supra*, note (*x*).

(*a*) *Howard* v. *Patent Ivory Co.*, *supra*, *Re Dale and Plant*, *supra*.

(*b*) *Hagedorn* v. *Oliverson*, 1814, 2 M. & S. 485, 15 R. R. 317.

(*c*) *Lyell* v. *Kennedy*, 1889, 14 App. Cas. 437, 59 L. J. Q. B. 268; 62 L. T. 77, 38 W. R. 353, H. L., *Foster* v. *Bates*, 1843, 1 D. & L. 400, 12 M. & W. 226, 13 L. J. Ex. 88.

(*d*) *Watson* v. *Swann*, 1862, 11 C. B. N. S. 756, 31 L. J. C. P. 210.

Article 26.

CIRCUMSTANCES UNDER WHICH, AND WITHIN WHAT TIME, AN ACT MAY BE RATIFIED.

Where an act depends for its validity upon being done within a certain time, it cannot be effectively ratified after that time has expired, so as to divest a right *in rem* which has in the meantime vested in a third person (*e*).

Where an act is done which, if it be not authorized by the person on whose behalf it is done, is a tort, the person on whose behalf it is done, in order by ratification to justify the person doing it, must ratify the act at a time when he might legally do it himself (*f*); but the fact that before the ratification an action for tort has been commenced against the person doing the act does not affect the validity of the ratification (*g*).

Where an offer is made to an agent, and is accepted by him without authority, the acceptance may be ratified by the principal, and the contract thereby be made binding on the person who made the offer, even if he has in the meantime given notice to the principal of the withdrawal of the offer (*h*).

Where a contract is made without authority, it must be ratified within a reasonable time after it is made,

---

(*e*) Illustrations 1 and 2. And see Article 29, Illustration 12.

(*f*) *Bird* v. *Brown*, 1850, 4 Ex. 786, 19 L. J. Ex. 154, 14 Jur. 132.

(*g*) Illustration 3.

(*h*) Illustration 4.

and certainly before the time fixed for the performance of the contract to commence, in order to render it binding on the other contracting party (*i*). But the mere fact that the person on whose behalf a contract is made refuses at first to recognize it does not estop him from afterwards ratifying it (*j*).

An insurance policy may be effectively ratified by the owner of the property insured, after the loss of the property, even if he has notice of the loss at the time of the ratification (*k*).

Illustrations.

1. A., without the authority of the landlord, gives a tenant notice to quit. The notice cannot be made binding on the tenant by the landlord's ratification after the time for giving notice has expired (*l*).

2. The agent of a consignor of goods, without the authority of his principal, gave notice of stoppage *in transitu* on the principal's behalf. The goods afterwards arrived at their destination, and were formally demanded by the trustee in bankruptcy of the consignee. It was held that the consignor could not subsequently ratify the stoppage *in transitu* and so divest the property in the goods, which had in the meantime vested in the consignee's trustee in bankruptcy (*m*).

(*i*) *Metropolitan Asylum Board* v. *Kingham*, 1890, 6 T. L. R. 217.

(*j*) *Soames* v. *Spencer*, 1822, 1 D. & R. 32.

(*k*) *Williams* v. *North China Assurance Co.*, 1876, 1 C. P. D. 757, 35 L. T. 884, C. A.

(*l*) *Doe* d. *Mann* v. *Warlters*, 1830, 10 B. & C. 626; 5 M. & R. 357; *Doe* d. *Lyster* v. *Goldwin*, 1841, 1 G. & D. 463, 2 Q. B. 143. The earlier case of *Goodtitle* v. *Woodward*, 3 B. & A. 689, must, to this extent, be considered overruled. See, however, *Roe* d. *Rochester* v. *Pierce*, 2 Camp. 96, 11 R. R. 673.

(*m*) *Bird* v. *Brown*, 1850, 4 Ex. 786, 19 L. J. Ex. 154, 14 Jur. 132; and see Article 29, illustration 12.

3. An agent, after the death of his principal, distrained in the principal's name for rent due. Held, that the executor might ratify the distress, and so justify the agent, although an action was at the time of the ratification pending against the agent for the trespass (*n*).

4. A. made an offer to B., the managing director of a company, and it was accepted by him on the company's behalf. B. had no authority to accept the offer. A. then gave the company notice that he withdrew his offer, and the company subsequently ratified B.'s unauthorized acceptance. Held, by the Court of Appeal, that the maxim "*omnis ratihabitio retrotrahitur et mandato priori æquiparatur*" applied, and that the ratification related back to the time of the acceptance, rendering the withdrawal of the offer inoperative; specific performance decreed against A. (*o*).

Article 27.

CONDITIONS NECESSARY FOR RATIFICATION.

No person is deemed to ratify an act done without his authority, unless at the time of the ratification he has a full knowledge of all the material circumstances under which the act was done (*p*), except where it appears that he intends to ratify the act, and take the

---

(*n*) *Whitehead* v. *Taylor*, 1839, 10 A. & E. 210; 2 P. & D. 367.

(*o*) *Bolton Partners* v. *Lambert*, 1888, 41 Ch. Div. 295, 58 L. J. Ch. 425, 60 L. T. 687, C. A. This case has been followed by the Court of Appeal in *Re Portuguese Copper Mines, Limited, ex p. Badman, ex p. Bosanquet*, 1890, 45 Ch. Div. 16; 62 L. T. 179, and must, therefore, be considered settled law, but it seems a somewhat unfair, even if a logical, application of the doctrine of ratification.

(*p*) Illustrations 1 and 2, *Edwards* v. *L. & N. W. Rail. Co.*, 1870, L. R. 5 C. P. 445, 39 L. J. C. P. 241, 22 L. T. 656, 18 W. R. 834, *Banque Jacques Cartier* v. *Banque D'Epargne*, 1887, 13 App. Cas. 111, 57 L. J. P. C. 42, P. C., *The Bonita* v. *The Charlotte*, 1861, Lush. 252, 30 L. J. Adm. 145, 5 L. T. 141, *Gunn* v. *Roberts*, 1874, L. R. 9 C. P. 331, 43 L. J. C. P. 233, 30 L. T. 424, 22 W. R. 652.

risk, whatever the circumstances may have been (*q*). But it is not necessary that he should be aware of all the collateral circumstances which affect the nature of the act (*r*).

Illustrations.

1. An agent wrongfully distrains certain goods without the authority of the principal, and pays over the proceeds to the principal. The principal is not deemed to have ratified the wrongful distress by receiving the proceeds, unless he received them with a full knowledge of the irregularity, or intended without inquiry to take the risk upon himself (*s*). So, a principal will not be deemed to ratify a voidable transaction unless he knows that it is voidable (*t*).

2. An agent, with authority to distrain for rent, wrongfully seized and sold a fixture, and paid the proceeds to the principal, who received them without notice of the illegality. Held, that the principal had not ratified the trespass (*u*).

3. An agent, without authority, signed a distress warrant, and, after the distress, informed his principal, who said that he should leave the matter in the agent's hands. Held, that that was a ratification of the whole transaction, though there had been irregularities in levying the distress of which the principal had no knowledge (*v*).

4. An agent entered into an agreement on behalf of his principal. A letter from the principal, saying that he did not know what the agent had agreed to, but that he must support

(*q*) Illustrations 3 and 4.

(*r*) Illustration 5.

(*s*) *Lewis* v. *Read*, 1845, 13 M. & W. 834, 14 L. J. Ex. 295.

(*t*) See *Spackman* v. *Evans*, 1868, L. R. 3 H. L. 171.

(*u*) *Freeman* v. *Rosher*, 1849, 13 Q. B. 780, 18 L. J. Q. B. 340. See, however, *Gauntlett* v. *King*, 1857, 3 C. B. N. S. 59.

(*v*) *Haselar* v. *Lemoyne*, 1858, 5 C. B. N. S. 530, 28 L. J. C. P. 103; 4 Jur. N. S. 1279.

him in all he had done, was held to be a sufficient ratification of the agreement, whatever it might be (*x*).

5. An agent purchased a chattel on his principal's behalf from a person who had no right to sell it, and the principal ratified the purchase. Held, that the principal was guilty of conversion, though he had no knowledge at the time of the ratification that the sale was unlawful. Here, the circumstances rendering the transaction a conversion were collateral to and did not form part of the contract ratified (*y*).

Article 28.

HOW AN ACT MAY BE RATIFIED.

The ratification by a person of an act or transaction done or entered into on his behalf may be express or implied. It will be implied whenever his conduct is such as to show that he intends to adopt the act or transaction (*z*). Any act done by him with a full knowledge of the circumstances, in recognition of the act or transaction in whole or in part (*a*), is sufficient evidence of such an intention; and where an agent exceeds his authority, a ratification of his acts may be implied from the mere silence or acquiescence of the

---

(*x*) *Fitzmaurice* v. *Bayley*, 1856, 6 El. & Bl. 868, 26 L. J. Q. B. 114; 3 Jur. N. S. 264.

(*y*) *Hilberry* v. *Hatton*, 1864, 2 H. & C. 822, 33 L. J. Ex. 190, 10 L. T. 39.

(*z*) Illustrations 1 to 8.

(*a*) Illustrations 2 to 4, *Benham* v. *Batty*, 1865, 12 L. T. 266, 13 W. R. 636, *Hawley* v *Sentance*, 1863, 7 L. T. 745, 11 W. R. 311, *Bigg* v. *Strong*, 1858, 4 Jur. N. S. 983, 6 W. R. 536, *Clarke* v. *Perrier*, 1679, 2 Freem. 48; *Keay* v. *Fenwick*, 1876, 1 C. P. D. 745; *Smith* v. *Cologan*, 1788, 2 T. R. 189.

principal (*b*). The adoption of part of a transaction operates as a ratification of the whole (*c*).

A written contract may be ratified verbally or by conduct, even where the contract is required by statute to be in writing (*d*), but it is doubtful whether a deed can be ratified otherwise than by deed (*e*).

Ratification by companies.—An act or transaction done or entered into on behalf of a company may be ratified by the directors, if they have power to do or enter into such an act or transaction on behalf of the company (*f*); and a ratification by the directors may be implied from part performance (*f*). Where the act or transaction is beyond the powers of the directors, it can only be effectively ratified by the shareholders (*g*). An act done by the directors in excess of their powers, but within the scope of the memorandum of associa-

---

(*b*) Illustration 5, *Prince* v. *Clark*, 2 D. & R. 266, 1 B. & C. 186, *Pott* v. *Bevan*, 1844, 1 C. & K. 335, *The Australia*, 1859, Swab. 480, 13 Moo. P. C. C. 132, P. C., *Robinson* v. *Gleadow*, 1835, 2 Bing. N. C. 156, 2 Scott, 250, 1 Hodges, 245.

(*c*) Illustrations 2 to 4, *Hovil* v. *Pack*, 1806, 7 East, 164, 3 Smith, 164, *Ferguson* v. *Carrington*, 1829, 9 B. & C. 59, 3 C. & P. 457, *Keay* v. *Fenwick*, 1876, 1 C. P. D. 745, C. A., *Bristow* v. *Whitmore*, 1861, 9 H. L. Cas. 391, 31 L. J. Ch. 467, 4 L. T. 622, 8 Jur. N. S. 291, 9 W. R. 621, H. L., *Frixione* v. *Tagliafferro*, 1856, 10 Moo. P. C. C. 175, 4 W. R. 373, P. C.

(*d*) *Maclean* v. *Dunn*, 1828, 1 M. & P. 761, 4 Bing. 722, *Soames* v. *Spencer*, 1822, 1 D. & R. 32.

(*e*) See *Oxford* v. *Crow*, (1893) 3 Ch. 535, 69 L. T. 228, 42 W. R. 200.

(*f*) *Wilson* v. *West Hartlepool, &c. Rail. Co.*, 1864, 2 De G., J. & S. 475, 34 L. J. Ch. 241, 11 Jur. N. S. 124, 11 L. T. 692, 13 W. R. 361, *Reuter* v. *Electric Telegraph Co.*, 1856, 6 El. & Bl. 341, 26 L. J. Q. B. 46, 2 Jur. N. S. 1245.

(*g*) *Spackman* v. *Evans*, 1868, L. R. 3 H. L. 171, H. L.

tion, may be ratified by ordinary resolution of the shareholders (*h*), and a ratification by the shareholders is implied if they acquiesce in such an act with a full knowledge of the circumstances (*i*).

Illustrations.

1. A shipmaster unnecessarily, and without authority, sells his ship. The owners receive the purchase-money with a full knowledge of the circumstances under which the ship was sold. The receipt of the purchase-money is a ratification of the sale (*k*).

2. A. is a bankrupt. B., at the request of A.'s wife, purchases certain bonds with A.'s money, and hands them to her. The trustee in bankruptcy seizes some of the bonds as part of A.'s estate. The trustee in bankruptcy has ratified the act of B., and thereby discharged him from liability (*l*).

3. A. is a bankrupt. B. wrongfully sells part of A.'s property. The trustee in bankruptcy accepts the proceeds, or otherwise recognizes B. as his agent in the transaction. B. is deemed to have been duly authorized by the trustee to sell the property (*m*).

4. An agent purchases hemp on behalf of his principal at a price exceeding his limit. The principal objects to the contract, but disposes of some of the hemp as his own. He is deemed to have ratified the contract, and is bound by it (*n*).

(*h*) *Grant* v. *United Kingdom Switchback Rail. Co.*, 1888, 40 Ch. Div. 135.

(*i*) *London Financial Association* v. *Kelk*, 1883, 26 Ch. Div. 107; *Evans* v. *Smallcombe*, 1868, L. R. 3 H. L. 249; 37 L. J. Ch. 793; 19 L. T. N. S. 207, H. L., *Re Magdalena Steam Navigation Co.*, 1860, 29 L. J. Ch. 667; Johns. 690.

(*k*) *The Bonita* v. *The Charlotte*, 1861, Lush. 252, 30 L. J. Adm. 145; 5 L. T. 141, *Hunter* v. *Parker*, 1840, 7 M. & W. 322.

(*l*) *Wilson* v. *Poulter*, 1724, 2 Str. 859.

(*m*) *Brewer* v. *Sparrow*, 1827, 7 B. & C. 310, 1 M. & R. 2.

(*n*) *Cornwall* v. *Wilson*, 1750, 1 Ves. 510.

5. A wife purchases goods, which are not necessaries, in the name of her husband. The husband has control over the goods, and does not return them to the seller. He is deemed to ratify the contract, and must pay for the goods (*o*).

6. A party to a contract which is fraudulent and voidable as against him sues on the contract. He is deemed to ratify the entire contract (*p*).

7. The steward of a corporation gives a tenant notice to quit on their behalf. The corporation bring an action of ejectment against the tenant. The action is a sufficient ratification of the notice to quit to dispense with the necessity of proving that the steward was duly authorized to give such notice (*q*).

8. A. receives the rents of certain property for many years without the authority of the owner. The owner sues A. for possession, and for an account of the rents and profits. The action is a sufficient ratification to render A. the agent of the owner from the commencement (*r*).

Article 29.

EFFECT OF RATIFICATION.

The effect of ratification is to invest the person on whose behalf the act ratified was done, the person who did the act, and third persons, with the same rights, duties, and liabilities in all respects as if the act had been done with the previous authority of the person on whose behalf it was done (*s*); provided, that

---

(*o*) *Waithman* v. *Wakefield*, 1807, 1 Camp. 120; 10 R. R. 654.

(*p*) *Ferguson* v. *Carrington*, 1829, 9 B. & C. 59; 3 C. & P. 457.

(*q*) *Roe* d. *Rochester* v. *Pierce*, 1809, 2 Camp. 96; 11 R. R. 673.

(*r*) *Lyell* v. *Kennedy*, 1889, 14 App. Cas. 437, 59 L. J. Q. B. 268, 62 L. T. 77, 38 W. R. 353, H. L.

(*s*) See the judgments in *Wilson* v. *Tunman*, 1843, 6 M. & G. 236, 6 Scott, N. R. 894, and *Bird* v. *Brown*, 1850, 4 Ex. 786, 19 L. J. Ex. 154, 14 Jur. 132; and illustrations 1 to 11.

no ratification can operate to divest rights *in rem* vested in third persons at the time of the ratification (*t*).

No ratification gives any new authority to the person whose act is ratified (*u*).

Illustrations.

1. A British naval commander destroyed certain property and released certain slaves belonging to a Spanish subject. The foreign and colonial Secretaries of State ratified the act of the commander. Held, that the ratification rendered the act an act of state, for which no action would lie at the suit of the Spanish subject (*x*).

2. A. purchases a chattel on behalf of B., under such circumstances that the dealing with the property in the chattel is a conversion. B. ratifies the purchase. A. and B. are jointly and severally liable for the conversion (*y*).

3. A., an agent of a corporation, assaults B., for the supposed benefit of the corporation. The corporation ratify the assault. They are liable to B. in an action for damages (*z*).

4. A., on B.'s behalf, but without his authority, distrains goods belonging to C. B. ratifies the distress. If B. had a right to distrain, A. is discharged from liability, the ratification having a retroactive effect, and rendering the distress lawful

(*t*) Illustration 12, and see Article 26, illustration 2.

(*u*) *Irvine* v. *Union Bank of Australia*, 1877, 2 App. Cas. 366; 46 L. J. P. C. 87, 37 L. T. 176; 25 W. R. 682, P. C.

(*x*) *Buron* v. *Denman*, 1848, 2 Ex. 167. See also *Secretary of State for India* v. *Kamachee Boye Sahaba*, 1859, 7 Moo. Ind. App. 476; 13 Moo. P. C. 22, P. C.

(*y*) *Hilberry* v. *Hatton*, 1864, 2 H. & C. 822; 33 L. J. Ex. 190; 10 L. T. 39.

(*z*) *Eastern Counties Rail. Co.* v. *Broom*, 1851, 6 Ex. 314; 6 Railw. Cas. 743, 20 L. J. Ex. 196, Ex. Ch.

ab initio (*a*). If B. had no right to distrain, A. and B. are jointly and severally liable as trespassers (*b*).

5. A. makes a contract on behalf of B. without his authority. B. ratifies the contract. B. is liable on the contract, and A. is discharged from liability unless he contracted personally (*c*).

6. An agent does an act in excess of his authority. The principal ratifies the act. The agent is not liable to the principal for having exceeded his authority (*d*).

7. A. converts the property of a bankrupt by selling or disposing of it without the authority of the trustee in bankruptcy. The trustee ratifies the sale or disposition by receiving the proceeds or otherwise. A. is discharged from liability in respect of the conversion (*e*).

8. A factor contracts to purchase goods on his principal's behalf at a price exceeding his limit. The principal ratifies the contract. He must pay the factor the full price (*f*).

9. A. insures goods, in which he has no insurable interest, on behalf of B. B., who has an insurable interest in the goods, ratifies the insurance. A. is deemed to have had an insurable interest (*g*).

10. The managing owner of a ship sells her through his agent. His co-owners ratify the sale. The owners are jointly liable to the agent for his commission (*h*). So, if a principal

---

(*a*) *Whitehead* v. *Taylor*, 1839, 10 A. & E. 210, 2 P. & D. 367, *Hull* v. *Pickersgill*, 1819, 1 Brod. & B. 282, 3 Moore, 612, 21 R. R. 598.

(*b*) See *Bird* v. *Brown*, 1850, 4 Ex. 786, 19 L. J. Ex. 154, 14 Jur. 132.

(*c*) *Spittle* v. *Lavender*, 1821, 2 Brod. & Bing. 452, 5 Moore, 270.

(*d*) *Clarke* v. *Perrier*, 1679, 2 Freem. 48, *Smith* v. *Cologan*, 1788, 2 T. R. 189, *Anderson* v. *Watson*, 1827, 3 C. & P. 214, *Cornwall* v. *Wilson*, 1750, 1 Ves. 510, *Risbourg* v. *Bruckner*, 1858, 3 C. B. N. S. 822, 27 L. J. C. P. 90.

(*e*) *Brewer* v. *Sparrow*, 1827, 7 B. & C. 310; 1 M. & R. 2, *Wilson* v. *Poulter*, 1724, 2 Str. 859.

(*f*) *Cornwall* v. *Wilson*, 1750, 1 Ves. 510.

(*g*) *Wolff* v. *Horncastle*, 1798, 1 B. & P. 316; 4 R. R. 808.

(*h*) *Keay* v. *Fenwick*, 1876, 1 C. P. D. 745, C. A.

ratifies the act of a sub-agent, he is liable to the sub-agent for his commission (*i*).

11. An agent defends an action brought against him for breach of a contract entered into by him on behalf of his principal. The principal ratifies what he has done. The principal must indemnify the agent against the damages and costs recovered by the plaintiff in the action (*k*).

12. A commodore in the navy, without authority to do so, appointed a captain. The Crown ratified the appointment. Held, that the ratification did not give the captain the right to share, as such, in prizes taken before the date of the ratification, because at the time of the ratification the rights to the various shares in those prizes were already vested in others (*l*).

(*i*) *Mason* v. *Clifton*, 1863, 3 F. & F. 899.

(*k*) *Frixione* v. *Tagliafferro*, 1856, 10 Moo. P. C. C. 175, 4 W. R. 373, P. C.

(*l*) *Donelly* v. *Popham*, 1807, 1 Taunt. 1, 9 R. R. 687.

CHAPTER V.

AUTHORITY OF AGENTS.

THE authority of an agent may be express or implied. Its nature and extent may be defined by a power of attorney, a formal instrument under seal, by writing not under seal, or by verbal instructions, or may be inferred from a course of dealing between the parties (*a*). Authority may be implied from the situation of the parties, the circumstances of the particular case, the usage of trade or business, or the conduct of the principal.

Article 30.

AUTHORITY CANNOT EXCEED POWERS OF PRINCIPAL.

The authority, whether express or implied, of every agent is confined within the limits of the powers of his principal (*b*).

Thus, an agent of a corporation cannot have any authority, express or implied, to do any act on behalf of the corporation which is *ultra vires* (*b*).

(*a*) See *Pole* v. *Leask*, 1860, 28 Beav. 562, 6 Jur. N. S. 1104; 29 L. J. Ch. 888.

(*b*) *Montreal Assurance Co.* v. *M'Gillivray*, 1859, 13 Moo. P. C. C. 87, 8 W. R. 165, P. C.; *Poulton* v. *S. W. Rail.* 1867, L. R. 2 Q. B. 534, 36 L. J. Q. B. 294, 8 B. & S. 616, 17 L. T. 11.

Article 31.

CONSTRUCTION OF AUTHORITY GIVEN IN GENERAL TERMS.

Authority conferred in general terms is construed as authority to act only in the usual way and ordinary course of business.

Illustrations.

1. A stockbroker is authorized to sell stock or shares. He has no authority to sell on credit, because it is not usual to sell stock or shares on credit (*c*).

2. A. is authorized to sell and warrant certain goods. He cannot bind his principal by a warranty given at any other time than at the sale of the goods (*d*).

3. On the dissolution of a partnership, authority is given to one of the partners by his co-partners—(1) to settle the partnership affairs (*e*), or (2) to receive all debts owing to, and to pay all debts owing by, the firm (*f*). In neither case has he authority to draw, accept, or indorse bills of exchange in the name of the firm.

Authority to receive payment of money.

4. A. is authorized to receive payment of money. He has no authority—(1) to receive payment before the money is due, and if his authority be revoked before that time, the debtor is not discharged by such a payment (*g*); (2) to receive payment by cheque, unless he can prove that in the particular business in which he is employed, it is usual to receive payment by cheque (*h*);

(*c*) *Wiltshire* v. *Sims*, 1808, 1 Camp. 258; 10 R. R. 673.

(*d*) *Helyear* v. *Hawke*, 1803, 5 Esp. 72.

(*e*) *Abel* v. *Sutton*, 1800, 3 Esp. 108, 6 R. R. 818.

(*f*) *Kilgour* v. *Finlayson*, 1789, 1 H. Bl. 155.

(*g*) *Breming* v. *Mackie*, 1862, 3 F. & F. 197.

(*h*) *Bridges* v. *Garrett*, 1870, L. R. 5 C. P. 451; 39 L. J. C. P. 251; 22 L. T. 448, Ex. Ch.

the burden of proving any such custom lies on the person who seeks to establish the authority (*i*); or (3) to receive payment by way of set-off or settlement of accounts between himself and the debtor (*k*).

5. It is provided by the conditions at a sale by auction that the purchase-money for the goods sold shall be paid to the auctioneer. The auctioneer has no authority to receive a bill of exchange in payment, and if his authority to receive payment is revoked during the currency of the bill, such a payment does not discharge the purchaser (*l*).

6. An agent is authorized to receive payment of an account, and to retain part of the amount in discharge of a debt due to him from the principal. He has authority, to the extent of his debt, to settle in his own way with the debtor of his principal (*m*).

7. A. authorizes B., a stockbroker, to receive money due from C., also a stockbroker. B. has no authority to settle with C. by way of set-off, and such a settlement does not bind A. (*n*).

8. A. authorizes B., an insurance broker, to receive the amount due under a policy of insurance from the underwriters. The underwriters in good faith settle with B. by setting off a debt due to them from him, and their names are struck out of the policy. By a custom at Lloyds', a set-off is considered equivalent to payment as between broker and underwriter. If A. was aware of the custom when he authorized B. to receive payment, he is bound by the settlement. If he was not aware

---

(*i*) *Pape* v *Westacott*, 1893, 10 L. T. R. 51, (1894) 1 Q. B. 272, 63 L. J. Q. B. 222, 9 R. 55, C. A.

(*k*) *Underwood* v. *Nicholls*, 1855, 17 C. B. 239, 25 L. J. C. P. 79, *Sweeting* v. *Pearce*, 1859, 7 C. B. N. S. 449, 29 L. J. C. P. 265.

(*l*) *Williams* v. *Evans*, 1866, L. R. 1 Q. B. 352, 35 L. J. Q. B. 111, 13 L. T. 753, 14 W. R. 330, *Sykes* v. *Giles*, 1839, 5 M. & W. 645.

(*m*) *Barker* v. *Greenwood*, 1836, 2 Y. & C. 414, 6 L. J. (N. S.) Eq. 54, 1 Jur. 541.

(*n*) *Pearson* v. *Scott*, 1878, L. R. 9 Ch. Div. 198, 47 L. J. Ch. 705, 38 L. T. 747, 26 W. R. 796, *Blackburn* v. *Mason*, 1893, 68 L. T. 510, 9 T. L. R. 286, 4 R. 297, C. A.

of the custom, he is not bound by the settlement (*o*). Such a custom is considered unreasonable, and the principal is, therefore, not deemed to have authorized the broker to follow it unless it was known to him (*o*).

Article 32.

AUTHORITY CONFERRED IN AMBIGUOUS TERMS.

Where the authority of an agent is conferred in such ambiguous terms, or the instructions given to him are so uncertain, as to be fairly capable of more than one construction, every act done by him in good faith, which is warranted by any one of those constructions, is deemed to have been duly authorized, though the construction adopted was not the one intended by the principal (*p*).

Illustrations.

1. An agent was instructed to sell goods at such a price as would realize 15*s*. per ton, net cash. He sold them at 15*s*. 6*d*. per ton, subject to two months' credit. Held, that the instructions might fairly be construed as meaning either 15*s*. net cash, such a price as would eventually realize 15*s*. after allowing for interest, or a *del credere* commission; and that the sale at 15*s*. 6*d*., two months, was within the authority (*q*).

2. A commission agent was authorized to buy and ship 500

(*o*) *Sweeting* v. *Pearce*, 1859, 7 C. B. N. S. 449, 29 L. J. C. P. 265, *Todd* v. *Reid*, 1821, 4 B. & Ald. 210, *Bartlett* v. *Pentland*, 1830, 10 B. & C. 760, *Stewart* v. *Aberdein*, 1838, 4 M. & W. 211, 1 H. & H. 284.

(*p*) *Ireland* v. *Livingstone*, 1872, L. R. 5 H. L. 395, 41 L. J. Q. B. 201; 27 L. T. 79, H. L., *Loring* v. *Davis*, 1886, 32 Ch. Div. 625, 55 L. J. Ch. 725, 54 L. T. 899, *Johnstone* v. *Kershaw*, 1867, L. R. 2 Ex. 82, 36 L. J. Ex. 44, 15 L. T. 485, 15 W. R. 354, and see Illustrations.

(*q*) *Boden* v. *French*, 1851, 10 C. B. 886.

tons of sugar (subject to a certain limit in price, to cover cost, freight, and insurance), 50 tons more or less of no moment, if it enabled him to secure a suitable vessel. Held, by the House of Lords, reversing the Exchequer Chamber, that a shipment of 400 tons was a good execution of the authority (*r*).

3. An agent undertook to sell and transfer certain stock when the funds should be at 85 or over. Held, that he was bound to sell when the funds reached 85, and had no discretion to wait until they went higher than that price (*s*).

Article 33.

CONSTRUCTION OF POWERS OF ATTORNEY.

Powers of attorney must be strictly pursued, and are construed as giving only such authority as they confer expressly or by necessary implication (*t*). The following are the most important rules of construction—

(1.) The operative part of the deed is controlled by the recitals (*u*).

(2.) Where authority is given to do particular acts, followed by general words, the general words are restricted to what is necessary for the proper performance of the particular acts (*v*).

(*r*) *Ireland* v. *Livingstone*, 1872, L. R. 5 H. L. 395, 41 L. J. Q. B. 201; 27 L. T. 79, H. L.

(*s*) *Bertram* v. *Godfray*, 1830, 1 Knapp, 381, P. C.

(*t*) *Bryant* v. *La Banque du Peuple*, *Bryant* v. *Quebec Bank*, (1893) A. C. 170, 62 L. J. P. C. 68, 68 L. T. 546, 41 W. R. 600, P. C., *Jonmenjoy Coondoo* v *Watson*, 1884, 9 App. Cas. 561, 53 L. J. P. C. 80, 50 L. T. 411, P. C., and see Illustrations 1 to 7.

(*u*) Illustration 1.

(*v*) Illustration 2, *Perry* v. *Holl*, 1860, 2 De G. F. & J. 38, 29 L. J. Ch. 677, 6 Jur. N. S. 661, 8 W. R. 570.

(3.) General words do not confer general powers, but are limited to the purpose for which the authority is given, and are construed as enlarging the special powers when necessary, and only when necessary, for that purpose (*x*).

(4.) The deed must be construed so as to include all medium powers necessary for its effective execution (*y*).

Illustrations.

1. A power of attorney recited that the principal was going abroad, and the operative part gave authority in general terms. Held, that the authority subsisted only during the principal's absence abroad (*z*).

2. Power was given "to demand and receive all moneys due to the principal on any account whatsoever, and to use all means for the recovery thereof, to appoint attorneys to bring actions, and to revoke such appointments, and to do all other business." Held, that "all other business" must be construed to mean all other business necessary for the recovery of the moneys, or in connection therewith; and that the power of attorney gave the agent no authority to indorse a bill of exchange received by him thereunder (*a*). So, power "to demand, sue for, recover and receive, by all lawful ways and means, all moneys, debts

---

(*x*) *Lewis* v. *Ramsdale*, 1886, 55 L. T. 179, 35 W. R. 8; *Attwood* v. *Mannings*, 1827, 7 B. & C. 278; *Re Bowles*, 1874, 31 L. T. 365, *Harper* v. *Godsell*, 1870, L. R. 5 Q. B. 422, 39 L. J. Q. B. 185, 18 W. R. 954; *Bryant* v. *La Banque du Peuple*, *Bryant* v. *Quebec Bank*, *supra*, note (*t*).

(*y*) *Withington* v. *Herring*, 1829, 5 Bing. 442; *Howard* v. *Baillie*, 1796, 2 H. Bl. 618.

(*z*) *Danby* v. *Coutts*, 1885, 29 Ch. Div. 500; 54 L. J. Ch. 577; 52 L. T. 401.

(*a*) *Hogg* v. *Snaith*, 1808, 1 Taunt. 347, 9 R. R. 788. And see *Hay* v. *Goldsmidt*, 1804, 1 Taunt. 349; 2 Smith, 79; 9 R. R. 790, *Esdaile* v. *La Nauze*, 1840, 1 Y. & C. 394.

and dues whatsoever, and to give sufficient discharges, and to transact all business," was held to give no authority to indorse bills of exchange on behalf of the principal (*b*).

3. A resident director and manager of a mining company was authorized by deed "to direct the mine so as most effectually to promote the interests of the company, to employ workmen, provide needful implements, &c., but not to engage the credit of the company for more than 50*l.* without the express authority in writing of the managing directors." Held, that he had no authority to bind the company by accepting bills of exchange (*c*).

4. An executor gave a power of attorney to transact in his name all the affairs of the testator. Held, that the agent had no authority to accept a bill of exchange in the name of the executor so as to bind him personally (*d*).

5. A power of attorney "from time to time to negotiate, make sale, dispose of, assign and transfer," gives no authority to "pledge" (*e*). But a power "to sell, indorse and assign," does authorize an indorsement to a bank as security for a loan to the agent; such a power is construed as giving (1) authority to sell, (2) authority to indorse, and (3) authority to assign (*f*).

Article 34.

CONSTRUCTION OF AUTHORITY NOT GIVEN UNDER SEAL.

Where the authority of an agent is given by an instrument not under seal, or is given verbally, it is

---

(*b*) *Murray* v. *East India Co.*, 1821, 5 B. & Ald. 204.

(*c*) *Brown* v. *Byers*, 1847, 16 M. & W. 252, 16 L. J. Ex. 112.

(*d*) *Gardner* v. *Baillie*, 1796, 6 T. R. 591, 1 Bos. & P. 32, 3 R. R. 531, 538. (*Howard* v. *Baillie*, 2 H. Bl. 618, 3 R. R. 531, was decided on the ground of ratification.)

(*e*) *Jonmenjoy Coondoo* v *Watson*, 1884, 9 App. Cas. 561, 53 L. J. P. C. 80, 50 L. T. 411, P. C., *De Bouchout* v. *Goldsmid*, 1800, 5 Ves. 211.

(*f*) *Bank of Bengal* v. *Macleod*, 1849, 5 Moo. Ind. App. 1, *Bank of Bengal* v. *Fagan*, 1849, 5 Moo. Ind. App. 27, P. C.

construed liberally, having due regard to the object of the authority and to the usages of trade or business (*g*).

IMPLIED AUTHORITY.

Article 35.

TO DO WHAT IS NECESSARY FOR OR INCIDENTAL TO EFFECTIVE EXECUTION OF EXPRESS AUTHORITY.

Every agent has implied authority to do whatever is necessary for or ordinarily incidental to the effective execution of his express authority in the usual way (*h*).

Illustrations.

1. A. is authorized to enter into a binding contract. He has implied authority to sign a memorandum thereof to satisfy the Statute of Frauds, or the Sale of Goods Act, 1893 (*i*).

2. A. is authorized to buy certain railway shares. He has implied authority to do everything in the usual course of business necessary to complete the bargain (*k*).

3. A. is employed to get a bill of exchange discounted. He

(*g*) See *Pole* v. *Leask*, 1860, 28 Beav. 562, 6 Jur. N. S. 1104; 29 L. J. Ch. 888, *Entwistle* v. *Dent*, 1848, 1 Ex. 812, 18 L. J. Ex. 138; *Pariente* v. *Lubbock*, 1855, 5 De G. M. & G. 5, 20 Beav. 588, *Gillow* v. *Aberdare*, 1893, 9 T. L. R. 12, *Ex p. Howell*, 1865, 12 L. T. 785.

(*h*) *Beaufort* v. *Neeld*, 1845, 12 C. & F. 248, *Pole* v. *Leask*, 1860, 28 Beav. 562, 6 Jur. N. S. 1104; 29 L. J. Ch. 888; *Dingle* v. *Hare*, 1859, 7 C. B. N. S. 145, 29 L. J. C. P. 143, 16 Jur. N. S. 679, 1 L. T. 38; *Stevens* v. *Hinshelwood*, 1891, 55 J. P. 341, C. A., *Capel* v. *Thornton*, 1828, 2 C. & P. 352, and see Illustrations.

(*i*) *Durrell* v. *Evans*, 1862, 1 H. & C. 174, 31 L. J. Ex. 337, 9 Jur. N. S. 104, 7 L. T. 97, 10 W. R. 665.

(*k*) *Bayley* v. *Wilkins*, 1849, 7 C. B. 886, 18 L. J. C. P. 273.

has implied authority to warrant it a good bill, but not to indorse it in the name of the principal (*l*).

4. A. is authorized to receive and sell certain goods, and to pay himself a debt out of the proceeds. He has implied authority to bring an action against a third person wrongfully withholding possession of the goods (*m*).

5. An agent is employed to find a purchaser for certain property. He has implied authority to describe the property, and state to an intending purchaser any facts or circumstances which may affect its value (*n*).

6. A horse-dealer or other person who is accustomed to buying and selling horses authorizes A. to sell a horse privately. A. has implied authority to give a warranty on the sale of the horse (*o*).

7. A., a person who is not accustomed to buying and selling horses, authorizes his servant to sell a horse privately. The servant has no implied authority to warrant the horse (*p*).

8. A., a person who is not accustomed to buying and selling horses, authorizes his servant to sell a horse at a fair or public market-place. The servant has implied authority to warrant the horse (*q*).

9. A. is authorized merely to deliver a horse. He has no implied authority to warrant it (*r*).

10. An agent is employed to find a purchaser and to contract

(*l*) *Fenn* v. *Harrison*, 1791, 3 T. R. 757, 4 T. R. 177.

(*m*) *Curtis* v. *Barclay*, 1826, 7 D. & R. 539, 5 B. & C. 141.

(*n*) *Mullens* v. *Miller*, 1882, 22 Ch. Div. 194, 52 L. J. Ch. 380, 48 L. T. 103, 31 W. R. 559.

(*o*) *Howard* v. *Sheward*, 1866, L. R. 2 C. P. 148, 36 L. J. C. P. 42, 12 Jur. N. S. 1015, *Bank of Scotland* v. *Watson*, 1813, 1 Dow. 45, 14 R. R. 11, H. L., *Baldry* v. *Bates*, 1885, 52 L. T. 620.

(*p*) *Brady* v *Todd*, 1861, 9 C. B. N. S. 592; 30 L. J. C. P. 223, 7 Jur. N. S. 827, 4 L. T. 212; 9 W. R. 483 overruling *Alexander* v. *Gibson*, 1811, 2 Camp. 555, 11 R. R. 797.

(*q*) *Brooks* v. *Hassell*, 1883, 49 L. T. 569.

(*r*) *Woodin* v. *Burford*, 1834, 2 C. & M. 391, 4 Tyr. 264.

for the sale of an estate. He has no implied authority, as such, to receive the purchase-money (*s*).

Article 36.

IMPLIED AUTHORITY OF GENERAL AGENTS.

Every agent who is authorized to conduct a particular trade or business (*t*), or generally to act for his principal in matters of a particular nature, or to do a particular class of acts (*u*) has implied authority to do whatever is incidental to the ordinary conduct of such a trade or business (*t*), or of matters of that nature, or is within the scope of that class of acts (*u*), and whatever is necessary for the proper and effective performance of his duties (*x*); but not to do anything that is outside the ordinary scope of his employment and duties (*y*).

Illustrations.

1. A. is the manager of an estate. He has implied authority to contract for the usual and customary leases (*z*), and to give and receive notices to quit to and from the tenants (*a*).

(*s*) *Mynn* v. *Joliffe*, 1834, 1 M. & Rob. 326.

(*t*) Illustrations 1 to 3.

(*u*) *Ex p. Howell*, 1865, 12 L. T. 785; *Peers* v. *Sneyd*, 1853, 17 Beav. 151, *Jones* v. *Phipps*, 1868, L. R. 3 Q. B. 567, 37 L. J. Q. B. 198, 9 B. & S. 761, 18 L. T. 813. For implied authority of shipmasters, see *post*, pp. 74 to 80.

(*x*) Illustrations 11 and 12; *Langan* v. *G. W. Rail. Co.*, 1874, 30 L. T. 173, 26 L. T. 577, Ex. Ch.

(*y*) *Linford* v. *Provincial, &c. Ins. Co.*, 1864, 34 Beav. 291, 11 L. T. 330, 10 Jur. N. S. 1066, *Cox* v. *Midland Counties Rail. Co.*, 1849, 3 Ex. 268; Illustrations 7 to 12.

(*z*) *Peers* v. *Sneyd*, 1853, 17 Beav. 151.

(*a*) *Papillon* v. *Brunton*, 1860, 5 H. & N. 518, 29 L. J. Ex. 265, *Jones* v. *Phipps*, *supra*, note (*u*).

2. A. is the manager of a beerhouse. He has implied authority to order cigars for such beerhouse (*b*).

3. A. is the manager of a business which he carries on in his own name as apparent principal. Drawing and accepting bills of exchange are incidental to the ordinary conduct of such a business. A. has implied authority to accept a bill in the name in which the business is carried on (*i.e.*, his own name), and the principal is liable on a bill so accepted (*c*).

4. A. is the general manager of a railway company. He has implied authority to order medical attendance for a servant of the company, on the company's credit (*d*).

5. A. is the foreman of a saw-mill. He has implied authority to enter into a written contract for the sale of staves (*e*).

6. A. is a traveller for the sale of goods in the provinces on behalf of a principal in London. A. has implied authority to receive payment in money for the goods sold by him, but not to accept other goods by way of payment (*f*).

7. A. is a rent collector. He has no implied authority, as such, to receive notice to quit from a tenant (*g*). So, a steward has no implied authority, as such, to grant leases (*h*); nor the cashier of a picture engraver to sell his master's engravings (*i*).

8. *Insurance agents.*—A. is the agent of an insurance company, and has authority to receive the payment of premiums within fifteen days of their becoming due. He has no implied authority to accept payment after the expiration of that time (*k*). So, a local agent of an insurance company has no implied

---

(*b*) *Watteau* v. *Fenwick*, 1892, (1893) 1 Q. B. 346, 56 J. P. 839, 67 L. T. 831, 9 T. L. R. 133, C. A.

(*c*) *Edmunds* v. *Bushell*, 1865, L. R. 1 Q. B. 97, 35 L. J. Q. B. 20, 12 Jur. N. S. 332.

(*d*) *Walker* v. *G. W. Rail. Co.*, 1867, L. R. 2 Ex. 228.

(*e*) *Richardson* v. *Cartwright*, 1844, 1 C. & K. 328.

(*f*) *Howard* v. *Chapman*, 1831, 4 C. & P. 508.

(*g*) *Pearse* v. *Boulter*, 1860, 2 F. & F. 133.

(*h*) *Collen* v. *Gardner*, 1856, 21 Beav. 540.

(*i*) *Graves* v. *Masters*, 1883, 1 C. & E. 73.

(*k*) *Acey* v. *Fernie*, 1840, 7 M. & W. 151.

authority, as such, to grant, or contract to grant, policies on behalf of the company, that being outside the ordinary scope of his employment and duties (*l*).

9. A. is a station master. He has no implied authority, as such, to pledge the credit of the railway company for medical attendance to an injured passenger (*m*).

10. *Directors and agents of unincorporated companies.*—A. is the resident agent and manager of a mine for an unincorporated company. He has no implied authority to borrow money on the credit of the shareholders, however pressing may be the necessity for a loan (*n*). So, directors of an unincorporated mining company have no implied authority to bind the members of the company by negotiable instruments, or to borrow money on their credit, either for the purpose of carrying on the mine or for any other purpose, however useful and necessary, the general rule being that directors of unincorporated companies have only such powers as are expressly or by necessary implication conferred upon them by the members (*o*).

11. *Arresting offenders, &c.*—A. is a bank manager. He has no implied authority to arrest or prosecute supposed offenders, on behalf of the bank (*p*). Authority to arrest or give persons into custody is only implied when the duties of the agent would not be efficiently performed without such authority (*p*). Thus, a servant has implied authority, as a general rule, to give persons into custody when such a step is necessary for the protection of his master's property, but not merely for the purpose of punishing a supposed wrongdoer (*q*).

(*l*) *Linford* v. *Provincial, &c. Ins. Co.*, 1864, 34 Beav. 291; 11 L. T. 330, 10 Jur. N. S. 1066.

(*m*) *Cox* v. *Midland Counties Rail. Co.*, 1849, 3 Ex. 268. Compare *Langan* v. *G. W. Rail. Co.*, 1874, 30 L. T. 173; 26 L. T. 577, Ex. Ch.

(*n*) *Hawtayne* v. *Bourne*, 1841, 5 Jur. 118, 7 M. & W. 595.

(*o*) *Dickinson* v. *Valpy*, 1829, 5 M. & R. 126, 10 B. & C. 128, *Burmester* v. *Norris*, 1851, 6 Ex. 796, 21 L. J. Ex. 43.

(*p*) *Bank of New South Wales* v. *Owston*, 1879, 4 App. Cas. 270; 48 L. J. P. C. 25, 40 L. T. 500, P. C. And see Illustration 12.

(*q*) *Stevens* v. *Hinshelwood*, 1891, 55 J. P. 341, C. A. And see Illustration 12.

12. *Servants of railway companies.*—The servants of a railway company have implied authority to remove passengers from carriages in which they are misconducting themselves or travelling without having paid the fare (*r*), and to do whatever else is necessary for the enforcement of the company's bye-laws (*s*). They have, therefore, implied authority to arrest persons infringing the bye-laws, where that remedy is prescribed by statute (*s*). So, a railway booking clerk, part of whose duty is to keep in a till under his charge money belonging to the company, has implied authority to do all acts necessary for the protection of such money; but he has no implied authority to give into custody a person whom he suspects of having attempted to steal from the till, after the attempt has ceased and there is no further danger to the property of the company (*t*). In *Edwards* v. *L. & N. W. Rail. Co.* (*u*), it was held that a foreman porter, who was in charge of a station in the absence of the station master, had no implied authority to give into custody a person whom he suspected to be stealing the company's property, because such an act was not within the ordinary scope of his employment or duties.

Article 37.

IMPLIED AUTHORITY WHERE EMPLOYED IN COURSE OF BUSINESS AS AGENT.

Every agent who is authorized to do any act in the course of his trade, profession, or business as an agent, has implied authority to do whatever is usually inci-

---

(*r*) *Lowe* v. *G. N. Rail. Co.*, 1892, 62 L. J. Q. B. 524; 9 T. L. R. 516.

(*s*) *Edwards* v. *L. & N. W. Rail. Co.*, 1870, L. R. 5 C. P. 445, 39 L. J. C. P. 241, 22 L. T. 656, 18 W. R. 834.

(*t*) *Allen* v. *L. & S. W. Rail. Co.*, 1870, L. R. 6 Q. B. 65, 40 L. J. Q. B. 55, 23 L. T. 612, 19 W. R. 127.

(*u*) See *ante*, note (*s*).

dental, in the ordinary course of such trade, profession, or business, to the execution of his express authority (x), but not to do anything which is unusual in such trade, profession, or business, or which is neither necessary for nor incidental to the execution of his express authority (y).

Illustrations.

1. A solicitor is authorized to sue for a debt. He has implied authority to receive payment thereof (z).

2. A solicitor is authorized to appear in an action. He has implied authority to refer the subject-matter to arbitration (a), or to enter into a compromise on behalf of his client (b).

3. Counsel is employed to conduct a case. He has implied authority to do everything belonging to the conduct of the case that he thinks best for the client (c).

4. A bailiff is authorized to distrain for rent. He has implied authority to receive the rent and expenses due, and a tender thereof to him operates as a tender to the principal (d).

(x) *Young* v. *Cole*, 1837, 3 Bing. N. C. 724; 4 Scott, 489, 3 Hodges, 126, *Sutton* v. *Tatham*, 1839, 10 Ad. & E. 27; Illustrations 1 to 7. See, also pp. 68 to 80 for implied authority of factors, brokers, auctioneers, solicitors, &c.

(y) *Wiltshire* v. *Sims*, 1808, 1 Camp. 258; 10 R. R. 673, *Daun* v. *Simmons*, 1879, 41 L. T. 783, 28 W. R. 129, 44 J. P. 264, C. A.; *Pourier* v. *Morris*, 1853, 3 El. & Bl. 89, 22 L. J. Q. B. 313, *Smith* v. *Webster*, 1876, 3 Ch. Div. 49, 45 L. J. Ch. 528, 35 L. T. 44, 24 W. R. 894, C. A., Illustrations 8 to 14. See, also, pp. 68 to 80.

(z) *Yates* v. *Freckleton*, 1781, 2 Doug. 623.

(a) *Faviell* v. *Eastern Counties Rail. Co.*, 1848, 2 Ex. 344; 6 D. & L. 54; 17 L. J. Ex. 297; *Smith* v. *Troup*, 1849, 6 D. & L. 679, 7 C. B. 757, 18 L. J. C. P. 209.

(b) *Butler* v. *Knight*, 1867, L. R. 2 Ex. 109, 36 L. J. Ex. 66, 15 L. T. 621, 15 W. R. 407. And see p. 73.

(c) *Strauss* v. *Francis*, 1866, L. R. 1 Q. B. 379; 35 L. J. Q. B. 133; 12 Jur. N. S. 486; 14 L. T. 326, 14 W. R. 634. And see p. 72.

(d) *Hatch* v. *Hale*, 1850, 15 Q. B. 10, 19 L. J. Q. B. 289, 14 Jur. 459.

5. An insurance broker is authorized to subscribe a policy for an underwriter. He has implied authority to adjust a loss arising thereunder (*e*), and to refer a dispute about such a loss to arbitration (*f*).

6. A horse-dealer is authorized to sell a horse. He has implied authority to warrant it (*g*).

7. A commission agent is authorized to make a bet in his own name on behalf of his principal. He has implied authority to pay the bet if he loses it (*h*). (No action now lies, however, for the recovery from the principal of any amount so paid, in consequence of the provisions of the Gaming Act, 1892 (*i*).)

8. An auctioneer is employed to sell goods by auction. He has no implied authority to sell them by private contract, even if the public sale proves abortive, and proof of a custom amongst auctioneers, to sell privately in such an event, is inadmissible (*k*).

9. A. is employed as a general agent for the sale of goods intrusted to his possession. He has no implied authority to pledge the goods (*l*).

10. A solicitor is authorized to sue for a debt. He has no implied authority to interplead, or agree to postpone execution, after judgment for his client (*m*).

11. A solicitor is authorized to send a draft contract for perusal and approval. He has no implied authority to sign a

---

(*e*) *Richardson* v. *Anderson*, 1805, 1 Camp. 43, n., 10 R. R. 628, n.

(*f*) *Goodson* v. *Brooke*, 1815, 4 Camp. 163.

(*g*) *Howard* v. *Sheward*, 1866, L. R. 2 C. P. 148; 36 L. J. C. P. 42, 12 Jur. N. S. 1015.

(*h*) *Read* v. *Anderson*, 1884, 13 Q. B. D. 779, 53 L. J. Q. B. 532, 51 L. T. 55; 49 J. P. 4, 32 W. R. 950, C. A.

(*i*) 55 Vict. c. 9. See *post*, Article 69.

(*k*) *Daniel* v. *Adams*, 1764, Ambl. 495, *Marsh* v. *Jelf*, 1862, 3 F. & F. 234. See, however, *Stein* v. *Cope*, 1883, 1 C. & E. 63.

(*l*) *City Bank* v. *Barrow*, 1880, 5 App. Cas. 664, 43 L. T. 393, H. L.

(*m*) *James* v. *Ricknell*, 1887, 20 Q. B. D. 164, 57 L. J. Q. B. 113, 58 L. T. 278, *Lovegrove* v. *White*, 1871, L. R. 6 C. P. 440, 40 L. J. C. P. 253, 24 L. T. 554, 19 W. R. 823.

memorandum of the contract, for the purpose of satisfying the 4th section of the Statute of Frauds (*n*).

12. A broker is authorized to effect a policy. He has no implied authority, after having effected the policy, to cancel it, it not being part of a broker's ordinary authority or duty to cancel contracts once completely and validly made (*o*).

13. A commission agent is authorized to buy goods in England on behalf of a foreign principal. It is not usual to pledge the credit of the foreign principal in such cases. The agent has no implied authority to pledge the principal's credit, and the fact that they have agreed to share the profit and loss does not affect this rule (*p*).

14. An estate agent is instructed to find a purchaser for certain property. He receives an offer, which he submits to his principal. The principal then instructs him to withdraw part of the property, and names the lowest price for the remainder. He has no implied authority to enter into a contract for the sale of the property, though the price is specified, because it is not usual for estate agents to enter into contracts on behalf of their principals, unless expressly authorized to do so, their duty being merely to submit to their principals any offers which may be made to them (*q*).

Article 38.

AUTHORITY IMPLIED FROM SPECIAL CUSTOMS.

Every agent has implied authority to act, in the execution of his express authority, according to the

(*n*) *Smith* v. *Webster*, 1876, 3 Ch. Div. 49; 45 L. J. Ch. 528, 35 L. T. 44, C. A.

(*o*) *Xenos* v. *Wickham*, 1866, L. R. 2 H. L. 296, 36 L. J. C. P. 313; 16 L. T. 800, 16 W. R. 38, H. L.

(*p*) *Hutton* v. *Bullock*, 1874, L. R. 9 Q. B. 572; 30 L. T. 648; 22 W. R. 956, Ex. Ch.; *Pourier* v. *Morris*, 1853, 3 El. & Bl. 89, 22 L. J. Q. B. 313, 17 Jur. 1116.

(*q*) *Chadburn* v. *Moore*, 1893, 61 L. J. Ch. 674, 67 L. T. 257, 41 W. R. 39, *Hamer* v. *Sharp*, 1875, L. R. 19 Eq. 108, 44 L. J. Ch. 53, 31 L. T. 643.

usage and customs of the particular place or business in which he is employed (*r*), except where the usage or custom is illegal or unreasonable (*s*), or changes the intrinsic character of the contract of agency (*t*). Where the usage or custom is unreasonable, or changes the intrinsic character of the contract of agency, the agent has no implied authority to act in accordance therewith, unless the principal had at the time that he gave the agent authority to act on his behalf notice of the existence of such usage or custom (*u*).

Illustrations.

1. A. is authorized to sell manure. The jury find that it is customary to sell manure with a warranty. A. has implied authority to give a warranty on a sale of the manure (*x*).

2. A. is authorized to sell a certain class of goods. It is customary to sell goods of that class on credit. A. has implied authority to sell the goods on credit (*y*).

3. A share broker is employed to transact business at a particular place. He has implied authority to act in accordance with the reasonable usages of that place (*z*).

4. A broker, a member of the Stock Exchange, is authorized to sell certain bonds. He has implied authority, if the bonds

---

(*r*) Illustrations 1 to 6; *Sutton* v. *Tatham*, 10 Ad. & E. 27; *Harker* v. *Edwards*, 1887, 57 L. J. Q. B. 147, C. A.

(*s*) Illustration 9; *Campbell* v. *Hassell*, 1816, 1 Stark. 233.

(*t*) Illustrations 7 and 8.

(*u*) *Pollock* v. *Stables*, 1848, 5 Railw. Cas. 352, 12 Q. B. 765; 17 L. J. Q. B. 352, 12 Jur. 1043, *Robinson* v. *Mollett*, 1874, L. R. 7 H. L. 802; 44 L. J. C. P. 362, 33 L. T. 544, H. L., Illustrations 7 to 9.

(*x*) *Dingle* v. *Hare*, 1859, 7 C. B. N. S. 145, 29 L. J. C. P. 143, 6 Jur. N. S. 679, 1 L. T. 38.

(*y*) *Pelham* v. *Hilder*, 1849, 1 Y. & Coll. C. C. 3.

(*z*) *Pollock* v. *Stables*, *supra*, note (*u*).

turn out not to be genuine, to rescind the sale and repay the purchaser the price, in accordance with the usage of the Stock Exchange (*a*).

5. A broker is authorized to sell shares on the Stock Exchange. He has implied authority to sell under the rules and regulations there in force, except so far as they are unreasonable and unknown to the principal (*b*).

6. A broker is authorized to buy wool in the Liverpool market. By a custom of that market, a broker so authorized may buy either in his own name or in the name of the principal without giving his principal notice whether he has bought in his own name or not. Such a custom is not unreasonable, and the principal is bound by a contract made in the name of the broker, though he had no notice of the custom or of the fact that the contract was made by the broker in his own name (*c*).

7. A broker is authorized to buy 50 bales of cotton. It is customary in the cotton trade for a broker to make a single contract in his own name for the purchase of a sufficiently large quantity of cotton to supply the orders of several principals, and to parcel it out amongst them. The broker has no implied authority to purchase a larger quantity than 50 bales and allocate 50 bales thereof to the principal, unless the principal was aware of the custom at the time that he gave the authority, because the effect of such a custom is to change the intrinsic character of the contract of agency by turning the agent into a principal, and thus giving him an interest at variance with his duty (*d*).

(*a*) *Young* v. *Cole*, 1837, 3 Bing. N. C. 724, 4 Scott, 489, 3 Hodges, 126.

(*b*) *Harker* v. *Edwards*, 1887, 57 L. J. Q. B. 147, C. A.; *Hodgkinson* v. *Kelly*, 1868, 37 L. J. Ch. 837; L. R. 6 Eq. 496, 16 W. R. 1078, *Coles* v. *Bristowe*, 1868, L. R. 4 Ch. 3; 38 L. J. Ch. 81; 19 L. T. 403, 17 W. R. 105.

(*c*) *Cropper* v. *Cook*, 1868, L. R. 3 C. P. 199, 16 W. R. 596.

(*d*) *Bostock* v. *Jardine*, 1865, 3 H. & C. 700, 34 L. J. Ex. 142; 11 Jur. N. S. 586, 12 L. T. 577. followed by the House of Lords in *Robinson* v.

8. A broker is authorized to sell stock. A custom of the Stock Exchange, whereby he is himself permitted to take over the stock at the price of the day if he is unable to find a purchaser, is unreasonable, and such a transaction is not binding on the principal unless he is proved to have been aware of the custom (*e*).

9. An insurance broker is authorized to receive from the underwriters payment of money due under a policy. A custom at Lloyds' whereby the broker may settle with the underwriters by way of set-off is unreasonable, and the principal is not bound by such a settlement unless he was aware of the custom when he authorized the broker to receive payment (*f*). The same rule applies to stockbrokers settling with agents (*g*).

Implied authority of particular classes of agents, as incidental to their employment.

1. Factors.

Where goods are intrusted to a factor for sale, he has implied authority—

1. To sell them in his own name (*h*).

2. To sell at such times and for such prices as he thinks best (*i*).

Mollett, 1874, L. R. 7 H. L. 802; 44 L. J. C. P. 362, 33 L. T. 544, where a similar custom in the tallow market was rejected on the same ground.

(*e*) *Hamilton* v. *Young*, 1881, L. R. 7 Ir. 289.

(*f*) *Sweeting* v. *Pearce*, 1859, 7 C. B. N. S. 449, 29 L. J. C. P. 265. See, also, cases cited under Article 31, Illustration 8.

(*g*) *Pearson* v. *Scott*, 1878, 9 Ch. Div. 198, 47 L. J. Ch. 705, 38 L. T. 747, 26 W. R. 796, *Blackburn* v. *Mason*, 1893, 68 L. T. 510, 9 T. L. R. 286, 4 R. 297, C. A.

(*h*) *Baring* v. *Corrie*, 1818, 2 B. & A. 137, 20 R. R. 383, *Ex p. Dixon, re Henley*, 1876, 4 Ch. Div. 133, 46 L. J. Bk. 20; 35 L. T. 644, 25 W. R. 105, C. A.

(*i*) *Smart* v. *Sandars*, 1846, 3 C. B. 380, 16 L. J. C. P. 39, 10 Jur. 841.

3. To sell on reasonable credit (*k*).

4. To warrant the goods sold, if it is usual to warrant that class of goods (*l*).

5. To receive payment of the price, if he sells in his own name (*m*).

A factor has no implied authority, as such—

1. To delegate his authority, whether acting under a *del credere* commission or not (*n*).

2. To barter (*o*) or pledge goods (*p*), or the bill of lading for goods (*q*), intrusted to him for sale; even if he has accepted bills drawn by the principal to be provided for out of the proceeds of the goods, he has no implied authority to raise money by pledging the goods for the purpose of meeting the bills (*r*).

2. Brokers.

A broker has implied authority—

1. Where he has entered into a contract, to sign an entry in his book, or to sign bought and sold notes, on behalf of both buyer and seller, as a memorandum of the contract for the purpose of satisfying the provisions of the 4th section of the Sale of Goods Act, 1893 (*s*).

(*k*) *Houghton* v. *Matthews*, 1803, 3 B. & P. 485, 489, 7 R. R. 815; *Scott* v. *Surman*, Willes, 406.

(*l*) *Dingle* v. *Hare*, 1859, 7 C. B. N. S. 145, 29 L. J. C. P. 143, 6 Jur. N. S. 679, 1 L. T. 38.

(*m*) *Drinkwater* v. *Goodwin*, 1775, Cowp. 251.

(*n*) *Cochran* v. *Irlam*, 1814, 2 M. & S. 301; 15 R. R. 257, *Solly* v. *Rathbone*, 1814, 2 M. & S. 298.

(*o*) *Guerreiro* v. *Peile*, 1820, 3 B. & A. 616; 22 R. R. 500.

(*p*) *Martini* v. *Coles*, 1813, 1 M. & S. 140, *Paterson* v. *Tash*, Str. 1178. See, however, Article 82 as to the rights of third persons dealing with him in good faith.

(*q*) *Guichard* v. *Morgan*, 1819, 4 Moore, 36, *Newson* v. *Thornton*, 1805, 6 East, 17, 2 Smith, 207, 8 R. R. 378.

(*r*) *Gill* v. *Kymer*, 1821, 5 Moore, 503, *Fielding* v. *Kymer*, 1821, 2 B. & B. 639.

(*s*) *Parton* v. *Crofts*, 1864, 16 C. B. N. S. 11, 33 L. J. C. P. 189, 10

2. To sell on reasonable credit, where there is no usage to the contrary (*t*).

3. Where he sells for an undisclosed principal, to receive payment of the price in accordance with the terms of the contract (*u*).

4. To act in accordance with the usage, and the rules and regulations of the market in which he deals, except so far as the usage, rules or regulations are illegal or unreasonable, or alter the intrinsic nature of the contract of agency (*x*).

5. To close his account with the principal, but not to close part of it only, if the principal fails to duly pay differences (*y*).

A broker has no implied authority, as such—

1. To contract in his own name (*z*).

2. To cancel contracts made by him (*a*).

3. To pay total or partial losses on behalf of his underwriters (*b*).

4. To include the orders of several principals in one contract (*c*).

5. To receive payment for an undisclosed principal otherwise than in accordance with the terms of the original contract, or to receive payment by way of set-off (*d*).

L. T. 34, 12 W. R. 553, *Thompson* v. *Gardiner*, 1876, 1 C. P. D. 777. See other cases cited under Article 90.

(*t*) *Boorman* v. *Brown*, 1842, 3 Q. B. 511, 2 G. & D. 793, 11 C. & F. 1, *Wiltshire* v. *Sims*, 1808, 1 Camp. 258, 10 R. R. 673.

(*u*) *Campbell* v. *Hassell*, 1816, 1 Stark. 233.

(*x*) See cases cited under Article 38.

(*y*) *Samuel* v. *Rowe*, 1892, 8 T. L. R. 488.

(*z*) *Baring* v. *Corrie*, 1818, 2 B. & A. 137.

(*a*) *Xenos* v. *Wickham*, 1866, L. R. 2 H. L. 296, 36 L. J. C. P. 313, 16 L. T. 800, 16 W. R. 38, H. L.

(*b*) *Bell* v. *Auldjo*, 1784, 4 Doug. 48.

(*c*) *Bostock* v. *Jardine*, 1865, 3 H. & C. 700, 34 L. J. Ex. 142, 11 Jur. N. S. 586, 12 L. T. 577.

(*d*) *Campbell* v. *Hassell*, 1816, 1 Stark. 233, *Pearson* v. *Scott*, 1878, 9 Ch. Div. 198, 47 L. J. Ch. 705, 38 L. T. 747, 26 W. R. 796.

6. To delegate his authority, whether acting under a *del credere* commission or not (*e*).

7. To pledge a bill intrusted to him to get discounted (*f*).

8. To sell stock or shares on credit, even if he considers it for the principal's benefit (*g*).

3. Auctioneers.

An auctioneer has implied authority at a sale by auction to sign a contract or memorandum thereof on behalf of both vendor and purchaser, and his signature is a sufficient compliance with the provisions of the 4th section of the Statute of Frauds, or of the 4th section of the Sale of Goods Act, 1893, in an action against either party either for specific performance or for damages for breach of contract (*h*).

An auctioneer has no implied authority, as such—

1. To rescind a sale made by him (*i*).

2. To warrant goods sold by him (*k*).

3. To make any verbal declarations which are inconsistent with the written conditions (*l*).

4. To take a bill of exchange in payment, where it is provided that the price shall be paid to him (*m*).

5. To sign the vendor's name to any contract except the contract of sale (*n*).

(*e*) *Henderson* v. *Barnewell*, 1827, 1 Y. & J. 387; *Cochran* v. *Irlam*, 1814, 2 M. & S. 301; 15 R. R. 257.

(*f*) *Haynes* v. *Foster*, 1833, 2 C. & M. 237; 4 Tyr. 65.

(*g*) *Wiltshire* v. *Sims*, 1808, 1 Camp. 258, 10 R. R. 673.

(*h*) *Kemeys* v. *Proctor*, 1820, 1 Jac. & Walk. 350, 3 Ves. & B. 57; *Shelton* v. *Livius*, 1832, 2 C. & J. 411; 2 Tyr. 420, *Emmerson* v. *Heelis*, 1809, 2 Taunt. 38, 11 R. R. 520; *White* v. *Proctor*, 1811, 4 Taunt. 209; 13 R. R. 580.

(*i*) *Nelson* v. *Aldridge*, 1818, 2 Stark. 435, 20 R. R. 709.

(*k*) *Payne* v. *Leconfield*, 1882, 51 L. J. Q. B. 642; 30 W. R. 814.

(*l*) *Gunnis* v. *Erhart*, 1789, 1 H. Bl. 290; 2 R. R. 769; *Shelton* v. *Livius*, 1832, 2 C. & J. 411, 2 Tyr. 420.

(*m*) *Williams* v. *Evans*, 1866, L. R. 1 Q. B. 352, 35 L. J. Q. B. 111; 13 L. T. 753, 14 W. R. 330, *Sykes* v. *Giles*, 1839, 5 M. & W. 645.

(*n*) *Megaw* v. *Molloy*, 1878, L. R. 2 Ir. 530.

6. To sell by private contract, even if the public sale proves abortive and he is offered more than the reserve price (*o*).

7. To deliver goods sold, without payment, or to allow a set-off due from the vendor to the purchaser (*p*).

8. To deal, after sale, with the terms on which a title shall be made (*q*). He is an agent for sale only (*q*).

4. Counsel.

Where counsel is employed to conduct a case, he has implied authority—

1. To consent to a nonsuit (*r*), or to the withdrawal of a juror (*s*).

2. To compromise or abandon the claims of his client, or give an undertaking on his behalf, in respect of all matters within the scope of the suit or matter (*t*).

3. To enter into an agreement with the counsel on the other side as to the subject-matter of the suit or matter, or as to costs (*u*).

4. To consent to an order (*x*).

5. Generally, to do all other things appertaining to the conduct of the case, according to his absolute discretion (*y*).

(*o*) *Marsh* v. *Jelf*, 1862, 3 F. & F. 234, *Daniel* v. *Adams*, 1764, Ambl. 495.

(*p*) *Brown* v. *Staton*, 1816, 2 Chit. 353.

(*q*) *Seton* v. *Slade*, 1802, 7 Ves. 276, 6 R. R. 124.

(*r*) *Lynch* v. *Coel*, 1865, 12 L. T. 548, 13 W. R. 846.

(*s*) *Strauss* v *Francis*, 1866, L. R. 1 Q. B. 379, 35 L. J. Q. B. 133, 12 Jur. N. S. 486, 14 L. T. 326, 14 W. R. 634.

(*t*) *Re Wood, ex p. Wenham*, 1872, 21 W. R. 104.

(*u*) *Strauss* v. *Francis*, *supra*, *Swinfen* v *Swinfen*, 1858, 2 De G. & J. 381, 3 Jur. N. S. 1109; 4 Jur. N. S. 774, 27 L. J. Ch. 35, 491.

(*x*) *Mole* v. *Smith*, 1820, 1 Jac. & Walk. 673, *Re Hobler*, 1844, 8 Beav. 101, *Furnival* v. *Bogle*, 1827, 4 Russ. 142.

(*y*) *Strauss* v. *Francis*, *supra*, note (*s*), *Lynch* v. *Coel*, *supra*, note (*r*).

5. Solicitors.

A solicitor has implied authority—

1. To receive payment of a debt for which he is instructed to sue (*z*).

2. To receive the consideration for a deed upon its production duly executed and containing a receipt for such consideration by the person entitled to give a receipt therefor (*a*).

3. Where he is authorized to appear in an action—

(a) to compromise (*b*), or refer the subject-matter thereof to arbitration (*c*);

(b) to abandon the claims of his client, provided that they are within the scope of the action, but not where they are collateral thereto (*d*);

(c) to enter into an undertaking in reference to the subject-matter thereof (*e*).

4. Where he is authorized to proceed to satisfaction—

(a) to issue and indorse a writ of *fi. fa.*, and do all other acts necessary to obtain the fruits of the judgment (*f*);

(b) to order the sheriff to withdraw from possession under a writ of *fi. fa.* (*g*);

(*z*) *Yates* v. *Freckleton*, 1781, 2 Doug. 623. Also the solicitor's London agent who issues and indorses the writ *Weary* v. *Alderson*, 1837, 2 M. & Rob. 127.

(*a*) Conveyancing Act, 1881, s. 56, Trustee Act, 1893, s. 17, extending the principle to solicitors of trustees.

(*b*) *Butler* v. *Knight*, 1867, L. R. 2 Ex. 109; 36 L. J. Ex. 66, 15 L. T. 621, 15 W. R. 407, *Prestwick* v. *Poley*, 1865, 18 C. B. N. S. 806, 34 L. J. C. P. 189, 11 Jur. N. S. 583, 12 L. T. 390.

(*c*) *Faviell* v. *Eastern Counties Rail. Co.*, 1848, 2 Ex. 344, 6 D. & L. 54, 17 L. J. Ex. 297, *Smith* v. *Troup*, 1849, 6 D. & L. 679; 7 C. B. 757, 18 L. J. C. P. 209.

(*d*) *Re Wood, ex p. Wenham*, 1872, 21 W. R. 104.

(*e*) *Re Commonwealth Land, &c. Co., ex p. Hollington*, 1873, 43 L. J. Ch. 99, 29 L. T. 502, 22 W. R. 106.

(*f*) *Jarmain* v. *Hooper*, 1843, 1 D. & L. 769, 6 M. & G. 827; 13 L. J. C. P. 63, 8 Jur. 127, *Morris* v. *Salberg*, 1889, 22 Q. B. D. 614, 61 L. T. 283, C. A.

(*g*) *Levi* v. *Abbott*, 1849, 4 Ex. 588; 19 L. J. Ex. 62.

(c) to compromise, after judgment (*h*).

A solicitor has no implied authority, as such—

1. To interplead or agree to postpone execution after a judgment in his client's favour, he being then *functus officio*, unless authorized to proceed (*i*).

2. To direct the sheriff to seize particular goods, when issuing a writ of *fi. fa.*, or otherwise to interfere with the sheriff in the performance of his duties (*k*).

3. To institute any action or suit (*l*).

4. To sign a memorandum of a contract of which he is instructed to prepare a draft, so as to satisfy the provisions of the Statute of Frauds (*m*).

5. To receive the purchase-money for an estate (except on production of a deed, as above (*n*).)

6. To pledge the credit of his client to counsel for fees (*o*).

7. To take special journeys, or go to foreign parts, on his client's behalf (*p*).

6. Shipmasters.

The extent of a shipmaster's authority to sell or hypothecate the ship or cargo (*q*), or to bind his principals personally by con-

(*h*) *Butler* v. *Knight*, 1867, L. R. 2 Ex. 109, 36 L. J. Ex. 66, 15 L. T. 621, 15 W. R. 407.

(*i*) *James* v. *Ricknell*, 1887, 20 Q. B. D. 164, 57 L. J. Q. B. 113, 58 L. T. 278, *Lovegrove* v. *White*, 1871, L. R. 6 C. P. 440, 40 L. J. C. P. 253, 24 L. T. 554, 19 W. R. 823.

(*k*) *Smith* v. *Keal*, 1882, 9 Q. B. D. 340, 47 L. T. 142, 31 W. R. 76.

(*l*) *Wright* v. *Castle*, 1817, 3 Meriv. 12, 17 R. R. 3.

(*m*) *Howard* v. *Braithwaite*, 1812, 1 Ves. & B. 202, *Smith* v. *Webster*, 1876, 3 Ch. Div. 49, 45 L. J. Ch. 528; 35 L. T. 44, 24 W. R. 894.

(*n*) *Viney* v. *Chaplin*, 1858, 2 De G. & J. 468, 27 L. J. Ch. 434, 4 Jur. N. S. 619.

(*o*) *Mostyn* v. *Mostyn*, 1870, L. R. 5 Ch. 457, 39 L. J. Ch. 780, 22 L. T. 461, 18 W R. 657.

(*p*) *Re Snell*, 1877, 5 Ch. Div. 815, 36 L. T. 534 25 W. R. 736.

(*q*) *The Karnak*, 1869, L. R. 2 P. C. 505, 38 L. J. Adm. 57, 21 L. T. 159, 6 Moo. P. C. C. (N. S.) 136, P. C., *The Gaetano and Maria*, 1882, 7 P. D. 137, 51 L. J. Ad. 67, 46 L. T. 835, 4 Asp. M. C. 470, C. A., *The August*, (1891) P. 328; 60 L. J. P. 57, 66 L. T. 32.

tract (*r*), is determined by the law of the country to which the ship belongs (*s*), and the ship's flag operates as notice to all the world that the master's authority is limited by the law of that flag (*r*). Thus, if an English cargo be hypothecated by the master of an Italian ship, the validity of the bond is governed by Italian law, and if found to be valid by that law, it will be enforced by the English Courts, although the conditions required for its validity by English law were not fulfilled (*t*).

A shipmaster is appointed for the purpose of conducting the voyage on which the ship is engaged to a favourable termination, and has implied authority to do all things necessary for the due and proper prosecution of that voyage (*u*). He has also implied authority to enter into contracts in respect of the usual employment of the ship (*v*). But he can only bind personally those owners who appointed him or were privy to his appointment (*x*). The mere fact that a person is a registered owner of the vessel is not sufficient to render him liable on the master's contracts; it must appear that the master is or has been held out as his agent (*x*).

The master of a British ship has implied authority—

1. To contract for the conveyance of merchandise according to the usual employment of the ship (*y*).

2. To enter into a charter-party on behalf of the owners when he is in a foreign port and there is difficulty in communicating with the owners (*z*).

(*r*) *Lloyd* v. *Guibert*, 1865, 6 B. & S. 100; 33 L. J. Q. B. 241, 35 L. J. Q. B. 74, 10 Jur. N. S. 949; 10 L. T. 570, 6 B. & S. 120.

(*s*) See note (*q*), *supra*, p. 74.

(*t*) *The Gaetano and Maria*, *supra*, note (*q*).

(*u*) *Arthur* v. *Barton*, 1840, 6 M. & W. 138, *Beldon* v. *Campbell*, 1851, 6 Ex. 886.

(*v*) *Grant* v. *Norway*, 1851, 10 C. B. 665; 20 L. J. C. P. 93, 15 Jur. 296, *McLean* v. *Fleming*, 1871, 2 H. L. Sc. App. 128, 25 L. T. 317, H. L.

(*x*) *Mackenzie* v. *Pooley*, 1856, 11 Ex. 638, 25 L. J. Ex. 124; *Mitcheson* v. *Oliver*, 5 E. & B. 419.

(*y*) *Rinquist* v. *Ditchell*, 3 Esp. 64.

(*z*) *The Fanny*, *The Matilda*, 5 Asp. M. C. 75, 48 L. T. 771, *Grant* v. *Norway*, *supra*, note (*v*).

3. To enter into reasonable towage agreements (*a*).

4. To enter into salvage agreements, if necessary for the owners' benefit; but not merely for the purpose of saving the lives of the master and crew without regard to saving the owners' property. A salvage agreement operates as a charge on the property saved, and is only binding to the extent of the value of that property (*b*).

5. To pledge the owners' credit, at home or abroad, for fit and proper repairs and stores necessary for the equipment of the vessel on her voyage, and such as a prudent owner himself would order (*c*), provided that it is reasonably necessary to obtain them on the owners' credit (*d*).

6. To borrow money on the owners' credit, at home or abroad, if the advance is necessary for the prosecution of the voyage, communication with the owners is not practicable, and there is no solvent agent of the owners on the spot (*e*). To render the owners liable for such an advance, the lender must prove—(1) that there was a reasonable necessity, according to the ordinary course of prudent conduct, to borrow on the owners' credit (*d*) (this is a question of fact for the jury (*e*)); (2) that the amount was advanced expressly for the use of the ship (*f*); and (3) that the money was expended on the ship (*g*). There is no implied authority to pledge the credit of the owners when they can reasonably be communicated with (*e*), or for the purpose of paying for services already rendered (*e*), or when there is a solvent

---

(*a*) *Wellfield* v. *Adamson* (*The Alfred*), 1884, 5 Asp. M. C. 214; 50 L. T. 511.

(*b*) *The Renpor*, 1883, 8 P. D. 115, 52 L. J. P. 49, 5 Asp. M. C. 98.

(*c*) *Frost* v. *Oliver*, 1853, 1 C. L. R. 1003, 22 L. J. Q. B. 353, 18 Jur. 166, *Webster* v. *Seekamp*, 1821, 4 B. & A. 352.

(*d*) *Gunn* v. *Roberts*, 1874, L. R. 9 C. P. 331, 43 L. J. C. P. 233, 30 L. T. 424, 22 W. R. 652, *Edwards* v. *Havill*, 1853, 14 C. B. 107, 2 C. L. R. 1343, 23 L. J. C. P. 8, 17 Jur. 1103.

(*e*) *Arthur* v. *Barton*, 1840, 6 M. & W. 138, *Beldon* v. *Campbell*, 1851, 6 Ex. 886, *Stonehouse* v. *Grant*, 1841, 2 Q. B. 431; *Johns* v. *Simons*, 1842, 2 Q. B. 425, *Edwards* v. *Havill*, 1853, 14 C. B. 107, 2 C. L. R. 1343, 23 L. J. C. P. 8, 17 Jur. 1103, *Rocher* v. *Busher*, 1815, 1 Stark. 27, 18 R. R. 742.

(*f*) *Thacker* v. *Moates*, 1831, 1 M. & Rob. 79.

(*g*) *Boyle* v. *Atty*, 1818, Gow, 50.

agent on the spot (*h*). But the state of accounts between the owners and the master does not affect his implied authority to borrow on their credit (*i*).

7. To hypothecate the ship, cargo, and freight (bottomry) when communication with the respective owners is impracticable (*j*), and it is necessary to obtain supplies or repairs in order to prosecute the voyage, and impossible to obtain them on personal credit, or in any other way than by hypothecation (*k*). But there is no implied authority to hypothecate either ship or cargo for necessaries already supplied (*k*), or without communicating with the respective owners where practicable (*j*), or for the purpose of obtaining personal freedom from arrest (*l*), or where it is possible to obtain supplies in any other way (*k*). Where ship and cargo are hypothecated for repairs, the shipowners are bound to indemnify the owners of the cargo from liability under the bond (*m*).

8. To hypothecate the cargo alone (*respondentia*), when it is necessary for the benefit of the cargo or for the prosecution of the voyage (*n*), and communication with the owners is impracticable (*o*). The master has no implied authority to hypothecate or do any act seriously affecting the value of the cargo without first communicating, if practicable, with the owners thereof (*o*).

(*h*) See note (*d*), *supra*, p. 76.

(*i*) *Williamson* v. *Page*, 1844, 1 C. & K. 581.

(*j*) *Kleinwort* v. *Cassa Marrittima Genoa*, 1877, 2 App. Cas. 156, 36 L. T. 118, 25 W. R. 608, P. C.

(*k*) *The Hersey*, 1837, 3 Hagg. Ad. 404, *Hussie* v. *Christie*, 1807, 13 Ves. 599, 9 East, 426, 9 R. R. 585.

(*l*) *Smith* v. *Gould*, 1842, 4 Moo. P. C. C. 21, 6 Jur. 543, P. C.

(*m*) *Duncan* v. *Benson*, 1849, 1 Ex. 537; 17 L. J. Ex. 238. Affirmed sub nom. *Benson* v. *Duncan*, 3 Ex. 644, 18 L. J. Ex. 169, Ex. Ch.

(*n*) *Cargo* v. *Sultan*, 1859, 5 Jur. N. S. 1060, Swa. 504, *The Gratitudine*, 1801, 3 Rob. 240.

(*o*) *The Onward*, 1873, L. R. 4 Ad. 38, 42 L. J. Ad. 61, 28 L. T. 204; 21 W. R. 601, *The Hamburgh*, 1863, 2 Moo. P. C. C. (N. S.) 289; 33 L. J. Ad. 116, 10 Jur. N. S. 600, 10 L. T. 206, 12 W. R. 628, P. C.

9. To sell the ship, in cases of absolute or urgent necessity, when it is not practicable to communicate with the owners (*p*). The master is justified in selling the ship only in cases of urgent necessity, and the burden of proof lies on the party seeking to uphold the sale (*q*). It must be such a necessity as leaves him no alternative as a prudent and skilful man, acting in good faith for the best interests of all concerned, and with the best judgment that can be formed under the circumstances, except to sell the ship as she lies. If he sells hastily, either without sufficient examination into the condition of the ship, or without having previously made every exertion in his power with the means then at his disposal to extricate her, the sale is invalid, even if the danger at the time appeared exceedingly imminent (*r*). But if in consequence of damage it is impossible to prosecute the voyage, or there is no prospect of completing it (*s*), or if the ship is in a foreign port, and cannot be repaired except at such a cost as no prudent person would venture to incur, the master has implied authority to sell her (*t*).

10. To sell part of the cargo—but not the whole—where repairs are absolutely necessary for the prosecution of the voyage, and communication with the owners of the cargo is imprac-

---

(*p*) *The Australia*, 1859, Swa. 480; 13 Moo. P. C. C. 132, P. C.; *The Margaret Mitchell*, 1858, Swa. 382, 4 Jur. N. S. 1193.

(*q*) *Cobequid Marine Ins. Co.* v. *Barteaux*, 1875, L. R. 6 P. C. 319; 32 L. T. 510, 23 W. R. 892, *Knight* v. *Faith*, 1850, 15 Q. B. 649; 19 L. J. Q. B. 509, 14 Jur. 1114, *Cammell* v. *Sewell*, 1860, 5 H. & N. 728; 29 L. J. Ex. 350, 6 Jur. N. S. 918, 8 W. R. 639, Ex. Ch. Held necessary in *The Glasgow*, 1856, Swa. 145, *The Victor*, 1865, 13 L. T. 21, *The Australia*, 1859, Swa. 480, 13 Moo. P. C. C. 132, P. C., *Ireland* v. *Thomson*, 1847, 4 C. B. 149, 17 L. J. C. P. 241. Sale set aside as unnecessary in *The Bonita* v. *The Charlotte*, 1861, 30 L. J. Ad. 145, 5 L. T. 141; Lush. 253, *The Eliza Cornish*, or *The Segreda*, 1853, 1 Spinks, 36; 17 Jur. 738.

(*r*) *Cobequid Marine Ins. Co.* v. *Barteaux*, *supra*.

(*s*) *Ireland* v *Thomson*, 1847, 4 C. B. 149, 17 L. J. C. P. 241, *Hunter* v. *Parker*, 1840, 7 M. & W. 322.

(*t*) *The Australia*, 1859, 13 Moo. P. C. C. 132; Swa. 480, P. C.

ticable (*u*). But it is only in cases of extreme necessity, and only after he has done everything in his power to carry the cargo to its destination, that he has implied authority to sell any portion thereof (*x*). He has no implied authority, in any case, to stop the voyage and sell the whole of the cargo in a foreign port, even if it is impossible to prosecute the original voyage, and the sale is most beneficial for the owners under the circumstances (*x*).

The master of a British ship has no implied authority—

1. To vary any contract made by the owners (*y*).

2. To agree for the substitution of another voyage in place of that agreed upon between the owners and freighters, or make any contract outside the scope of that voyage (*z*).

3. To hold out any person as an agent to charter the vessel (*a*).

4. To sign a bill of lading for goods not actually received (*b*), or for a greater quantity than are actually received on board (*c*), or at a lower freight than the owners contracted for (*d*). His authority is limited to signing for goods actually received on board, and all persons taking a bill of lading, by indorsement or otherwise, are deemed to have notice that his authority is so limited (*c*). The 3rd section of the 18 & 19 Vict. c. 111—providing that every bill of lading, in the hands of a consignee

---

(*u*) *The Gratitudine*, 1801, 3 Rob. 240; *Australian Steam Navigation Co.* v. *Morse*, 1872, L. R. 4 P. C. 222; 27 L. T. 357, 20 W. R. 728, 8 Moo. P. C. C. (N. S.) 482, P. C., *Duncan* v. *Benson*, 1849, 1 Ex. 537; 17 L. J. Ex. 238. affirmed *sub nom. Benson* v. *Duncan*, 3 Ex. 644, 18 L. J. Ex. 169, Ex. Ch.

(*x*) *Atlantic Marine Ins. Co.* v. *Huth*, 1879, 16 Ch. D. 474; 44 L. T. 67; 29 W. R. 387, C. A., *Wilson* v. *Millar*, 1816, 2 Stark. 1; 19 R. R. 670; *Joseph* v. *Knox*, 1813, 3 Camp. 320; *Van Omeron* v. *Dowick*, 1809, 2 Camp. 42, 11 R. R. 656.

(*y*) *Grant* v. *Norway*, 1851, 10 C. B. 665, 20 L. J. C. P. 93, 15 Jur. 296.

(*z*) *Burgon* v. *Sharpe*, 1810, 2 Camp. 529; 11 R. R. 788.

(*a*) *The Fanny*, *The Matilda*, 5 Asp. M. C. 75; 48 L. T. 771.

(*b*) *Grant* v. *Norway*, *supra*, note (*y*).

(*c*) *Hubbersty* v. *Ward*, 1853, 8 Ex. 330, 22 L. J. Ex. 113.

(*d*) *Pickernell* v. *Jauberry*, 1862, 3 F. & F. 217.

or indorsee for valuable consideration, representing goods to have been shipped on board a vessel, shall be conclusive evidence of such shipment against the master or other person signing the same, notwithstanding such goods or part thereof may not have been shipped—applies only as against the persons who have actually signed the bill of lading (*e*), and does not make the master's signature conclusive evidence against the owners (*f*). The master's signature is *primâ facie* evidence against the owners that the goods were put on board (*g*), but they are permitted to prove that in fact they were not (*f*).

Article 39.

DELEGATION OF AUTHORITY.

No agent has power to delegate his authority to a sub-agent, or to appoint a deputy or substitute to do any act on behalf of the principal, except with the express or implied authority of the principal. The authority of the principal is implied—

(1) Where the employment of a sub-agent is justified by the usage of the particular trade or business in which the agent is employed, provided that such usage is not inconsistent with the express terms of the agent's authority or instructions (*h*).

(*e*) *Jessel* v. *Bath*, 1867, L. R. 2 Ex. 267, 36 L. J. Ex. 149; 15 W. R. 1041.

(*f*) *Meyer* v. *Dresser*, 1864, 16 C. B. N. S. 646; 33 L. J. C. P 289, 10 L. T. 612, 12 W. R. 983, *Brown* v. *Powell Duffryn Steam Coal Co.*, 1875, L. R. 10 C. P. 562; 44 L. J. C. P. 289, 32 L. T. 621, 23 W. R. 549.

(*g*) *M'Lean* v. *Fleming*, 1871, 2 H. L. Sc. App. 128, 25 L. T. 317, H. L.

(*h*) *De Bussche* v. *Alt*, 1877, 8 Ch. Div. 286, 47 L. J. Ch. 381, 38 L. T. 370, C. A.

(2) Where the principal knows, at the time of the agent's appointment, that the authority will be executed by a substitute (*i*).

(3) Where, from the conduct of the principal and agent, it may reasonably be presumed to have been their intention that the agent should have power to delegate his authority (*k*).

(4) Where, in the course of the agent's employment, unforeseen emergencies arise which impose upon him the necessity of appointing a substitute (*k*).

(5) Where the authority conferred is of such a nature as to necessitate its execution by means of a deputy (*i*).

(6) Where the act done is purely ministerial, and does not involve confidence or discretion (*l*).

The maxim "*Delegatus non potest delegare*" is founded on the confidential character of the contract of agency, and whenever authority is coupled with a discretion or confidence, it must, as a general rule, be executed by the agent in person (*m*). Thus,

---

(*i*) *Quebec and Richmond Rail. Co.* v. *Quinn*, 1858, 12 Moo. P. C. C. 232, P. C.

(*k*) *De Bussche* v. *Alt*, *supra*, note (*h*).

(*l*) *Mason* v. *Joseph*, 1804, 1 Smith, 406; *Rossiter* v. *Trafalgar Life Assurance Co.*, 1859, 27 Beav. 377, *Coles* v. *Trecothick*, 1804, 9 Ves. 234; 1 Smith, 233, 7 R. R. 167.

(*m*) *Combe's case*, 9 Co. R. 75 (vol. 5, p. 135); *Blore* v. *Sutton*, 1816, 3 Meriv. 237; 17 R. R. 74.

auctioneers (*n*), factors (*o*), directors (*p*), liquidators (*q*), brokers (*r*), arbitrators (*s*), &c., have, in general, no implied authority to act through sub-agents. So, where a shipmaster was authorized to sell certain goods, it was held that he had no implied authority to send them on to another person for sale, though he was unable himself to find a purchaser (*t*).

So, it was held that four liquidators had no power to authorize one of their number to accept bills of exchange on behalf of them all, but that they might authorize him to accept a particular bill on their behalf (*u*). The execution of the former authority required discretion; the latter was an authority to do a purely ministerial act. So, where a tenant for life had a power to lease, and a memorandum of a contract for a lease was signed by his agent's clerk with the approval of the agent and in the ordinary course of business, it was held that the memorandum was not sufficient to satisfy the provisions of the 4th section of the Statute of Frauds, not having been signed by a duly authorized agent, within the meaning of that statute (*x*). On the other hand, authority to draw bills of exchange in the principal's name may be exercised through the agent's clerk (*y*), and an authority to indorse a particular bill in the principal's name may be delegated (*z*), because such acts are purely ministerial and involve no discretion.

(*n*) *Coles* v. *Trecothick*, 1804, 9 Ves. 234, 1 Smith, 233, 7 R. R. 167.

(*o*) *Cochran* v. *Irlam*, 1814, 2 M. & S. 301, 15 R. R. 257; *Catlin* v. *Bell*, 1815, 4 Camp. 183.

(*p*) *Howard's case*, 1866, L. R. 1 Ch. 561.

(*q*) *Ex p. Birmingham Banking Co.*, 1868, L. R. 3 Ch. 651.

(*r*) *Henderson* v. *Barnewell*, 1827, 1 Y. & J. 387; *Cochran* v. *Irlam*, 1814, 2 M. & S. 301, 15 R. R. 257.

(*s*) *Little* v. *Newton*, 1841, 2 M. & G. 351, 2 Scott, N. R. 159.

(*t*) *Catlin* v *Bell*, 1815, 4 Camp. 183.

(*u*) *Ex p. Birmingham Banking Co.*, *supra*.

(*x*) *Blore* v. *Sutton*, 1816, 3 Meriv. 237, 17 R. R. 74. And see *Doe* v. *Robinson*, 1837, 3 Bing. N. C. 677.

(*y*) *Ex p. Sutton*, 1788, 2 Cox, 84.

(*z*) *Lord* v. *Hall*, 1848, 2 C. & K. 698.

Acquiescence of principal.—Where the highest bidder at a sale by auction was an agent, and the auctioneer entered his name as buyer without objection by the principal, who was present at the sale, it was held that such entry was a sufficient memorandum of the contract to satisfy the Statute of Frauds as against the principal, on the ground of his acquiescence in the appointment of the auctioneer as a sub-agent (*a*).

Solicitors' town agents.—A country solicitor has implied authority to act through his London agent when necessary or usual in the ordinary course of business, and the acts of such agent in reference to the matters intrusted to him bind the client (*b*). But a solicitor cannot delegate his entire employment to his London agent so as to make the agent his client's solicitor (*c*).

Article 40.

PRINCIPAL AND SUB-AGENT.

Where an agent delegates his entire employment to a substitute, with the knowledge and consent of the principal, privity of contract may arise between the principal and the substitute, so as to render the substitute responsible to the principal for the proper performance of his duties (*d*). But there is no privity of contract between a principal and sub-agent, as such, whether the sub-agent was appointed with the autho-

---

(*a*) *White* v. *Proctor*, 1811, 4 Taunt. 209; 13 R. R. 580; *Coles* v. *Trecothick*, 1804, 9 Ves. 234, 1 Smith, 233; 7 R. R. 167.

(*b*) *Griffiths* v. *Williams*, 1787, 1 T. R. 710; *Weary* v. *Alderson*, 1837, 2 M. & Rob. 127. See Article 40, Illustrations 7 and 8.

(*c*) *Wray* v. *Kemp*, 1883, 26 Ch. Div. 169; 53 L. J. Ch. 1020; 50 L. T. 552.

(*d*) *De Bussche* v. *Alt*, 1877, 8 Ch. Div. 286; 47 L. J. Ch. 381; 38 L. T. 370, C. A., Illustration 1. It is not easy to reconcile this decision with the cases cited in Illustrations 2 and 3.

rity of the principal or not, and the rights and duties arising out of the contracts between the principal and agent and between the agent and sub-agent respectively, are only enforceable by and against the immediate parties thereto (*e*).

Where a sub-agent is appointed without the authority, express or implied, of the principal, the principal is not bound by his acts (*f*).

Illustrations.

1. A ship was consigned to A., an agent in China, for sale, a minimum price being fixed. A., with the knowledge and consent of the principal, employed B. to sell the ship. B., being unable to find a purchaser, bought the ship himself at the minimum price, and subsequently resold her at a large profit. It was held that privity of contract existed between the principal and B., and that B. was liable to account to the principal for the profit made on the re-sale (*g*).

2. A factor was employed to sell goods on a *del credere* commission. The factor, with the principal's authority, employed a broker on an ordinary commission to sell the goods. The broker sold the goods and received the proceeds, and made payments on account to the factor from time to time. While the balance of the proceeds was still in the hands of the broker, the factor, being then indebted to the broker in respect of other independent transactions, became bankrupt. Held—(1) that there

---

(*e*) *New Zealand and Australian Land Co.* v. *Watson*, 1881, 7 Q. B. D. 374, 50 L. J. Q. B. 433, 44 L. T. 675, 29 W. R. 694, C. A., *Robbins* v. *Fennell*, 1847, 11 Q. B. 248, 17 L. J. Q. B. 77, 12 Jur. 157, *Schmaling* v. *Tomlinson*, 1815, 6 Taunt. 147, 1 Marsh. 500, Illustrations 2 to 8.

(*f*) See *Doe* v. *Robinson*, 1837, 3 Bing. N. C. 677, *Blore* v. *Sutton*, 1816, 3 Meriv. 237.

(*g*) *De Bussche* v. *Alt*, 1877, 8 Ch. Div. 286, 47 L. J. Ch. 381, 38 L. T. 370, C. A. Compare with Illustration 2.

was no privity of contract between the principal and the broker; (2) that the broker was not liable to account to the principal for the proceeds of the goods sold; (3) that the principal was not entitled to recover the balance of the proceeds from the broker in the factor's name without allowing the amount due from the factor to the broker in respect of other transactions to be set off, though the broker had reason to believe that the factor was acting as an agent (*h*).

3. An agent appointed a sub-agent to manage the principal's affairs. The sub-agent took over the entire management thereof, and communicated with the principal direct. Held, that the sub-agent was not liable to render an account of his agency to the principal (*i*). The general rule is that sub-agents must account to the agents employing them, and the agents to their principals (*k*). An agent is only liable to account to his own principal (*l*).

4. A. employs B. to transport goods to a foreign market. B., without A.'s knowledge or consent, delegates his entire employment to C. There is no privity of contract between A. and C., and A. is not liable to C. for his charges, even if he has not paid B. for the services rendered (*m*).

5. A. employs B. to procure a loan on usual terms. B. employs C., who obtains a loan on terms which are unusual. A. is

---

(*h*) *New Zealand and Australian Land Co.* v. *Watson*, 1881, 7 Q. B. D. 374, 50 L. J. Q. B. 433, 44 L. T. 675, 29 W. R. 694, C. A. See, however, *Blackburn* v. *Mason*, 1893, 68 L. T. 510, 9 T. L. R. 286, 4 R. 297, C. A.

(*i*) *Lockwood* v. *Abdy*, 1845, 14 Sim. 437, 9 Jur. 267. And see *Cartwright* v. *Hateley*, 1791, 1 Ves. jun. 292, 3 Bro. C. C. 238.

(*k*) *Stephens* v. *Badcock*, 1831, 3 B. & Ad. 354, *Sims* v. *Brittain*, 1832, 1 N. & M. 594, 4 B. & Ad. 375, *Montagu* v. *Forwood*, (1893) 2 Q. B. 350, 69 L. T. 371, 9 T. L. R. 634, 42 W. R. 124, 4 R. 579, C. A.

(*l*) *Att.-Gen.* v. *Chesterfield*, 1854, 18 Beav. 596, 18 Jur. 686, 2 W. R. 499, *Pinto* v. *Santos*, 1814, 1 Marsh. 132, 5 Taunt. 447. See also *Kinloch* v. *Secretary of State for India*, 1882, 7 App. Cas. 619, 51 L. J. Ch. 885, 47 L. T. 133, 30 W. R. 845, H. L., *Maw* v. *Pearson*, 1860, 28 Beav. 196.

(*m*) *Schmaling* v. *Tomlinson*, 1815, 1 Marsh. 500, 6 Taunt. 147.

not liable to C. for commission, unless he ratifies the terms of the loan and recognizes C.'s employment (*n*).

6. A factor delegates his employment without the authority of the principal. The sub-agent has no lien for duties, &c., paid by him, as against the principal (*o*).

Solicitors' town agents.

7. The London agent of a country solicitor, in the ordinary course receives, as such, the proceeds of a cause in which he is engaged. There is no privity of contract between the client and the London agent, and the client cannot recover the proceeds from him as money received to the client's use (*p*). So, a London agent, in the ordinary course, gives credit to the country solicitor and not to the client, and has no remedy, except his lien, against the client for costs, and such lien, as against the client, is limited to the amount due from the client to the country solicitor (*q*). The Court may, however, in exercise of its summary jurisdiction over its own officers, order a London agent to pay over to the client money received, the agent claiming to retain the amount in satisfaction of a debt due to him from the country solicitor (*q*), or having received it without the authority of either the country solicitor or the client (*r*).

8. A client gives money to his solicitor to pay a debt and costs. The solicitor remits the amount, by means of his own cheque, to his London agent for the purpose of paying such debt and costs. The agent retains the amount in satisfaction of a debt due to him from the solicitor. The agent is not liable to the client in an action for money had and received to

---

(*n*) *Mason* v. *Clifton*, 1863, 3 F. & F. 899.

(*o*) *Solly* v. *Rathbone*, 1814, 2 M. & S. 298.

(*p*) *Robbins* v. *Fennell*, 1847, 11 Q. B. 248, 17 L. J. Q. B. 77, 12 Jur. 157.

(*q*) *Ex p. Edwards, re Johnson*, 1881, 7 Q. B. D. 155, 8 Q. B. D. 262, 51 L. J. Q. B. 108, 45 L. T. 578, C. A., *Waller* v *Holmes*, 1860, 1 Johns. & H. 239, 30 L. J. Ch. 24, 6 Jur. N. S. 1367.

(*r*) *Robbins* v. *Fennell*, *supra*.

the client's use (*s*). So, if a London agent receives money improperly, the remedy of the client is against his own solicitor, not against the agent (*t*).

(*s*) *Cobb* v. *Becke*, 1845, 6 Q. B. 930; 14 L. J. Q. B. 108; 9 Jur. 439. See, however, *Ex p. Edwards*, *supra*, note (*q*).

(*t*) *Gray* v. *Kirby*, 1834, 2 D. P. C. 601. See, however, *Robbins* v. *Fennell*, *supra*, note (*p*).

CHAPTER VI.

Duties of Agents.

Article 41.

DUTY TO PERFORM HIS UNDERTAKING.

Every agent who enters into an undertaking for valuable consideration is bound to perform the undertaking (*a*); but no agent is bound to perform what he has undertaken to do gratuitously (*b*). Every agent must act in person, unless he is expressly or impliedly authorized by the principal to delegate his duties (*c*).

Article 42.

DUTY TO OBEY INSTRUCTIONS, OR ACT ACCORDING TO USAGE AND FOR THE PRINCIPAL'S BENEFIT.

It is the duty of every agent to strictly pursue the terms of his authority and obey the instructions of his principal (*d*), except where the instructions are

---

(*a*) *Turpin* v. *Bilton*, 1843, 5 Man. & G. 455, 6 Scott, N. R. 447, 12 L. J. C. P. 167, 7 Jur. 950.

(*b*) *Coggs* v. *Bernard*, 2 Ld. Raym. 909, Smith, L. C. (9th ed.), 201; *Balfe* v. *West*, 1853, 13 C. B. 466, 22 L. J. C. P. 175, *Elsee* v. *Gatward*, 1793, 5 T. R. 143.

(*c*) See Article 39.

(*d*) Illustrations 1 to 4. *Smart* v. *Sandars*, 1846, 3 C. B. 380; 16 L. J. C. P. 39, 10 Jur. 841; *Pariente* v. *Lubbock*, 1855, 20 Beav. 588, 5 De G. M. & G. 5, *Bertram* v. *Godfray*, 1830, 1 Knapp, P. C. C. 381.

illegal (*e*); and, in the absence of express instructions, to act according to usage (*f*), or where there is no special usage, and in all matters left to his discretion, to act in good faith to the best of his judgment solely for the benefit of the principal (*g*).

Illustrations.

1. An agent is instructed to sell certain shares when the funds reach 85 or more. He is bound to sell when the funds reach 85, and has no discretion to wait until they go higher (*h*).

2. A. by letter requests B. to purchase 150 bales of cotton and forward a bill of lading, in exchange for which A. undertakes to accept B.'s draft. B. accepts the commission. B. is bound to forward the bill of lading as soon as possible, and is not entitled to retain it until A. gives security for payment. If he does so retain it, A. is justified in refusing to accept the cotton (*i*).

3. A foreign merchant sends a bill of lading to his correspondent in England with instructions to insure the goods. If the correspondent accepts the bill of lading he is bound to insure (*k*).

4. A solicitor, retained to conduct an action, is expressly in-

---

(*e*) Illustration 5. *Bexwell* v. *Christie*, 1776, Cowp. 395, *Ex p. Mather*, 1797, 3 Ves. 373.

(*f*) Illustrations 6 to 9. *Lambert* v. *Heath*, 1846, 15 M. & W. 486; *Solomon* v. *Barker*, 1862, 2 F. & F. 726, *Foster* v. *Pearson*, 1835, 1 C. M. & R. 849, 5 Tyr. 255; *Moore* v. *Mourgue*, 1776, Cowp. 479.

(*g*) *Gray* v. *Haig*, 1854, 20 Beav. 219; *General Exchange Bank* v. *Horner*, 1869, L. R. 9 Eq. 480, 39 L. J. Ch. 393, 22 L. T. 693, 18 W. R. 414, *Henchman* v. *East India Co.*, 1791, 1 Ves. jun. 289, *Gwatkin* v. *Campbell*, 1854, 1 Jur. N. S. 131; *Pariente* v. *Lubbock*, 1855, 20 Beav. 588, 5 De G. M. & G. 5, *Clarke* v. *Tipping*, 1846, 9 Beav. 284, *Comber* v. *Anderson*, 1808, 1 Camp. 523, *Dyas* v. *Cruise*, 1845, 2 J. & L. 460; 8 Ir. Eq. R. 407.

(*h*) *Bertram* v. *Godfray*, 1830, 1 Knapp, P. C. C. 381, P. C.

(*i*) *Barber* v. *Taylor*, 1839, 5 M. & W. 527.

(*k*) *Smith* v. *Lascelles*, 1788, 2 T. R. 187, 1 R. R. 457.

structed by the client not to enter into any compromise. It is his duty to obey his client's instructions, even if the counsel engaged in the case advise a compromise (*l*).

5. An auctioneer, at a sale without reserve, is instructed by the vendor not to sell for less than a certain sum. Such instructions are illegal, and it is the duty of the auctioneer to accept the highest *bonâ fide* bid even if it be less than the sum mentioned (*m*).

6. A stockbroker is instructed to sell certain shares. It is his duty to sell for ready money, according to usage, in the absence of special directions to the contrary (*n*).

7. It is the duty of an auctioneer, in the absence of special instructions, to sell for ready money only (*o*), but he may take a cheque in lieu of cash in payment of the deposit, according to the usual custom (*p*). An agent ought not, however, to accept a cheque in lieu of cash that he has been authorized to receive, unless it is customary to do so in the particular business in which he is employed (*q*).

8. Goods are intrusted to a broker for sale. It is usual in the particular trade to send an estimate of the value to the principal, in order that he may fix a reserve price. It is the broker's duty to send such an estimate to his principal (*r*).

9. It is the duty of a house or estate agent, where he is

(*l*) *Fray* v. *Voules*, 1859, 1 El. & El. 839, 28 L. J. Q. B. 232; 5 Jur. N. S. 1253, 33 L. T. O. S. 133, 7 W. R. 446. And see *Swinfen* v. *Swinfen*, 1858, 2 De G. & J. 381, 4 Jur. N. S. 774, 27 L. J. Ch. 491, as to the duty of counsel to act according to his client's wishes.

(*m*) *Bexwell* v. *Christie*, 1776, Cowp. 395.

(*n*) *Wiltshire* v. *Sims*, 1808, 1 Camp. 258, 10 R. R. 673.

(*o*) *Ferrars* v. *Robins*, 1835, 2 C. M. & R. 152, 1 Gale, 70; 5 Tyr. 705, *Williams* v. *Evans*, 1866, L. R. 1 Q. B. 352; 35 L. J. Q. B. 111; 13 L. T. 753; 14 W. R. 330.

(*p*) *Farrer* v. *Lacy*, 1885, 31 Ch. Div. 42; 55 L. J. Ch. 149; 53 L. T. 515, 34 W. R. 22, C. A.

(*q*) *Papè* v. *Westacott*, 1893, (1894) 1 Q. B. 272, 63 L. J. Q. B. 222, 9 R. 55, 10 T. L. R. 51, C. A., where a house agent accepted a cheque and was held liable for breach of duty.

(*r*) *Solomon* v. *Barker*, 1862, 2 F. & F. 726.

instructed to find a purchaser for property at a minimum price, to submit any offers which may be made to him to his principal, and not to enter into a contract for the sale of the property unless the principal has expressly authorized him to do so (*s*).

Execution of deeds under powers of attorney.—It was formerly necessary, in order to render a deed executed under a power of attorney binding on the principal, or to entitle him to sue thereon, that the deed should be executed in his name (*t*). But the Conveyancing Act, 1881 (44 & 45 Vict. c. 41), s. 46, provides that the donee of a power of attorney may, if he thinks fit, execute or do any assurance, instrument, or thing, in and with his own name and signature, and his own seal, where sealing is required, by the authority of the donor of the power; and every assurance, instrument, and thing so executed and done shall be as effectual in law, to all intents, as if it had been executed or done by the donee of the power in the name and with the signature and seal of the donor thereof.

Article 43.

DUTY TO KEEP PRINCIPAL'S PROPERTY SEPARATE, AND TO PRESERVE CORRECT ACCOUNTS.

It is the duty of every agent—

(a) to keep the money and property of his principal separate from his own and that of third persons (*u*);

(b) to preserve and be constantly ready with cor-

(*s*) *Chadburne* v. *Moore*, 1893, 61 L. J. Ch. 674, 67 L. T. 257; 41 W. R. 39; *Hamer* v. *Sharp*, 1874, L. R. 19 Eq. 108; 44 L. J. Ch. 53, 31 L. T. 643.

(*t*) See *White* v. *Cuyler*, 1795, 6 T. R. 176; 1 Esp. 200, 3 R. R. 147; *Wilks* v. *Back*, 1802, 2 East, 142, 6 R. R. 409, *Berkeley* v. *Hardy*, 1826, 8 D. & R. 102, 5 B. & C. 355, *Frontin* v. *Small*, 1726, 2 Ld. Raym. 1419, 2 Str. 705, *Combe's case*, 9 Co. R. 75.

(*u*) *Gray* v. *Haig*, 1854, 20 Beav. 219; *Clarke* v. *Tipping*, 1846, 9 Beav. 284, *Guerreiro* v. *Peile*, 1820, 3 B. & Ald. 616; 22 R. R. 500.

rect accounts of all his dealings and transactions in the course of his agency (*x*);

(c) to produce to the principal, or to a proper person appointed by the principal, all documents in his hands relating to the principal's affairs (*y*); and

(d) to pay over to the principal, on request, money received in the course of the agency to the use of the principal (*z*).

Where an agent is permitted to retain for investment money belonging to his principal, he is in the position of, and is under the same duties and liabilities as, a trustee (*a*).

Where an agent fails to keep and preserve correct accounts, and is called upon for an account of his agency, everything will be presumed against him that is consistent with established facts (*b*). So, if he mixes the property of the principal with his own, everything not proved to be his own will be deemed to be the principal's (*c*).

Where an agent pays his principal's money into his own

(*x*) *Gray* v. *Haig*, 1854, 20 Beav. 219, *Clarke* v. *Tipping*, 1846, 9 Beav. 284, *Pearse* v. *Green*, 1819, 1 Jac. & W. 135; 20 R. R. 258, *Turner* v. *Burkinshaw*, 1867, L. R. 2 Ch. 488, 15 W. R. 753, *Collyer* v. *Dudley*, 1823, T. & R. 421.

(*y*) *Dadswell* v. *Jacobs*, 1887, 34 Ch. Div. 278, 56 L. J. Ch. 233, 55 L. T. 857, 35 W. R. 261, C. A. (The principal cannot call upon him to produce documents, &c., to an improper person, such as a rival or unfriendly person. *Ibid.*)

(*z*) *Harsant* v. *Blaine*, 1887, 56 L. J. Q. B. 511, C. A., *Pearse* v. *Green*, 1819, 1 Jac. & W. 135, 20 R. R. 258, *Edgell* v. *Day*, 1865, L. R. 1 C. P. 80, 35 L. J C. P. 7, 12 Jur. N. S. 27, 13 L. T. 328, H. & R. 8.

(*a*) *Burdick* v. *Garrick*, 1870, L. R. 5 Ch. 233, 39 L. J. Ch. 369, 18 W. R. 387, *Power* v. *Power*, 1884, L. R. 13 Ir. 281.

(*b*) *Gray* v. *Haig*, *supra*.

(*c*) *Lupton* v. *White*, 1808, 15 Ves. 432, 10 R. R. 94.

banking account, he is responsible for the amount, in the event of the failure of the banker, even if acting gratuitously (*d*).

An agent who improperly refuses to pay over money on request is chargeable with interest from the date of the request (*e*).

Article 44.

DUTY TO EXERCISE DUE SKILL, CARE AND DILIGENCE (*f*).

Every agent acting for reward is bound to exercise such skill, care, and diligence in the performance of the undertaking for which he is paid as is usual or necessary in or for the ordinary or proper pursuance of the profession or business in which he is employed (*g*).

Every agent acting gratuitously is bound to exercise such skill as he actually possesses, and such care and diligence as he would exercise in his own affairs (*h*); and if he has held himself out for the careful and skilful performance of a particular undertaking, then such care and skill as might reasonably be expected from one so holding himself out (*i*).

(*d*) *Massey* v. *Banner*, 1820, 1 Jac. & W. 241, 4 Madd. 413, 21 R. R. 150.

(*e*) *Harsant* v. *Blaine*, 1887, 56 L. J. Q. B. 511, C. A.

(*f*) See also Article 54, and illustrations thereto.

(*g*) *Beal* v. *South Devon Rail. Co.*, 1864, 3 H. & C. 337; 11 L. T. 184; 12 W. R. 1115, Ex. Ch., *Cassaboglou* v. *Gibbs*, 1882, 9 Q. B. D. 220; 51 L. J. Q. B. 593; 47 L. T. 98: affirmed 11 Q. B. D. 797, C. A.; *Solomon* v. *Barker*, 1862, 2 F. & F. 726, *Russell* v. *Hankey*, 1794, 6 T. R. 12, 3 R. R. 102, *Harmer* v. *Cornelius*, 1858, 5 C. B. N. S. 236, 4 Jur. N. S. 1110. And see Illustrations 1 to 11, in all of which the agent was acting for reward.

(*h*) *Moffatt* v. *Bateman*, 1869, L. R. 3 P. C. 115, 22 L. T. 140, 6 Moo. P. C. C. (N. S.) 369, P. C., *Wilson* v. *Brett*, 1843, 12 L. J. Ex. 264, 11 M. & W. 113, Illustrations 12 to 14.

(*i*) *Beal* v. *South Devon Rail. Co.*, *supra*; Illustration 14.

Every agent is bound to take as much care in looking after the property and money of his principal as a reasonable degree of diligence would induce him to take in looking after his own property or money (*k*).

Illustrations.

1. A house agent is employed to let houses, and is paid a commission of 5 per cent. He is bound to use reasonable care to ascertain the solvency of the tenants (*l*).

2. An insurance broker undertakes to effect a policy. He is bound to use due diligence to perform what he has undertaken within a reasonable time (*m*).

3. An agent is employed to purchase a public-house. It is his duty to examine the takings, &c., and the fact that the principal has himself examined them on the advice of the agent does not exonerate him from liability for a breach of that duty (*n*).

4. An insurance broker is employed to insure from a particular point. It is his duty to insert in the policy all the clauses usually inserted in an insurance from that point (*o*).

5. A broker is employed on commission to purchase and ship scrap iron. He is not bound to inspect the iron for the purpose of ascertaining whether it is of the quality bought, because it is not part of a broker's ordinary business to inspect goods bought by him, as such (*p*).

(*k*) *Massey* v. *Banner*, 1820, 1 Jac. & W. 241, 4 Madd. 413, 21 R. R. 150, *Maltby* v. *Christie*, 1795,1 Esp. 340, *Reeve* v. *Palmer*, 1858, 5 C. B. N. S. 91, 28 L. J. C. P. 168, 5 Jur. N. S. 916, Illustrations 12 to 14.

(*l*) *Hayes* v *Tindall*, 1861, 1 B. & S. 296, 2 F. & F. 444; 30 L. J. Q. B. 362, 4 L. T. 403.

(*m*) *Turpin* v. *Bilton*, 1843, 5 Man. & G. 455, 6 Scott, N. R. 447, 12 L. J. C. P. 167, 7 Jur. 950.

(*n*) *Smith* v. *Barton*, 1866, 15 L. T. 294.

(*o*) *Mallough* v. *Barber*, 1815, 4 Camp. 115.

(*p*) *Zwilchenbart* v. *Alexander*, 1860, 1 B. & S. 234, 30 L. J. Q. B. 254, 7 Jur. N. S. 1157, 4 L. T. 412, 9 W. R. 670, Ex. Ch.

6. An insurance broker is instructed in general terms to insure certain goods. He insures them "free from particular average" in the usual way. He is not liable to the principal merely because the insurance might have been effected on better terms (*q*).

7. A share broker is employed to buy certain railway scrip. He buys on the market, in the ordinary course of business, what is usually sold as such scrip. He is not responsible to the principal because the scrip turns out not to be genuine, having had no notice that it was not genuine, and having bought it in the ordinary course of business (*r*).

8. An insurance broker retains in his own hands a policy effected by him. He is bound to use due diligence to procure a settlement and payment of a loss arising thereunder (*s*).

9. A. acts as a patent agent. He is bound to know the law relating to the practice of obtaining patents, and is responsible to his principal for injury caused through his ignorance of such law. Every person who acts as a skilled agent is bound to bring reasonable skill and knowledge to the performance of his duties (*t*).

10. A. acts as a valuer of ecclesiastical property. He is bound to know the general rules applicable to the valuation of dilapidations, but is not expected to have an accurate and precise knowledge of the law relating thereto (*u*).

11. A broker was employed to sell certain goods "to arrive," of "fair average quality in the opinion of the selling broker." A dispute having arisen, the broker inspected the goods and reported that they were not of fair average quality. Held, that he was not bound to exercise any skill in order to form a correct

---

(*q*) *Moore* v. *Mourgue*, 1776, Cowp. 479.

(*r*) *Lambert* v. *Heath*, 1846, 15 M. & W. 486.

(*s*) *Bousfield* v. *Cresswell*, 1810, 2 Camp. 545; 11 R. R. 794.

(*t*) *Lee* v. *Walker*, 1872, L. R. 7 C. P. 121; 41 L. J. C. P. 91; 26 L. T. 70.

(*u*) *Jenkins* v. *Betham*, 1854, 15 C. B. 168, 24 L. J. C. P. 94; 1 Jur. N. S. 237.

opinion, it not being part of the ordinary business of a broker to act as an arbitrator (*x*).

12. A. rides a horse gratuitously for the purpose of exhibiting it. He is bound to exercise such skill as he actually possesses, and is responsible to his principal for any injury caused by his neglect to do so. Whether he in fact exercised such skill or not is a question for the jury (*y*).

13. A general merchant undertakes, without reward, to enter a parcel of A.'s goods with a parcel of his own. He enters both parcels, by mistake, under a wrong denomination, and the goods are seized. He is not responsible to A. for the loss, having taken the same care of A.'s goods as of his own (*z*).

14. A. offers, without reward, to lay out 700*l.* in the purchase of an annuity, and undertakes to obtain good security. He is bound to use due care to lay out the money securely (*a*).

Article 45.

DUTY TO PAY OVER MONEY RECEIVED TO USE OF PRINCIPAL.

Every agent who receives money to the use of his principal is bound to pay over or account for such money to the principal, notwithstanding claims made by third persons in respect thereof (*b*), even if the money was received under a void (*c*) or illegal (*d*) contract. Provided that, where money is obtained by an agent wrongfully, or is paid to him under a mistake of

---

(*x*) *Pappa* v. *Rose*, 1872, L. R. 7 C. P. 32, 525, 41 L. J. C. P. 11, 187; 25 L. T. 468, 27 L. T. 348, 20 W. R. 62, 784, Ex. Ch.

(*y*) *Wilson* v. *Brett*, 1843, 11 M. & W. 113, 12 L. J. Ex. 264.

(*z*) *Shiells* v. *Blackburne*, 1789, 1 H. Bl. 158, 2 R. R. 750.

(*a*) *Whitehead* v. *Greetham*, 1825, 2 Bing. 464, M'Clel. & Y. 205, 10 Moo. 183, Ex. Ch.

(*b*) *Nicholson* v. *Knowles*, 1820, 5 Madd. 47; 21 R. R. 276, Illustrations 1 and 2.

(*c*) Illustration 5.

(*d*) Illustration 4.

fact or for a consideration which fails, he may show that he has repaid it to the person from whom he so obtained it or who so paid it to him (*e*); and where money is paid to him in respect of a voidable contract, he may show that the contract has been rescinded, and the money repaid, even if the contract was rescinded solely on the ground of his own fraud (*f*).

When an agent is accounting for money received to the use of his principal, he is entitled to take credit for any sums expended by him with the consent or subsequent acquiescence of the principal, even if they were expended for an illegal purpose (*g*); but authority to deal with money in an illegal manner may be revoked at any time before the money has been actually paid away (*h*).

Illustrations.

1. A ship which is the property of A. is transferred to B. as security for a debt. B. insures the ship for and on behalf of A. & Company, and charges them with the premiums. The ship is lost, and B. receives the insurance money. B. must pay over the money, after deducting the amount of his debt, to A. & Company, and cannot set up A.'s title, having insured for and on behalf of A. & Company (*i*). So, an insurance broker who receives money under a policy cannot dispute the claim of his principal on the ground that other persons are interested in the subject-matter of the insurance, their claims being a matter

(*e*) See Article 117.
(*f*) Illustration 6.
(*g*) *Bayntun* v. *Cattle*, 1833, 1 M. & Rob. 265.
(*h*) *Bone* v. *Ekless*, 1860, 5 H. & N. 925, 29 L. J. Ex. 438.
(*i*) *Dixon* v. *Hammond*, 1819, 2 B. & A. 310.

between them and the assured, with which the broker has nothing to do (*k*).

2. A. sells a ship as agent for three joint owners. He must account to his principals jointly for the proceeds, and cannot be compelled to pay one of them the amount of his share without the consent of the others (*l*).

3. A. deposits bank notes with his banker, who sends them to the issuing bank and receives credit for the amount. That is equivalent to actual payment, and A.'s banker must account to A. for the amount, though he never actually received payment of the notes, in consequence of the failure of the issuing bank (*m*).

4. An agent receives money on his principal's behalf under an illegal contract. The agent must account to the principal for the money, and cannot set up the illegality of the contract, which the other contracting party has waived by paying the money (*n*).

5. A turf commission agent is employed to make bets. He must pay over to the principal the amount of any winnings actually received by him in respect of such bets, though the bets themselves are void by statute (8 & 9 Vict. c. 109), and though, in consequence of the provisions of the Gaming Act, 1892, he would not be able to recover from the principal the amount of any losses paid in respect of the bets (*o*).

6. An agent sells a horse and receives the purchase-money. The sale is subsequently rescinded on the ground of the agent's fraud, and the purchase-money is repaid. The agent is not

---

(*k*) *Roberts* v. *Ogilby*, 1821, 9 Price, 269.

(*l*) *Hatsall* v. *Griffith*, 1834, 2 C. & M. 679, 4 Tyr. 487.

(*m*) *Gillard* v. *Wise*, 1826, 7 D. & R. 523, 5 B. & C. 134.

(*n*) *Bousfield* v. *Wilson*, 1846, 16 M. & W. 185, 16 L. J. Ex. 44; *Farmer* v. *Russell*, 1798, 1 B. & P. 296, *Tenant* v. *Elliott*, 1797, 1 B. & P. 3, 4 R. R. 755.

(*o*) *De Mattos* v. *Benjamin*, 1894, 63 L. J. Q. B. 248, 70 L. T. 560, 10 R. 103, *Bridger* v. *Savage*, 1885, 15 Q. B. D. 363; 54 L. J. Q. B. 464, 53 L. T. 129, 33 W. R. 891, C. A. overruling *Beyer* v *Adams*, 1857, 26 L. J. Ch. 841. As to the Gaming Act, 1892, see *post*, Article 69.

liable to the principal for the amount of the purchase-money (*p*).

7. An insurance broker receives notice that the assured under a policy is entitled to the return of a portion of certain premiums held by the broker. The broker is entitled to deduct such portion in an action by the underwriters for the full premiums, because he is a common agent acting for both parties (*q*).

8. A factor raises money by wrongfully pledging the goods of his principal. The principal may, if he thinks fit, adopt the transaction, and treat the money raised as money had and received to his use (*r*).

Article 46.

ESTOPPED FROM DENYING PRINCIPAL'S TITLE.

Where a person is in possession of property as an agent, his possession, as evidence of title, and for the acquisition of title by prescription, is deemed to be the possession of the principal (*s*).

No agent is permitted to deny the title of his principal, or to set up the title of any third person in opposition to that of the principal, to any goods intrusted to him by, or which he has agreed to hold on behalf of, the principal (*t*), except where the goods were wrongfully obtained by the principal from a third person, who claims them from the agent, and of whose claim the agent had no notice at the time that they were so intrusted to him, or that he so agreed to

(*p*) *Murray* v. *Mann*, 1848, 2 Ex. 538; 12 Jur. 634; 17 L. J. Ex. 256.

(*q*) *Shee* v. *Clarkson*, 1810, 12 East, 507, 11 R. R. 473.

(*r*) *Bonzi* v. *Stewart*, 1842, 4 M. & G. 295, 5 Scott, N. R. 1, 26.

(*s*) Illustrations, 1 to 3; *Cooper* v. *De Tastet*, 1829, Tamlyn, 177.

(*t*) Illustrations 4 to 8; *Dixon* v. *Hammond*, 1819, 2 B. & A. 310; *Roberts* v. *Ogilby*, 1821, 9 Price, 269.

hold them, in which case he may set up the title of that third person (u). Provided that the agent may in all cases show that he has been compelled to deliver up the goods to a person who had a good title thereto as against the principal (x).

Illustrations.

1. An agent is allowed, for the convenient performance of his duties, as such, to occupy premises belonging to his principal. The agent cannot acquire any estate therein, by reason of such occupation, even if he is permitted to use the premises for an independent business of his own (y). No agent can acquire an adverse title to his principal unless he can distinctly show that the acts upon which he relies were done in respect of his title, and not of his agency (z).

2. A. receives the rents of certain properties as an agent, and pays them into a separate account at his own bank. The principal dies intestate. A. continues to receive the rents for more than twelve years after the death of the principal, stating to several of the tenants that he is acting for the heir, whoever he may be. Subsequently, within a reasonable time after the heir is ascertained, his assignee brings an action against A., claiming possession of the property and an account of the rents and profits. A. claims the property as his own, and pleads the Statute of Limitations. The plaintiff is entitled to possession of the property, and an account of all the rents and profits received by A. since the principal's death (a).

(u) *Biddle* v. *Bond*, 1865, 6 B. & S. 225; 34 L. J. Q. B. 137, 11 Jur. N. S. 425, 12 L. T. 178, 13 W. R. 561, *Ex p. Davis, re Sadler*, 1881, 19 Ch. Div. 86, 45 L. T. 632, 30 W. R. 237, C. A., Illustrations 9 and 10.

(x) *Biddle* v. *Bond*, *supra*, *Hunt* v. *Maniere*, 1864, 11 Jur. N. S. 28, 73, 34 L. J. Ch. 142, 13 W. R. 363, 11 L. T. 723.

(y) *White* v. *Bayley*, 1861, 10 C. B. N. S. 227; 30 L. J. C. P. 253; 7 Jur. N. S. 948.

(z) *A.-G.* v. *Corporation of London*, 1845, 2 Mac. & G. 247, 2 H. & Tw. 1, 19 L. J. Ch. 314, 14 Jur. 205.

(a) *Lyell* v. *Kennedy*, 1889, 14 App. Cas. 437, 59 L. J. Q. B. 268, 62 L. T. 77, 38 W. R. 353, H. L.

3. A. receives the rents of certain property as B.'s agent for more than twelve years, and duly pays them over to B. B. thereby acquires a good prescriptive title to the property, in the absence of fraud, even if A. was the true owner (*b*). Possession by an agent, as such, does not preserve his adverse rights (*b*).

4. A. makes advances for the purposes of a mine, in order to obtain the ore, which he consigns to B. for sale, B. undertaking to account to him for the proceeds. B. cannot set up any paramount title to the ore, or dispute A.'s right to the proceeds on the ground that there are rights of third persons existing independently of the contract between A. and B. (*c*).

5. A. buys goods on B.'s behalf, and delivers them to carriers at B.'s risk. A. is estopped from disputing B.'s title to the goods (*d*).

6. The servant of a wharfinger gives a receipt for certain goods, in which there is an undertaking to deliver the goods to A. The wharfinger will not be permitted to deny A.'s title to the goods on their arrival (*e*).

7. A wharfinger agrees to hold certain goods, described in a delivery order, on behalf of the transferee of such order. In an action by the transferee against the wharfinger for conversion of the goods, it is no defence that the goods in question were not separated from the bulk, and that therefore the property in the goods had not passed to the plaintiff (*f*). A wharfinger is an agent for the person in whose name he holds the goods, and is not permitted to set up the title of any other person (*g*).

8. A. delivers goods to a carrier, consigned to B. The pro-

(*b*) *Williams* v. *Potts*, 1871, 12 L. R. Eq. 149, 40 L. J. Ch. 775.

(*c*) *Zulueta* v. *Vinent*, 1851, 1 De G. M. & G. 315.

(*d*) *Green* v. *Maitland*, 1842, 4 Beav. 524.

(*e*) *Evans* v. *Nichol*, 1841, 4 Scott, N. R. 43, 3 M. & G. 614, 5 Jur. 1110.

(*f*) *Woodley* v. *Coventry*, 1863, 32 L. J. Ex. 185, 9 Jur. N. S. 548, 8 L. T. 249, 11 W. R. 599. See *Gosling* v. *Birnie*, 1831, 7 Bing. 339; 5 M. & P. 160.

(*g*) *Betteley* v. *Reed*, 1843, 3 G. & D. 561, 4 Q. B. 511, 12 L. J. Q. B. 172; 7 Jur. 507, *Holl* v. *Griffin*, 1833, 10 Bing. 246, 3 M. & Scott, 732.

perty in the goods has not, in fact, passed to B. A. countermands his instructions, and the carrier re-delivers the goods to him. The carrier may set up A.'s title, in an action by B., carriers not being, as such, agents of their consignees (*h*).

9. A. wrongfully distrains B.'s goods and delivers them to C., an auctioneer, for sale, C. having at the time no knowledge of B.'s adverse claim. B. subsequently gives notice of his title to C., and claims the proceeds. C. may set up the title of B., in an action by A. for the proceeds (*i*). The estoppel of a bailee ceases when the bailment on which it is founded is determined by title paramount or its equivalent (*j*).

10. A. sells goods as B.'s agent, having at the time that the goods are intrusted to him notice that C. claims them. A. cannot, in an action by B. for the proceeds, set up the title of C., even if C. was wrongfully deprived of the goods by B., A. having elected to act as B.'s agent for the sale of the goods after receiving notice of C.'s adverse claim (*k*).

DUTIES ARISING FROM THE FIDUCIARY CHARACTER OF THE RELATIONSHIP.

Article 47.

DUTY TO MAKE FULL DISCLOSURE WHERE ANY PERSONAL INTEREST.

No agent is permitted to enter, as such, into any transaction in which he has a personal interest in conflict with his duty to his principal, unless the principal, with a full knowledge of all the material circumstances, and of the exact nature and extent of the agent's

(*h*) *Sheridan* v. *New Quay Co.*, 1858, 4 C. B. N. S. 618, 28 L. J. C. P. 58, 5 Jur. N. S. 248.

(*i*) See note (*b*), *supra*, p. 101.

(*j*) *Biddle* v. *Bond*, 1865, 6 B. & S. 225, 34 L. J. Q. B. 137, 11 Jur. N. S. 425, 12 L. T. 178, 13 W. R. 561.

(*k*) *Ex p. Dixon, re Sadler*, 1881, 19 Ch. Div. 86, 45 L. T. 632, 30 W. R. 237, C. A.

interest, consents (*l*). Where any transaction is entered into in violation of this principle, the principal, when the circumstances come to his knowledge, may repudiate the transaction, or may adopt it and claim an account of the profit made by the agent (*m*).

Illustrations.

1. A stockbroker was employed to purchase certain shares. He purchased the shares from his own trustee without informing the principal of the fact. The transaction was set aside, after an interval of many years, without inquiry whether a fair price was charged or not (*n*).

2. A director of a company enters into a contract on behalf of the company with a firm of which he is a member. The contract is voidable in equity by the company, quite apart from the question of its fairness or unfairness (*o*). It is the duty of a director to promote the interests of the company, and he cannot be permitted to enter into engagements in which his own interest is in conflict with that duty (*o*).

3. A solicitor entered into an arrangement under which he was to receive a share of certain property, and also a share of the profit arising from the sale of such property. He subsequently acted as solicitor in purchasing a large portion of the property, without disclosing his interest therein to the client for whom he so acted. Held, that he was a trustee for the client for a proportionate part of the share taken by him, and that he

---

(*l*) *Rothschild* v. *Brookman*, 1831, 5 Bli. N. S. 165, 2 Dow. & Cl. 188, H. L., *Parker* v. *McKenna*, 1874, L. R. 10 Ch. 96, 44 L. J. Ch. 425, 31 L. T. 739, 23 W. R. 271, *Gardner* v. *McCutcheon*, 1842, 4 Beav. 534; *Henchman* v. *E. I. Co.*, 1791, 1 Ves. jun. 289. And see Illustrations, and cases there cited.

(*m*) *Rothschild* v. *Brookman*, *supra*. And see Illustrations to this Article and to Article 51.

(*n*) *Gillett* v. *Peppercorne*, 1840, 3 Beav. 78.

(*o*) *Aberdeen Rail. Co.* v. *Blakie*, 1854, 2 Eq. R. 1281, H. L.

must account for the full amount of the profit made by him upon the sale, with interest at the rate of 5 per cent. (*p*).

4. An auctioneer who was employed to sell an estate, purchased it himself. The transaction was set aside, after an interval of thirteen years (*q*). No agent for the sale of goods is permitted to purchase them himself, and no agent to purchase is permitted to buy his own goods on the principal's behalf, unless he makes full disclosure to the principal; and the fact that he pays or charges a fair price is immaterial in the application of this rule (*r*). So, an agent of a trustee for sale cannot purchase the property sold (*s*); and a solicitor who conducts a sale of property must not purchase it without a full explanation to the vendor (*t*). But the auctioneer is not deemed to be an agent of the purchaser at a sale by auction, for this purpose, and may (probably) sell his own property at such a sale without disclosing that he is the owner (*u*).

5. A broker is employed to sell goods. He sells them, ostensibly to A., really to A. and himself jointly. Whilst the goods are still in the possession of the broker, he becomes bankrupt, A. also being insolvent. The principal may repudiate the contract and recover the goods specifically from the trustee in bankruptcy of the broker (*x*).

6. A firm of brokers were authorized to purchase iron. They delivered bought notes to the principal, which purported to be notes of a contract of which the brokers guaranteed performance, but which did not disclose the sellers. The principal paid the

---

(*p*) *Tyrrell* v. *Bank of London*, 1862, 10 H. L. Cas. 26, 31 L. J. Ch. 369, 6 L. T. 1, 8 Jur. N. S. 849, 10 W R. 359, H. L.

(*q*) *Oliver* v. *Court*, 1820, Dan. 301, 8 Price, 127, 22 R. R. 720.

(*r*) *Lowther* v. *Lowther*, 1806, 13 Ves. 95, 102, *Massey* v. *Davies*, 1794, 2 Ves. jun. 317, 2 R. R. 218, *Bentley* v. *Craven*, 1853, 18 Beav. 75; *Rothschild* v. *Brookman*, 1831, 5 Bli. N. S. 165, 2 Dow. & Cl. 188, H. L.

(*s*) *Whitcomb* v. *Minchin*, 1820, 5 Madd. 91.

(*t*) *Re Bloye's Trust*, 1849, 1 Mac. & G. 488, 2 H. & Tw. 140, 19 L. J. Ch. 89, 14 Jur. 49, *Ex p. James*, 1803, 8 Ves. 337, 7 R. R. 56.

(*u*) *Flint* v. *Woodin*, 1852, 9 Hare, 618, 16 Jur. 719.

(*x*) *Ex p. Huth, re Pemberton*, 1840, Mont. & Ch. 667; 4 Dea. 294.

brokers their commission and a deposit, and subsequently discovered that one of the brokers intended to perform the contract himself. The principal was held to be entitled to repudiate the contract, and the brokers were ordered to repay the deposit and commission, with interest (*y*). No agent can become a principal and deal on that footing without full and fair disclosure (*z*).

7. An agent for sale sells to a company of which he is a director or shareholder. The sale is not binding on the principal (*a*). Where an agent for sale takes any interest in a purchase negotiated by him, he must fully disclose all the material facts, and the exact nature and extent of his interest. It is not sufficient to merely disclose that he has an interest, or to make such statements as would put the principal on inquiry (*b*).

8. A director of a railway company purchased, on the company's behalf, the concession of a line of which he was the concealed owner. Held, that the company might repudiate the transaction (*c*). So, where a director sold a vessel to his company as from a stranger, it was held that he must account to the company for the profit made by him, with interest (*d*). In such cases, the principal may rescind the transaction, or may affirm it and claim the profit made, at his option (*e*).

9. *Special customs inconsistent with this Article are unreasonable.*—A broker is authorized to sell certain shares and pay himself certain advances out of the proceeds. A custom whereby he

---

(*y*) *Wilson* v. *Short*, 1847, 6 Hare, 366, 17 L. J. Ch. 289, 12 Jur. 301.

(*z*) *Ibid.*, *Williamson* v. *Babour*, 1877, 9 Ch. Div. 529, 50 L. J. Ch. 147, 37 L. T. 698, *Bostock* v. *Jardine*, 1865, 3 H. & C. 700; 11 Jur. N. S. 586, 34 L. J. Ex. 142, 12 L. T. 577, 13 W. R. 970.

(*a*) *Salomans* v. *Pender*, 1865, 3 H. & C. 639, 34 L. J. Ex. 95, 11 Jur. N. S. 432, 12 L. T. 267, 13 W. R. 637.

(*b*) *Dunne* v. *English*, 1874, L. R. 18 Eq. 524, 31 L. T. 75.

(*c*) *Gt. Luxemburg Rail. Co.* v. *Magnay*, 1858, 25 Beav. 586, 4 Jur. N. S. 839.

(*d*) *Benson* v. *Heathorn*, 1842, 1 Y. & Col. C. C. 326.

(*e*) *Re Cape Breton Co.*, 1884, 26 Ch. Div. 221, 29 Ch. Div. 795, C. A.; *Cavendish Bentinck* v. *Fenn*, 12 App. Cas. 652. And see Article 51, and Illustrations thereto.

may himself take over the shares at the price of the day in the event of his being unable to find a purchaser at an adequate price is unreasonable, and such a transaction is not binding on the principal unless he was aware of the custom at the time that he gave the broker the authority, even if it is proved that a forced sale of the shares would certainly have realised less than the price given by the broker (*f*). So, a custom whereby an agent for sale may purchase at the minimum price if he cannot find a purchaser is illegal (*g*). Every usage which converts an agent into a principal, or otherwise gives him an interest at variance with his duty, is unreasonable, and is not binding on persons who are ignorant of it (*h*).

Article 48.

AGENT WHO PURCHASES PROPERTY, AS SUCH, IN OWN NAME, IS A TRUSTEE.

Where an agent who is employed to purchase property purchases it in his own name or on his own behalf, and it is conveyed or transferred to him, he is a trustee thereof for the principal (*i*).

(*f*) *Hamilton* v. *Young*, 1881, 7 L. R. Ir. 289.

(*g*) *De Bussche* v. *Alt*, 1877, 8 Ch. Div. 286, 47 L. J. Ch. 381, 38 L. T. 370, C. A.

(*h*) *Robinson* v *Mollett*, 1874, L. R. 7 H. L. 802, 44 L. J. C. P. 362, 33 L. T. 544, H. L.

(*i*) *Lees* v. *Nuttall*, 1834, 2 Myl. & K. 819, *Austin* v. *Chambers*, 1837, 6 Cl. & F. 1, H. L., *Bartlett* v. *Pickersgill*, 1 Cox, 15, 4 East, 577, 1 R. R. 1, *James* v. *Smith*, (1891) 1 Ch. 384, 65 L. T. 544. See Article 21, as to the right of the agent to plead the 7th section of the Statute of Frauds, where verbally appointed to purchase land. See also *Taylor* v. *Salmon*, 1838, 4 Myl. & Cr. 139.

Article 49.

DUTY TO MAKE FULL DISCLOSURE WHERE HE DEALS WITH THE PRINCIPAL.

Where an agent enters into any contract or transaction with his principal, or with his principal's representative in interest, he must deal with him at arm's length, and make a full and fair disclosure of all the material circumstances, and of all his knowledge respecting the subject-matter of the contract (*k*).

Where any question arises as to the validity of any such transaction, or of any gift made by a principal to his agent, the burden of proving that no advantage was taken by the agent of his position, or of the confidence reposed in him, and that the transaction was entered into in perfectly good faith and after full disclosure lies upon the agent (*k*).

Where a principal desires to set aside a contract or transaction entered into with his agent, on the ground of want of full disclosure or good faith, he must take proceedings for that purpose within a reasonable time after he becomes aware of the facts on which he relies (*l*).

Illustrations.

1. A manager of a bank, who was permitted to carry on a separate business on his own account, made advances for the

---

(*k*) *Molony* v. *Kernan*, 1842, 2 Dr. & War. 31; *Waters* v. *Shaftesbury*, 1866, 12 Jur. N. S. 311, 14 L. T. 184, 14 W. R. 572, *Charter* v. *Trevelyan*, 1842, 11 Cl. & F. 714, 8 Jur. 1015, H. L., *Savery* v. *King*, 1856, 5 H. L. Cas. 627, 2 Jur. N. S. 503, 25 L. J. Ch. 482, H. L., *Ward* v. *Sharp*, 1883, 53 L. J. Ch. 313, 50 L. T. 557. And see Illustrations 1 to 12.

(*l*) See Illustration 11.

purposes of such business, upon bills which he had not indorsed. The drawers and acceptors of the bills became insolvent. Held, that the manager was bound to make good the loss. He ought not to grant himself any accommodation or acquire any personal benefit in the course of his agency, without bringing the whole circumstances most fully and fairly before the directors (*m*).

2. An agent for the management of trust property purchases part of such property from the *cestui que trust*. The agent, to support the transaction, must show, not only that he gave full value, but also that he dealt at arm's length, and fully disclosed everything that he knew which tended to enhance the value of the property (*n*).

3. A steward contracts with his employer for a lease. He must show that he is giving as high a rent as it would have been his duty to obtain from a third person, and that his employer was fully informed of every circumstance tending to demonstrate the value of the property which was, or ought to have been, within the steward's knowledge (*o*).

4. A director proposes a contract to his company, it being provided by the articles of association that directors may contract with the company on disclosing their interest. It is his duty to declare the full extent and exact nature of his interest, not merely that he has an interest (*p*).

5. A solicitor purchases property from his client's trustee in bankruptcy. He must make a full disclosure of all the knowledge acquired by him respecting such property during the time that he was acting as solicitor for the bankrupt (*q*).

6. A solicitor purchased property from a former client, and concealed a material fact. The transaction was set aside, although there was another solicitor acting on behalf of the

(*m*) *Gwatkin* v. *Campbell*, 1854, 1 Jur. N. S. 131.

(*n*) *King* v. *Anderson*, 1874, 8 Ir. R. Eq. 147.

(*o*) *Selsey* v. *Rhoades*, 1824, 2 S. & S. 41.

(*p*) *Imperial and Mercantile Credit Co.* v. *Coleman*, 1873, L. R. 6 H. L. 189, 42 L. J. Ch. 644, 29 L. T. 1, H. L.

(*q*) *Luddy's Trustees* v. *Peard*, 1886, 33 Ch. Div. 500, 55 L. J. Ch. 884, 55 L. T. 137.

plaintiff (*r*). But the rule that an agent must disclose knowledge acquired by him, as such, does not, in general, apply where the agent has ceased to act, and there is another agent, with equal means of knowledge, acting for the principal in the transaction (*s*).

7. An agent purchases his principal's property in the name of a third person. The transaction will be set aside without inquiry as to the adequacy of the price. An agent may purchase property from his principal, provided that he deals at arm's length and fully discloses all that he knows respecting the property; but if any underhand dealing or concealment appears, the transaction will at once be set aside on the application of the principal (*t*).

8. A director of a railway company contracted with the company to take refreshment rooms. The Court refused to decree specific performance of the contract against the company (*u*).

9. A solicitor takes a mortgage from his client. The Court will not enforce any unusual stipulations in the mortgage disadvantageous to the client (*x*), and will restrain the solicitor from exercising his rights as mortgagee in an unfair or inequitable manner (*y*). Where a power of sale exerciseable at any time was inserted in such a mortgage without the usual proviso requiring interest to be in arrear or notice to be given, and the solicitor sold the property under the power, he was held liable to the client in damages as for an improper sale, it not being shown that he had explained to the client the unusual nature of

---

(*r*) *Gibbs* v. *Daniel*, 1862, 4 Giff. 1; 9 Jur. N. S. 636, 10 W. R. 688; 7 L. T. 27.

(*s*) *Scott* v. *Dunbar*, 1828, 1 Moll. 442.

(*t*) *McPherson* v. *Watt*, 1877, 3 App. Cas. 254, H. L., *Murphy* v. *O'Shea*, 1845, 2 J. & L. 422; 8 Ir. Eq. Rep. 329; *Crowe* v. *Ballard*, 1790, 2 Cox, 253, 1 Ves. jun. 215; 3 Bro. C. C. 117, 1 R. R. 122.

(*u*) *Flanagan* v. *G. W. Rail. Co.*, 1868, 19 L. T. 345.

(*x*) *Cowdry* v. *Day*, 1859, 1 Giff. 316; 5 Jur. N. S. 1199; 29 L. J. Ch. 39.

(*y*) *McLeod* v. *Jones*, 1883, 24 Ch. Div. 289; 53 L. J. Ch. 145, C. A.

the power (*z*). Prior to the Mortgagees Legal Costs Act, 1895 (58 & 59 Vict. c. 25), if the solicitor himself prepared the mortgage deed, he was only permitted to charge out of pocket expenses, unless there was an express agreement to the contrary (*a*); but that Act provides that he shall be entitled in such a case to his usual remuneration as a solicitor.

10. A solicitor purchases property from his client. He must show that the price was adequate, that he took no advantage of his position, and that the sale was as advantageous to the client as any that the solicitor could have obtained, with the exercise of due diligence, from a third person (*b*).

11. A bill to set aside the purchase of property by an agent was dismissed, with costs, on proof that the principal had distinct notice, at the time of the transaction, that the agent was one of the beneficial purchasers, no proceedings having been taken to set it aside for more than six years, and the property having advanced in value in the meantime (*c*).

Gifts to agents.

12. A client, who had recovered certain property after protracted litigation, shortly afterwards conveyed, by deed of gift, a valuable portion of such property to the counsel engaged on

---

(*z*) *Readdy* v. *Prendergast*, 1887, 56 L. T. 790, C. A., *Cockburn* v. *Edwards*, 1881, 18 Ch. Div. 449, 51 L. J. Ch. 46, C. A., *Craddock* v. *Rogers*, 1884, 53 L. J. Ch. 968, 51 L. T. 191.

(*a*) *Re Wallis, ex p. Lickorish*, 1890, 25 Q. B. D. 176, 59 L. J. Q. B. 500, 62 L. T. 674; 38 W. R. 482, 6 T. L. R. 291, C. A., *Re Roberts*, 1889, 43 Ch. Div. 52, 59 L. J. Ch. 25, 62 L. T. 33, 38 W. R. 225.

(*b*) *Savery* v. *King*, 1856, 5 H. L. Cas. 627, 2 Jur. N. S. 503, 25 L. J. Ch. 482, H. L., *Pisani* v. *Gibraltar*, 1874, L. R. 5 P. C. 516, P. C., *Spencer* v. *Topham*, 1856, 22 Beav. 573; 2 Jur. N. S. 865, *Gibson* v. *Jeyes*, 1801, 6 Ves. 266, 5 R. R. 295, *Montesquieu* v. *Sandys*, 1811, 18 Ves. 313, 11 R. R. 197, *Coaks* v. *Boswell*, 1886, 11 App. Cas. 232; 55 L. J. Ch. 761, 55 L. T. 32, H. L.

(*c*) *Wentworth* v. *Lloyd*, 1864, 10 H. L. Cas. 589; 10 Jur. N. S. 961; 32 Beav. 467, H. L. See *De Bussche* v. *Alt*, 1877, 8 Ch. Div. 286; 47 L. J. Ch. 381, 38 L. T. 370, C. A.

his behalf, in consideration of services, &c. rendered in connection with its recovery. The deed was set aside on the ground of want of independent advice (*d*). A solicitor is not permitted to bargain with his client for any benefit beyond the amount of his legal remuneration, and during the time he is acting as solicitor for the client, is incapable of accepting any gift or reward besides such remuneration, even if there is no suspicion of any fraud, misrepresentation or undue influence (*e*). A promise by a client to give his solicitor a large sum, in the event of success in an action, is void, and for any gift from the client to be permitted to stand, there must be a previous severance of the confidential relationship, as well as an absence of all suspicion of undue influence (*e*). The executor of a deceased client was held to be entitled to have a gift from the deceased to her solicitor set aside, although the deceased, after the confidential relationship had ceased, had expressed her intention to abide by the gift, the circumstances not being such as would have debarred her, at the time of her death, from having it set aside (*f*). But, except in the case of solicitor and client, the general rule is that a gift from principal to agent is valid if the agent proves that there was no undue influence on his part (*g*).

Article 50.

DUTY TO ACCOUNT IN EQUITY.

It is the duty of every agent to render just and true accounts of his agency to the principal, and in

---

(*d*) *Brown* v. *Kennedy*, 1864, 4 De G. J. & S. 217; 33 L. J. Ch. 342; 10 Jur. N. S. 141, 13 C. B. N. S. 677, 32 L. J. C. P. 137.

(*e*) *Morgan* v. *Minett*, 1877, 6 Ch. Div. 638, 36 L. T. 948, 25 W. R. 744, *O'Brien* v. *Lewis*, 1863, 32 L. J. Ch. 569; 9 Jur. N. S. 528; 8 L. T. 179, 11 W. R. 318, *Wright* v. *Proud*, 1806, 13 Ves. 138; *Tomson* v. *Judge*, 1855, 3 Drew. 306; 1 Jur. N. S. 583, 24 L. J. Ch. 785, *Middleton* v. *Welles*, 1785, 4 Bro. P. C. 245, P. C.; *Saunderson* v. *Glass*, 1742, 2 Atk. 297.

(*f*) *Tyars* v. *Alsop*, 1888, 59 L. T. 367; 37 W. R. 339.

(*g*) *Hunter* v. *Atkins*, 1832, 3 Myl. & K. 113.

cases of general agency of a fiduciary character the principal has a right to have an account taken in a court of equity (*h*). In the case of a single agency transaction untainted with fraud (*i*), or where the agency is not of a fiduciary character, the agent is not bound to render an account in a court of equity, unless the accounts are so complicated that they cannot be properly investigated in an action at law (*k*).

No principal has a right to have settled accounts re-opened unless the agent has been guilty of fraud, but he may be given leave to surcharge and falsify them (*l*). Where the agent has been guilty of fraud, his accounts will be re-opened from the commencement of the agency, and in such a case the Statute of Limitations does not constitute a defence (*m*).

The illegality of a transaction between principal and agent is not necessarily a bar to an action in the Chancery Division for an account thereof (*n*).

The right of a principal to have an account taken in equity

(*h*) *Makepeace* v. *Rogers*, 1865, 4 De G. J. & S. 649, 34 L. J. Ch. 396, 11 Jur. N. S. 215, 12 L. T. N. S. 12, 221, 13 W. R. 450, 566, *Hemmings* v. *Pugh*, 1863, 4 Giff. 456, 9 L. T. 283, 9 Jur. N. S. 1124, 12 W. R. 44.

(*i*) *Navulshaw* v. *Brownrigg*, 1852, 2 De G. M. & G. 441, 21 L. J. Ch. 908, 16 Jur. 979, *Phillips* v. *Phillips*, 9 Hare, 471, 22 L. J. Ch. 141.

(*k*) *Barry* v. *Stevens*, 1862, 31 Beav. 258, 31 L. J. Ch. 785, 10 W. R. 822, 6 L. T. 568, *Hemmings* v. *Pugh*, *supra*, note (*h*), *King* v. *Rossett*, 1827, 2 Y. & J. 33, *Blyth* v. *Whiffin*, 1872, 27 L. T. 330.

(*l*) *Hunter* v. *Belcher*, 1864, 2 De G. J. & S. 194.

(*m*) *Beaumont* v. *Boultbee*, 1802, 7 Ves. 599, 5 Ves. 485, 4 R. R. 244; *Clarke* v. *Tipping*, 1846, 9 Beav. 284, *Middleditch* v. *Sharland*, 1799, 5 Ves. 87.

(*n*) *Williams* v. *Trye*, 1854, 23 L. J. Ch. 860, 18 Jur. 442.

rests upon the trust and confidence reposed in the agent (*o*), and in all cases of general agency, the fiduciary character of the relationship is sufficient to support an action for an account, whether the accounts are complicated or not, and even if the receipts and payments are all on the one side (*p*). Thus, where an agent is employed to sell property, he may be compelled to account in equity for the proceeds (*q*). But the bare relationship of principal and agent is not sufficient, in the absence of fraud, where the agent is not employed in a fiduciary capacity, and the transaction can be fairly and properly investigated in a common law action (*r*). Thus, bankers are not bound to account in equity to their customers, unless the accounts in question are intricate and complicated (*s*). So, it was held that a person who was occasionally employed as a clerk by a solicitor was not bound to account in equity, though there had been mutual receipts and payments (*t*). Damages for neglect of duty cannot be passed in taking an account, the proper remedy for such damages being an action at law (*u*).

Fraud.—In cases of fraud, accounts long since settled will be reopened from the commencement of the agency. Proof of one fraudulent overcharge has been held sufficient to entitle the principal to have the agent's accounts reopened for a period of twenty years (*v*). So, where there were incorrect entries, and amounts unexplained and unaccounted for, in the accounts of a deceased agent of a company, who was also a large shareholder

---

(*o*) *Padwick* v. *Stanley*, 1852, 9 Hare, 627, 16 Jur. 586.

(*p*) See note (*h*), *supra*.

(*q*) *Mackenzie* v. *Johnston*, 1819, 4 Madd. 373.

(*r*) See note (*k*), *supra*.

(*s*) *Foley* v. *Hill*, 1844, 1 Ph. 399, 13 L. J. Ch. 182; 8 Jur. 347; *Bowles* v. *Orr*, 1835, 1 Y. & Coll. 464.

(*t*) *Fluker* v. *Taylor*, 1855, 3 Drew. 183.

(*u*) *G. W. Ins. Co. of New York* v. *Cunliffe*, 1874, L. R. 9 Ch. 525; 43 L. J. Ch. 741, 30 L. T. 661.

(*v*) *Williamson* v. *Babour*, 1877, 9 Ch. Div. 529; 50 L. J. Ch. 147; 37 L. T. 698.

in the company, his accounts were reopened after his death, for a period of twenty-five years (*u*).

Statutes of Limitations.—Formerly, where an agent was sued in a fiduciary capacity, he was not permitted to plead the Statutes of Limitations (*x*), but by virtue of the 8th section of the Trustee Act, 1888, he may now plead and is entitled to the benefit of the statutes, except where he is sued for property intrusted to him as an agent, or for the proceeds or value of any such property converted by him to his own use, or where he has been guilty of fraud (*y*).

Article 51.

DUTY TO ACCOUNT FOR ALL SECRET PROFITS.

No agent is permitted to acquire any personal benefit in the course of his agency without the knowledge and consent of the principal (*z*).

Every agent must account to the principal for every benefit, and pay over to the principal every profit, acquired by him in the course of the agency without the consent of the principal (*z*), even if, in acquiring the benefit or profit, the agent incurred a possibility

---

(*u*) *Stainton* v. *Carron Co.*, 1857, 24 Beav. 346, 27 L. J. Ch. 89, 3 Jur. N. S. 1235.

(*x*) *Teed* v. *Beere*, 1859, 28 L. J. Ch. 782, 5 Jur. N. S. 381, *Padwick* v. *Hurst*, 1854, 18 Beav 575, 18 Jur. 763, 23 L. J. Ch. 657, *Burdick* v. *Garrick*, 1870, L. R. 5 Ch. 233, 39 L. J. Ch. 369, 18 W R. 387, *Power* v. *Power*, 1884, 13 L. R. Ir. 281.

(*y*) See *Re Lands Allotments Co.*, (1894) 1 Ch. 616, 63 L. J. Ch. 291; 70 L. T. 286, 7 R. 115, C. A.

(*z*) *Parker* v. *McKenna*, 1874, L. R. 10 Ch. 96, 44 L. J. Ch. 425, 31 L. T. 739, 23 W. R. 271, *Morrison* v. *Thompson*, 1874, L. R. 9 Q. B. 480, 43 L. J. Q. B. 215, 30 L. T. 869, 22 W. R. 859, *Re North Australian Territory Co., Archer's case*, (1892) 1 Ch. 322, 65 L. T. 800, C. A., *Imp. Mercantile Credit Co.* v *Coleman*, 1873, L. R. 6 H. L. 189, 42 L. J. Ch. 644, 29 L. T. 1, H. L., Illustrations 1 to 12.

of loss (a), and the principal suffered no injury thereby (b).

Where the principal is aware that the agent is paid for his services by third persons, but is under a misapprehension as to the extent of the remuneration, such remuneration is not a benefit or profit acquired without the consent of the principal within the meaning of this Article, unless the agent misinformed or intentionally misled the principal as to the extent thereof (c).

Illustrations.

1. An agent purchases a debt due from his principal to a third person. He is only entitled to recover from his principal the amount he actually paid for the debt (d).

2. A barrister who was employed as a legal adviser and confidential agent, having acquired a knowledge of his client's property and liabilities, purchased certain charges on the client's estates for less than their nominal value, after he had ceased to act for the client. Held, that he was only entitled to recover from the client the amount actually paid for the charges, with interest, he having purchased them without the consent of the client (e). The employment of a person in such a capacity disables him from purchasing any such charges, or otherwise obtaining a personal benefit in the course of his employment, except with the principal's permission, and the disability continues for so long after the fiduciary relation has ceased as the reasons on which it is founded continue to operate (e).

3. A. consigned a ship to B. for sale at a minimum price.

(a) *Williams* v. *Stevens*, 1866, L. R. 1 P. C. 352, 36 L. J. P. C. 21; 4 Moo. P. C. C. (N. S.) 235, 15 W. R. 409, P. C.

(b) *Parker* v. *McKenna*, *supra*, note (z).

(c) Illustration 13.

(d) *Reed* v. *Norris*, 1837, 2 M. & C. 361, 374; 1 Jur. 233.

(e) *Carter* v. *Palmer*, 1841, 8 Cl. & F. 657, H. L.

B., with A.'s consent, employed C. to sell the ship. C., being unable to find a purchaser, bought the ship himself at the minimum price without the consent of A., and subsequently resold her at a large profit. Held, that C. must account to A. for the profit (*f*). So, where a broker is instructed to buy shares at a certain price, he must account for the profit if he obtains the shares at less than that price (*g*). Where an agent makes a secret profit in the course of his employment, and there are no accounts remaining to be taken between him and his principal, he is bound to pay over such profit as money had and received to the use of the principal (*h*).

4. A partner, in negotiating the transfer of a lease on behalf of the firm, stipulated for a personal benefit. Held, that he must account to the firm for the benefit received (*i*).

5. A., having bought certain shares at 2*l.* each, and knowing that B. desired to purchase some, represented that he could obtain them at 3*l.* or less, and asked B. to authorize him to buy at 3*l.* B. gave him the authority A. then transferred his own shares to B. at 3*l.* each, representing that C. was the vendor. Held, that A. must account to B. for the profit of 1*l.* per share (*k*).

6. A. requested B. to provide an outfit for A.'s son. B. did so, and obtained certain discounts, but charged A. the full prices. The discounts were disallowed, although B. did not charge any commission as an agent (*l*).

7. A shipmaster, being authorized to employ his vessel to the best advantage, and being unable to procure remunerative

---

(*f*) *De Bussche* v. *Alt*, 1877, 8 Ch. Div. 286, 47 L. J. Ch. 381, 38 L. T. 370, C. A. And see *Barker* v. *Harrison*, 1846, 2 Coll. 546.

(*g*) *Thompson* v. *Meade*, 1891, 7 T. L. R. 698.

(*h*) *Morrison* v. *Thompson*, 1874, L. R. 9 Q. B. 480, 43 L. J. Q. B. 215; 30 L. T. 869, 22 W. R. 859.

(*i*) *Fawcett* v. *Whitehouse*, 1829, 1 Russ. & M. 132, 4 L. J. Ch. 64, 8 L. J. Ch. 50.

(*k*) *Kimber* v. *Barber*, 1872, L. R. 8 Ch. 56, 27 L. T. 526, 21 W. R. 65.

(*l*) *Turnbull* v. *Garden*, 1869, 20 L. T. 218. See *Queen of Spain* v. *Parr*, 1869, 39 L. J. Ch. 73.

freight, loaded her with a cargo of his own. Held, that he must account to the owners for the profit made by the sale of the cargo, and not merely for reasonable freight (*m*).

8. Commission agents, who are also merchants, are employed to ship and sell goods abroad. They do so, and purchase other goods with the proceeds. They are not bound to account for the profit on the sale of the goods bought with the proceeds, because such profit is not made in the course of the agency. They are only bound to account for the proceeds of the goods sold on the principal's behalf (*n*).

9. The vendor to a company gives the secretary 600 fully paid up shares. The secretary must account to the company for the highest value of the shares during the time that he is the holder thereof (*o*).

Directors of companies (*o*).

10. The directors of a company, on the transfer of the business to another company, receive from the transferees, without the knowledge of the transferors, a large sum by way of compensation. They must pay over such sum to the first-mentioned company (*p*). Neither directors nor officers of a company are permitted to retain any pecuniary benefits acquired in the con-

(*m*) *Shallcross* v. *Oldham*, 1862, 2 Johns. & H. 609, 5 L. T. 824, 10 W. R. 291.

(*n*) *Kirkham* v. *Peel*, 1881, 44 L. T. 195, 43 L. T. 171; 28 W. R. 941, C. A.

(*o*) *McKay's case*, 1875, 2 Ch. Div. 1; 45 L. J. Ch. 148, 33 L. T. 517, C. A. Promoters of a company are not allowed to make secret profits in their dealings with the company. See *Erlanger* v. *New Sombrero Phosphate Co.*, 1878, 3 App. Cas. 1218, 48 L. J. Ch. 73, 39 L. T. 269, 27 W R. 65, H. L., *Bagnall* v. *Carlton*, 1877, 6 Ch. Div. 371, 47 L. J. Ch. 30, 26 W R. 243, 37 L. T. 481, C. A., *Sydney and Wigpool Iron Ore Co.* v. *Bird*, 1886, 33 Ch. Div. 85, 55 L. J. Ch. 875, 55 L. T. 558, C. A., *Emma Silver Mining Co.* v *Lewis*, 1879, 4 C. P. D. 396, 48 L. J. C. P. 257, 40 L. T. 168, 27 W. R. 836, *Same* v. *Grant*, 1877, 11 Ch. Div. 918, 40 L. T. 804, *Whaley Bridge Calico Co.* v. *Green*, 1879, 5 Q. B. D. 109; 49 L. J. Q. B. 326, 41 L. T. 674, 28 W. R. 351.

(*p*) *Gaskell* v. *Chambers*, 1858, 26 Beav. 360, 5 Jur. N. S. 52, 28 L. J. Ch. 385.

duct of the company's business, unless the particulars of such benefits are fully explained to, and are approved of by, the shareholders (*q*). So, a solicitor-director is not permitted to receive any remuneration for his services, professional or otherwise, unless such remuneration is sanctioned by resolution of the shareholders (*r*).

11. A. agreed to become a director of a company on condition that the promoters indemnified him in respect of the amount paid for qualification shares. A. afterwards resigned, and the promoters, in pursuance of the agreement, purchased the shares (which had become valueless) from him at the original price. Held, that A. must account to the company for the value of the indemnity constituted by his secret agreement with the promoters—*i.e.*, for the original price of the shares (*s*).

12. The first five directors of a company, being bound to each hold twenty qualification shares, accepted that number from the promoter with the knowledge and approval of each other. Held, that the directors were jointly and severally liable to pay to the liquidator of the company the original value of such shares (*t*). Every director who receives a gift from the promoters of his company is bound to account to the company either for the gift or for its highest value during the time it is held by him, at the option of the company (*u*). Thus, where a director received his qualification shares from the promoter, and the company was afterwards wound up, it was held that he must account to the liquidator for the nominal value of the shares (*x*); where a

(*q*) *General Exchange Bank* v. *Horner*, 1869, L. R. 9 Eq. 480, 39 L. J. Ch. 393, 22 L. T. 693, 18 W. R. 414.

(*r*) *N. E. Rail. Co.* v. *Jackson*, 1870, 19 W. R. 198.

(*s*) *In re North Australian Territory Co., Archer's case*, (1892) 1 Ch. Div. 322, 65 L. T. 800, C. A.

(*t*) *In re Carriage Cooperative Supply Association*, 1884, 27 Ch. Div. 323; 51 L. T. 286, 53 L. J. Ch. 1154, 33 W. R. 411.

(*u*) *Eden* v. *Ridsdale's Lamp, &c. Co.*, 1889, 58 L. J. Q. B. 579, 61 L. T. 444, C. A.

(*x*) *Pearson's case*, 1877, 5 Ch. Div. 336, 46 L. J. Ch. 339, 25 W. R. 618, C. A.

director received the money to pay for his qualification shares, it was held that he must account for the amount received, with interest from the date of its receipt (*y*).

13. *Misapprehension as to extent of remuneration.*—It is usual for underwriters to allow insurance brokers, for punctual payment of premiums, ten per cent. cash discount, or twelve per cent. calculated on the yearly profits, in addition to the ordinary commission of five per cent. on each re-insurance. A company, having made no inquiry as to the remuneration paid by the underwriters, and not being aware of the twelve per cent. allowance, employed an insurance agent to negotiate its business. After the agent (who received no remuneration from the company) had been paid the usual allowance of twelve per cent. for more than eight years, the company discovered it and claimed to have it paid over to them as secret profit. It was held that they were not entitled to recover (*z*). This decision has been followed by the Court of Appeal in a later case, on the ground that every person who employs another as his agent with the knowledge that the agent receives his remuneration from third persons, and who does not choose to inquire what the charges of the agent will be, must allow all the usual and customary charges of such an agent, and is not entitled to dispute them on the ground that he is a foreigner and was not aware of the extent of the remuneration usually received by such agents (*a*).

In *Re Cape Breton Co.* (*b*), the Court of Appeal, affirming the decision of Pearson, J., held that where an agent secretly sells to his principal goods which were the property of the agent before the commencement of the agency, and the principal declines to rescind the contract, or rescission has become impos-

(*y*) *Hay's case*, 1875, L. R. 10 Ch. 593, 33 L. T. 466, 44 L. J. Ch. 721, *In re Drum Slate Quarry Co.*, 1885, 55 L. J. Ch. 36, 53 L. T. 250.

(*z*) *Great Western Insurance Co. of New York* v. *Cunliffe*, 1869, L. R. 9 Ch. 525, 30 L. T. 661, 43 L. J. Ch. 741, Ch. App.

(*a*) *Baring* v. *Stanton*, 1876, 3 Ch. Div. 502, 35 L. T. 652, 25 W. R. 237, C. A.

(*b*) 1884, 26 Ch. Div. 221, 29 Ch. Div. 795, C. A.

sible, the agent cannot, in the absence of fraud, be called upon to account for the profit made by him upon the transaction, or for the difference between the contract price and the market value. On appeal to the House of Lords (*c*) this doctrine was disapproved, but the decision was affirmed upon another ground. The doctrine appears to be irreconcilable with *Kimber* v. *Barber* (*d*); but the Court of Appeal have followed it in a later case (*e*), the judges remarking that, as the former decision had not been definitely overruled, it was binding upon them (*e*). Where it is clear that an agent has acquired a profit by secretly selling his own goods to his principal, it is difficult to see why the fact that the goods belonged to him before the commencement of the agency should entitle him to retain such profit, especially if rescission of the contract became impossible before the principal acquired a knowledge of the circumstances.

SPECIAL DUTIES OF PARTICULAR CLASSES OF AGENTS.

1.—*Factors.*

It is the duty of a factor—

(1) to give his principal the free and unbiassed use of his judgment and discretion (*f*);

(2) to act in person, unless authorized to delegate his authority (*g*);

(3) to keep and render just and true accounts (*f*);

(4) to keep the property of the principal separate from his own and that of others (*f*);

(5) to keep each sale distinct and separate from other transactions (*h*);

(*c*) *Sub nomine Cavendish Bentinck* v. *Fenn*, 12 App. Cas. 652.

(*d*) 1872, L. R. 8 Ch. 56, 27 L. T. 526, 21 W. R. 65, Ch. App., *ante*, Illustration 5.

(*e*) *Ladywell Mining Co.* v. *Brooks*, 1887, 35 Ch. Div. 400, 56 L. J. Ch. 684, 56 L. T. 677, 35 W. R. 785, C. A.

(*f*) *Clarke* v. *Tipping*, 1846, 9 Beav. 284.

(*g*) *Cochran* v. *Irlam*, 1814, 2 M. & S. 301, 15 R. R. 257. And see Article 39.

(*h*) *Guerreiro* v. *Peile*, 1820, 2 B. & Ald. 616, 22 R. R. 500.

(6) to account for goods sold, pay over the proceeds, and deliver unsold goods to the principal on demand (*i*) ;

(7) to keep goods intrusted to him for sale with as much care as would be taken by a prudent man in respect of his own goods (*j*), and not to barter (*k*) or pledge them (*l*) unless expressly authorized to do so ;

(8) to insure goods consigned to him, if instructed to do so, or if he has been in the habit of doing so (*m*).

2.—*Brokers.*

It is the duty of a broker—

(1) to contract in the name of the principal, subject to any special instructions or usage to the contrary (*n*) ;

(2) to execute contracts in such a way as to be legally binding on both parties (*o*), and so as to give each party a right to sue thereon (*p*) ;

(3) to comply with statutory provisions, in entering into contracts, notwithstanding a custom amongst brokers to disregard such provisions (*q*) ;

(4) to make a careful estimate of the value of goods which he is instructed to sell, so that he may not sell them for less than their value (*r*) ;

(5) to exercise his skill, and fairly communicate his opinion to his principal (*s*) ;

(*i*) *Topham* v. *Braddick*, 1809, 1 Taunt. 572, 10 R. R. 610.

(*j*) *Coggs* v. *Bernard*, 2 Ld. Raym. 909, 918.

(*k*) See note (*h*), *supra*.

(*l*) *Martini* v. *Coles*, 1813, 1 M. & S. 140, *Gill* v. *Kymer*, 1821, 5 Moo. 503, *Fielding* v. *Kymer*, 1821, 2 B. & B. 639.

(*m*) *Smith* v. *Lascelles*, 1788, 2 T. R. 187, 1 R. R. 457.

(*n*) *Baring* v. *Corrie*, 1818, 2 B. & A. 137, 20 R. R. 383. See Article 38, Illust. 6.

(*o*) *Grant* v. *Fletcher*, 1826, 5 B. & C. 436.

(*p*) *Bostock* v. *Jardine*, 1865, 3 H. & C. 700; 34 L. J. Ex. 142; 12 L. T. 577.

(*q*) *E.g.*, Leeman's Act (30 Vict. c. 29), *Neilson* v. *James*, 1882, 9 Q. B. D. 546, 51 L. J. Q. B. 369, 46 L. T. 791, C. A.

(*r*) *Solomon* v. *Barker*, 1862, 2 F. & F. 726.

(*s*) *Ex p. Dyster*, 1816, 2 Rose, 349.

(6) not to deliver goods sold by him, except in accordance with the terms of sale (*t*);

(7) not to sell his own goods to his principal, nor buy the principal's goods himself, without full and fair disclosure (*u*).

It is not part of his duty, in the absence of a special contract or custom, to examine goods bought by him, for the purpose of ascertaining whether they are of the quality bought (*x*).

3.—*Shipmasters.*

It is the duty of a shipmaster to give the whole of his time to the service of his principal, and therefore not to trade on his own account (*y*), nor give any portion of his personal services to another (*z*). A custom for shipmasters to trade on their own account is, apparently, illegal (*y*).

4.—*Auctioneers.*

It is the duty of an auctioneer—

(1) to act in person (*a*);

(2) to sell for ready money only, in the absence of instructions to the contrary (*b*);

(3) to disclose his principal (*c*);

(4) to see that the deposit is duly paid (*d*), and, if it be paid

---

(*t*) *Boorman* v. *Brown*, 1842, 2 G. & D. 793, 3 Q. B. 511, 11 C. & F. 1.

(*u*) *Wilson* v. *Short*, 1847, 6 Hare, 366, 17 L. J. Ch. 289, 12 Jur. 301, *Tetley* v *Shand*, 1872, 25 L. T. 658, 20 W R. 206, *Rothschild* v *Brookman*, 1831, 2 Dow. & C. 188, 5 Bli. N. S. 165, H. L., *Ex p. Huth, re Pemberton*, 1840, Mont. & Ch. 667, 4 Dea. 294.

(*x*) *Zwilchenbart* v. *Alexander*, 1860, 1 B. & S. 234, 30 L. J. Q. B. 254; 7 Jur. N. S. 1157, 4 L. T. 412, Ex. Ch.

(*y*) *Gardner* v. *M'Cutcheon*, 1842, 4 Beav. 534.

(*z*) *Thompson* v. *Havelock*, 1808, 1 Camp. 527, 10 R. R. 744.

(*a*) *Coles* v *Trecothick*, 1804, 9 Ves. 234, 1 Smith, 233, 7 R. R. 167.

(*b*) *Ferrars* v. *Robbins*, 1835, 2 C. M. & R. 152, 1 Gale, 70, 5 Tyr. 705, *Sykes* v. *Giles*, 1839, 5 M. & W. 645.

(*c*) *Franklyn* v. *Lamond*, 1847, 4 C. B. 637, 16 L. J. C. P. 221, 11 Jur. 780.

(*d*) *Hibbert* v. *Bayley*, 1860, 2 F. & F. 48.

to him, to hold it as stakeholder until the completion of the transaction (*e*);

(5) to sell to a third person (*f*);

(6) to accept the highest *bonâ fide* bid, where he sells without reserve, notwithstanding express instructions from his principal to the contrary (*g*);

(7) to account for the proceeds of goods sold, to the person from whom he received them (*h*);

(8) not to deliver goods sold until paid for, nor allow any deduction from the price, unless authorized to do so by the principal (*i*);

(9) if appointed to conduct a sale by the Court, to pay into Court any money received by him (*k*).

5.—*Solicitors.*

It is the duty of a solicitor—

(1) to obey the express instructions of his clients notwithstanding counsel's advice to the contrary (*l*);

(2) to give his clients his personal superintendence and judgment (*m*);

(3) to know and observe the rules of practice and procedure in the Courts (*n*);

(*e*) *Gray* v. *Gutteridge*, 1827, 3 C. & P. 40, *Yates* v. *Farebrother*, 1819, 4 Madd. 239, *Burrough* v. *Skinner*, 1770, 5 Burr. 2639.

(*f*) *Oliver* v. *Court*, 1820, Dan. 301, 8 Price, 127, 22 R. R. 720.

(*g*) *Warlow* v. *Harrison*, 1858, 1 El. & El. 309, 29 L. J. Q. B. 14; 6 Jur. N. S. 66, Ex. Ch., *Bexwell* v. *Christie*, 1776, Cowp. 395.

(*h*) *Crosskeys* v. *Mills*, 1834, 1 C. M. & R. 298, *Crowther* v. *Elgood*, 1887, 34 Ch. Div. 691; 56 L. J. Ch. 416, 56 L. T. 415, 35 W. R. 369, C. A.

(*i*) *Brown* v. *Staton*, 1816, 2 Chit. 353.

(*k*) *Biggs* v. *Bree*, 1882, 51 L. J. Ch. 64, 263; 45 L. T. 648; 46 L. T. 8, 30 W. R. 132, 278, C. A.

(*l*) *Fray* v *Voules*, 1859, 1 El. & El. 839, 28 L. J. Q. B. 232, 5 Jur. N. S. 1253, 7 W. R. 446, *Butler* v. *Knight*, 1867, L. R. 2 Ex. 109; 36 L. J. Ex. 66, 15 L. T. 621, 15 W. R. 407.

(*m*) *Hopkinson* v. *Smith*, 1822, 1 Bing. 13.

(*n*) *Godefroy* v. *Dalton*, 1830, 6 Bing. 460.

(4) to check useless litigation (*o*), and before instituting proceedings, especially on behalf of a wife against her husband, to carefully ascertain the facts of the case, and whether there is a reasonable prospect of success (*p*);

(5) to keep secret all confidential communications made to him by his client, and all information and knowledge of his client's affairs acquired in the course of his employment (*q*);

(6) not to act for the opponent of his client, or of a former client, in any matter in which such client or former client has an interest (*r*). An injunction will be granted to restrain a solicitor from acting for the opponent of a former client, whenever the transaction in reference to which the injunction is sought so flows out of or is connected with that in which he acted for the former client, that the same matter of dispute may probably arise (*s*). Where a solicitor had acted for the executor and devisee of a deceased client, he was at their instance restrained from acting for a creditor of the estate, although such creditor had been a client of his before he had acted for the deceased (*t*). In the application of this principle it is quite immaterial whether the solicitor was discharged by his former client, or ceased to act for him voluntarily (*r*).

(*o*) *Ottley* v. *Gilby*, 1845, 8 Beav. 602; 14 L. J. (N. S.) Ch. 177.

(*p*) *Re Hooper*, *Baylis* v. *Watkins*, 1864, 33 L. J. Ch. 300, 10 Jur. N. S. 114, 9 L. T. 741, 12 W. R. 324.

(*q*) *Davies* v. *Clough*, 1836, 8 Sim. 262, 6 L. J. (N. S.) Ch. 113; *Biggs* v. *Head*, 1837, Sau. & Sc. 335, *Taylor* v. *Blacklow*, 1836, 3 Scott, 614, 3 B. N. C. 235, 2 Hodges, 224.

(*r*) *Little* v. *Kingswood Colliery Co.*, 1882, 20 Ch. Div. 733, 52 L. J. Ch. 56, 47 L. T. 323, 21 W. R. 178, C. A., *Hutchins* v *Hutchins*, 1825, 1 Hog. 315, *Davies* v. *Clough* (cited in last note), *Cholmondeley* v. *Clinton*, 1815, 19 Ves. 261, 13 R. R. 183, *Biggs* v. *Head*, 1837, Sau. & Sc. 335, and cases reported in notes thereto.

(*s*) *Little* v. *Kingswood Colliery Co.*, *supra*.

(*t*) *Biggs* v. *Head*, *supra*.

(7) to continue, until its termination, the conduct of any cause undertaken by him, unless there is good reason to abandon it (*e.g.*, the failure of the client, after reasonable notice, to supply him with funds for out of pocket expenses), and when there is such good reason, to give his client reasonable notice of his intention to abandon the cause (*u*);

(8) not to bargain for nor accept any gift or reward from his client during the continuance of his employment, beyond the amount of his proper professional remuneration (*x*);

(9) if he prepares a deed in which he takes a personal interest, to insert all the usual clauses and fully explain to the client the effect of the deed (*y*);

(10) if he contracts with a client, to fully explain the transaction and make a full and fair disclosure of everything known to him respecting the subject matter (*z*);

(11) if he receives the deposit at a sale by auction, to pay it over to his client on demand, and not retain it as a stakeholder (*a*).

(*u*) *Nicholls* v. *Wilson*, 1843, 2 D. N. S. 1031, 11 M. & W. 106; 12 L. J. Ex. 266, *Harris* v. *Osborn*, 1834, 2 C. & M. 629, 4 Tyr. 445; *Whitehead* v. *Lord*, 1852, 7 Ex. 691; 21 L. J. Ex. 239, *Van Sandau* v. *Brown*, 1832, 9 Bing. 402, 2 M. & Scott, 543, 1 D. P. C. 715, *Hoby* v. *Built*, 1832, 3 B. & Ad. 350, *Wadsworth* v. *Marshall*, 1832, 2 C. & J. 665, *Underwood* v. *Lewis*, (1894) 2 Q. B. 306, 64 L. J. Q. B. 60, 70 L. T. 833, 9 R. 440, C. A.

(*x*) *O'Brien* v. *Lewis*, 1863, 32 L. J. Ch. 569, 9 Jur. N. S. 528, 8 L. T. 179, 11 W. R. 318. See Article 49, Illustration 12.

(*y*) *Cockburn* v. *Edwards*, 1881, 18 Ch. Div. 449, 51 L. J. Ch. 46, C. A. This principle applies also to counsel *Segrave* v. *Kirwan*, 1828, Beat. 157.

(*z*) *Pisani* v. *Gibraltar*, 1874, L. R. 5 P. C. 516, P. C., *Savery* v. *King*, 1856, 5 H. L. Cas. 627, 2 Jur. N. S. 503, 25 L. J. Ch. 482, H. L.; *Ward* v. *Sharp*, 1883, 53 L. J. Ch. 313, 50 L. T. 557, *Luddy* v. *Peard*, 1886, 33 Ch. Div 500, 55 L. J. Ch. 884, 55 L. T. 137. See Article 49, Illustrations, 5, 6, 9, and 10.

(*a*) *Edgell* v. *Day*, 1865, L. R. 1 C. P. 80, 35 L. J. C. P. 7, 12 Jur. N. S. 27, 13 L. T. 328, 14 W. R. 87, H. & R. 8.

CHAPTER VII.

Liabilities of Agents to their Principals.

Article 52.

IN RESPECT OF CONTRACTS ENTERED INTO ON BEHALF OF THE PRINCIPAL.

Except in the case of insurance brokers, who are, by usage, personally liable to the underwriters for premiums payable under policies effected by them (*a*), no agent incurs any personal liability to his principal in respect of any contract entered into by him on the principal's behalf, and in pursuance of his authority, unless he was acting under a *del credere* commission (*b*). Where an agent enters into a contract under a *del credere* commission, he is personally responsible to the principal for the due performance of the contract by the other contracting party (*c*).

Right of set-off by insurance brokers.—It has been held that where an insurance broker is sued by the trustee of a bankrupt

(*a*) *Baker* v. *Langhorn*, 1816, 6 Taunt. 519, 4 Camp. 396; 2 Marsh. 215; 16 R. R. 662, *Lee* v. *Bullen*, 1858, 27 L. J. Q. B. 161; 8 El. & Bl. 692, n., 4 Jur. N. S. 557.

(*b*) *Varden* v. *Parker*, 1799, 2 Esp. 710; *Alson* v. *Sylvester*, 1823, 1 C. & P. 107.

(*c*) *Hornby* v. *Lacy*, 1817, 6 M. & S. 166, 18 R. R. 345, *Morris* v. *Cleasby*, 1816, 4 M. & S. 566, 16 R. R. 544.

underwriter for premiums due to the bankrupt, the broker has a right to set off the amount of a loss which occurred prior to the bankruptcy under a policy underwritten by the bankrupt, and effected by the broker in his own name under a *del credere* commission, even if the bankrupt was not aware that the broker was acting under a *del credere* commission, on the ground that such transactions are mutual dealings within the meaning of the Bankruptcy Acts (*d*).

It was laid down by Lord Mansfield in *Grove* v. *Dubois*, 1 T. R. 112, that an agent who sold goods under a *del credere* commission was liable in the first instance to the principal for the price, but it is now settled that such an agent is in the position of a surety, and only becomes liable on the purchaser's default (*e*).

Article 53.

LIABILITY ON BILLS OF EXCHANGE SIGNED WITHOUT QUALIFICATION.

Where an agent, in the course of his employment, signs a bill of exchange in his own name, without qualification, as drawer or indorser, the question whether he is personally liable to the principal, as the holder of the bill, depends upon what was the real intention of the parties. If the agent intended to bind himself, or if, by signing without qualification, he led the principal to believe that such was his intention, and to act in a way in which he would not have acted but for such belief, the agent is liable to the holder on the bill, even if the principal is the holder thereof.

(*d*) *Lee* v. *Bullen*, 1858, 27 L. J. Q. B. 161, 8 El. & Bl. 692, n., 4 Jur. N. S. 557, limiting the effect of *Baker* v. *Langhorn*, 1816, 6 Taunt. 519; 16 R. R. 664.

(*e*) See note (*c*) *supra*.

Otherwise the agent is not liable to the principal on the bill (*e*).

Thus, where a broker, who had no authority to draw bills on behalf of the principal, was employed to sell goods, and sold them for a bill at a given date, and drew on the purchaser for the amount, he was held liable to the principal on the bill, on the ground that his signature, as drawer, might have misled the principal, and prevented him from making inquiries as to the solvency of the purchaser (*e*). So, if an agent who is instructed to purchase foreign bills for his principal, indorses such bills, intending to guarantee them, or indorses and sends his own bills in execution of the order, he is liable to the principal on the indorsement (*e*). But, where it is not intended that the agent shall be bound, the mere fact that he signs a bill without qualification does not render him liable to the principal, but only to third parties who become holders thereof in due course (*e*).

Article 54.

LIABILITY FOR NEGLIGENCE AND OTHER BREACHES OF DUTY.

Except in the case of counsel, who are under no legal liability to their clients for negligence or other breaches of duty in the course of their employment, as such (*f*), every agent is liable to make good any legal damage suffered by his principal as a reasonable or probable consequence of the agent's negligence,

---

(*e*) *Castrique* v. *Buttigieg*, 1855, 10 Moo. P C. C. 94, P. C., *Goupy* v. *Harden*, 1816, 2 Marsh. 454, 7 Taunt. 159, Holt, 342, 17 R. R. 478; *Le Feuvre* v. *Lloyd*, 1814, 1 Marsh, 318, 5 Taunt. 749, 15 R. R. 644.

(*f*) *Fell* v. *Brown*, 1791, 1 Peake, 131, 3 R. R. 663, *Mulligan* v. *M'Donough*, 1860, 2 L. T. 136, 5 Ir. Jur. N. S. 101.

want of due skill, or other breach of duty in the course of his employment.

Provided that—

(a) where an agent is clearly authorized to do a particular act, he is not liable to the principal for injurious consequences arising from the imprudent or improper nature of that act (*g*);

(b) where an agent strictly follows the instructions of the principal (*h*), or, in the absence of express instructions, acts in accordance with usage and in the ordinary course of business (*i*), or upon the best advice he can obtain under the circumstances (*k*), or uses his best judgment in a matter of pure discretion (*l*), he is not liable to the principal for any damage resulting therefrom.

Actionable negligence, in the case of an unpaid agent, is neglect to exercise such skill as he actually possesses, or has held himself out to possess, and such care and diligence as he would exercise in regard to his own affairs (*m*). Actionable negligence, in the

(*g*) Illustration 12.

(*h*) *Pariente* v. *Lubbock*, 1855, 8 De G. M. & G. 5, 20 Beav. 588; *Warwick* v. *Noakes*, 1790, 1 Peake, 98, 3 R. R. 653.

(*i*) *Russell* v. *Hankey*, 1794, 6 T. R. 12, 3 R. R. 102, *Lambert* v. *Heath*, 1846, 15 M. & W. 486, *Moore* v. *Mourgue*, 1776, Cowp. 479; Illustrations 8 and 11.

(*k*) *Miles* v. *Bernard*, 1795, 2 Peake, 61.

(*l*) *Comber* v. *Anderson*, 1808, 1 Camp. 523.

(*m*) See Article 44, and cases there cited. *Beal* v. *South Devon Rail. Co.*, 1864, 3 H. & C. 337, 11 L. T. 184, 12 W. R. 1115, Ex Ch, Illustration 16.

case of a paid agent, is neglect to exercise such skill, care, and diligence as is usual in the ordinary and proper course of the particular business in which he is employed (*n*).

Illustrations.

Disobedience to instructions.

1. A solicitor enters into a compromise on behalf of his client, notwithstanding express instructions from the client not to do so. He is liable to the client for damages, though the compromise was reasonable, and was entered into in good faith for the benefit of the client, and on the advice of the counsel engaged in the case (*o*).

2. An agent was instructed, and undertook, to warehouse certain goods at a particular place. He warehoused a portion of such goods at another place, where they were destroyed, without negligence. Held, that the loss of the goods was a natural consequence of the agent's disobedience to instructions, and that he was liable to the principal for their value (*p*).

3. An agent is instructed to insure certain goods, which he neglects to do. He is liable to the principal for the value of the goods, in the event of their being lost (*q*).

Other breaches of duty.

4. An agent pays his principal's money into his own account at the bank, it being his duty to pay it into a separate account. He is responsible for the failure of the banker, though acting gratuitously (*r*).

(*n*) See Article 44, and cases there cited. As to liability of solicitors for negligence, see *post*, p. 135.

(*o*) *Butler* v. *Knight*, 1867, L. R. 2 Ex. 109, 36 L. J. Ex. 66, 15 L. T. 621, 15 W. R. 407, *Fray* v *Voules*, 1859, 1 El. & El. 839; 28 L. J. Q. B. 232, 5 Jur. N. S. 1253, 7 W R. 446.

(*p*) *Lilley* v. *Doubleday*, 1881, 7 Q. B. D. 510, 51 L. J Q. B. 310, 44 L. T. 814, C. A.

(*q*) *Smith* v. *Lascelles*, 1788, 2 T. R. 187, 1 R. R. 457.

(*r*) *Wren* v. *Kirton*, 1805, 11 Ves. 377, 8 R. R. 174, *Massey* v. *Banner*, 1820, 1 Jac. & Walk. 241, 4 Madd. 413, 21 R. R. 150.

5. A broker was authorized to sell and deliver certain goods. He contracted to sell them for cash on delivery. It then became his duty not to deliver the goods without payment. Held, that he was liable to the principal in damages for having delivered the goods without payment (*s*).

6. A broker is authorized to sell goods at a certain price. He sells them at a lower price. He is liable to the principal in damages for the breach of duty (*t*). So, a broker who sold goods by auction at much below their real value, not having made an estimate of the value in accordance with usage, was held liable in an action for negligence (*u*). But an auctioneer is not liable to his principal for accepting the highest *bonâ fide* bid at a sale without reserve in opposition to the principal's express instructions, because such instructions are illegal, and it is not his duty to obey them (*x*).

7. An auctioneer takes a bill of exchange in payment of the price of goods sold by him. He is liable to the principal for the amount, if the bill be dishonoured (*y*). So, an estate agent who accepts a cheque in lieu of cash is liable to the principal for the amount, in the event of the cheque being dishonoured (*z*).

8. A London banker receives bills from a correspondent in the country, to be presented for payment. He gives up the bills to the acceptor, in exchange for a cheque for the amount, that being the usual and ordinary course amongst bankers. The cheque is dishonoured. The banker is not liable in an action for negligence, having acted in the ordinary course of business and in accordance with usage (*a*).

9. A solicitor, employed to procure a mortgage, discovers a defect in his client's title, which he afterwards discloses to

(*s*) *Boorman* v. *Brown*, 1842, 2 G. & D. 793; 3 Q. B. 511; 11 C. & F. 1.

(*t*) *Dufresne* v. *Hutchinson*, 1810, 3 Taunt. 117.

(*u*) *Solomon* v. *Barker*, 1862, 2 F. & F. 726.

(*x*) *Bexwell* v. *Christie*, 1776, Cowp. 395.

(*y*) *Ferrars* v. *Robbins*, 1835, 2 C. M. & R. 152; 1 Gale, 70; 5 Tyr. 705.

(*z*) *Papè* v. *Westacott*, (1894) 1 Q. B. 272, 63 L. J. Q. B. 222; 70 L. T. 18, 42 W. R. 131, 9 R. 55, 10 T. L. R. 51.

(*a*) *Russell* v. *Hankey*, 1794, 6 T. R. 12, 3 R. R. 102.

another client, causing damage to the first-mentioned client. He is liable for the damage caused by his breach of duty (*b*). So, where a solicitor without reasonable cause, or without giving his client reasonable notice of his intention to do so, abandons the prosecution or defence of an action, he is liable to the client for any loss occasioned thereby (*c*).

10. An auctioneer sells property under conditions requiring the payment of an immediate deposit. He is liable in an action for negligence, if he permits the highest bidder to go away without paying the deposit (*d*).

Negligence.

11. An insurance broker was employed to insure certain goods from a particular point in the voyage. He insured them "at and from that point, beginning the adventure from the loading thereof on board." Held, that he had been guilty of actionable negligence, for the consequences of which he was liable to his principal (*e*). Actions for negligence against insurance brokers have also been held to lie—(a) for not effecting a policy within a reasonable time (*f*); (b) for an omission to insert a clause usually inserted when insuring from the particular point (*g*); and (c) for an omission to communicate a material letter to the underwriters, in consequence of which the principal failed in an action on the policy (*h*). But, where a broker acts in good faith and in accordance with usage in effecting a policy, the mere fact that the insurance might possibly have been effected on better terms is not sufficient to render the broker

---

(*b*) *Taylor* v. *Blacklow*, 1836, 3 Scott, 614, 3 B. N. C. 235, 2 Hodges, 224.

(*c*) *Hoby* v. *Built*, 1832, 3 B. & Ad. 350.

(*d*) *Hibbert* v. *Bayley*, 1860, 2 F. & F. 48.

(*e*) *Park* v. *Hammond*, 1816, 6 Taunt. 495, 2 Marsh. 189, 4 Camp. 344; Holt, 80; 16 R. R. 658.

(*f*) *Turpin* v. *Bilton*, 1843, 5 Man. & G. 455, 6 Scott, N. R. 447, 12 L. J. C. P. 167, 7 Jur. 950.

(*g*) *Mallough* v. *Barber*, 1815, 4 Camp. 150.

(*h*) *Maydew* v *Forrester*, 1814, 5 Taunt. 615, 15 R. R. 597.

liable to the principal for damages. To render him liable, it must appear that he has been guilty of negligence or of some breach of duty (*i*).

12. *Act in itself imprudent.*—The directors of a limited company whose object was to purchase a certain business were authorized by the articles of association "to purchase or acquire the said business as it then stood, upon such terms and under such stipulations as might be agreed upon." Held, that the directors were not liable, in the absence of proved gross negligence on their part, for the consequences of so carrying out the object of the company, the business, in fact, being in a state of insolvency at the time, they being clearly authorized to purchase the business as it stood, which was an act in itself imprudent (*k*).

13. *Damage must not be too remote.*—Certain bankers who were employed to receive the dividends on certain shares for a customer, for which they charged him a small commission, negligently allowed their manager to have the key of the safe where the certificates of the shares were kept. The manager fraudulently sold the shares, and forged the customer's name to a transfer thereof. Held, that although the bankers would have been liable to the customer for any loss occasioned to him as a reasonable or probable consequence of their negligence, the costs of an action to recover the shares from the transferee were too remote a consequence, for which they were not liable (*l*).

14. *Damage must be legal damage.*—A. employs B., a turf commission agent, to make bets on his behalf. B. undertakes the commission, and neglects to make the bets. A. has suffered no legal damage, because the bets would have been void, and A. would not have been able to recover them by action, even if B. had duly made them on his behalf. A. therefore cannot main-

(*i*) *Moore* v. *Mourgue*, 1776, Cowp. 479, *Comber* v. *Anderson*, 1808, 1 Camp. 523.

(*k*) *Overend, Gurney & Co.* v. *Gibb*, 1872, L. R. 5 H. L. 480, 42 L. J. Ch. 67, H. L.

(*l*) *In re United Service Co., Johnston's claim*, 1870, L. R. 6 Ch. 212, 40 L. J. Ch. 286, 24 L. T. 115, 19 W. R. 457.

tain an action against B. for breach of duty, though it may be customary to pay such bets without action (*m*). So, where an agent who was instructed to insure certain slaves neglected to do so, it was held that he was not liable to his principal in an action for negligence, although it was customary for underwriters to pay in respect of such a policy, because, by reason of its illegality, the principal would have been unable to recover upon the policy at law (*n*).

15. *Nominal damages, though no actual loss.*—An agent is instructed to present a bill for acceptance. He neglects to do so. The principal is entitled to recover nominal damages for the breach of duty, though he suffered no actual loss thereby, the bill having been paid by other parties thereto. In such a case legal damage is presumed (*o*).

16. *Negligence of gratuitous agent.* — A customer deposited certain securities with his bankers for safe keeping, the bankers receiving no reward for taking care of them. The securities were stolen by a clerk in the bankers' employ Held, that the bankers, having acted gratuitously, were not liable, unless they had been guilty of gross negligence (*p*). A gratuitous agent is liable for gross negligence in the course of his employment (*q*); but not for mere want of skill (*r*), unless he is in a situation from which skill may be implied (*s*). But an omission to exercise such skill as he actually possesses, or has held himself out to possess, or such skill as may reasonably be implied from

---

(*m*) *Cohen* v. *Kittell*, 1889, 22 Q. B. D. 680, 58 L. J. Q. B. D. 241, 60 L. T. 932, 37 W. R. 400.

(*n*) *Webster* v. *De Tastet*, 1797, 7 T. R. 157, 4 R. R. 402. See, also, *Duncan* v. *Skipwith*, 1809, 2 Camp. 68.

(*o*) *Wait* v. *Wolley*, 1830, M. & M. 520.

(*p*) *Giblin* v. *McMullen*, 1869, L. R. 2 P C. 317, 38 L. J. P. C. 25, P. C.

(*q*) *Elsee* v. *Gatward*, 1793, 5 T. R. 143, *Wilkinson* v. *Coverdale*, 1793, 1 Esp. 75, *Beauchamp* v *Powley*, 1831, 1 M. & Rob. 38, *Doorman* v. *Jenkins*, 1834, 2 A. & E. 256, 4 N. & M. 170.

(*r*) *Moffatt* v *Bateman*, 1869, L. R. 3 P. C. 115, 6 Moo. P. C. C. (N. S.) 369, 22 L. T. 140, P. C.

(*s*) *Shiells* v. *Blackburne*, 1789, 1 H. Bl. 158, 2 R. R. 750.

his profession or employment, or to exercise such care and diligence as he is in the habit of exercising in regard to his own affairs, is deemed to be gross negligence, for the consequences of which he is responsible to the principal (*t*).

Liability of Solicitors for Negligence.

A solicitor is not liable to his client for negligence in the performance of his duties, as such, unless he has been guilty of gross negligence or gross ignorance (*u*). Where, however, there is any evidence at all of negligence, the question whether there has been gross negligence or not ought to be submitted to the jury (*x*). A lessee consulted a solicitor in reference to the building of a certain wall, to the erection of which the lessor objected. The lease was shown to the solicitor, who, without making any inquiries as to whether there was any obstacle other than what might be contained in the lease, advised that the lessee might build the wall, there being, in fact, a restrictive covenant in favour of the original vendors. Held, that there was no evidence of negligence for the jury (*y*). So, a solicitor is not liable merely because he has made a mistake, or has given his client erroneous or bad advice (*z*); or has misinterpreted a rule of Court, the meaning of which is obscure (*a*). Nor is he liable for an error of judgment upon a point of new occurrence, or of nice or doubtful construction, or in respect of a matter such as is usually

---

(*t*) *Wilson* v. *Brett*, 1843, 11 M. & W. 113, 12 L. J. Ex. 264, *Dartnall* v. *Howard*, 1825, 4 B. & C. 345, 6 D. & R. 438, *Whitehead* v. *Greetham*, 1825, 2 Bing. 464, 10 Moo. 183, M'Clel. & Y. 205, Ex. Ch.

(*u*) *Purves* v. *Landell*, 1845, 12 C. & F. 91, H. L., *Chapman* v. *Van Toll*, *Van Toll* v. *Chapman*, 1857, 8 E. & B. 396, 27 L. J. Q. B. 1, 3 Jur. N. S. 1126, *Dooby* v. *Watson*, 1888, 39 Ch. Div. 178, 57 L. J. Ch. 865, 58 L. T. 943, *Lowry* v. *Guildford*, 1832, 5 C. & P. 234, *Pitt* v. *Zalden*, 4 Burr. 2060.

(*x*) *Ireson* v. *Pearman*, 1825, 3 B. & C. 799, 5 D. & R. 687.

(*y*) *Pitman* v. *Francis*, 1884, 1 C. & E. 355.

(*z*) *Purves* v. *Landell*, *supra*.

(*a*) *Laidler* v. *Elliott*, 1825, 3 B. & C. 738.

intrusted to counsel (*b*). But he is liable for the consequences of his ignorance or non-observance of the rules of practice; for want of reasonable care in the preparation of a cause for trial, or for neglecting to attend at the trial with his witnesses; or for the mismanagement of so much of the cause as is usually intrusted to his department (*b*). Thus, where a solicitor was employed to take proceedings against certain apprentices for misconduct, and proceeded on the section of the statute relating to servants, he was held liable for the damages and costs incurred by reason of the error (*c*). So, where a solicitor allowed a case to be called on without ascertaining whether a material witness, whom his client had promised to bring, was in Court, that was held sufficient evidence of want of reasonable care to go to the jury (*d*). Where a solicitor allowed judgment to go against his client by default, it was held that the solicitor must show that there was no defence, in order to rebut the inference of negligence, and that it was not necessary for the client to prove that he had a good defence (*e*). Solicitors have been held liable in actions for negligence—(1) for lending money on insufficient security (*f*); (2) for suing where the Court had no jurisdiction (*g*); (3) for not duly filing certain writs, in accordance with the practice of the Court (*h*); (4) for not using due diligence to obtain satisfaction of a judgment (*i*); (5) for investing trust moneys in improper securities (*k*), and (6) for missing a case which had been transferred to another judge, without the

---

(*b*) *Godefroy* v. *Dalton*, 1830, 6 Bing. 460.

(*c*) *Hart* v. *Frame*, 1839, 6 Cl. & F. 193, Macl. & R. 595, H. L.

(*d*) *Reece* v. *Rigby*, 1821, 4 B. & A. 202.

(*e*) *Godefroy* v. *Jay*, 1831, 7 Bing. 413, 5 M. & P. 284.

(*f*) *In re Partington*, *Partington* v. *Allen*, 1887, 57 L. T. 654.

(*g*) *Williams* v. *Gibbs*, 1836, 5 Ad. & E. 208, 6 N. & M. 788, 2 H. & W. 241.

(*h*) *Hunter* v. *Caldwell*, 1847, 10 Q. B. 69, 83, 12 Jur. 285, 16 L. J. Q. B. 274, Ex. Ch.

(*i*) *Russell* v. *Palmer*, 1767, 2 Wils. 325.

(*k*) *Blyth* v. *Fladgate*, *Morgan* v. *Blyth*, *Smith* v. *Blyth*, (1891) 1 Ch. 337, 60 L. J. Ch. 66, 63 L. T. 546, 39 W. R. 422.

solicitor's knowledge, by order of the Lord Chancellor (*l*). If property comes to a solicitor in consequence of his ignorance, or of a breach of duty on his part, he is a trustee thereof for the persons who would have been entitled if he had known and done his duty. No solicitor is permitted to take advantage of his own ignorance or breach of duty (*m*).

Article 55.

MEASURE OF DAMAGES FOR NEGLIGENCE OR OTHER BREACH OF DUTY.

The measure of damages in an action by a principal against his agent for negligence or any other breach of duty in the course of the agent's employment is the loss actually sustained by the principal as a reasonable or probable consequence of such negligence or breach of duty (*n*).

Illustrations.

1. A commission agent in Hong Kong was instructed to purchase a quantity of a certain kind of opium. He purchased and shipped to his principal opium of an inferior kind. Held, that the proper measure of damages was the loss actually sustained by the principal in consequence of the opium not being of the description ordered, and not the difference between the value of the description ordered and of that shipped (*o*).

(*l*) *Burgoine* v. *Taylor*, 1878, 9 Ch. Div. 1, 47 L. J. Ch. 542, 38 L. T. 438, 26 W. R. 568, C. A.

(*m*) *Bulkeley* v. *Wilford*, 1834, 2 Cl. & F. 102, 8 Bli. N. S. 111, H. L.

(*n*) *In re United Service Co., Johnston's claim*, 1870, L. R. 6 Ch. 212, 40 L. J. Ch. 286, 24 L. T. 115; 19 W. R. 457, Ch. App., *Cassaboglou* v. *Gibb*, 1882, 9 Q. B. D. 220, 51 L. J. Q. B. 593, 47 L. T. 98, 11 Q. B. D. 797, 52 L. J. Q. B. 538, 48 L. T. 850, C. A., *Fisher* v. *Val de Travers Co.*, 1876, 1 C. P. D. 511, 45 L. J. C. P. 479, 35 L. T. 366; *Hadley* v. *Baxendale*, 1854, 9 Ex. 341, 23 L. J. Ex. 182, *Bertram* v. *Godfray*, 1830, 1 Knapp P. C. C. 381, P. C. And see Illustrations.

(*o*) *Cassaboglou* v. *Gibb*, *supra*.

2. An agent is instructed to insure his principal's goods, and wilfully or negligently omits to do so. He is liable to the same extent as the underwriters would have been if the goods had been duly insured (*p*).

3. An insurance broker, in effecting a policy, omitted to disclose a material letter, the consequence being that his principal failed in an action against the underwriters on the policy. Held, that the broker was liable for the actual loss sustained by the principal in consequence of the omission, including the costs of the action against the underwriters (*q*).

4. A. employs B. to buy tobacco of the best quality. B. delegates his employment to C., who buys an inferior quality. A. recovers damages from B. for the breach of duty. B. is entitled to recover from C. the full amount of the damages and costs incurred by him in the action by A. (*r*).

5. A solicitor, employed to effect a mortgage, neglected to ascertain that a third person had an equitable charge thereon to the extent of 46*l*. The client had to pay the amount of the charge, on a sale of the property, to enable him to convey it to the purchaser. Held, that 46*l*. was the proper measure of damages for the negligence, in the absence of evidence reducing the amount (*s*).

6. A stockbroker, employed to sell joint stock bank shares, omitted to insert in the contract the number of the shares, or the name of the registered proprietor thereof, as required by Leeman's Act, the omission rendering the contract void. Held, that the principal was entitled to recover, as damages for the breach of duty, the amount he would have obtained for the shares if they had been validly sold (*t*).

(*p*) *Smith* v. *Price*, 1862, 2 F. & F. 748; *Tickel* v. *Short*, 1750, 2 Ves. 239.

(*q*) *Maydew* v. *Forrester*, 1814, 5 Taunt. 615; 15 R. R. 597.

(*r*) *Mainwaring* v. *Brandon*, 1818, 2 Moore, 125; 19 R. R. 497.

(*s*) *Whiteman* v. *Hawkins*, 1878, 4 C. P. D. 13; 39 L. T. 629; 27 W. R. 262.

(*t*) *Neilson* v. *James*, 1882, 9 Q. B. D. 546; 51 L. J. Q. B. 369; 46 L. T. 791, C. A.

7. An agent was instructed not to part with the possession or control of certain goods until they were paid for. He parted with them, and the purchaser failed to pay the price. Held, that the measure of damages was the value of the goods, which the principal had lost in consequence of the breach of duty (*u*).

8. An agent, acting under a power of attorney, wrongfully transferred to himself certain shares belonging to his principal, in satisfaction of a claim which the principal partly admitted and partly disputed. Held, that the principal was entitled to recover the full value of the shares (*x*).

Article 56.

LIABILITY OF AGENTS ACCEPTING BRIBES.

Where an agent accepts any money or property in the course of his agency by way of a bribe, he is liable to account for and pay over the amount or value thereof, as money received to the use of the principal, with interest from the date of its receipt; and if he has been induced by the bribe to depart from his duty to the principal, he is also liable, jointly and severally with the person who bribed him, to make good any loss suffered by the principal in consequence of such departure from duty, without taking into consideration the amount of the bribe so accounted for or paid over to the principal (*y*).

The claim of a principal in respect of a bribe received

(*u*) *Stearine Co.* v. *Heintzmann*, 1864, 17 C. B. N. S. 56, 10 Jur. N. S. 881, 11 L. T. 272.

(*x*) *Dantra* v. *Stiebel*, 1863, 3 F. & F. 951.

(*y*) *Mayor of Salford* v. *Lever*, 1890, (1891) 1 Q. B. 168, 60 L. J. Q. B. 39, 63 L. T. 658, C. A., *Morgan* v. *Elford*, 1876, 4 Ch. Div. 352, *Phosphate Sewage Co.* v. *Hartmont*, 1875, 5 Ch. Div. 394, 457, C. A., *E. I. Co.* v. *Henchman*, 1 Ves. jun. 289.

by his agent is barred by the Statute of Limitations, in equity as well as at law, after the expiration of six years from the time when the principal became aware of the bribery (*z*).

The principal is justified in dismissing without notice any agent who accepts a bribe in the course of his agency (*a*).

Illustrations.

1. An agent, in consideration of a bribe, induces his principal to contract with the person bribing him. The principal is entitled to recover from the agent the amount of the bribe, as money received to his use, and from the agent and the person bribing him, jointly and severally, any loss incurred through having been so induced to contract (*b*).

2. A director of a company, who was a shareholder in two other companies, accepted bonuses from such other companies, in consideration of his giving them orders for goods on behalf of the first-mentioned company. The articles of association provided that the directors might contract with the company Held, that the bonuses were bribes, and that the director must account to the company for them, with interest. Held, further, that the bribery justified the dismissal of the director, though the bribery was not discovered until after the dismissal, and had taken place several months prior thereto (*a*).

3. An agent, who was employed to purchase goods, accepted large sums from the vendor by way of bribery, and invested part of the amount. The principal claimed to follow the money, and prayed for an injunction to restrain the agent from dealing

(*z*) *Metropolitan Bank* v. *Herron*, 1880, 5 Ex. Div. 319, C. A. But the Statute of Limitations is no defence in case of fraud *Walsham* v. *Stainton*, 1863, 12 W R. 63, Ch. App., *Hardwicke* v. *Vernon*, 1808, 14 Ves. 504, 9 R. R. 329.

(*a*) *Boston Deep Sea Co.* v. *Ansell*, 1888, 39 Ch. Div. 339, 59 L. T. 345, C. A.

(*b*) *Salford* v. *Lever*, *supra*, note (*y*).

with the investment, and an order directing him to bring the amount into court. Held, that the relation between the parties was that of debtor and creditor, not that of trustee and *cestui que trust*, and that the plaintiff was not entitled to follow the money (*c*).

Article 57.

WHERE LIABLE TO PAY INTEREST.

No agent is liable to pay interest upon money received by him to the use of his principal, except where he receives or deals with the money improperly, and in breach of his duty (*d*), or refuses to pay it over to the principal on demand (*e*). Where he refuses to pay it over on demand, he is liable to pay interest from the date of the refusal (*e*).

Illustrations.

1. An agent, at the request of his principal, retained large sums of money in his hands, and duly accounted for the same. Held, that he was not liable to pay interest, though he had made use of the money for his own purposes (*f*). But, in general, where an agent applies the principal's money to his own use, he is bound to pay interest thereon, it being his duty to act in the agency solely for the principal's benefit (*g*).

2. A solicitor was authorized by power of attorney to sell certain property and invest the proceeds. He paid the proceeds

---

(*c*) *Lister* v. *Stubbs*, 1890, 45 Ch. Div. 1, 59 L. J. Ch. 570, 62 L. T. 654, C. A.

(*d*) *Wolfe* v. *Findlay*, 1847, 6 Hare, 66, 16 L. J. Ch. 241, 11 Jur. 82; *Fry* v. *Fry*, 1864, 10 Jur. N. S. 983; Illustrations 1 to 6.

(*e*) *Harsant* v. *Blaine*, 1887, 56 L. J. Q. B. 511, C. A., *Pearse* v. *Green*, 1819, 1 Jac. & W. 135.

(*f*) *Chedworth* v. *Edwards*, 1802, 8 Ves. 48; 6 R. R. 212.

(*g*) *Rogers* v. *Boehm*, 1799, 2 Esp. 704.

into the account of his firm, who made use of the money. Held, that he must pay interest at the rate of five per cent. (*h*).

3. An agent, who undertook to invest his principal's money in the funds, kept large balances in his hands. Held, that he must pay interest on such balances (*i*).

4. An agent had the entire management of his principal's affairs for many years without being called upon for an account. Errors were then discovered, and upon a bill being filed for an account, a large sum was found to be due. Held, that, in the absence of fraud, the agent was not liable to pay interest upon the balances in his hands (*k*).

5. A stakeholder is not liable to pay interest, even if he uses, and himself obtains interest on, the money. Thus, where an auctioneer received a deposit, and invested and obtained interest upon the amount, it was held that he was not liable to pay over the interest, on the completion of the sale. In this respect, there is an essential difference between an agent and a stakeholder (*l*).

6. An agent is bound to pay interest upon bribes (*m*), and profits made in the course of his agency without the principal's knowledge (*n*), and in all cases of fraud or wilful concealment (*o*).

Article 58.

LIABILITY TO ATTACHMENT.

Where an agent is ordered by a court of equity to pay over money received by him in a fiduciary

(*h*) *Burdick* v. *Garrick*, 1869, L. R. 5 Ch. 233, 39 L. J. Ch. 369; 18 W. R. 387, Ch. App.

(*i*) *Brown* v. *Southhouse*, 1790, 3 Bro. C. C. 107.

(*k*) *Turner* v. *Burkinshaw*, 1867, L. R. 2 Ch. 488, 15 W. R. 753, Ch. App.

(*l*) *Harington* v. *Hoggart*, 1830, 1 B. & Ad. 577.

(*m*) *In re Drum Slate Quarry Co.*, 1885, 55 L. J. Ch. 36, 53 L. T. 250, *Boston Deep Sea Fishing Co.* v. *Ansell*, 1888, 39 Ch. Div. 339, 59 L. T. 345, C. A.

(*n*) *Benson* v. *Heathorn*, 1842, 1 Y. & Coll. C. C. 326, *Tyrrell* v. *Bank of London*, 1862, 10 H. L. Cas. 26, 8 Jur. N. S. 849, 31 L. J. Ch. 369, 10 W. R. 359, 6 L. T. 1, H. L.

(*o*) *Hardwicke* v. *Vernon*, 1808, 14 Ves. 504, 9 R. R. 329.

capacity, he is liable to attachment, on default in such payment, though he may have parted with the money, and become a bankrupt or insolvent (*p*).

Article 59.

LIABILITY FOR ACTS OF SUB-AGENTS.

Where an agent employs a sub-agent, the agent is liable to the principal for money received by the sub-agent to the principal's use (*q*), and is responsible to the principal for the negligence and other breaches of duty of the sub-agent in the course of his employment (*r*).

Illustrations.

1. A solicitor was held liable to his client for the negligence of his town agent (*s*).

2. A banker was employed to obtain payment of a bill of exchange. His agent obtained payment, and became bankrupt before handing the money over. Held, that the banker was

(*p*) Debtors Act, 1869, sect. 4, sub-sect. 3; *Crowther* v. *Elgood*, 1887, 34 Ch. Div. 691, 56 L. J. Ch. 416, 56 L. T. 415, 35 W. R. 369, C. A. (auctioneer attached for not paying over the price of goods sold by him); *Litchfield* v. *Jones*, 1887, 36 Ch. Div. 530, 57 L. J. Ch. 100; 58 L. T. 20 (town agent, in an action for an account of his agency by country solicitor). See, also, *Re Edge*, 1891, 63 L. T. 762, 39 W. R. 198; 7 T. L. R. 183, *In re Dudley, ex p. Monet*, 1883, 12 Q. B. D. 44; 53 L. J. Q. B. 16, 49 L. T. 737; 32 W. R. 264, C. A., *Jacob* v. *Magnay*, 1842, 12 L. J. Q. B. 93, 7 Jur. 326, as to the attachment of solicitors for breach of their duty as officers of the court. As to the criminal liability of an agent who fraudulently appropriates or deals with money or goods intrusted to him, as such, see 24 & 25 Vict. c. 96, ss. 75—79.

(*q*) *Matthews* v. *Haydon*, 1796, 2 Esp. 509, *In re Mitchell*, 1884, 54 L. J. Ch. 342; 52 L. T. 178.

(*r*) *Lord North's case*, Dy. 161a, *Eccossaise S.S. Co.* v. *Lloyd*, 1891, 7 T. L. R. 76, Illustrations 1 to 4.

(*s*) *Collins* v. *Griffin*, Barnes, 37.

liable to his customer for the amount (*t*). The general rule of law, that an agent is responsible for the acts of a sub-agent employed by him, is not confined to cases where the principal supposes that the agent will act in person (*t*), but applies even where the sub-agent is appointed with the principal's knowledge (*u*).

3. A. employs B., as an agent, to make advances upon goods. B. employs C. to make the advances, and authorizes him to draw upon A. for the amounts. C. fraudulently draws upon A. for an amount which he has not advanced. B. is liable to A. for the fraudulent act of C. in the course of his employment (*x*).

4. Moneys are handed, with the approbation of the secretary of a company, to the secretary's private clerk, who is not an officer of the company. The clerk misappropriates the money. The secretary is liable to the company for the amount so misappropriated (*y*).

Article 60.

RIGHTS OF PRINCIPAL ON AGENT'S BANKRUPTCY.

On the bankruptcy of an agent the principal is entitled, as against the trustee in bankruptcy and creditors of the bankrupt, to any money intrusted by him to the bankrupt for application in a particular way and still in the hands of the bankrupt (*z*), and to all goods and securities in the possession of (*a*), and all

---

(*t*) *Mackersy* v. *Ramsays*, 1843, 9 C. & F. 818, H. L.

(*u*) *Skinner* v. *Weguelin*, 1882, 1 C. & E. 12.

(*x*) *Swire* v. *Francis*, 1877, 3 App. Cas. 106, 47 L. J. P. C. 18, 37 L. T. 554, P. C.

(*y*) *In re Mutual Aid Permanent Building Society, ex p. James*, 1883, 49 L. T. 530.

(*z*) Illustration 1.

(*a*) Illustrations 2 to 5.

outstanding debts due to, the bankrupt, as his agent (*b*), subject to any lien of the bankrupt thereon. Provided, that this principle does not extend to goods, or debts due or growing due to the bankrupt in the course of his trade or business, which are, at the commencement of the bankruptcy, in the possession, order, or disposition of the bankrupt in his trade or business, by the consent and permission of the true owner, under such circumstances that the bankrupt is the reputed owner thereof (*c*).

Where an agent misapplies money intrusted to him for application in a particular way, or fraudulently converts the property of his principal into some other form, the principal is entitled, as against the agent and his trustee in bankruptcy and creditors, to the proceeds of such money or property, of whatsoever nature they may be, provided that they can be clearly traced (*d*).

Where an agent fraudulently mixes the money or property of his principal with his own, the principal is entitled, as against the agent and his trustee in bankruptcy and creditors, to a first charge on the mixed fund or property, or on the proceeds thereof, provided that they can be clearly traced (*e*).

(*b*) Illustrations 2 to 5.

(*c*) Bankruptcy Act, 1883 (46 & 47 Vict. c. 52), s. 44. See *Re Fawcus, ex p. Buck*, 1876, 3 Ch. Div. 795; 34 L. T. 807. And see Illustrations 5 and 7.

(*d*) Illustrations 6 and 7.

(*e*) Illustrations 8 and 9.

Illustrations.

1. Money is paid to a broker by his principal for application in a particular way. The broker pays the money into his own account at a bank, and becomes bankrupt before applying it as directed. The principal is entitled to the money, as against the broker's trustee in bankruptcy (*f*). If, in such a case, the agent has drawn on the account, the principal has a charge on the balance in the banker's hands, the amounts so drawn being deemed to be drawn out of the agent's own moneys, whenever they were paid in (*g*).

2. An agent becomes bankrupt, it being a matter of notoriety that he is an agent. Goods in his hands for sale (*h*), and unmatured bills and notes received by him as the price of goods sold (*i*), must, subject to his lien, be returned to the principal, and may be recovered by him from the trustee in bankruptcy. The price of goods already sold may, subject to the agent's lien, be recovered by the principal from the purchaser (*k*), and if received by the trustee in bankruptcy, may be recovered from him by the principal as money received to his use (*k*).

3. Bills are remitted to a factor or banker for a particular purpose, or to be dealt with for the use of the remitter. The factor or banker becomes bankrupt. The bills must be returned to the remitter (*l*).

(*f*) *Ex p. Cooke, re Strachan*, 1876, 4 Ch. Div. 123, 46 L. J. Bk. 52; 35 L. T. N. S. 649, 25 W. R. 171, C. A. And see *Farley* v. *Turner*, 1857, 26 L. J. Ch. 710, 3 Jur. N. S. 532; *Massey's case*, 1870, 39 L. J. Ch. 635.

(*g*) *Re Hallett's Estate, Knatchbull* v. *Hallett*, 1878, 13 Ch. Div. 696; 49 L. J. Ch. 415; 42 L. T. 421, 28 W. R. 732, C. A.

(*h*) *Scott* v. *Surman*, 1742, Willes, 400, *Ex p. Boden, re Wood*, 1873, 28 L. T. 174, *Whitfield* v. *Brand*, 1847, 16 M. & W. 282, *Stafford* v. *Clark*, 1823, 1 C. & P. 24, *Ex p. Dumas*, 1754, 1 Atk. 231, *Godfrey* v. *Furzo*, 1733, 3 P. W. 186.

(*i*) *Scott* v. *Surman, supra*, *Mace* v. *Cadell*, 1718, Cowp. 233, *Whitecomb* v. *Jacob*, 1 Salk. 160.

(*k*) *Scott* v. *Surman, supra*; *Ex p. Boden*, 1873, 28 L. T. 174; *Ex p. Carlow*, 1834, 2 Mon. & A. 39, 4 Deac. & Ch. 120, *Burdett* v. *Willett*, 1708, 2 Vern. 638.

(*l*) *Ex p. Oursell*, 1756, Ambl. 297, *Ex p. Smith*, 1819, Buck. 355;

4. A foreign merchant remitted bills to a factor in London, with instructions to sell them. The factor sold and indorsed them in his own name, and became bankrupt before receiving the price. Held, that the principal was entitled to the proceeds, as against the trustee in bankruptcy (*m*).

5. Books are left with a publisher for sale in the course of his trade. The books do not pass to his trustee in bankruptcy (*n*). So, where an agent was described, on a brass plate at his place of business and on his invoices, as a merchant and manufacturer's agent, that was held to be sufficient notice of the agency to exclude the operation of the reputed ownership clause of the Bankruptcy Acts, and the trustee in bankruptcy was ordered to deliver up to the manufacturers goods of theirs in the hands of the agent, and to pay over to them the proceeds of goods which had been sold on their behalf (*o*).

6. A broker misapplied his principal's money by purchasing stock and bullion, and absconded. He was adjudicated bankrupt on the same day that he received the money and so misapplied it. Upon being arrested he surrendered the securities for the stock and bullion to the principal. Held, that the principal was entitled to retain the securities as against the trustee in bankruptcy (*p*).

7. Malting agents sent in to their principal fictitious accounts of barley alleged to have been bought on his account, and misapplied the money. They subsequently absconded, leaving barley and malt on their premises of less value than the amount misapplied, and became bankrupt. The principal seized the malt and barley. Held, that he was entitled to hold it as against the trustee in bankruptcy. It is notorious that malting

---

Ex p. Pease, 1812, 19 Ves. 49; 1 Rose, 232; *Zinck* v. *Walker*, 1777, W. Bl. 1154; *Ex p. Gregory*, 1842, 2 M. D. & De G. 613.

(*m*) *Ex p. Pauli, re Trye*, 1838, 3 Dea. 169; 2 Jur. 208.

(*n*) *Ex p. Greenwood, re Thickbroom*, 1862, 6 L. T. N. S. 558, *Whitfield* v. *Brand*, 1847, 16 M. & W. 282.

(*o*) *Ex p. Bright, re Smith*, 1879, 10 Ch. Div. 566; 48 L. J. Bk. 81, 39 L. T. 649, 27 W. R. 385, C. A.

(*p*) *Taylor* v. *Plumer*, 1815, 3 M. & S. 562; 2 Rose, 457; 16 R. R. 361.

agents are, in many instances, not the owners of barley and malt on the malting premises, and it was, therefore, not in the order and disposition of the agents as reputed owners; and though much of it was bought with their own money, they were estopped, by their representation that they were buying it with the money intrusted to them by the principal, from saying so, and the trustee in bankruptcy was, in this respect, in no better position (*q*).

8. An agent, who was intrusted with bills to get discounted, mixed them with his own property, absconded, and became bankrupt. He was arrested with money in his possession which was clearly shown to be the produce of portions of the mixed property. Held, that the principal was entitled, in preference to the other creditors, to a first charge on such money for the amount of the bills (*r*).

9. An agent, who was employed to sell certain goods, mixed them with goods of his own, and consigned the whole of the goods together to a factor for sale, representing to his principal that he had sold his goods, and debiting himself with the amount of the supposed prices. The agent having become bankrupt, the principal was held entitled to have the proceeds of the mixed property marshalled, so as to throw advances made by the factor, as far as possible, on the agent's own goods (*s*).

(*q*) *Harris* v. *Truman*, 1882, 9 Q. B. D. 264, 51 L. J. Q. B. 338; 46 L. T. 844; 30 W. R. 533, C. A.

(*r*) *Frith* v. *Cartland*, 1865, 34 L. J. Ch. 301; 11 Jur. N. S. 238; 13 W. R. 493, 12 L. T. N. S. 175.

(*s*) *Broadbent* v. *Barlow*, 1861, 3 De G. F. & J. 570; 30 L. J. Ch. 569.

CHAPTER VIII.

Rights of Agents against their Principals.

Sect. 1.—*Right of Remuneration.*

Article 61.

FOUNDED ON AN EXPRESS OR IMPLIED CONTRACT.

Every right of remuneration that any agent has against his principal is founded on an express or implied contract (*a*). A contract to pay remuneration for services rendered may be implied from custom or usage, from the conduct of the principal, or from the circumstances of the particular case (*b*).

Where there is an express contract providing for remuneration, no other contract which is inconsistent therewith, whether founded on custom or otherwise, will be implied (*c*); but evidence of a particular custom may be given for the purpose of explaining any ambiguity in the terms of the express contract, or for the

(*a*) See Illustration 2.

(*b*) Illustrations 1 to 3.

(*c*) Illustrations 4 and 5. And see *Moore* v. *Maxwell*, 1848, 2 C. & K. 554, *Marshall* v. *Parsons*, 1841, 9 C. & P. 656, *Ward* v. *Stuart*, 1856, 1 C. B. N. S. 88, *Fullwood* v. *Akerman*, 1862, 11 C. B. N. S. 737, *Harris* v. *Petherick*, 1878, 39 L. T. 543; *Biggs* v. *Gordon*, 1860, 8 C. B. N. S. 638, *Battams* v. *Tompkins*, 1892, 8 T. L. R. 707, C. A.; *Caine* v. *Horsefall*, 1847, 1 Ex. 519, 17 L. J. Ex. 25.

purpose of adding a provision which is not inconsistent therewith (*b*).

Where there is no express contract providing for remuneration, and the circumstances of the agent's employment are such that a contract to remunerate him may be implied (*c*), the amount of the remuneration, and the conditions under which it becomes payable, must be ascertained from the custom or usage of the particular business (*d*). Where there is no particular custom or usage, the implied contract is to pay reasonable remuneration.

No barrister has any legal right to recover any fee or remuneration for services rendered by him, as such, nor is any promise to pay him for any such services binding, either at law or in equity (*e*).

Illustrations.

1. A. entered into an agreement in the following terms—"I hereby agree to enter your service as weekly manager, and the amount of payment I am to receive I leave entirely to you"—and served in that capacity for six weeks. Held, that there was an implied contract to make some payment, at all events, and that A. was entitled, in an action on a *quantum meruit*, to recover such an amount as the employer, acting in good faith, ought to have awarded (*f*).

(*b*) See note (*c*), *supra*, p. 149.

(*c*) Illustrations 1 to 3.

(*d*) Illustration 6; *Cohen* v. *Paget*, 1814, 4 Camp. 96, *Burnett* v. *Bouch*, 1840, 9 C. & P. 620; *Broad* v. *Thomas*, 1830, 7 Bing. 99, 4 M. & P. 732; 4 C. & P. 338, *Rucker* v. *Lunt*, 1863, 3 F. & F. 959, *Baring* v. *Stanton*, 1876, 3 Ch. Div. 502, 35 L. T. 652, 25 W. R. 237.

(*e*) *Brown* v. *Kennedy*, 1864, 4 De G. J. & S. 217, 33 L. J. Ch. 342; 10 Jur. N. S. 141; 13 C. B. N. S. 677; 32 L. J. C. P. 137, Ch. App.

(*f*) *Bryant* v. *Flight*, 1839, 5 M. & W. 114.

2. A committee resolved that any services rendered by A. should be taken into consideration, and such remuneration be paid to him as should be deemed right. Held, that no action would lie at the suit of A. to recover such remuneration, the resolution importing that the committee were to judge whether any, and if so, what remuneration was due for his services (*g*). Service, however long continued, creates no right to remuneration unless there is a contract to pay it; and such a contract will only be implied where the circumstances are such as to indicate an understanding between the parties that there should be remuneration (*h*).

3. A. employs an auctioneer to sell property on his behalf. A contract by A. to pay the auctioneer the usual commission is implied (*i*). So, the mere employment of a professional man, as such, raises a presumption of an intention to remunerate him, and an agreement to do so is always implied from such an employment, in the absence of other circumstances rebutting the presumption (*j*).

4. It was agreed that an agent should receive commission on "all sales effected or orders executed by him." By a custom of trade, no commission was payable in respect of bad debts. Held, that the agent was, nevertheless, entitled to commission on all sales effected by him, including those resulting in bad debts, the custom being inconsistent with the terms of the contract (*k*).

5. An agent was employed to find a purchaser for certain property at a fixed commission, to be payable only in the event of success. Held, that he was not entitled to a *quantum meruit*, in the absence of success, such a claim being excluded by the express contract (*l*). So, where it was agreed that a sailor should

---

(*g*) *Taylor* v. *Brewer*, 1813, 1 M. & S. 290. See, also, *Roberts* v. *Smith*, 1859, 4 H. & N. 315, 28 L. J. Ex. 164.

(*h*) *Reeve* v. *Reeve*, 1858, 1 F. & F. 280.

(*i*) *Miller* v. *Beale*, 1879, 27 W. R. 403.

(*j*) See *Manson* v. *Baillie*, 1855, 2 Macq. H. L. Cas. 80, H. L.

(*k*) *Bower* v. *Jones*, 1831, 8 Bing. 65, 1 M. & Scott, 140.

(*l*) *Green* v. *Mules*, 1861, 30 L. J. C. P. 343; *M'Leod* v. *Artola*, 1889, 6 T. L. R. 68.

be paid a fixed sum, provided he continued to serve, and did his duty, during the whole voyage, it was held that no wages could be claimed, either on a *quantum meruit* or otherwise, in the event of his dying before the completion of the voyage (*m*).

6. A London shipbroker negotiated for the hire of a vessel, and a memorandum of charter was duly signed, but the contract afterwards went off. By a custom of the City of London, shipbrokers who negotiate the hire of vessels are entitled to a certain commission on the amount of the freight, where the contracts are completed, the rate of payment being higher than would fairly compensate them for their services; but are not entitled to any remuneration with respect to contracts which are not completed. Held, that the broker was not entitled to recover either commission or a *quantum meruit* for the services rendered, even if the contract went off owing to the act of the principal. The implied contract to pay an agent reasonable remuneration for his services does not arise when there is an express agreement, or one to be inferred from custom, which is inconsistent therewith (*n*).

Article 62.

COMMISSION ONLY ON TRANSACTIONS DIRECTLY RESULTING FROM THE AGENCY.

No agent is entitled to commission upon any transaction, unless he shows that the transaction is a direct, though not necessarily an immediate, result of his agency (*o*). It is necessary, in order to establish a claim for commission, that there should be a con-

---

(*m*) *Cutter* v. *Powell*, 1795, 6 T. R. 320, 3 R. R. 185.

(*n*) *Read* v. *Rann*, 1830, 10 B. & C. 438, *Broad* v. *Thomas*, 1830, 7 Bing. 99; 4 M. & P. 732; 4 C. & P. 338.

(*o*) *Wilkinson* v. *Alston*, 1879, 48 L. J. Q. B. 733; 41 L. T. 394, C. A.; *Bailey* v. *Chadwick*, 1878, 39 L. T. 429, H. L., *Bray* v. *Chandler*, 1856, 18 C. B. 718, *White* v. *Baxter*, 1883, 1 C. & E. 199, *Jeffrey* v. *Crawford*, 1890, 7 T. L. R. 618, C. A., Illustrations 1, 2 and 8.

tractual, and not merely a casual, relation between the acts of the agent and the transaction in respect of which the claim is made (*p*). But it is not necessary that he should complete the transaction, or even that he should be acting for the principal at the time of the completion, provided that he was the direct cause of the business being done, and was acting for the principal during some portion of the negotiations (*q*).

The question whether an agent is entitled to commission upon business arising wholly after his employment has ceased, as a result of his introduction, depends upon the nature and terms of his employment. *Primâ facie*, he is not so entitled (*r*).

Illustrations.

1. A. employs B., a broker, to obtain a contract for a charter-party. B. introduces C., who is also a broker. C. introduces D., who obtains a contract. B. has no claim upon A. for commission, the transaction being too remote a consequence of his introduction. A custom for a broker to be paid commission in such a case is invalid (*s*).

2. A house agent lets a house for a term of years, the tenant having the option of taking it for a further term. The tenant afterwards, through the intervention of another agent, takes the house for a further term at a different rent. The first-mentioned agent is not entitled to commission in respect of the further term, and a trade custom to pay commission to the original

(*p*) *Toulmin* v. *Millar*, 1887, 58 L. T. 96, H. L.; Illustrations 3, 7, 8 and 9.

(*q*) Illustrations 4 to 8; *Wilkinson* v. *Martin*, 1837, 8 C. & P. 1.

(*r*) Illustration 10.

(*s*) *Gibson* v. *Crick*, 1862, 1 H. & C. 142; 31 L. J. Ex. 304, 6 L. T. 392; 10 W. R. 525; 2 F. & F. 766.

agent, under such circumstances, is invalid. He is entitled to commission only upon the rent obtained as a proximate consequence of his own acts (*t*).

3. A. entered into an agreement with B. in the following terms:—"In case of your introducing a purchaser (of a certain business) of whom I approve, or capital which I should accept, I could pay you five per cent. commission, provided no one else is entitled to commission in respect of the same introduction." B. introduced C., who advanced 10,000*l*. by way of loan, and B. was duly paid his commission in respect of that advance. Some months afterwards, A. and C. entered into an agreement for a partnership, C. advancing a further 4,000*l*. by way of capital. Held, that B. was not entitled to commission on the 4,000*l*., that amount having been advanced in consequence of the negotiations between A. and C. for a partnership, with which B. had nothing to do (*u*). It is not sufficient for the agent to show that the transaction would not have been entered into but for his introduction. He must show that the introduction is the direct cause of the transaction (*u*).

4. An estate agent, who was employed to find a purchaser for certain property, introduced a person to his principal on January 7th. A few days afterwards, the principal became a bankrupt. On January 17th, further negotiations took place between the person introduced and the trustee in bankruptcy, resulting in a sale of the property on January 24th. Held, that the sale was brought about by the agent's introduction, and that he was entitled to prove in the bankruptcy for the amount of his commission (*v*).

5. An auctioneer and estate agent was employed to sell an estate, a reserve price being fixed, commission to be paid if the estate should be sold. He put it up for sale, but it was not sold. A person, who attended the sale, afterwards asked the auctioneer who was the owner of the property, was referred by him to the

(*t*) *Curtis* v. *Nixon*, 1871, 24 L. T. 706.
(*u*) *Tribe* v. *Taylor*, 1876, 1 C. P. D. 505.
(*v*) *Ex p. Durrant, re Beale*, 1888, 5 M. B. R. 37.

principal, and eventually became the purchaser of the estate. Held, that the auctioneer was the *causa causans* of the sale, and was therefore entitled to his commission, although, before the actual sale, the vendor had withdrawn the property from him (*x*). An agent who really brings about the relationship of buyer and seller is entitled to commission, though he does not actually complete the contract (*x*).

6. A house agent was instructed to offer a house for sale, and it was agreed that he should receive 2½ per cent. commission on the price if he found a purchaser, or a guinea for his services if the house was sold without his intervention. A person called on the agent and obtained an order to view, but thought that the price was too high. The same person subsequently renewed negotiations with a friend of the principal's, and ultimately bought the house. Held, that there was evidence for the jury that the house was sold through the intervention of the agent, so as to entitle him to his commission (*y*).

7. An agent introduced a person to his principal as a possible purchaser of certain property, but no terms were arrived at. The principal subsequently sold the property by auction, the person introduced by the agent being the purchaser. Held, that the agent was not entitled to commission (*z*).

8. A. employed B. to sell an estate in lots. C. bought certain lots, and B. received commission thereon. A. then withdrew B.'s authority, and C. subsequently bought the remaining lots by private contract. Held, that the jury were entitled to find that the ultimate sale was not due to B.'s introduction (*a*). But if it appears that the agent's introduction is the foundation of the negotiations resulting in an ultimate sale, the principal cannot deprive him of his commission by withdrawing the property from his hands. The proper question for the jury is—

(*x*) *Green* v. *Bartlett*, 1863, 14 C. B. N. S. 681, 32 L. J. C. P. 261; 8 L. T. 503, 11 W. R. 834.

(*y*) *Mansell* v. *Clements*, 1874, L. R. 9 C. P. 139.

(*z*) *Taplin* v. *Barrett*, 1889, 6 T. L. R. 30.

(*a*) *Lumley* v. *Nicholson*, 1886, 34 W. R. 716.

"Did the sale really and substantially proceed from the agent's acts?" (*b*).

9. An agent claims commission for procuring a loan. It is not sufficient to show that the loan indirectly resulted from his intervention. He must show that it was obtained, by means of the agency, from the parties to whom he applied. If third persons casually heard that a loan was wanted, and lent the money directly to the principal, the agent cannot claim commission thereon (*c*). So, in order to found a claim for commission upon a sale, there must be a contractual, and not merely a casual, relation between the introduction of the purchaser by the agent and the ultimate sale (*d*).

10. An agent is employed to sell goods on commission, and the principals agree "to allow him commission upon all orders executed by them and paid for by the customers arising from his introduction." He is entitled to commission on all orders executed for customers introduced by him, even if the orders are received after his dismissal from the principals' employment (*e*.) But, apart from any express stipulation, the general rule is that a principal is not liable to pay commission upon orders sent by his agent's customers after the agent has ceased to represent him (*f*).

Article 63.

REMUNERATION MAY BE PAYABLE, THOUGH THE PRINCIPAL ACQUIRES NO BENEFIT.

Where an agent contracts or is employed to perform an undertaking for a fixed remuneration, he is entitled to that remuneration so soon as he has done all that he

---

(*b*) *Wilkinson* v. *Martin*, 1837, 8 C. & P. 1.
(*c*) *Antrobus* v. *Wickens*, 1865, 4 F. & F. 291.
(*d*) *Toulmin* v. *Millar*, 1887, 58 L. T. 96, H. L.
(*e*) *Bilbee* v. *Hasse*, 1889, 5 T. L. R. 677.
(*f*) *Nayler* v. *Yearsley*, 1860, 2 F. & F. 41.

contracted to do (*g*), or has substantially performed the undertaking (*h*), even if the principal acquires no benefit from his services (*g*), and, except where there is an express agreement or special custom to the contrary (*i*), even if the transaction in respect of which the remuneration is claimed falls through in consequence of circumstances over which the agent has no control (*g*).

Illustrations.

1. A. employed B. to procure a loan, and entered into the following agreement:—"In the event of your obtaining me the sum of 2,000*l.*, or such other sum as I shall accept, I agree to pay you a commission of 2½ per cent. on the amount received." B. introduced A. to a building society, who offered to lend 1,625*l.* upon certain terms, which were accepted by A. The transaction afterwards went off because A. would not satisfy certain requirements of the society, and failed to show a sufficient title to the property upon which the loan was to have been made. Held, that B. was entitled to his commission of 2½ per cent. upon 1,625*l.*, the amount the society offered to advance (*j*).

2. An agent who was employed to borrow a certain sum upon leasehold security, found a person able and willing to lend that sum, but the transaction fell through in consequence of unusual covenants in the leases, of which covenants the agent had no knowledge. Held, that he was entitled to the whole of the agreed commission for procuring the loan (*k*). If an agent, employed to negotiate a loan, brings the principals together, and nothing more remains for him to do, he is entitled to his com-

---

(*g*) Illustrations 1 to 5.
(*h*) Illustration 6.
(*i*) Illustration 7.
(*j*) *Fisher* v. *Drewitt*, 1879, 48 L. J. Ex. 32; 39 L. T. 253; 27 W. R. 12, C. A.
(*k*) *Green* v. *Lucas*, 1876, 33 L. T. 584; 31 L. T. 731, C. A.

mission, even if the contract afterwards goes off without any default by his principal (*l*).

3. It was agreed that an agent should receive commission upon "all goods bought through him." He obtained an order for goods, which the principal accepted but was unable to execute, so that no benefit resulted therefrom. Held, that the agent was entitled to commission upon the order (*m*). As a general rule, the agent is entitled to his commission whenever he procures a binding bargain which the principal accepts (*m*).

4. A. promised to pay B. 5*l.* if he should succeed in obtaining a purchaser for a lease at a certain price. B. introduced C., who entered into a contract with A., and paid a deposit. C. was unable to complete the purchase, and A. permitted the contract to be cancelled, A. retaining the deposit. Held, that B. had substantially performed his undertaking, and was entitled to payment of the 5*l.* promised (*n*). But the agent has no right to commission in such a case, unless the contract made is complete and binding (*o*).

5. An agent was employed on commission to purchase certain property. He purchased the property, subject to his principal's solicitor's approval of the title. The principal broke off the transaction, and the title was never submitted to his solicitor. Held, that in order to maintain an action for the commission, the agent ought to show either that the principal's solicitor approved the title, or that such a title was submitted to him as he could not reasonably disapprove, and that unless the agent could prove that the seller had a good title, he could not recover the commission (*p*).

(*l*) *Fuller* v. *Eames*, 1892, 8 T. L. R. 278. See judgment of Bramwell, L. J., in *Fisher* v. *Drewitt*, *supra*, *Platt* v. *Depree*, 9 T. L. R. 194.

(*m*) *Lockwood* v. *Levick*, 1860, 8 C. B. N. S. 603, 29 L. J. C. P. 340, 7 Jur. N. S. 102, *Caruthers* v. *Graham*, 1811, 14 East, 578, *Hill* v. *Kitching*, 1846, 3 C. B. 299; 15 L. J. C. P. 251.

(*n*) *Horford* v. *Wilson*, 1807, 1 Taunt. 12, *Lara* v. *Hill*, 1863, 15 C. B. N. S. 45.

(*o*) *Grogan* v. *Smith*, 1890, 7 T. L. R. 132, C. A.; *Maester* v. *Atkins*, 1814, 1 Marsh. 76, 5 Taunt. 381.

(*p*) *Clack* v. *Wood*, 1882, 9 Q. B. D. 276; 47 L. T. 144; 30 W. R. 931, C. A.

6. A. promised to pay B. 2½ per cent. commission in the event of his finding a purchaser of certain land at the price of 3,000*l.* B. introduced C., who took a lease for 1,000 years at a yearly rent of 150*l.*, with an option to purchase the land, within twenty years, for 3,000*l.* Held, that B. had practically found a purchaser, and was therefore entitled to the commission (*q*).

7. An agent was employed to sell an advowson, and it was expressly agreed that the commission should be paid when the abstract of conveyance was drawn out. He found a purchaser, who entered into a contract, but the abstract was not delivered, and negotiations were dropped. Held, that the agent was not entitled to recover the commission, the event upon which it was to become payable not having happened (*r*). So, where it was agreed that commission should be paid "upon the sum which might be obtained," it was held that it could not be recovered until the principal had actually received the amount, because it was impossible to calculate the commission until then (*s*). So, if there is a special trade custom whereby the agent is not entitled to commission unless the transaction in respect of which it is claimed be completed, he cannot recover the commission until completion, even if the transaction falls through in consequence of the principal's default (*t*).

Article 64.

PRINCIPAL LIABLE IN DAMAGES IF HE WRONGFULLY PREVENTS AGENT FROM EARNING REMUNERATION.

Where a principal, in breach of an express or implied contract with his agent (*u*), refuses to complete a transaction, or otherwise prevents the agent from

(*q*) *Rimmer* v. *Knowles*, 1874, 30 L. T. 496, 22 W. R. 574.

(*r*) *Alder* v. *Boyle*, 1847, 4 C. B. 635; 16 L. J. C. P. 232; 11 Jur. 591.

(*s*) *Bull* v. *Price*, 1831, 5 M. & P. 2, 7 Bing. 237.

(*t*) *Read* v. *Rann*, 1830, 10 B. & C. 438; *Broad* v. *Thomas*, 1830, 7 Bing. 99, 4 M. & P. 732; 4 C. & P. 338. See Article 61, Illustration 6.

(*u*) See Illustrations 2 to 7.

earning his commission, the agent is entitled to recover, by way of damages, the loss actually sustained by him in consequence of such breach of contract (*v*). The measure of damages, where nothing further remains to be done by the agent, is the full amount that he would have earned if the principal had duly completed the transaction, or otherwise carried out his contract with the agent (*w*).

Where the authority of an agent is revoked by the principal after it has been partially executed, or after the agent has endeavoured to execute it, the question whether the agent is entitled to remuneration for what he has already done, depends upon the nature and terms of his employment, and the custom or usage of the particular business in which he is employed (*x*).

Illustrations.

1. A. employs B. to find a purchaser for certain property at a fixed price, and promises to pay him commission in the event of a sale being effected. B. finds a purchaser at the price fixed, but A. refuses to complete the transaction. B. is entitled, in an action against A. for wrongfully preventing him from earning his commission, to recover the full amount that he would have been entitled to if the transaction had been duly completed (*w*). But this rule does not apply if there is a special custom whereby the agent is entitled to remuneration only in the event of the transaction in respect of which it is claimed being completed,

---

(*v*) Illustrations 1, 2, 5 and 6.

(*w*) *Prickett* v. *Badger*, 1856, 1 C. B. N. S. 296; 3 Jur. N. S. 66; 26 L. J. C. P. 33; *Roberts* v. *Barnard*, 1884, 1 C. & E. 336, Illustration 1.

(*x*) See *Queen of Spain* v. *Parr*, 1869, 39 L. J. Ch. 73, *Simpson* v. *Lamb*, 1856, 17 C. B. 603; 25 L. J. C. P. 113, 2 Jur. N. S. 91, Illustration 9.

the rate of remuneration being higher than would fairly compensate him for the services rendered (*y*).

2. A. contracted to employ B., and B. to serve A., as agent for the sale of such goods as should be forwarded or submitted to B. by sample from time to time, the agreement to be determined at the end of five years by notice from either party. Before the expiration of the five years, A.'s factory was burnt down, and the business was not resumed. In an action by B. for breach of contract, the Court of Appeal held that there was no implied condition that the contract should determine on the destruction of the factory, and that B. was entitled to substantial damages (*z*).

3. A. and B. agreed, in consideration of the services and payments to be mutually rendered and made, that for seven years, or so long as A. should continue business at L., A. should be sole agent there for the sale of B.'s coals. About four years afterwards B. sold his colliery. Held, by the House of Lords, that B. was under no obligation to continue the business, but only to employ A. as agent for the sale of such coals as he might send to L., and that the agency necessarily determined when the subject matter thereof was gone (*a*). It is not easy to reconcile this decision with the decision in the preceding illustration.

4. A firm agreed to employ an agent for a specified term. During the term, one of the partners died. Held, that the parties contracted with reference to the existing partnership, subject to an implied condition that all the parties should so

(*y*) *Broad* v. *Thomas*, 1830, 7 Bing. 99; 4 M. & P. 732; 4 C. & P. 338; *Read* v. *Rann*, 1830, 10 B. & C. 438. Article 61, Illustration 6.

(*z*) *Turner* v. *Goldsmith*, (1891) 1 Q. B. 544; 60 L. J. Q. B. D. 247; 64 L. T. 301, C. A. See also *Emmens* v. *Elderton*, 1852, 4 H. L. Cas. 624; 13 C. B. 495, 18 Jur. 21.

(*a*) *Rhodes* v. *Forwood*, 1876, 1 App. Cas. 256; 47 L. J. Ex. 396; 24 L. T. 890; 24 W. R. 1078, H. L. See *Brace* v. *Calder*, (1895) 2 Q. B. 253, 64 L. J. Q. B. 582; 72 L. T. 829, 11 T. L. R. 450. As to the meaning of "sole agent" see *Snelgrove* v. *Ellringham Colliery Co.*, 1881, 45 J. P. 408.

long live, and that, therefore, the agent was not entitled to damages from the other partners for refusing to continue the employment (*b*).

5. A company employed a broker to dispose of their shares, and agreed to pay him 100*l.* down, and a further 400*l.* on the allotment of all the shares. The broker disposed of a considerable number of the shares, and then the company was voluntarily wound up. Held, that the broker was prevented earning the 400*l.* by the act of the company, and was entitled to recover such damages for the breach of contract as the jury thought reasonable. The jury awarded him 250*l.* (*c*).

6. A. was engaged for a fixed term by a company as a traveller, and it was agreed that he should receive by way of remuneration a commission upon all orders obtained, but no salary. After A. had established a connection, and before the expiration of the term for which he was engaged, the company wound up voluntarily. Held, that A. was entitled to recover damages for the loss of the commission that he would have earned during the remainder of the term (*d*). It was pointed out that, had the case been otherwise decided, the company might have immediately commenced business again, and so obtained the benefit of A.'s connection without paying for it (*d*).

7. An agent was employed by an insurance company for a term of five years, at a fixed salary of 500*l.* a year and a commission on the profits, the agent undertaking to transact no other business during the term. The company wound up voluntarily before the expiration of the term. Held, that the agent was not entitled to prove in the winding up for prospective commission, the contract merely importing that a commission on the profits was to be paid if the company found it profitable to

---

(*b*) *Tasker* v. *Shepherd*, 1861, 6 H. & N. 575; 30 L. J. Ex. 207; 4 L. T. 19, 9 W. R. 476.

(*c*) *Inchbald* v. *Western Neilgherry Coffee, &c. Co.*, 1864, 17 C. B. N. S. 733, 34 L. J. C. P. 15.

(*d*) *In re Patent Floor Cloth Co., Dean and Gilbert's claim*, 1872, 41 L. J. Ch. 476, 26 L. T. 467.

carry on the business, and chose to do so. Such a contract gives the agent no right to insist upon the business being carried on (*e*). It will be observed that, in this case, a salary was paid, whereas, in the last illustration, the agent received commission only. But it is not easy to reconcile the decisions, and it would seem that each case must depend upon the particular circumstances, and the presumed intention of the parties (*e*).

8. The articles of association of a company provided that in the event of the manager being dismissed for any cause other than gross misconduct, he should be paid a certain sum by way of compensation. Held, that he was entitled to prove for such sum in the winding up of the company (*f*).

9. An agent was employed to sell an advowson. Before he succeeded in finding a purchaser, the principal sold it privately. Held, in an action for wrongful revocation of authority, that the agent was not entitled to recover anything, in the absence of evidence of expense incurred by him (*g*). Where the authority of an agent for sale is revoked before a sale is effected, the question whether he has a right to remuneration for what he has done in trying to effect a sale, depends upon the terms of his employment. Unless there is an express contract to pay the agent remuneration for his trouble, or the circumstances are such as to show that that was the intention of the parties, he is not entitled to recover in such a case; at all events, without proof of damage (*g*).

(*e*) *In re English and Scottish Marine Insurance Co., ex p. Maclure*, 1870, L. R. 5 Ch. 737; 39 L. J. Ch. 685; 23 L. T. 685, Ch. App.

(*f*) *In re London and Scottish Bank, ex p. Logan*, 1870, L. R. 9 Eq. 149; *In re Imperial Wine Co., Shirreff's case*, 1872, L. R. 14 Eq. 417; 42 L. J. Ch. 5.

(*g*) *Simpson* v. *Lamb*, 1856, 17 C. B. 603; 25 L. J. C. P. 113; 2 Jur. N. S. 91.

Article 65.

NO REMUNERATION IN RESPECT OF ILLEGAL OR WAGERING TRANSACTIONS.

No agent can recover any remuneration unless he is legally qualified to act in the capacity in which he claims the remuneration (*h*).

No agent can recover any remuneration in respect of any transaction which is apparently, or to his knowledge, illegal (*i*), or in respect of any wagering contract or agreement rendered null and void by the 8 & 9 Vict. c. 109, or of any services in relation thereto or connection therewith (*j*).

Illustrations.

1. A solicitor cannot maintain an action for costs unless his certificate was in force at the time the work for which the costs are claimed was done (*k*). So, a broker (*l*) or appraiser (*m*) cannot maintain any action for commission or remuneration as such, unless he was duly licensed to act in that capacity.

2. An action was brought for work performed and money expended in buying shares in a certain company. The company affected to act as a body corporate without authority by charter or statute, and was, therefore, illegal. Held, that the action was not maintainable, because it arose out of an illegal transaction (*n*). So, a broker cannot recover commission for effecting

(*h*) Illustration 1.

(*i*) Illustrations 2 and 3.

(*j*) 55 Vict. c. 9. Illustration 4.

(*k*) *Brunswick* v. *Crowl* (or *Ex p. Brunswick, re Crowl*), 1849, 4 Ex. 492; 19 L. J. Ex. 112; 13 Jur. 1058.

(*l*) *Cope* v. *Rowlands*, 1836, 2 M. & W. 149, 2 Gale, 231.

(*m*) *Palk* v. *Force*, 1848, 12 Q. B. 666, 17 L. J. Q. B. 299; 12 Jur. 797.

(*n*) *Josephs* v. *Pebrer*, 1825, 3 B. & C. 639; 1 C. & P. 341.

an illegal insurance (*o*), or in respect of an illegal sale of offices (*p*). Every agreement to pay remuneration in respect of any such illegal transaction is absolutely void (*p*). But a contract by a broker is not rendered illegal, so as to preclude him from recovering commission, by his omission to send a contract note to the principal, though he is liable to a penalty for the omission (*q*).

3. Commission was claimed by a broker for procuring freight. Held, that the fact that the charter-party, in respect of which the commission was claimed, would be illegal unless the charterer obtained certain licences, was no answer to the action, it not being part of the broker's duty to see that the licences were obtained (*r*).

4. The Gaming Act, 1892 (55 Vict. c. 9), provides that any promise, express or implied, to pay any sum by way of commission, fee, or reward, or otherwise, in respect of any contract or agreement rendered null and void by the 8 & 9 Vict. c. 109, or of any services in relation thereto or connection therewith, shall be null and void, and no action shall be brought or maintained to recover any such sum. Prior to this Act it was held that a plea of "gaming and wagering" was no answer to an action by a stockbroker for commission upon purchases and sales of stock or shares (*s*). The 8 & 9 Vict. c. 109 does not make gaming or wagering illegal, but merely renders any such contract null and void (*s*). In the case of Stock Exchange speculation, the question whether particular transactions are gaming or wagering

---

(*o*) *Allkins* v. *Jupe*, 1877, 2 C. P. D. 375; 46 L. J. C. P. 824; 36 L. T. 851.

(*p*) *Stackpole* v. *Erle*, 1761, 2 Wils. 133; *Waldo* v. *Martin*, 1825, 4 B. & C. 319; 6 D. & R. 364; 2 C. & P. 1, *Parsons* v. *Thompson*, 1790, 1 H. Bl. 322, 2 R. R. 773.

(*q*) *Learoyd* v. *Bracken*, (1894) 1 Q. B. 114, 63 L. J. Q. B. 96, 69 L. T. 668; 9 R. 92.

(*r*) *Haines* v. *Busk*, 1814, 5 Taunt. 521; 1 Marsh. 191.

(*s*) *Knight* v. *Fitch*, 1855, 15 C. B. 566, 3 C. L. R. 567, 24 L. J. C. P. 122, 1 Jur. N. S. 526.

transactions, or are genuine dealings in the stocks and shares, is a question of fact for the jury.

Article 66.

NO REMUNERATION IN CASES OF MISCONDUCT OR BREACH OF DUTY.

No agent is entitled to remuneration—

(a) in respect of any unauthorized transaction, unless the principal ratifies it (*t*);

(b) in respect of any transaction entered into by him in violation of the duties arising from the fiduciary character of the relationship between him and the principal, even if the transaction is adopted by the principal (*u*);

(c) where he has been guilty of wilful breach of duty or misconduct in the course of his employment (*v*); or

(d) where the principal derives no benefit from his services, in consequence of his negligence or other breach of duty (*w*).

Illustrations.

1. A. is employed on commission to procure a loan upon certain terms. Before anything is done the principal varies the

(*t*) Illustrations 1 to 3. *Toppin* v. *Healey*, 1863, 11 W. R. 466; *Gillow* v. *Aberdare*, 1893, 9 T. L. R. 12; *Keay* v. *Fenwick*, 1876, 1 C. P. D. 745. And see *Beaumont* v. *Boultbee*, 1805, 11 Ves. 358. As to ratification see Article 29, Illustration 10.

(*u*) Illustration 4. *Etna Insurance Co., re Owens*, 1873, 7 Ir. R. Eq. 235, 424, *Gray* v. *Haig*, 1854, 20 Beav. 219.

(*v*) Illustration 5. *White* v. *Chapman*, 1815, 1 Stark. 113, *Hurst* v. *Holding*, 1810, 3 Taunt. 32; 12 R. R. 587, *Palmer* v. *Goodwin*, 13 Ir. Ch. R. 171.

(*w*) Illustrations 6 to 8.

terms. A. is unable to procure the loan on the terms as varied, but obtains an offer on the original terms, which the principal refuses to accept. A. is not entitled to any commission (*x*).

2. An agent is employed on commission to sell certain property. His authority is revoked by the death of the principal, but he subsequently sells the property, and the principal's executors confirm the sale. The agent is not entitled to recover the agreed commission from the executors unless they ratify and recognize the terms of his employment, but he may be entitled to a *quantum meruit* (*y*).

3. An auctioneer, who is employed to sell property by auction, sells it by private contract. He is not entitled to commission (*z*).

4. An agent, who is employed to sell certain land, sells it to a company in which he is a director and shareholder. He is not entitled to commission upon the sale, even if it be adopted and confirmed by the principal (*a*).

5. A solicitor, having undertaken the conduct of a suit, abandons it without reasonable cause, or without giving his client reasonable notice of his intention to do so. He is not entitled to recover any costs, even for the work already done (*b*). So, a solicitor cannot recover his costs for conducting a suit, unless he has given the client the benefit of his personal judgment and superintendence (*c*). So, where a solicitor and confidential agent neglected to keep regular and proper accounts, he was deprived of his costs and charges (*d*).

(*x*) *Toppin* v. *Healey*, 1863, 11 W. R. 466.

(*y*) *Campanari* v. *Woodburn*, 1854, 15 C. B. 400; 3 C. L. R. 140; 24 L. J. C. P. 13.

(*z*) *Marsh* v. *Jelf*, 1862, 3 F. & F. 234.

(*a*) *Salomans* v. *Pender*, 1865, 3 H. & C. 639; 34 L. J. Ex. 95; 11 Jur. N. S. 432; 12 L. T. 267; 13 W. R. 637.

(*b*) *Whitehead* v. *Lord*, 1852, 7 Ex. 691; 21 L. J. Ex. 239; *Nicholls* v. *Wilson*, 1843, 2 D. N. S. 1031; 11 M. & W. 106; 12 L. J. Ex. 266; *Van Sandau* v. *Brown*, 1832, 9 Bing. 402; 2 M. & Scott, 543, 1 D. P. C. 715; *Underwood* v. *Lewis*, (1894) 2 Q. B. 306, 9 R. 440; 64 L. J. Q. B. 60; 70 L. T. 833, C. A.

(*c*) *Hopkinson* v. *Smith*, 1822, 1 Bing. 13.

(*d*) *White* v. *Lincoln*, 1803, 8 Ves. 363; 7 R. R. 71.

6. A broker is employed to negotiate a contract for the hire of a vessel. The contract goes off in consequence of his negligence or default. He is not entitled to recover any remuneration, or even the expenses incurred by him (*e*). If an agent performs his duties in so slovenly a manner that no benefit results from his services, he is not entitled to any remuneration whatever (*f*).

7. An auctioneer, who was employed to sell an estate, negligently omitted to insert in the conditions a certain proviso usually inserted therein, and in consequence of the omission the sale was rendered nugatory. Held, that he was not entitled to any compensation or remuneration for his services, although the particulars of the sale had been submitted to the principal, and were not objected to by him. It is the duty of every agent to exercise such skill and care as is usually exercised by similar agents (*g*).

8. A solicitor, who was retained to prosecute an appeal, neglected to see that the appeal was duly entered, and failed to give notice thereof, as required by statute. At the subsequent sessions the justices refused to entertain the appeal. Held, that the solicitor was not entitled to recover any costs (*h*). So, if a solicitor, in conducting a suit, commits a negligent act whereby all the previous steps become useless in the result, he cannot recover costs for any part of the work done (*i*); and, generally, in the taxation of costs as between solicitor and client, the taxing master ought to disallow any costs occasioned by the negligence or ignorance of the solicitor (*j*).

(*e*) *Dalton* v. *Irwin*, 1830, 4 C. & P. 289.

(*f*) *Hamond* v. *Holiday*, 1824, 1 C. & P. 384.

(*g*) *Denew* v. *Deverell*, 1813, 3 Camp. 451.

(*h*) *Huntley* v. *Bulwer*, 1839, 8 Scott, 325, 6 Bing. N. C. 111; 3 Jur. 1105.

(*i*) *Bracey* v. *Carter*, 1840, 12 Ad. & E. 373. See, also, *Stokes* v. *Trumper*, 1855, 2 Kay & J. 232, 2 W. R. 503, 615; *Cox* v. *Leech*, 1857, 1 C. B. N. S. 617; 26 L. J. C. P. 125, 3 Jur. N. S. 442.

(*j*) *Re Massey and Carey*, 1884, 26 Ch. Div. 459, 53 L. J. Ch. 705; 51 L. T. 390, 32 W. R. 1008, C. A.; *Shaw* v. *Arden*, 1832, 9 Bing. 287; 2 M. & Scott, 341; 1 D. P. C. 705.

Sect. 2.—*Rights of Reimbursement and Indemnity.*

Article 67.

INDEMNITY FROM ALL LIABILITIES, AND REIMBURSEMENT OF ALL EXPENSES, INCURRED IN COURSE OF AGENCY.

Subject to the provisions of Articles 68 and 69, every agent has a right against his principal, founded upon an implied contract, to be indemnified against all losses and liabilities, and to be reimbursed all expenses, incurred by him in the execution of his authority (*k*); and where the agent is sued for money due to his principal, he has a right to set off the amount of any such losses, liabilities, or expenses (*l*).

Illustrations.

1. A. employs B. to find a purchaser for certain bark. C. agrees with B. to purchase the bark, subject to its turning out equal to sample. B., being offered a *del credere* commission by A., accepts A.'s draft for the price of the bark, and in due course pays the amount of the draft. C. then refuses the bark as not being equal to sample. B. is entitled to recover from A. the amount of the draft paid by him (*m*).

2. A. instructs B., a stockbroker, to buy and sell various shares and stock, intending to receive or pay the differences. B.

(*k*) Illustrations 1 to 9. *Thacker* v. *Hardy*, 1878, 4 Q. B. D. 685; 48 L. J. Q. B. 289; 39 L. T. 595, 27 W. R. 158, C. A., *Toplis* v. *Grane*, 1839, 5 Bing. N. C. 636; 7 Scott, 620; *Campbell* v. *Larkworthy*, 1894, 9 T. L. R. 528, C. A.; *Graham* v. *Ackroyd*, 1852, 10 Hare, 192; 22 L. J. Ch. 1046. And see Article 68, and Illustrations thereto. See, however, *Farebrother* v. *Ansley*, 1808, 1 Camp. 342.

(*l*) Illustrations 8 and 9.

(*m*) *Hooper* v. *Treffrey*, 1847, 1 Ex. 17; 16 L. J. Ex. 233.

is entitled to recover the amount of any losses paid by him in respect of such shares or stock, although he does not make separate contracts on behalf of A., but appropriates to him portions of larger amounts of shares and stock, which he buys as principal with a view of dividing it amongst various clients for whom he is acting (*n*).

3. A. purchases shares as a broker, not being duly licensed to act as a broker. He is entitled to recover from the principal the price of the shares, which he has been compelled to pay, such payment not being an essential part of the duty of a broker, although, in consequence of not being licensed, he cannot recover any commission or remuneration (*o*).

4. A stockbroker incurs liabilities on the Stock Exchange on behalf of his principal. The stockbroker subsequently pays a composition on the amount of his debts (including such liabilities), and by a rule of the Stock Exchange he cannot be sued for the balance of such debts without the permission of the committee. The principal is bound to indemnify him to the full extent of the liabilities incurred on his behalf. The implied contract to indemnify an agent extends to all liabilities incurred by him, not merely to actual losses (*p*).

5. An auctioneer is instructed to sell certain property, and after he has contracted liabilities in reference to his employment, his authority is revoked by the principal. The principal must indemnify him against the liabilities (*q*).

6. An agent incurs damages and expenses in defending an action on behalf of his principal. He is entitled to reimburse-

(*n*) *Ex p. Rogers, re Rogers*, 1880, 15 Ch. Div. 207, 43 L. T. 163, 29 W. R. 29, C. A., distinguishing *Robinson* v. *Mollett*, 1874, L. R. 7 H. L. 802, H. L. This is, however, subject to provisions of the Gaming Act, 1892, where the transactions are of a gambling nature. See Article 69.

(*o*) *Smith* v. *Lindo*, 1858, 5 C. B. N. S. 587, 27 L. J. C. P. 335; 4 Jur. N. S. 974, Ex. Ch.

(*p*) *Lacey* v. *Hill, Crawley's claim*, 1870, L. R. 18 Eq. 182; 43 L. J. Ch. 551; 30 L. T. 484, 22 W. R. 586.

(*q*) *Warlow* v. *Harrison*, 1858, 1 El. & El. 309, 29 L. J. Q. B. 14, 6 Jur. N. S. 66, Ex. Ch.

ment of such damages and expenses if he was acting within the scope of his authority in defending the action, and the loss was not caused by his own default (*r*).

7. An accommodation bill is drawn and accepted for the purpose of raising money for the benefit of the drawer and acceptor. The drawer instructs a bill broker to get the bill discounted. It is the common practice for bill brokers to give a general guarantee to the bankers who discount their bills, and not to indorse each bill discounted on behalf of their customers. The bill is dishonoured, and the broker becomes liable to the bankers upon such a guarantee. The broker is entitled to recover from the acceptor the amount that he is compelled to pay in pursuance of such guarantee, with interest, it being a liability incurred in the execution of his authority in the ordinary course of his business as a bill broker (*s*).

8. A broker, in accordance with a reasonable custom of the particular market in which he was employed, rendered himself personally responsible for the price of goods bought on behalf of his principal, and subsequently duly paid for the goods. Held, that he was entitled to set off the amount so paid, in an action by the principal's trustee in bankruptcy for money due to the principal (*t*).

9. An agent, who had general authority to receive and sell goods on behalf of the principal, in good faith brought an action against a third person who wrongfully withheld possession of the goods. In an action by the principal for the proceeds of the goods it was held that the agent was entitled to set off the amount of the costs incurred by him in the proceedings to recover the goods (*u*).

(*r*) *Frixione* v. *Tagliaferro*, 1855, 10 Moo. P. C. C. 175; 4 W. R. 373, P. C. See Article 69.

(*s*) *Ex p. Bishop, re Fox*, 1880, 15 Ch. Div. 400; 50 L. J. Ch. 18; 43 L. T. 165, 29 W. R. 144, C. A.

(*t*) *Cropper* v. *Cook*, 1868, L. R. 3 C. P. 199; 16 W. R. 596. See also *Lee* v. *Bullen*, 1858, 27 L. J. Q. B. 161; 4 Jur. N. S. 557.

(*u*) *Curtis* v. *Barclay*, 1826, 7 D. & R. 539; 5 B. & C. 141.

Article 68.

LIABILITIES INCURRED UNDER RULES OR USAGES OF PARTICULAR MARKETS.

Where an agent is authorized to deal in a particular market, he is entitled to be indemnified by the principal against all liabilities, and to be reimbursed all expenses, incurred by him in the execution of his authority under the rules or regulations, or according to the customs or usages of that market (*v*). Provided that, where the rules or regulations, or customs or usages are unreasonable, the principal is not bound by them unless he was aware of their existence at the time that he conferred the authority (*w*).

Illustrations.

1. A. authorized B., a broker in Liverpool, to sell certain shares. B. sold the shares to C., who was also a broker. A. failed to deliver the shares, and B. therefore bought some on the market and completed the contract with C. By the usage of Liverpool, of which A. had knowledge, it was customary for brokers to render themselves personally liable when contracting

---

(*v*) Illustrations 1 to 10. *Paxton* v. *Courtnay*, 1860, 2 F. & F. 131; *Kirchner* v. *Venus*, 1858, 12 Moo. P. C. C. 361, 5 Jur. N. S. 395; 7 W. R. 455, P. C.; *Sentance* v. *Hawley*, 1863, 13 C. B. N. S. 458, 7 L. T. 745, *Harker* v. *Edwards*, 1887, 57 L. J. Q. B. 147, C. A.; *Smith* v. *Reynolds*, 1892, 66 L. T. 808, 8 T. L. R. 137, 391, C. A.; *Martin* v. *Gibbon*, 1875, 33 L. T. 561; 24 W. R. 87, C. A.; *Sutton* v. *Tatham*, 1839, 10 Ad. & E. 27, *Reynolds* v. *Smith*, 9 T. L. R. 494, H. L.

(*w*) Illustrations 9 and 10. *Blackburn* v. *Mason*, 1893, 9 T. L. R. 286, 68 L. T. 510; 4 R. 297, C. A.

with each other. Held, that A. was liable to B. for the loss incurred by him in completing the contract (*x*).

Usages of the Stock Exchange.

2. A. employs B., a stockbroker, to purchase shares on the Stock Exchange. B. purchases the shares, and is compelled to refund to the seller the amount of a "call" which the latter had to pay in order to enable him to transfer the shares. A. must indemnify B. (*y*).

3. A. employs B., a stockbroker, to purchase, for the next settling day, shares in a certain bank. Before the settling day the bank stops payment and goes into liquidation. A. gives notice to B. not to pay for the shares. B. nevertheless pays for them, in accordance with the rules of the Stock Exchange. A. must indemnify B. even if the directors of the bank refuse to consent to a transfer of the shares (*z*).

4. A. employs B., a stockbroker, to purchase shares in a certain company. On settling day A. gives B. the name of an infant transferee, to whom the shares are transferred. The company is subsequently wound up, and the name of the infant is struck out and that of the transferor substituted as a contributory. The Stock Exchange committee order B. to indemnify the transferor, and B. does so. A. must indemnify B. (*a*).

5. A. employs B., a stockbroker, to buy, for next settling day, shares in a certain company. Before the settling day the company is being wound up under a statute which provides that every transfer of shares after the commencement of the winding up shall be void unless the Court otherwise orders. B. pays for and takes a transfer of the shares on settling day, in

---

(*x*) *Bayliffe* v. *Butterworth*, 1847, 1 Ex. 425. And see *Pollock* v. *Stables*, 1848, 12 Q. B. 765; 5 Railw. Cas. 352; 17 L. J. Q. B. 352.

(*y*) *Bayley* v. *Wilkins*, 1849, 7 C. B. 886; 18 L. J. C. P. 273.

(*z*) *Taylor* v. *Stray*, 1857, 2 C. B. N. S. 175, 197; 3 Jur. N. S. 540, 964; 26 L. J. C. P. 287, Ex. Ch.

(*a*) *Peppercorne* v. *Clench*, 1872, 26 L. T. 656.

accordance with the rules of the Stock Exchange. A. must indemnify B. (*b*).

6. A. employs B., a stockbroker, to purchase shares. B. purchases the shares, but the transfer, in consequence of the winding up of the company, cannot be registered. B. is compelled to indemnify the seller against "calls," according to the rules of the Stock Exchange. A. must indemnify B. (*c*).

7. A. employs B., a stockbroker, to sell certain bonds. B. sells the bonds, and pays over the proceeds to A. The bonds are subsequently discovered to be unmarketable, and B., in accordance with the rules of the Stock Exchange, takes them back and repays the price to the purchaser. A. must repay the price to B. (*d*).

8. By the usage of the Stock Exchange, a broker who contracts, as such, to buy stock is justified in immediately reselling the stock in the event of the death, bankruptcy, or insolvency of the principal. A broker who so acts in such a case is entitled to recover from the principal or his representatives the amount of any loss incurred on the resale (*e*).

9. A. employs B., a stockbroker, to purchase shares in a joint stock banking company. B. purchases the shares and sends a contract note to A., in which the numbers of the shares are not inserted as required by Leeman's Act (30 Vict. c. 29), the contract, therefore, being void in law. Before the settling day, A. repudiates the contract. B. nevertheless duly completes the contract, and pays for the shares, to avoid being declared a defaulter and expelled from the Exchange, it being the usual custom for members of the Stock Exchange to ignore Leeman's Act. If A. was aware of the custom when he employed B., he

---

(*b*) *Chapman* v. *Shepherd*, 1867, L. R. 2 C. P. 228; 36 L. J. C. P. 113, 15 L. T. 477; 15 W. R. 314.

(*c*) *Hodgkinson* v. *Kelly*, 1868, 37 L. J. Ch. 837, L. R. 6 Eq. 496.

(*d*) *Young* v. *Cole*, 1837, 3 Bing. N. C. 724; 4 Scott, 489, 3 Hodges, 126.

(*e*) *Lacey* v. *Hill*, *Crawley's claim*, 1870, L. R. 18 Eq. 182; 43 L. J. Ch. 551, 30 L. T. 484, 22 W. R. 586; *Scrimgeour's claim*, 1870, L. R. 8 Ch. 921; 42 L. J. Ch. 657, Ch. App.

must indemnify B. (*f*). But if A. had no knowledge of the custom, and was not aware that, by the rules of the Exchange, B. was bound to complete such a contract, though it was void in law (*g*), or if he knew neither of Leeman's Act nor of the custom (*h*), he is not bound to indemnify B., because the custom is an unreasonable one.

10. A. instructs B., his broker, to carry over certain stock to the next settlement, but fails, after receiving due notice of the amount, to pay on the current pay day the balance due for differences, or to place sufficient security at B.'s disposal. By the usage of the Stock Exchange, a broker may in such a case close the principal's account. B. closes A.'s account, according to usage, and sues him for the losses. The usage is reasonable, and A. must indemnify B., whether the usage was known to him or not (*i*).

Article 69.

NO INDEMNITY OR REIMBURSEMENT IN RESPECT OF ILLEGAL, WAGERING, OR UNAUTHORIZED TRANSACTIONS, OR OF LIABILITIES OR EXPENSES INCURRED IN CONSEQUENCE OF OWN DEFAULT.

No agent is entitled to indemnity against any losses or liabilities, or reimbursement of any expenses incurred by him—

(a) in respect of any transaction obviously, or to his knowledge, illegal (*j*);

(*f*) *Seymour* v. *Bridge*, 1885, 14 Q. B. D. 460; 54 L. J. Q. B. 347.

(*g*) *Perry* v. *Barnett*, 1885, 15 Q. B. D. 388; 54 L. J. Q. B. 466; 53 L. T. 585; 34 W. R. 154, C. A.

(*h*) *Coates* v. *Pacey*, 1892, 8 T. L. R. 474, C. A.

(*i*) *Davis* v. *Howard*, 1890, 24 Q. B. D. 691; 59 L. J. Q. B. 133; *Druce* v. *Levy*, 1891, 7 T. L. R. 259.

(*j*) Illustrations 1 to 4.

(b) in respect of any gaming or wagering transaction (*k*);

(c) in respect of anything done by him without the express or implied authority of the principal (*l*);

(d) in consequence of his own obviously illegal act (*m*); or

(e) in consequence of his own negligence, default, insolvency, or breach of duty (*n*).

Illustrations.

1. An agent expends money on behalf of his principal in purchasing shares in a company which affects to act as a body corporate without authority by charter or statute, and which is, therefore, an illegal company. The agent is not entitled to recover from the principal the amount so expended, because the transaction is obviously illegal (*o*).

2. A broker effects an illegal insurance on behalf of his principal, and pays the premium thereon. The broker is not entitled to recover from the principal the amount of the premiums, or any other payments made by him in respect of such insurance (*p*).

(*k*) 55 Vict. c. 9. Illustration 5.

(*l*) Illustrations 6 to 9. *Johnston* v. *Usborne*, 1840, 3 P. & D. 236; 11 A. & E. 549, 1 Jur. 943; *Frixione* v. *Tagliaferro*, 1855, 10 Moo. P. C. C. 175; 4 W. R. 373, P. C.; *Coates* v. *Pacey*, 1892, 8 T. L. R. 474, C. A.; *Service* v. *Bain*, 1893, 9 T. L. R. 95.

(*m*) Illustrations 1 to 4. *Thacker* v. *Hardy*, 1878, 4 Q. B. D. 685; 48 L. J. Q. B. 289, 39 L. T. 595; 27 W. R. 158, C. A.

(*n*) Illustrations 10 to 12. *Toplis* v. *Grane*, 1839, 5 Bing. N. C. 636, 7 Scott, 620; *Simpson* v. *Swan*, 1812, 3 Camp. 291, 13 R. R. 805, *Frixione* v. *Tagliaferro*, 1855, 10 Moo. P. C. C. 175, 4 W. R. 373, P. C.

(*o*) *Josephs* v. *Pebrer*, 1825, 3 B. & C. 639; 1 C. & P. 341.

(*p*) *Allkins* v. *Jupe*, 1877, 2 C. P. D. 375, 46 L. J. C. P. 824; 36 L. T. 851; *Ex p. Mather*, 1797, 3 Ves. 373.

3. A. employs B. to purchase smuggled goods. B. purchases the goods and pays for them. B. cannot recover the price from A., even if A. obtains possession of the goods (*q*).

4. A. instructs B., an auctioneer, to sell certain goods of which A. has no right to dispose, B. having no knowledge of any defect in A.'s title. B. sells the goods, and duly pays over the proceeds to A. B. is afterwards compelled to pay to the true owner the value of the goods. A. must indemnify B., the transaction not being obviously, or to B.'s knowledge, illegal (*r*). The rule that a tortfeasor cannot recover upon either an express or implied promise of indemnity by the person at whose request or on whose behalf the tort is committed, is confined to cases where the tortious act is obviously illegal, and does not apply when there is a *bonâ fide* doubt about the matter (*s*).

5. The Gaming Act, 1892 (55 Vict. c. 9), provides that any contract, express or implied, to pay any person any sum paid by him under or in respect of any contract or agreement rendered null and void by 8 & 9 Vict. c. 109, shall be null and void, and no action shall be brought or maintained to recover any such sum. Gaming and wagering contracts are not illegal, but merely void, and prior to the Act of 1892 it was held that money paid by an agent in pursuance of such a contract was recoverable from the principal, even if he had repudiated the transaction before the money was actually paid, the agent being entitled to be indemnified against the moral liability incurred by him in executing his authority (*t*). So, it was held that a plea of "gaming and wagering" was no answer to an action by a stockbroker for differences paid on his client's behalf (*u*). In

(*q*) *Ex p. Mather*, 1797, 3 Ves. 373.

(*r*) *Adamson* v. *Jarvis*, 1827, 4 Bing. 66; 12 Moo. 241.

(*s*) *Betts* v. *Gibbins*, 1834, 2 Ad. & El. 57; 4 N. & M. 64.

(*t*) *Read* v. *Anderson*, 1884, 13 Q. B. D. 779, 53 L. J. Q. B. 532; 51 L. T. 55, 32 W. R. 950, C. A. (bets paid by a turf commission agent). The Act is not retrospective. *Knight* v. *Lee*, (1893) 1 Q. B. 41, 62 L. J. Q. B. 28, 67 L. T. 688, 41 W. R. 125.

(*u*) See *Thacker* v. *Hardy*, 1878, 4 Q. B. D. 685, 48 L. J. Q. B. 289;

the case of Stock Exchange speculations, it is a question of fact for the jury whether particular transactions are gaming and wagering contracts or not.

6. A. authorizes B., a broker, to effect an insurance policy. After the underwriters have signed the slip, but before a binding contract is made, A. revokes B.'s authority. B., nevertheless, effects the policy, and pays the premiums. B. cannot recover the premiums from A., having acted without authority. (The contract does not become binding until the policy is subscribed by the underwriters) (*v*).

7. A. authorizes B. and C. to insure his life in their names. They insure in the names of B., C., and D., and pay the premiums. They are not entitled to recover the amount of the premiums from A., not having strictly pursued their authority (*w*).

8. A., a broker, contracted on behalf of B. to sell certain shares to C. In consequence of the non-delivery of the shares, C. bought against B., without having tendered a transfer to him, and A. paid C. the difference, although B. had given him express notice not to do so. Held, that C. could not have recovered the difference until a transfer had been tendered by him, and that as A. had paid the amount without B.'s authority, he was not entitled to indemnity from B. Otherwise, if the payment had been made in discharge of a liability incurred by A. (*x*).

9. A. draws a cheque on his banker. The amount of the cheque is altered without A.'s authority, and the banker, in good faith, pays the increased amount. The banker is only entitled to charge A. with the amount for which the cheque was originally drawn, unless it was drawn so negligently as to facili-

---

39 L. T. 595; 27 W. R. 158, C. A.; *Rosewarne* v. *Billing*, 1863, 15 C. B. N. S. 316, 33 L. J. C. P. 55, 10 Jur. N. S. 496, 9 L. T. 441.

(*v*) *Warwick* v. *Slade*, 1811, 3 Camp. 127; 13 R. R. 772. See *Service* v. *Bain*, 1893, 9 T. L. R. 95, C. A.

(*w*) *Barron* v. *Fitzgerald*, 1840, 6 Bing. N. C. 201.

(*x*) *Bowlby* v. *Bell*, 1846, 3 C. B. 284, 16 L. J. C. P. 18.

tate the alteration, in which case A. would not be permitted to deny that he authorized the alteration (*y*).

10. A solicitor undertook a prosecution for perjury, and agreed that he would only charge out of pocket expenses. The prosecution failed in consequence of the negligent way in which the indictment was drawn. Held, that the solicitor was not entitled to recover the disbursements (*z*). So, an agent is not entitled to be indemnified against a loss incurred by him in consequence of his own mistake on a point of law as to which he ought to have been competent (*a*).

11. A stockbroker is instructed by his principal to carry over stock to the next settlement. Before the next settling day the broker becomes insolvent and is declared a defaulter, in consequence of which the stock is sold at a loss. The principal is not bound to indemnify the broker, the loss having been caused by the broker's insolvency (*b*).

12. A broker is instructed to buy shares, and becomes a defaulter before settling day. He informs his principal that he may have the contract completed (the jobber is bound to complete in such a case if the principal wishes it), or may consider it closed at the official price at the time of the broker's default. The principal elects the latter alternative. He is bound to indemnify the broker against the loss, having ratified the closing of the transaction before settling day (*c*).

(*y*) *Hall* v. *Fuller*, 1826, 5 B. & C. 750; *Young* v. *Grote*, 1827, 4 Bing. 253; 12 Moo. 484.

(*z*) *Lewis* v. *Samuel*, 1846, 8 Q. B. 685; 15 L. J. Q. B. 218; 10 Jur. 429.

(*a*) *Capp* v. *Topham*, 1805, 6 East, 392; 2 Smith, 443.

(*b*) *Duncan* v. *Hill*, *Duncan* v. *Beeson*, 1873, L. R. 8 Ex. 242, 42 L. J. Ex. 179, 29 L. T. 268; 21 W. R. 797, Ex. Ch.

(*c*) *Hartas* v. *Ribbons*, 1889, 22 Q. B. D. 254, C. A.

Sect. 3.—*Right of Lien.*

Article 70.

DEFINITIONS OF PARTICULAR AND GENERAL POSSESSORY LIENS.

A possessory lien is a right of a person who has possession of goods or chattels belonging to another, to retain possession thereof until the satisfaction of some debt or obligation by the owner of the goods or chattels.

Where the right is to retain possession in respect of a general balance of account, or until the satisfaction of debts or obligations incurred independently of the goods or chattels subject to the right, it is called a general lien.

Where the right is confined to debts and obligations incurred in respect of the goods or chattels subject to the right, it is called a particular lien.

Article 71.

POSSESSORY LIEN OF AGENTS.

Every agent has a general or particular possessory lien on the goods and chattels of his principal, for what is due to him as such agent (*d*), provided—

(1) that the possession of the goods or chattels

(*d*) Illustrations 1 to 7. *Williams* v. *Millington*, 1788, 1 H. Bl. 81 2 R. R. 724; *M'Gillivray* v. *Simpson*, 1826, 9 D. & R. 35; 2 C. & P. 320 *Pulteney* v. *Keymer*, 1800, 3 Esp. 182.

was obtained by him lawfully (*e*), and in the same capacity in which he claims the lien (*f*);

(2) that there is no express agreement inconsistent with the existence of the lien (*g*); and

(3) that the goods or chattels were not delivered to him with express directions, or for a special purpose, inconsistent with the existence of the lien (*h*).

The possessory lien of every agent is a particular lien only, except where there is an express agreement for a general lien, or a course of dealing or special custom from which such an agreement may be implied (*i*). Factors (*j*), insurance (*k*) and other brokers (*l*), solicitors (*m*), bankers (*n*), wharfingers (*o*), and

(*e*) Illustration 8.

(*f*) Illustrations 7, 9, 14 and 15.

(*g*) Illustration 11. *Cowell* v. *Simpson*, 1809, 16 Ves. 280; 10 R. R. 181; *Bock* v. *Gorrisson*, 1861, 30 L. J. Ch. 39, 3 L. T. N. S. 424; 7 Jur. N. S. 81; 9 W. R. 209, 2 De G. F. & J. 434.

(*h*) Illustrations 12 to 16.

(*i*) *Bock* v. *Gorrisson*, 1861, 30 L. J. Ch. 39; 3 L. T. N. S. 424, 7 Jur. N. S. 81, 9 W. R. 209, 2 De G. F. & J. 434, *Walker* v. *Birch*, 6 T. R. 258.

(*j*) *Baring* v. *Corrie*, 1818, 2 B. & A. 137, 20 R. R. 383; *Godin* v. *London Assurance Co.*, 1758, 1 W. Bl. 103. And see Illustrations 4, 7, 9, and 11.

(*k*) *Snook* v. *Davidson*, 1809, 2 Camp. 218, 11 R. R. 696, *Mann* v. *Forrester*, 1814, 4 Camp. 60, 15 R. R. 724; *Westwood* v. *Bell*, 1815, 4 Camp. 349; 16 R. R. 800.

(*l*) *Jones* v. *Peppercorne*, 1858, Johns. 430; 5 Jur. N. S. 140; 28 L. J. Ch. 158.

(*m*) *Re Broomhead*, 1847, 5 D. & L. 52; 16 L. J. Q. B. 355. Illustrations 9, 10, and 16.

(*n*) *Chartered Bank of Australia* v. *White*, 1879, 4 App. Cas. 413; 48 L. J. P. C. 75, P. C.; *Brandeo* v. *Barnett*, 1846, 12 C. & F. 787; 3 C. B. 519, H. L., *Jourdaine* v. *Lefevre*, 1793, 1 Esp. 66, *Scott* v. *Franklin*, 1812, 15 East, 428; *Misa* v. *Currie*, 1876, 1 App. Cas. 554, 45 L. J. Ex. 852, 35 L. T. 414, H. L. And see Illustrations 9, 11, 12, and 15.

(*o*) *Naylor* v. *Mangles*, 1794, 1 Esp. 109; 5 R. R. 722, *Spears* v. *Hartley*, 1798, 3 Esp. 81; 6 R. R. 814.

packers (*p*), have a general lien by implication from custom.

Illustrations.

1. A. carries on a business in his own name as agent for B. B. becomes bankrupt. A. is liable to the creditors of the business by reason of his having carried it on in his own name. A. has a lien upon the goods in his possession belonging to B. to the extent of such liability (*q*).

2. A. carries on a business in his own name as agent for B., and deals with the possession of the goods of such business as if he were the owner thereof. A. accepts certain bills of exchange drawn by B. Both A. and B. become bankrupt. A.'s trustee in bankruptcy has a lien upon the goods in A.'s possession to the extent of A.'s liability upon current bills as well as for any other amounts due to him from B. (*r*).

3. *Property must be in agent's possession.*—A. bought goods as a factor for and on behalf of B., and it was agreed that the goods should remain upon the premises of the seller at a rent to be paid by B. After a time A. was requested by the seller to remove the goods, but did not do so. Subsequently, without B.'s authority or instructions, A. removed the goods to his own premises, and at about the same time a petition in bankruptcy was presented against B. Held, that the possession of the goods continued in B., and that A. had therefore no lien upon them (*s*). So, where a factor accepted bills upon the faith of a consignment of goods, and both he and the principal became bankrupt before the arrival of the cargo, it was held that the factor's trustee in bankruptcy had no lien upon the cargo, and therefore no claim against the principal's trustee, who had sold the cargo and received the price, because the goods had never

(*p*) *In re Witt*, 1876, 2 Ch. Div. 489, 45 L. J. Bk. 118, 34 L. T. 785, C. A.

(*q*) *Foxcroft* v. *Wood*, 1828, 4 Russ. 487.

(*r*) *In re Fawcus, Ex p. Buck*, 1876, 3 Ch. Div. 795; 34 L. T. 807.

(*s*) *Taylor* v. *Robinson*, 1818, 2 Moo. 730.

been in the factor's possession (*t*). Constructive possession of goods by the agent is, however, sufficient for the purpose of establishing his lien thereon (*u*).

4. A factor accepts bills of exchange on the faith of a consignment of goods, which are duly delivered to and sold by him. The principal dies during the currency of some of the bills. The factor has a lien upon the proceeds of the goods for the amount of the bills not yet due, as well as for the amount of those which he has paid (*v*). So, a factor who becomes a surety for his principal has a lien upon the proceeds of goods sold by him for the amount guaranteed (*w*).

5. An agent was appointed by a company to sell goods on their behalf in a shop taken for that purpose, and it was agreed that he should from time to time accept bills representing the value of the goods in his hands for sale. Goods were consigned to the agent, and he accepted a bill for their value. Before the bill became due the company was wound up, and the liquidators took possession of and sold the goods. Held, that the agent, having paid the bill, had a lien upon the goods for the amount, and was entitled to be repaid out of the proceeds thereof in preference to the other creditors of the company (*x*).

6. *Goods in the order and disposition of the principal.*—A. was appointed by a Glasgow firm to manage a warehouse in London, and it was expressly agreed that he should have a lien upon the goods stored in the warehouse. The business was carried on and the goods were stored in the name of the firm, which became bankrupt. Held, that the goods were in the order and disposition of the firm, and that, in consequence of the "order and disposition" clause of the Bankruptcy Acts, A.'s lien was not

---

(*t*) *Kinloch* v. *Craig*, 1790, 3 T. R. 119, 783; 4 Bro. P. C. 47, 1 R. R. 664, H. L.

(*u*) See *Bryans* v. *Nix*, 1839, 4 M. & W. 775; 1 H. & H. 480.

(*v*) *Hammond* v. *Barclay*, 1802, 2 East, 227.

(*w*) *Drinkwater* v. *Goodwin*, 1775, Cowp. 251.

(*x*) *In re Pavy's Patent Felted Fabric Co.*, 1876, 1 Ch. Div. 631; 45 L. J. Ch. 318; 24 W. R. 507.

effective, though he had physical possession and control of the goods (*y*).

7. *Debt or obligation must be incurred in course of the agency.*—A., a factor, sold goods in his own name on B.'s behalf to C. C. subsequently sent goods to A. for sale, never having employed him as a factor before. C. became bankrupt. Held, that A. had no lien upon C.'s goods for the price of the goods sold by him on B.'s behalf. The lien of an agent is confined to what is due to him as such agent, and does not extend to a debt incurred before the commencement of the agency (*z*). So, the general lien of a solicitor is confined to claims made by him in that capacity (*a*).

8. *The property must be obtained lawfully.*—A lien cannot be acquired by a tort or wrongful act. Thus, if an agent obtains goods from his principal by misrepresentations, he has no lien thereon, though the circumstances in other respects be such that he would have had a lien if the goods had been obtained lawfully (*b*). So, where an agent, who was employed by a ship's husband, made the freight payable to himself without authority to do so, it was held that he had no lien upon the freight received by him, for a debt due from the principal (*c*).

9. *The property must be acquired in the same capacity as that in which the lien is claimed.*—A factor insures a ship on his principal's behalf, the transaction being quite distinct and separate from his duties as factor. His general lien does not extend to the policy of insurance, because he did not acquire it in the capacity of factor (*d*). So, if a policy is left merely for safe custody in

---

(*y*) *Hoggard* v. *Mackenzie*, 1858, 25 Beav. 493, 4 Jur. N. S. 1008. See Bankruptcy Act, 1883, s. 44.

(*z*) *Houghton* v. *Matthews*, 1803, 3 B. & P. 485, 7 R. R. 815.

(*a*) *In re Galland*, 1885, 31 Ch. Div. 296, 55 L. J. Ch. 478, 53 L. T. 921; 34 W. R. 158, C. A.

(*b*) *Madden* v. *Kempster*, 1807, 1 Camp. 12.

(*c*) *Walshe* v. *Provan*, 1853, 1 C. L. R. 823, 8 Ex. 843; 22 L. J. Ex. 355.

(*d*) *Dixon* v. *Stansfield*, 1850, 10 C. B. 398.

an agent's hands, he has no general lien thereon for advances (*e*). So, the general lien of a solicitor does not extend to an original will left in his hands by the client (*f*). A banker's lien for the general balance due to him is confined to property deposited with him in the capacity of a banker, and does not extend, *e. g.*, to boxes of securities left with him merely for safe custody (*g*). But it extends to all bills, cheques, and money paid into the bank, and to all documents and securities deposited with him as a banker (*g*).

10. *Solicitor's general lien.*—Every solicitor has a lien, for his general bill of costs, upon all documents and chattels belonging to his client of which he obtains possession in his capacity of solicitor, and the Courts will not interfere with this general lien by ordering him to deliver up papers deposited with him for the purposes of a particular suit, upon payment of the costs in that suit, even if the possession of the papers is necessary to enable the client to go on with the proceedings (*h*).

11. *Must be no agreement inconsistent with the lien.*—A life policy was deposited at a bank, with a memorandum charging it with overdrafts not exceeding a specified amount. Held, that the banker's general lien was excluded by the special contract, such contract being inconsistent with the existence of a general lien on the policy (*i*). So, if a factor expressly agrees to deal in a particular way with the proceeds of goods deposited with him for sale, his general lien is thereby excluded (*k*). But the lien is not excluded unless it appears that the express contract is clearly inconsistent with its existence (*l*). Thus, where certain

---

(*e*) *Muir* v. *Fleming*, D. & R. N. P. C. 29.

(*f*) *Balch* v. *Symes*, 1 Turn. & R. 87, *Georges* v. *Georges*, 1811, 18 Ves. 294.

(*g*) *Misa* v. *Currie*, 1876, 1 App. Cas. 554, 45 L. J. Ex. 852; 35 L. T. 414, H. L.; *London Chartered Bank of Australia* v. *White*, 1879, 4 App. Cas. 413; 48 L. J. P. C. 75, P. C., *Scott* v. *Franklin*, 1812, 15 East, 428.

(*h*) *In re Broomhead*, 1847, 5 D. & L. 52, 16 L. J. Q. B. 355.

(*i*) *In re Bowes*, *Strathmore* v. *Vane*, 1886, 33 Ch. Div. 586; 56 L. J. Ch. 143; 55 L. T. 260; 35 W. R. 166.

(*k*) *Walker* v. *Birch*, 6 T. R. 258.

(*l*) *Brandeo* v. *Barnett*, 1846, 12 C. & F. 787; 3 C. B. 519, H. L.

securities were deposited with brokers for a specific loan, and they were given a power of sale, it was held that their general lien extended to such securities (*m*). So, an agreement that there shall be monthly settlements does not affect the lien of an insurance broker for premiums, upon policies in his hands (*n*). So, the general lien of a factor is not excluded merely because he acts under special instructions to sell in his principal's name and at a particular price (*o*).

No lien on property intrusted to him for special purpose inconsistent therewith.

12. Certain exchequer bills were deposited at a bank, to be kept in a box under lock and key. The bills were subsequently intrusted to the banker, with instructions to obtain the interest on them, and get them exchanged for new bills, and to deposit the new bills in the box as before. Held, that the banker's lien did not attach either on the original bills or on those for which they were exchanged, the special purpose for which they were placed in his hands being inconsistent with the existence of a general lien (*p*).

13. A. consigned certain goods to B. for sale, and in sending B. the bill of lading told him that those goods would cover a bill of exchange that he had drawn in favour of C., and asked him to duly honour such bill. C. presented the bill to B., who refused to accept it. The cargo duly arrived, and A. became bankrupt. Held, that the cargo was appropriated to meet the bill, and that C. had a lien thereon for the amount in priority

---

(*m*) *Jones* v. *Peppercorne*, 1858, Johns. 430, 5 Jur. N. S. 140; 28 L. J. Ch. 158.

(*n*) *Fisher* v. *Smith*, 1878, 4 App. Cas. 1, 48 L. J. Ex. 411; 39 L. T. 430; 27 W. R. 113, H. L.

(*o*) *Stevens* v. *Biller*, 1883, 25 Ch. Div. 31, 53 L. J. Ch. 249, 50 L. T. 36; 32 W. R. 419, C. A.

(*p*) *Brandeo* v. *Barnett*, 1846, 12 C. & F. 787, 3 C. B. 519, H. L.

to B.'s general lien (*q*). Where an agent accepts goods with express directions to apply them or their proceeds in a particular way, he cannot set up his general lien in opposition to those directions (*q*). So, where A. sent bills to B. to be discounted, and the proceeds applied in a particular way, and B. did not discount them, but received the amounts thereof after A. had become bankrupt, it was held that A.'s trustee in bankruptcy was entitled to recover such amounts as money had and received to A.'s use, and that B. had no right to set off a debt due to him from A. (*r*).

14. A factor, who acted as such for the owners of a ship, asked the master to let him have the certificate of registry for the purpose of paying certain duties at the custom house. Held, that his general lien as factor did not attach on the certificate (*s*).

15. A deed, dealing with two distinct properties, was deposited at a bank, with a memorandum pledging one of the properties to secure a specific sum and also the general balance due to the banker. Held, that the banker had no lien upon the other property, the deed having been deposited with a specific intention inconsistent therewith (*t*). So, a banker has no lien upon muniments of title casually left at the bank after a refusal by him to advance money upon their security (*u*).

16. A solicitor received a sum of money from a client to pay off a certain mortgage, and then claimed to have a lien thereon for costs. He was summarily ordered to repay the amount to the client, on the ground that he had received it for a specific purpose inconsistent with such a lien (*v*). A solicitor's general

---

(*q*) *Frith* v. *Forbes*, 1862, 4 De G. F. & J. 409, 32 L. J. Ch. 10, 8 Jur. N. S. 1115.

(*r*) *Buchanan* v. *Findlay*, 1829, 9 B. & C. 738; 4 M. & R. 593.

(*s*) *Burn* v. *Brown*, 1817, 2 Stark. N. P. C. 272, 19 R. R. 719.

(*t*) *Wylde* v. *Radford*, 1864, 33 L. J. Ch. 51, 9 Jur. N. S. 1169; 9 L. T. 471; 12 W. R. 38.

(*u*) *Lucas* v. *Dorrien*, 1817, 7 Taunt. 278; 1 Moo. 29, 18 R. R. 480.

(*v*) *Re Callen*, 1859, 27 Beav. 51.

lien for costs, however, attaches on papers deposited with him for a particular purpose, unless it is excluded by express agreement, or is clearly inconsistent with such purpose (*w*). It also attaches upon deeds allowed to remain in his possession after the special purpose for which they were left with him has failed (*x*).

Article 72.

CONFINED TO RIGHTS OF PRINCIPAL, EXCEPT IN THE CASE OF MONEY OR NEGOTIABLE SECURITIES.

The possessory lien of an agent attaches only upon property in respect of which the principal has, as against third persons, the right or power to create the lien, and except in the case of money or negotiable securities, is necessarily confined to the rights of the principal in the property at the time the lien arises (*y*), but it is not affected by subsequent dealings by the principal with the property, or by his subsequent bankruptcy (*z*). Money and negotiable securities deposited with an agent by or in the name of the principal are subject to the general or particular lien of the agent, even if they are the property of third persons, and are so deposited in fraud of such third persons, provided that the agent has no notice at the

---

(*w*) *Colmer* v. *Ede*, 1870, 40 L. J. Ch. 185; 23 L. T. 884; 19 W. R. 318. See *Re Lawrance, Bowker* v. *Austin*, (1894) 1 Ch. 556, 8 R. 102; 63 L. J. Ch. 205.

(*x*) *Ex p. Pemberton*, 1810, 18 Ves. 282.

(*y*) Illustrations 1 to 3. And see *Att.-Gen.* v. *Trueman*, 1843, 11 M. & W. 694, 13 L. J. Ex. 70; *Att.-Gen.* v. *Walmsley*, 1843, 12 M. & W. 179, 13 L. J. Ex. 66.

(*z*) Illustration 4.

time of the receipt of the money or securities of any defect in the title of the principal thereto (*a*).

Illustrations.

1. *Books, &c., of companies.*—No solicitor or other agent can have a lien on the share register or minute book of a joint stock company, because the directors have no power to create any lien that could interfere with the use of such register or book for the purposes of the company (*b*). So, no lien can attach upon such books of a company as, under the articles of association or the Companies Acts, ought to be kept at the registered office of the company (*c*). So, where documents come into the hands of a solicitor pending the winding up of a company, he cannot claim any lien thereon that would interfere with the winding up (*b*).

2. *Trust funds.*—An agent is employed by trustees. He has no lien on the trust funds for his expenses (*d*).

3. *No lien in excess of principal's rights.*—Goods were consigned to a factor for sale, the principal having committed an act of bankruptcy. The factor advanced moneys to the principal, and subsequently sold and received the proceeds of the goods. Held, that he had no lien upon the goods for the advances, and that he must account for the proceeds to the trustee in bankruptcy, because the principal had no power after the act of bankruptcy to create any lien (*e*). So, the lien of a solicitor upon papers deposited with him by a client is confined to the rights of the client therein (*f*).

(*a*) Illustration 5.

(*b*) *Re Capital Fire Insurance Association, ex p. Beall*, 1883, 24 Ch. Div. 408; 53 L. J. Ch. 71; 49 L. T. 697; 32 W. R. 260, C. A.

(*c*) *Re Anglo-Maltese Hydraulic Dock Co.*, 1885, 54 L. J. Ch. 730; 52 L. T. 841; 33 W. R. 652.

(*d*) *Worrall* v. *Harford*, 1802, 8 Ves. 4.

(*e*) *Copeland* v. *Stein*, 1799, 8 T. R. 199.

(*f*) *Hollis* v. *Claridge*, 1813, 4 Taunt. 807.

4. *Not affected by subsequent dealings or bankruptcy.*—Goods were consigned to a factor for sale, and after he had sold them the principal committed an act of bankruptcy. The factor subsequently received the price of the goods. Held, that he had a lien on the goods for the amount of a debt due to him from the principal, and that he was entitled, as against the trustee in bankruptcy, to retain the proceeds in payment of the debt (*g*). So, an order for the winding up of a company does not affect the lien of a solicitor upon documents of the company, if the lien was acquired before the presentation of the petition for the winding up (*h*). So, an assignment by the principal, of goods in the possession of a factor, does not affect the factor's general lien thereon (*i*).

5. *Negotiable instruments.*—A banker borrowed a specific sum of money from a stockbroker, with whom he deposited, as security, negotiable instruments belonging to third persons. The banker dealt as a principal with the broker, having had many previous transactions with him, and there was nothing to lead the broker to believe that the securities were not the property of the banker. Held, that the broker's general lien for the balance due to him from the banker attached upon the securities, although the banker had been guilty of gross fraud (*j*). So, the general lien of a banker upon negotiable instruments deposited with him is not affected by the fact that the customer who deposits them is acting as agent for a third person (*k*), nor by equities between the customer and third persons (*l*). But an agent has no lien upon a negotiable instrument, as against the

(*g*) *Robson* v. *Kemp*, 1802, 4 Esp. 233; 8 R. R. 831.

(*h*) *In re Capital Fire Insurance Association, ex p. Beall*, 1883, 24 Ch. Div. 408, 53 L. J. Ch. 71; 49 L. T. 697; 32 W. R. 260, C. A.

(*i*) *Godin* v. *London Assurance Co.*, 1758, 1 W. Bl. 103.

(*j*) *Jones* v. *Peppercorne*, 1858, Johns. 430; 5 Jur. N. S. 140; 28 L. J. Ch. 158.

(*k*) *Brandeo* v. *Barnett*, 1846, 12 C. & F. 787; 3 C. B. 519, H. L.

(*l*) *Misa* v. *Currie*, 1876, 1 App. Cas. 554, 45 L. J. Ex. 852; 35 L. T. 414, H. L.

true owner, for advances made after notice of a defect in the title of the principal (*m*).

Article 73.

LIEN OF SUB-AGENTS.

Where a sub-agent is employed without the express or implied authority of the principal, he has no lien, either general or particular, as against the principal (*n*).

Where a sub-agent is appointed with the express or implied authority of the principal, and

(a) has no notice, at the time of his appointment, that the agent employing him is not acting on his own behalf, he has the same right of general or particular lien, as against the principal, as he would have had against the agent if the agent had been acting on his own behalf (*o*);

(b) has notice, at the time of his appointment, that the agent employing him is not acting on his own behalf, he has a particular lien for his charges, as against the principal, even if the principal has settled with the agent (*p*); but his general lien, as against the principal, is limited to the amount due from the principal to the agent (*p*).

(*m*) *Solomons* v. *Bank of England*, 1810, 13 East, 135; 12 R. R. 341. And see *De la Chaumette* v. *Bank of England*, 1829, 9 B. & C. 208.

(*n*) Illustration 1.

(*o*) Illustrations 2 and 3.

(*p*) Illustrations 4 and 5.

Illustrations.

1. A factor delegates his authority to a sub-agent, without the assent of the principal. The sub-agent has no lien on the principal's goods, even for duties paid in respect of those goods (*q*).

2. An agent, on behalf and with the authority of his principal, employs an insurance broker to effect a policy, the broker having no notice, and being unaware, that he is dealing with an agent. The broker has a lien on the policy for the general balance due to him from the agent, and is entitled to apply the proceeds of the policy in payment of such balance, notwithstanding that he has, in the meantime, received notice of the principal's rights (*r*).

3. A. employed B. to collect general average contributions under an insurance policy. B., in the ordinary course of business, employed C., an insurance broker, to collect the contributions, C. being unaware that B. was acting as an agent. C. collected the contributions, and B. became bankrupt. Held, in an action by A. against C. for the contributions, as money had and received to his use, that C. was entitled to set off the amount of a debt due to him from B. (*s*).

4. An agent, on behalf of his principal, employs an insurance broker to effect a policy, the broker being aware that the agent is acting for a principal. The principal pays the agent the amount of the premiums due in respect of the policy. Notwithstanding such payment, the broker has a lien upon the policy for premiums in respect thereof paid by him, or for which he is liable (*t*). But he has no lien, as against the principal, for a

(*q*) *Solly* v. *Rathbone*, 1814, 2 M. & S. 298.

(*r*) *Mann* v. *Forrester*, 1814, 4 Camp. 60, 15 R. R. 724, *Maanss* v. *Henderson*, 1801, 1 East, 335; *Westwood* v. *Bell*, 1815, 4 Camp. 349; 16 R. R. 800.

(*s*) *Montagu* v. *Forwood*, (1893) 2 Q. B. 350; 69 L. T. 371; 42 W. R. 124; 9 T. L. R. 634, C. A. And see *New Zealand and Australian Land Co.* v. *Watson*, 1881, 7 Q. B. D. 374, 50 L. J. Q. B. 433, 44 L. T. 675, 29 W. R. 694, C. A.

(*t*) *Fisher* v. *Smith*, 1878, 4 App. Cas. 1; 48 L. J. Ex. 411, 39 L. T. 430; 27 W. R. 113, H. L.

general balance due from the agent in respect of other transactions (*u*).

5. As against the solicitor employing him, a London agent has a general lien upon all moneys recovered and documents deposited with him in the course of his employment (*v*), but as against the client, his general lien is limited to the amount due from the client to the country solicitor (*w*). As against both the country solicitor and the client, he has a lien upon money recovered and documents deposited with him in a particular suit, for the amount of his agency charges and disbursements in connection with that suit (*x*).

Solicitor's charging Lien on property recovered or preserved through his instrumentality.

Whenever a solicitor is employed to prosecute or defend any suit or proceeding in a court of justice, the Court or judge before whom the suit or proceeding has been heard, or is depending, may declare such solicitor entitled to a charge upon the property recovered or preserved, and upon such declaration being made, such solicitor has a charge upon and right to payment out of the property, of whatsoever nature it may be, which has been recovered or preserved through his instrumentality, for the taxed costs and expenses of or in reference to such suit or proceeding; and all conveyances made and acts done to defeat, or which operate to defeat, such charge or right, unless made to a *bonâ fide* purchaser for value without notice, are absolutely void as against such charge or right; provided, that no such declaration may be made in any case where the right to recover payment of

(*u*) *Man* v. *Shiffner*, 1802, 2 East, 523; *Snook* v. *Davidson*, 1809, 2 Camp. 218; 11 R. R. 696; *Maanss* v. *Henderson*, 1801, 1 East, 335.

(*v*) *Lawrence* v. *Fletcher*, 1874, 12 Ch. Div. 858; 27 W. R. 937.

(*w*) *Ex p. Edwards, re Johnson*, 1881, 8 Q. B. D. 262; 51 L. J. Q. B. 108; 45 L. T. 578, C. A.; *Moody* v. *Spencer*, 1822, 2 D. & R. 6; *Waller* v. *Holmes*, 1860, 1 Johns. & H. 239, 3 L. T. 289; 30 L. J. Ch. 24; 6 Jur. N. S. 1367, 9 W. R. 32.

(*x*) *Dicas* v. *Stockley*, 1836, 7 C. & P. 587, *Lawrence* v. *Fletcher*, *supra*.

the costs or expenses is barred by any Statute of Limitations (*y*). The right to such a declaration is often referred to as a "charging lien." The order is a matter of judicial discretion, and must be made in the Court to which the particular suit is attached (*z*). The Act applies only to costs and expenses connected with proceedings in a court of justice, not, *e. g.*, to the costs of an arbitration (*a*). All property recovered or preserved in any such proceedings by the instrumentality of a solicitor is subject to his charging lien for the costs of such proceedings, even if the verdict and judgment therein are against his client (*b*). Thus, it attaches upon money received by way of compromise (*b*), or awarded to the client upon a reference of the suit to arbitration (*c*). So, where, in a suit by a *cestui que trust* against his trustee, the plaintiff, after the appointment of a receiver, compromised with the defendant without consulting his solicitor, it was held that the solicitor was entitled to a first charge on the plaintiff's interest in the trust property (*d*). So, where a defendant was ordered to pay money into Court to abide the event of an action, and after he had paid it in the parties compromised the action, the plaintiff's solicitor was held entitled to a charging order on the amount so paid in (*e*). So, where an action was dismissed, with costs amounting to 298*l.*, which were duly paid, and upon an appeal by the plaintiff, the decision was

---

(*y*) 23 & 24 Vict. c. 127, s. 28.

(*z*) *Heinrich* v. *Sutton, Re Fiddey*, 1871, L. R. 6 Ch. 865; 25 L. T. 643; 19 W. R. 1075. See *Groom* v. *Cheesewright*, (1895) 1 Ch. 730, 72 L. T. 555; 43 W. R. 475.

(*a*) *Macfarlane* v. *Lister*, 1888, 37 Ch. Div. 88, 57 L. J. Ch. 92, 58 L. T. 201, C. A. See *Pritchard* v. *Roberts*, 1873, L. R. 17 Eq. 222, 43 L. J. Ch. 129; 29 L. T. 883; 22 W. R. 259.

(*b*) *Davies* v. *Lowndes*, 1847, 3 C. B. 823; *Ross* v. *Buxton*, 1889, 42 Ch. Div. 190; 58 L. J. Ch. 442; 60 L. T. 630; 38 W. R. 71.

(*c*) *Ormerod* v. *Tate*, 1801, 1 East, 464; 6 R. R. 327.

(*d*) *Twynam* v. *Porter*, 1870, L. R. 11 Eq. 181; 40 L. J. Ch. 30, 23 L. T. 551; 19 W. R. 151.

(*e*) *Moxon* v. *Sheppard*, 1890, 24 Q. B. D. 627, 59 L. J. Q. B. 286; 62 L. T. 726; 38 W. R. 704.

reversed and the defendant ordered to repay the 298*l.*, together with the costs of the appeal, amounting to 165*l.*, it was held that the solicitors who acted for the plaintiff on the appeal were entitled, in addition to the 165*l.*, to a charge on the 298*l.*, for the extra costs of the appeal as between solicitor and client (*f*). Money paid into Court by a plaintiff, as security for the defendant's costs, is not, however, on a judgment for the plaintiff, deemed to be property preserved, within the meaning of the Act (*g*).

Priority of charging lien.—A solicitor is entitled to a charging order, even if he was discharged before the trial, but subject to the lien for costs of the solicitor for the time being (*g*). Such a charge has priority to a garnishee order in reference to the fund recovered (*h*); and the right to a declaration of charge extends to the solicitor's assignee (*i*). But it is not such a charge as to give the solicitor the position or rights of a *cestui que trust*, so as to prevent the opponent from setting off the amount of the judgment against a debt or other judgment in his favour (*j*). The charge depends on the rights of the client, and is limited to the interest of the client in the sum recovered (*j*). Thus, if the defendant is entitled, as against the plaintiff, to be relieved from the verdict, the Court will not abstain from interfering and giving effect to the defendant's rights, merely because the

---

(*f*) *Guy* v. *Churchill*, 1887, 35 Ch. Div. 489; 56 L. J. Ch. 670; 57 L. T. 510; 35 W. R. 706, C. A.

(*g*) *Re Wadsworth, Rhodes* v. *Sugden*, 1885, 29 Ch. Div. 517; 54 L. J. Ch. 638, 52 L. T. 613; 33 W. R. 558.

(*h*) *Ex p. Adams, Dallow* v. *Garrold*, 1884, 14 Q. B. D. 543; 54 L. J. Q. B. 76; 52 L. T. 240, C. A.; *Shippey* v. *Gray*, 1880, 49 L. J. C. P. 524; 42 L. T. 673, C. A. And see *The Heinrich*, 1872, L. R. 3 A. & E. 505; 41 L. J. Adm. 68; 26 L. T. 372; 20 W. R. 759.

(*i*) *Briscoe* v. *Briscoe*, (1892) 3 Ch. 543; 61 L. J. Ch. 665; 67 L. T. 116; 40 W. R. 621.

(*j*) *Mercer* v. *Graves*, 1872, L. R. 7 Q. B. 499; 41 L. J. Q. B. 212; 26 L. T. 551; 20 W. R. 605.

plaintiff's solicitor has a lien on the subject-matter (*k*). So, where the client is a life tenant, his solicitor is not entitled to a charging order on the interest of the reversioner in the sum recovered (*l*). So, where a verdict for 25*l.* was entered, and a rule *nisi* was obtained to set it aside, it was held that a settlement for 10*l.*, made to avoid the expenses of a new trial, the plaintiff being a pauper, was not impeachable by the plaintiff's solicitor on the ground of his lien (*m*). So, where there is a counterclaim, the lien attaches only on the balance actually recovered by the plaintiff, after setting off the amount recovered by the defendant on the counterclaim (*n*). But the Court will not permit the solicitor's lien to be prejudicially affected by a collusive compromise (*m*), or by an agreement between the parties (*o*). Thus, where two actions were pending between the same parties, and they agreed to refer both actions to arbitration, the result being that 100*l.* was awarded to one of the parties, and 80*l.* to the other, it was held that the 80*l.* could not be set off against the 100*l.* to the prejudice of a solicitor who claimed a lien for the costs of the action in respect of which the 100*l.* was awarded to his client (*o*). Where the defendant in an action pays money to the plaintiff, either by way of compromise, or in pursuance of an award, or otherwise, after receiving notice from the plaintiff's solicitor of his claim to a charging lien thereon, the defendant is personally liable to such solicitor for his taxed costs in the proceedings, to the extent that the amount so paid by him would have satisfied such costs (*p*).

(*k*) *Symons* v. *Blake*, 1835, 2 C. M. & R. 416; 4 D. P. C. 263; 1 Gale, 182.

(*l*) *Berry* v. *Howitt*, 1869, L. R. 9 Eq. 1; 39 L. J. Ch. 119.

(*m*) *Sullivan* v. *Pearson, Ex p. Morrison*, 1868, L. R. 4 Q. B. 153; 38 L. J. Q. B. 65, 19 L. T. 430, 9 B. & S. 960.

(*n*) *Westacott* v. *Bevan*, (1891) 1 Q. B. 774, 60 L. J. Q. B. 536; 65 L. T. 263, 7 T. L. R. 290; 39 W. R. 363.

(*o*) *Cowell* v. *Betteley*, 1834, 4 M. & Scott, 265, 10 Bing. 432.

(*p*) *Ross* v. *Buxton*, 1889, 42 Ch. Div. 190, 58 L. J. Ch. 442; 60 L. T. 630, 38 W. R. 71; *Ormerod* v. *Tate*, 1801, 1 East, 464, 6 R. R. 327.

Town agents.—A London agent is not entitled, as against the client, to a charging order under the Act, because he is not the solicitor employed by the client (*q*); but the country solicitor may apply for such an order, and the Court will then direct the costs of the London agent to be paid out of the fund in question to the extent of the country solicitor's interest therein (*r*).

Shipmaster's lien.

Every shipmaster has a maritime lien on the ship and freight for his wages (*s*), and for disbursements (*t*) or liabilities properly made or incurred by him on account of the ship (*u*), and has a possessory lien on the cargo for freight and general average contributions due from the owners thereof (*v*).

Maritime liens do not depend upon possession, but remain attached to the ship, notwithstanding any changes in the ownership (*w*), and are effectual even against a purchaser for value without notice (*x*). Where the rights of third parties are affected, however, such a lien may be lost by negligence or delay (*x*). Maritime liens are enforced by an Admiralty action

---

(*q*) *Macfarlane* v. *Lister*, 1888, 37 Ch. Div. 88, 57 L. J. Ch. 92, 58 L. T. 201, C. A.

(*r*) *Tardrew* v. *Howell*, 1861, 3 Giff. 381; 31 L. J. Ch. 57, 7 Jur. N. S. 1120; 5 L. T. 276, 10 W. R. 32.

(*s*) Merchant Shipping Act, 1894 (57 & 58 Vict. c. 60), s. 167 (1), re-enacting 17 & 18 Vict. c. 104, s. 191, *The Neptune*, 1824, 1 Hagg. Adm. 227.

(*t*) See *The Castlegate*, (1893) A. C. 38, 62 L. J. P. C. 17, 68 L. T. 99; 41 W. R. 349, 7 Asp. M. C. 284, 1 R. 97, H. L.

(*u*) 57 & 58 Vict. c. 60, s. 167 (2), re-enacting 52 & 53 Vict. c. 46, s. 1, which made *Hamilton* v. *Baker*, 1889, 14 A. C. 209, H. L., *Wilkins* v. *Carmichael*, 1779, 1 Doug. 101, *Smith* v. *Plummer*, 1818, 1 B. & A. 575; 19 R. R. 391; *Bristow* v. *Whitmore*, 1861, 9 H. L. Cas. 391, H. L., no longer law.

(*v*) *Cargo* v. *Galam*, 1864, 33 L. J. Adm. 97, P. C.; *Kirchner* v. *Venus*, 1858, 12 Moo. P. C. C. 361, 5 Jur. N. S. 395; 7 W. R. 455, P. C. And see 57 & 58 Vict. c. 60, ss. 494 to 498.

(*w*) *The Charles Amelia*, 1868, L. R. 2 A. & E. 330, 38 L. J. Adm. 17; 19 L. T. 429.

(*x*) *Harmer* v. *Bell* (*The Bold Buccleugh*), 1850, 7 Moo. P. C. C. 267, P. C.

in rem, in which the Court arrests and takes possession of the ship, in order, by sale or otherwise, to realize the amount of the lien (*y*). They are payable in the inverse order of their attachment on the *res* (*z*). Thus, a bottomry bond has priority to a maritime lien for wages and disbursements earned and made in the previous voyage to that in which the bond was given; and *vice versâ* (*z*). The master's maritime lien for wages and disbursements, whenever earned and made, has priority to the claim of a purchaser or mortgagee (*a*), and, as a general rule, to all other claims, except for salvage and collision (*b*). Where the master of a foreign ship, who was also a part owner, ordered necessaries, it was held that the lien for the necessaries had priority to that of the master for his wages and disbursements (*c*); but the priority of a master's lien to the claim of a mortgagee is not affected by the circumstance that the master is also a part owner (*d*).

Article 74.

HOW LIEN EXTINGUISHED.

The lien of an agent is extinguished by his entering into any agreement (*e*), or acting in any capacity (*f*), which is inconsistent or incompatible with the continuance of the lien; or by his taking other security for the debt or obligation (*g*), if the nature of the

(*y*) *The Cella*, 1888, 57 L. J. Adm. 55; 13 P. Div. 82, 59 L. T. 125; 6 Asp. M. C. 293, C. A.

(*z*) *The Hope*, 1872, 28 L. T. 287.

(*a*) *The Ringdove*, 1886, 11 P. Div. 120; 55 L. J. P. 56, 55 L. T. 552; 6 Asp. M. C. 28, *The Mary Ann*, 1 A. & E. 8, *The Hope*, 28 L. T. 287.

(*b*) *The Panthea*, 1871, 25 L. T. 389.

(*c*) *The Jenny Lind*, 1872, L. R. 3 Adm. 529, 41 L. J. Adm. 63; 26 L. T. 591.

(*d*) *The Feronia*, 1868, 2 A. & E. 65.

(*e*) Illustration 1.

(*f*) Illustration 2.

(*g*) *Cowell* v. *Simpson*, 1809, 16 Ves. 275; 10 R. R. 181.

security and circumstances under which it is taken are inconsistent with the continuance of the lien (*h*), or are such that it appears to have been his intention to abandon the lien (*i*), but not otherwise (*i*). But the lien is not affected by the circumstance that the debt or obligation secured thereby is barred by the Statute of Limitations (*j*).

A possessory lien is extinguished by the agent giving up the possession of the goods or chattels subject thereto (*k*), except where he is induced by fraud to give up the possession (*l*), or it is obtained from him illegally (*m*).

Illustrations.

1. A shipmaster elects to allow the balance of his wages to remain in the hands of the managing owners at interest. He thereby surrenders his lien for such wages (*n*).

2. A solicitor acts for both mortgagor and mortgagee in carrying out a mortgage. The solicitor thereby loses his lien on the title deeds of the mortgaged property for costs due from the mortgagor, even if the costs were incurred prior to the mortgage, and the deeds are not permitted to be taken away from the solicitor's office (*o*).

(*h*) *Angus* v. *Maclachlan*, 1881, 23 Ch. Div. 330; 52 L. J. Ch. 587; 48 L. T. 863; 31 W. R. 641.

(*i*) *Re Taylor*, (1891) 1 Ch. 590; 60 L. J. Ch. 525; 64 L. T. 605; 39 W. R. 417; 7 T. L. R. 262.

(*j*) *Spears* v. *Hartley*, 1798, 3 Esp. 81; 6 R. R. 814; *Re Broomhead*, 1847, 5 D. & L. 52; 16 L. J. Q. B. 355.

(*k*) Illustrations 3 and 4; *Kruger* v. *Wilcox*, 1754, Ambl. 252; Dick. 269.

(*l*) *Wallace* v. *Woodgate*, 1824, R. & M. 193; 1 C. & P. 575.

(*m*) *Dicas* v. *Stockley*, 1836, 7 C. & P. 587.

(*n*) *The Rainbow*, 1885, 53 L. T. 91; 5 Asp. M. C. 479.

(*o*) *Re Nicholson, ex p. Quinn*, 1883, 53 L. J. Ch. 302; 49 L. T. 811; 32 W. R. 296: overruling *Re Messenger, ex p. Calvert*, 1875, 3 Ch. Div. 317.

3. An agent delivers goods, on which he has a lien, on board a ship, to be conveyed on account and at the risk of the principal. The agent thereby surrenders his lien on the goods, and he has no power to revive it by stopping the goods *in transitu* (p).

4. An insurance broker gave up to his principal the possession of a policy. The policy was afterwards returned to the broker for readjustment. Held, that the broker's particular lien for unpaid premiums re-attached on the policy, but that his general lien for the balance due from the principal did not (q).

Sect. 4.—*Rights of stoppage in transitu, interpleader, and account.*

Article 75.

RIGHT OF STOPPAGE IN TRANSITU.

Where an agent, by contracting personally (r), renders himself personally liable for the price of goods bought on behalf of his principal, he has the same right of stopping the goods *in transitu* as he would have had if the relation between him and his principal had been that of seller and buyer (s).

(p) *Sweet* v. *Pym*, 1800, 1 East, 4; 5 R. R. 497.

(q) *Levy* v. *Barnard*, 1818, 2 Moore, 34; 19 R. R. 484.

(r) See Articles 107 to 112.

(s) *Imperial Bank* v. *London & St. Katharine's Docks*, 1876, 5 Ch. Div. 195; 46 L. J. Ch. 335; 36 L. T. 233, *Feise* v. *Wray*, 1802, 3 East, 93; 6 R. R. 551, *The Tigress*, 1863, B. & L. 38; 9 Jur. N. S. 361, 8 L. T. 117; 11 W. R. 538; *Falk* v. *Fletcher*, 1865, 18 C. B. N. S. 403; 34 L. J. C. P. 146; 11 Jur. N. S. 176; *Hawkes* v. *Dunn*, 1831, 1 Tyr. 413; 1 C. & J. 519.

Article 76.

RIGHT TO INTERPLEAD.

Where adverse claims are made upon an agent in respect of any money, goods, or chattels in his possession, and he claims no interest in the subject-matter of the dispute other than for costs or charges, he may claim relief by way of interpleader (*t*), even as against his own principal whose title he has acknowledged (*u*), provided that he had no notice of the adverse claim at the time of such acknowledgment (*v*). Where the agent claims a lien on property as against the owner, whoever he may be, the lien is not such an interest as deprives him of the right to interplead in respect of the ownership of the property (*w*); but where he claims a lien or any other interest in the property, or part thereof, as against a particular claimant, he is not permitted to interplead (*x*).

Illustrations.

1. An agent has funds in his hands, upon which a third person claims to have been given a lien by the principal. The

(*t*) Rules S. C., 1883, Ord. LVII.; *Blyth* v. *Whiffin*, 1872, 27 L. T. 330.

(*u*) *Attenborough* v. *St. Katharine's Docks*, 3 C. P. D. 450, 47 L. J. C. P. 763; 38 L. T. 404; 26 W. R. 583; Illustrations 1 to 5. It would seem that, in so far as they are decisions to the contrary, *Crawshay* v. *Thornton*, 1836, 2 Myl. & C. 1; 6 L. J. Ch. 179; 1 Jur. 19; *Cooper* v. *De Tastet*, 1829, Tamlyn, 177; and *Nickolson* v. *Knowles*, 1820, 5 Madd. 47, are no longer law since the C. L. P. Act, 1860 (23 & 24 Vict. c. 126).

(*v*) *Ex p. Davies, re Sadler*, 1881, 19 Ch. Div. 86; 45 L. T. 632; 30 W. R. 237, C. A.

(*w*) Illustration 5; *Attenborough* v. *St. Katharine's Docks*, *supra.*

(*x*) Illustration 6.

agent may interplead as against his principal and the third person (*y*).

2. A., a part owner of a vessel, instructs B., a broker, to insure the vessel. B. receives an amount due under the policy in respect of a loss, and the whole of the amount is claimed by A. A. sues B. for the whole amount, and certain other part-owners sue him for part thereof. B. may interplead (*z*).

3. A. deposits goods with B., a wharfinger, and afterwards requests him to transfer them to the name of C., reserving to himself a right to draw samples. B. enters the goods in C.'s name. D. then claims them as paramount owner, and A. acquiesces in his claim. C. also claims them. B. may interplead as against C. and D. (*a*).

4. A. intrusted a policy to B. for a specified purpose. C., who had pledged the policy with A., and A. each brought an action against B. for the policy. Held, that B. was entitled to interplead (*b*).

5. A., an auctioneer, sold goods on behalf of B., and whilst a portion of the proceeds was still in his hands received notice of a claim by C. B. having sued A. for the balance of the proceeds, it was held that A. had a right to interplead as to the residue after the deduction of his expenses and charges, C. being willing to allow such expenses and charges (*c*).

6. An action is brought against an auctioneer for the amount of a deposit paid to him by the plaintiff. The auctioneer cannot interplead if he insists on retaining his commission, for which his own principal alone is liable (*d*). So, where a wharfinger

---

(*y*) *Smith* v. *Hammond*, 1833, 6 Sim. 10.

(*z*) *Stuart* v. *Welch*, 1838, 4 Myl. & C. 305, 3 Jur. 237.

(*a*) *Pearson* v. *Cardon*, 1831, 2 Russ. & M. 606, *Mason* v. *Hamilton*, 1831, 5 Sim. 19.

(*b*) *Tanner* v. *European Bank*, *Bowen* v. *Same*, L. R. 1 Ex. 261; 35 L. J. Ex. 151; 14 L. T. 414.

(*c*) *Best* v. *Heys*, 1862, 3 F. & F. 113, 1 H. & C. 718; 32 L. J. Ex. 129. See, also, *Martinius* v. *Helmuth*, 1815, Coop. 245, 2 Ves. & B. 412, 13 R. R. 126.

(*d*) *Mitchell* v. *Hayne*, 1824, 2 Sim. & S. 63.

has a lien upon goods as against only one of the parties claiming the goods, he cannot interplead (*e*). So, where the depositary of a fund had a personal interest in contesting with one of the claimants a question relating to part of the fund, it was held that he could not interplead respecting the fund (*f*).

Article 77.

RIGHT TO AN ACCOUNT.

Where the accounts between a principal and agent are of so complicated a nature that they cannot be satisfactorily disposed of in an action at law, the agent has a right to have an account taken in a court of equity (*g*); but it does not follow, merely because the principal has such a right, that the agent has a similar right (*h*). Where an agent is paid a salary or commission in proportion to the profits made or the business done, the question whether he is entitled to have an account taken in a court of equity depends upon whether or not the accounts are of too intricate or complicated a nature to be properly and conveniently gone into by a jury (*i*).

(*e*) *Braddick* v. *Smith*, 1832, 9 Bing. 84; 2 M. & Scott, 131.

(*f*) *Moore* v. *Usher*, 1835, 7 Sim. 383; 4 L. J. Ch. 205.

(*g*) *Padwick* v. *Hurst*, 1854, 18 Beav. 575, 18 Jur. 763; 23 L. J. Ch. 657; *Blyth* v. *Whiffin*, 1872, 27 L. T. 330; *Dinwiddie* v. *Bailey*, 1801, 6 Ves. 141.

(*h*) *Padwick* v. *Stanley*, 1852, 9 Hare, 627; 16 Jur. 586. Because the right of the principal may be founded on the fiduciary character of the agency.

(*i*) *Harrington* v. *Churchward*, 1860, 6 Jur. N. S. 576; 29 L. J. Ch. 521; 8 W. R. 302; *Smith* v. *Levaux*, 1863, 1 H. & M. 123; 9 Jur. N. S. 1140; 12 W. R. 31; 33 L. J. Ch. 167; 9 L. T. N. S. 313; 3 N. R. 18;

Article 78.

NO RIGHT TO SUE PRINCIPAL ON CONTRACTS ENTERED INTO ON HIS BEHALF.

Except in the case of insurance brokers, who may sue their principals for premiums due under policies effected by them even if they have not paid or settled with the underwriters (*j*), no agent has any right of action against his principal on any contract entered into on the principal's behalf, whether the agent is himself personally liable on the contract to the other contracting party or not (*k*).

Illustrations.

1. A., a foreign merchant, employs B. to buy goods on commission. B. buys the goods, and the vendors invoice them to him and take his acceptance for the price. B. cannot sue A., as for goods sold and delivered (*l*). (His only remedy is an action for indemnity.)

2. A broker buys goods on behalf of an undisclosed principal. He cannot sue the principal for not accepting the goods, although, having contracted without naming the principal, he is, by a custom of trade, personally liable on the contract (*m*). Nor can he sue as for goods bargained and sold (*n*).

Waters v. *Shaftesbury*, 1866, 14 L. T. 184, 12 Jur. N. S. 311; 14 W. R. 572; *Shepard* v. *Brown*, 1862, 7 L. T. 499, 9 Jur. N. S. 195; 11 W. R. 162.

(*j*) *Power* v. *Butcher*, 1829, 5 M. & R. 327.

(*k*) Illustrations 1 and 2.

(*l*) *Seymour* v. *Pychlau*, 1817, 1 B. & A. 14.

(*m*) *Tetley* v. *Shand*, 1872, 25 L. T. 658, 20 W. R. 206.

(*n*) *White* v. *Benekendorff*, 1873, 29 L. T. 475, *Ex p. Dyster*, 1816, 2 Rose, 349.

CHAPTER IX.

Relations between the Principal and Third Persons.

Sect. 1.—*What acts of agents bind their principals.*

Article 79.

ACTS WITHIN SCOPE OF APPARENT AUTHORITY.

Every act done by an agent on behalf of the principal, within the scope of his apparent authority and in the course of his employment, binds the principal, unless the agent is in fact unauthorized to do the particular act, and the person dealing with him has notice (*a*) that he is exceeding his authority (*b*).

Illustrations.

1. An agent was intrusted by his principal with a document containing a written consent signed by the principal to do a particular act, but the agent was told not to give the consent,

(*a*) See Article 84.

(*b*) Illustrations 1 to 10; *Royal British Bank* v. *Turquand*, 1857, 6 El. & Bl. 327; 24 L. J. Q. B. 327; 1 Jur. N. S. 1086; *Heyworth* v. *Knight*, 1864, 17 C. B. N. S. 298; 33 L. J. C. P. 298; *Dyas* v. *Cruise*, 1845, 2 J. & L. 460, Ir.; *Ex p. Dixon, re Henley*, 1876, 4 Ch. Div. 133; 46 L. J. Bk. 20; 35 L. T. 644; 25 W. R. 105; *Todd* v. *Robinson*, 1825, 1 R. & M. 217; *Gilman* v. *Robinson*, 1825, 1 R. & M. 226; *Waller* v. *Drakeford*, 1853, 1 El. & Bl. 749; 22 L. J. Q. B. 274; 17 Jur. 853; *Nickson* v. *Brohan*, 10 Mod. 109; *Strauss* v. *Francis*, 1866, L. R. 1 Q. B. 379, 35 L. J. Q. B. 133; 12 Jur. N. S. 486; 14 L. T. 326; 14 W. R. 634; *Curlewis* v. *Birkbeck*, 1863. 3 F. & F. 894; *Wright* v. *Bigg*, 1852, 15 Beav. 592.

except on certain conditions which were not specified in the document. The agent consented unconditionally. Held, that the principal was bound, though he had signed the document without having read it (*c*). So, where a principal wrote—"I have authorized A. to see you, and, if possible, to come to some amicable arrangement"—and gave A. private instructions not to settle for less than a certain amount, it was held that he was bound by A.'s settlement for less than that amount, the instructions not having been communicated to the other side (*d*). No private instructions given to an agent, of which the persons dealing with him have no notice, prevent the acts of the agent, within the scope of his ostensible authority, from binding the principal (*e*).

2. An agent was employed as manager of a business, which he carried on apparently as principal. It was incidental to the ordinary course of the business to draw and accept bills of exchange, but it had been expressly agreed between the principal and agent, that the agent should not draw or accept bills of exchange on the principal's behalf. The agent accepted a bill, in the name in which the business was carried on. Held, that the principal was liable on the bill (*f*). So, a horsedealer is bound by a warranty given by his agent for the sale of a horse (*g*), and a client by a compromise entered into by his solicitor (*h*), in the course of his employment, even if the warranty

---

(*c*) *Beaufort* v. *Neeld* (*Beaufort* v. *Taylor*), 1844, 12 C. & F. 248; 9 Jur. 813, H. L.

(*d*) *Trickett* v. *Tomlinson*, 1863, 13 C. B. N. S. 663; 7 L. T. 678.

(*e*) *National Bolivian Navigation Co.* v. *Wilson*, 1880, 5 A. C. at p. 209, 43 L. T. 70, H. L., *Smith* v. *M'Guire*, 1858, 3 H. & N. 554; 27 L. J. Ex. 465, 1 F. & F. 199.

(*f*) *Edmunds* v. *Bushell*, 1865, L. R. 1 Q. B. 97, 35 L. J. Q. B. 20, 12 Jur. N. S. 332. And see *Fuentes* v. *Montis*, 1868, L. R. 1 C. P. 268, 277.

(*g*) *Howard* v. *Sheward*, 1866, L. R. 2 C. P. 148, 36 L. J. C. P. 42, 12 Jur. N. S. 1015.

(*h*) *Butler* v. *Knight*, 1867, L. R. 2 Ex. 109, 36 L. J. Ex. 66; 15 L. T. 621; 15 W. R. 107, *Smith* v. *Troup*, 1849, 6 D. & L. 679, 7 C. B. 757, 18 L. J. C. P. 209.

was given, or the compromise was entered into, contrary to his express instructions.

3. An agent was given authority, in cases of emergency, to borrow money on exceptional terms outside the ordinary course of business. A third person, in good faith and without notice that the agent was exceeding his authority, lent money to him on such exceptional terms. Held, that the principal was bound, although in the particular case the emergency had not arisen (*i*).

4. An owner of certain deeds intrusted them to an agent, and authorized him to pledge them for a certain sum. The agent pledged them for a larger sum than was authorized to a person who took them in good faith, and without notice of the limit on the agent's authority. Held, that the owner was not entitled to recover the deeds except on repayment of the full amount advanced upon them (*j*).

5. An agent who is unable to read is authorized to contract on the principal's behalf. The principal is bound by a written contract signed by the agent, notwithstanding his inability to read the contract (*k*).

6. A solicitor is authorized to sue for a debt. A tender of the debt to his managing clerk operates as a tender to the client, even if the clerk was instructed not to receive payment of the particular debt (*l*), unless, at the time of the tender, he disclaims any authority to receive the money (*m*).

7. The manager of a business, which he carried on in his own name as apparent principal, ordered goods for the business. Held, that the undisclosed principal was liable for the price of

---

(*i*) *Montaignac* v. *Shitta*, 1892, 15 App. Cas. 357.

(*j*) *Brocklesby* v. *Permanent Temperance Building Society*, (1895) A. C. 173; 64 L. J. Ch. 433; 72 L. T. 477; 43 W. R. 406, H. L. And see *Tottenham* v. *Green*, 1863, 1 N. R. 466.

(*k*) *Foreman* v. *G. W. Rail.*, 1878, 38 L. T. 851.

(*l*) *Moffatt* v. *Parsons*, 1814, 1 Marsh. 55; 5 Taunt. 307; 15 R. R. 506.

(*m*) *Bingham* v. *Allport*, 1833, 1 N. & M. 398. See, also, *Kirton* v. *Braithwaite*, 1836, 1 M. & W. 310; 2 Gale, 48; *Wilmot* v. *Smith*, 1828, 3 C. & P. 453; *Goodland* v. *Blewitt*, 1808, 1 Camp. 477; 10 R. R. 731.

the goods, although in ordering them the manager had exceeded his actual authority (*n*).

8. A broker was permitted by his principal, on several occasions, to draw bills in his own name for the price of goods sold on the principal's behalf. A purchaser accepted a bill so drawn, having previously paid in a similar manner for goods supplied to him. Held, that the principal was bound by the payment, although the broker became bankrupt before the maturity of the bill (*o*).

9. A., an iron-dealer, on one occasion sent B., a waterman, to buy iron on credit from C., and in due course paid C. for it. On a subsequent occasion he sent him with ready money, but B. again bought on credit and misappropriated the money. Held, that A. was liable to C. for the price of the iron bought on the second occasion, B. having apparent authority to pledge his credit (*p*).

10. The assignee of a life policy which was voidable if the assured went beyond Europe, in paying the premiums to the local agent of the assurance company, told him that the assured was in Canada. The agent said that that would not avoid the policy, and continued to receive the premiums until the death of the assured. Held, that the company were estopped by the representation of their agent from saying that the policy was avoided by the absence of the assured (*q*).

Article 80.

NOT BOUND BY ACTS BEYOND SCOPE OF AUTHORITY, OR NOT DONE IN COURSE OF EMPLOYMENT.

No principal is bound by any act of his agent which is not done in the course of the agent's employment on

(*n*) *Watteau* v. *Fenwick*, (1893) 1 Q. B. 346, 67 L. T. 831, 9 T. L. R. 133, 56 J. P. 839, C. A.

(*o*) *Townsend* v. *Inglis*, 1816, Holt, 278, 17 R. R. 636.

(*p*) *Hazard* v. *Treadwell*, 1730, 1 Str. 506. See, however, *Gilman* v. *Robinson*, 1825, 1 R. & M. 226. Compare with Illustration 7 to Article 80.

(*q*) *Wing* v. *Harvey*, 1854, 5 De G. M. & G. 265, 18 Jur. 394, 23 L. J. Ch. 511; 2 W. R. 370.

his behalf (*r*), or by any act outside the scope of the agent's apparent authority, unless he in fact authorized him to do the particular act (*s*).

This article is subject to the provisions of Articles 81 and 82.

Illustrations.

1. A. agreed with a company to become surety for a debt owing by B., and indorsed a bill to the company for the amount, it being understood that he was to have funds to meet the bill out of a debt accruing due to B. from C. The managing director of the company, who knew of this arrangement between A. and B., had previously lent money privately to B., and held his acceptance. When the acceptance became due, the managing director obtained an order from B. for the payment to him of the debt due from C., and appropriated this payment to his own private debt. In an action by the company against A. on the bill indorsed by him as surety, it was held that the company were not responsible for the acts of the managing director in obtaining payment of his private debt, such acts not being done in the course of his employment on behalf of the company (*t*).

2. The manager and director of the business, in South America, of a company, gave a promissory note in the name of the company. It was not shown that it was necessary, or in the ordinary course of business of such a company when carried on

(*r*) Illustration 1.

(*s*) Illustrations 2 to 10; *Olding* v. *Smith*, 1852, 16 Jur. 497; *Graves* v. *Masters*, 1883, 1 C. & E. 73, *Acey* v. *Fernie*, 1840, 7 M. & W. 151; *Fitzgerald* v. *Dressler*, 1859, 7 C. B. N. S. 374, 29 L. J. C. P. 113, 5 Jur. N. S. 598; *East India Co.* v. *Hensley*, 1794, 1 Esp. 112; *Attwood* v. *Mannings*, 1827, 7 B. & C. 278, 1 M. & R. 66; *Att.-Gen.* v. *Jackson*, 1846, 3 Hare, 365, *Fenn* v. *Harrison*, 1790, 3 T. R. 757; *Levy* v. *Richardson*, 1889, 5 T. L. R. 236.

(*t*) *McGowan* v. *Dyer*, 1873, L. R. 8 Q. B. 141; 21 W. R. 560.

in the usual way, to give promissory notes. Held, that the company were not bound by the note (*u*).

3. The local agent of an insurance company contracted on behalf of the company to grant a policy. Held, that it was not within the ordinary scope of the authority of such an agent to make such a contract, and that, therefore, the company were not bound by the contract, unless it could be shown that the agent was, in fact, authorized to make it (*v*). So, where a house or estate agent who is employed to procure a purchaser at a certain price enters into a contract of sale, the principal is not bound unless he in fact authorized the agent to make the contract on his behalf, it not being within the ordinary scope of such an agent's authority to enter into binding contracts on his principal's behalf (*w*).

4. A stockbroker who was authorized to sell stock, in good faith, and for the benefit of the principal, sold it on credit. Held, that the principal was not bound by the contract, he not having expressly authorized a sale on credit, because it is not usual to sell stock on such terms (*x*).

5. The manager of a public-house, who had authority to deal with particular persons only, bought spirits from a person with whom he had no authority to deal. Held, that the principal was not bound, it being usual for such managers to be restricted to particular persons from whom to purchase spirits (*y*).

6. A. gave authority to an insurance broker in Liverpool to underwrite policies of marine insurance in his name, the risk not

---

(*u*) *Re Cunningham, Simpson's claim*, 1887, 36 Ch. Div. 532; 57 L. J. Ch. 169, 58 L. T. 16.

(*v*) *Linford* v. *Provincial Horse, &c. Ins. Co.*, 1864, 34 Beav. 291; 10 Jur. N. S. 1066; 11 L. T. 330.

(*w*) *Chadburn* v. *Moore*, 1893, 61 L. J. Ch. 674; 67 L. T. 257; 41 W. R. 39, *Hamer* v. *Sharp*, 1874, L. R. 19 Eq. 108; 44 L. J. Ch. 53; 31 L. T. 643.

(*x*) *Wiltshire* v. *Sims*, 1808, 1 Camp. 258, 10 R. R. 673.

(*y*) *Daun* v. *Simmons*, 1879, 41 L. T. 783, 28 W. R. 129; 44 J. P. 264, C. A. Compare *Watteau* v. *Fenwick*, (1893) 1 Q. B. 346, 67 L. T. 831; 9 T. L. R. 133, C. A.

to exceed 100*l.* by any one vessel. The broker underwrote a policy for 150*l.* on A.'s behalf. The assured was not aware of the limitation on the broker's authority, but it was notorious in Liverpool that in nearly all such cases certain limits were fixed. Held, that A. was not liable on the policy (*z*).

7. A principal, who is in the habit of paying cash for goods bought by his agent, gives the agent money to buy goods. The agent buys the goods on credit and embezzles the money. The principal is not liable for the price of the goods (*a*).

8. A partner, who is given authority to settle the affairs of the partnership on the winding up thereof, draws a bill of exchange in the name of the firm. The other partners are not liable on the bill, unless they expressly authorized him to bind them by drawing bills (*b*).

9. The secretary of a tramway company made a representation as to the financial relations of the company. It was not shown that he was authorized to make the representation. Held, that the company were not bound, it not being part of the ordinary duties of such a secretary to make any representations whatever on behalf of the company (*c*). So, where an auctioneer, at a sale by auction, makes verbal declarations which are inconsistent with the written conditions, the principal is not bound by the declarations unless he expressly authorized them to be made (*d*).

10. A principal cannot commit an act of bankruptcy by

(*z*) *Baines* v. *Ewing*, 1866, L. R. 1 Ex. 320; 35 L. J. Ex. 194; 14 L. T. 733, 14 W. R. 782, 4 H. & C. 511.

(*a*) *Stubbing* v. *Heintz*, 1791, 1 Peake, 66; 3 R. R. 651; *Rusby* v. *Scarlett*, 1803, 5 Esp. 76; *Pearce* v. *Rogers*, 1800, 3 Esp. 214. Compare with Illustration 9 to Article 79.

(*b*) *Kilgour* v. *Finlyson*, 1789, 1 H. Bl. 155; *Abel* v. *Sutton*, 1800, 3 Esp. 108.

(*c*) *Barnett* v. *South London Tram. Co.*, 1887, 18 Q. B. D. 815, 56 L. J. Q. B. 452; 57 L. T. 436, C. A.

(*d*) *Gunnis* v. *Erhart*, 1789, 1 H. Bl. 290; 2 R. R. 769; *Shelton* v. *Livius*, 1832, 2 C. & J. 411; 2 Tyr. 420.

an unauthorized act of his agent, done without his knowledge (*e*).

Article 81.

DEALINGS WITH MONEY AND NEGOTIABLE SECURITIES.

Where an agent, in consideration of an antecedent debt or liability, or for any other valuable consideration, pays or negotiates money or negotiable securities in his possession to a person who receives the same in good faith and without notice that the agent has not authority to so pay or negotiate the same, the payment or negotiation is as valid as if it had been expressly authorized by the owner of the money or securities.

A thing is deemed to be done in good faith within the meaning of this Article when it is in fact done honestly, whether it is done negligently or not (*f*).

Illustrations.

1. A., having bought on the Stock Exchange scrip which was issued in England by the agent of a foreign government, and which purported to entitle the bearer, on payment of 100*l.*, to receive a bond for that amount, intrusted the scrip to a broker. The broker pledged the scrip as security for a debt owing by himself, the pledgee taking it in good faith and without notice that the broker was not authorized to so pledge it. Held, that, the scrip being negotiable in the same manner as the bond which it represented would be, the pledgee acquired a good title,

(*e*) *Ex p. Blain, re Sawers*, 1879, 12 Ch. Div. 522, 41 L. T. 46, 28 W. R. 334, C. A., *Cotton* v. *James*, 1829, M. & M. 273, 3 C. & P. 505.

(*f*) 45 & 46 Vict. c. 61 (Bills of Exchange Act, 1882), sect. 90, *Goodman* v. *Harvey*, 1836, 4 A. & E. 870; 6 N. & M. 372. As to notice, see Article 84.

as against A., to the extent of the pledge (*g*). Every person who takes negotiable securities for valuable consideration, and in good faith, acquires a good title, although the person who negotiates them has no authority to do so (*h*).

2. An auctioneer, in the ordinary course of business, and not in breach of trust, paid the proceeds of sales into his own account at a bank. The bankers retained the amounts so paid in for an overdraft of the auctioneer, and closed the account. Held, that the principal had no remedy against the bankers, although they had notice that the money was substantially the proceeds of sales. Otherwise, if the auctioneer had been guilty of a breach of trust in so paying in the money, and the bankers had been aware of that (*i*).

Article 82.

DEALINGS PROTECTED BY THE FACTORS ACT, 1889.

Where a mercantile agent (*j*) is permitted by the owner of goods (*k*) to have possession (*l*) of the goods, or of the documents of title (*m*) thereto, any sale,

---

(*g*) *Goodwin* v. *Robarts*, 1876, 1 App. Cas. 476; 35 L. T. N. S. 179; 45 L. J. Ex. 748, H. L.; *Rumball* v. *Metropolitan Bank*, 1877, 2 Q. B. D. 194, 46 L. J. Q. B. 346, 36 L. T. 240.

(*h*) *Simmons* v. *London Joint Stock Bank*, (1892) A. C. 201 reversing, (1891) 1 Ch. 270, H. L.

(*i*) *Marten* v. *Roche*, 1885, 53 L. T. 946, 34 W. R. 253.

(*j*) For definition of mercantile agent, see Article 1.

(*k*) The expression "goods" includes wares and merchandize. sect. 1 (3). But not certificates of stock *Freeman* v. *Appleyard*, 1862, 1 N. R. 30; 32 L. J. Ex. 175; 7 L. T. 282.

(*l*) A person is deemed to be in possession of the goods or documents when they are in his actual custody, or are held by any other person subject to his control, or for him, or on his behalf: sect. 1 (2).

(*m*) "Documents of title" include any bill of lading, dock warrant, warehouse keeper's certificate, and warrant or order for the delivery of goods, and any other document used in the ordinary course of business as proof of the possession or control of goods, or authorizing, or purpledge (*n*), or other disposition of the goods for valuable consideration, made by him when acting in the ordinary course of business of a mercantile agent while the goods or documents of title, or any other documents of title to the goods obtained by means of the goods or of the first-mentioned documents of title, are in his possession is, as between the owner of the goods and the person taking under the disposition, as valid as if the agent were expressly authorized by the owner to make the same; provided that the person taking under the disposition acts in good faith, and has not at the time of the disposition notice that the agent has not authority to make the same, or that the goods or documents of title are in the possession of the agent without the consent of the owner, if such be the fact (*o*).

Provided always that—

(a) where the goods are pledged, without authority, for an antecedent debt or liability of the pledgor, the pledgee acquires no further right to the goods than could have been

porting to authorize, either by indorsement or delivery, the possessor of the document to transfer or receive goods thereby represented: sect. 1 (4).

(*n*) "Pledge" includes any contract pledging or giving a lien or security on goods, whether in consideration of an original advance, or of any further or continuing advance, or of any pecuniary liability: sect. 1 (5).

(*o*) 52 & 53 Vict. c. 45, s. 2 (1) to (4), Illustrations 1 to 3. See *Cole* v. *North Western Bank*, 1875, L. R. 10 C. P. 354, 32 L. T. 733, 44 L. J. C. P. 233, as to the scope and intention of the Factors Acts. The Act of 1889, superseding and repealing all the previous Acts, is set out in full in the Appendix, *post*. As to notice, see Article 84.

enforced by the pledgor at the time of the pledge (*p*);

(b) where the goods are pledged, without authority, in consideration of the delivery or transfer of other goods or documents of title to goods, or of a negotiable security, the pledgee acquires no right or interest in the goods so pledged in excess of the value of the goods, documents, or security when so delivered or transferred in exchange (*q*).

For the purposes of this article,—

(a) a pledge of the documents of title to goods is deemed to be a pledge of the goods (*r*).

(b) a person is not deemed to act in good faith and without notice if, in the opinion of the jury, the circumstances of the particular case are such as would lead a reasonable business man to believe that the agent is exceeding his authority or acting in bad faith (*s*).

This article applies only to mercantile agents and transactions (*t*).

(*p*) 52 & 53 Vict. c. 45, s. 4; Illustration 1.

(*q*) *Ibid.* s. 5.

(*r*) *Ibid.* s. 3, Illustration 1. The transfer of a document may be by indorsement, or, where the document is, by custom or by its express terms, transferable by delivery, or makes the goods deliverable to the bearer, then by delivery. sect. 11.

(*s*) *Gobind Chunder Sind* v. *Ryan*, 1861, 9 Moo. Ind. App. 140; 8 Jur. N. S. 343, 5 L. T. 559, P. C., *Navulshaw* v. *Brownrigg*, 1852, 2 De G. M. & G. 441; 21 L. J. Ch. 908, 16 Jur. 979; *Douglas* v. *Ewing*, 1857, 6 Ir. Ch. R. 395, Ir.

(*t*) Illustrations 4 and 5; *Lewis* v. *Ramsdale*, 1886, 55 L. T. 179, 35 W. R. 8.

Illustrations.

1. A factor is authorized to sell goods, and is intrusted with the bill of lading for them by the owner thereof. By means of the bill of lading he obtains dock warrants for the goods, and, without the authority of the principal, pledges the warrants with his banker as security for an overdraft, the banker taking them in good faith, and without notice that in so pledging them he is exceeding his authority. Before receiving notice of the want of authority, the banker, on the faith of the pledge, permits the overdraft to be increased. So far as concerns the overdraft existing at the time of the pledge, the principal is only bound by the pledge to the extent of any lien the factor had on the goods at that time, and may redeem the goods upon payment to that extent, and payment of the amount overdrawn since the date of the pledge. If the factor has a lien in excess of the full amount of the overdraft, the principal must, if required, also pay to the factor the amount of the excess before he is entitled to redeem the goods (*u*).

2. A broker is intrusted with the possession of goods for sale. The principal revokes his authority, and demands the return of the goods. The broker refuses to return the goods, and then fraudulently sells and delivers them to a person who purchases them in good faith, and without notice that in selling them the broker is exceeding his authority, or that he is in possession of the goods without the consent of the owner. The principal is bound by the sale, but may sue in his own name for the price, subject to any right of set-off the purchaser may have against the broker (*v*). The broker is civilly and criminally liable for the fraudulent breach of duty to the same extent as he would have been if the Factors Acts had not been passed (*w*).

3. A factor in possession of goods with the consent of the owner, pledges them for an advance. Subsequently, the pledgee makes a further advance to the factor, in respect of the same

---

(*u*) Sect. 12 (2). (*v*) Sect. 12 (3). (*w*) Sect. 12 (1).

goods. The principal is bound by both advances, provided that the pledgee acted in good faith, &c. (*x*).

4. An agent was employed to sell jewellery, retail, on commission. He fraudulently pledged some of the jewellery to a pawnbroker. Held, that the pledge was not protected by the Factors Act, 1889, not being made in the ordinary course of business of a mercantile agent (*y*).

5. An agent occupies a furnished house, and has the control of the furniture therein, with the consent of the owner of the furniture. A third person makes advances on the furniture, believing the agent to be the owner thereof. The transaction is not protected by the Factors Act (*z*).

Article 83.

LIEN OF CONSIGNEE FOR ADVANCES TO APPARENT OWNER OF GOODS.

Where the owner of goods has given possession thereof to an agent for the purpose of consignment or sale, or has shipped goods in the name of an agent, and the consignee of the goods has not had notice that the agent is not the owner thereof, the consignee, in respect of advances made to or for the use of the agent, has the same lien on the goods as if the agent were the owner thereof, and may transfer any such lien to another person; provided, that nothing in this article limits or affects the validity of any sale, pledge, or other disposition by a mercantile agent (*a*).

(*x*) *Portalis* v. *Tetley*, 1867, L. R. 5 Eq. 140; 37 L. J. Ch. 139, 17 L. T. 344.

(*y*) *Hastings* v. *Pearson*, (1893) 1 Q. B. 62; 62 L. J. Q. B. 75; 67 L. T. 553, 9 T. L. R. 18, 41 W. R. 127.

(*z*) *Wood* v. *Rowcliffe*, 1846, 6 Hare, 191.

(*a*) Factors Act, 1889, sect. 7 (1) and (2).

Article 84.

NO UNAUTHORIZED ACT BINDING WITH RESPECT TO PERSONS WITH NOTICE.

No act done by an agent in excess of his actual authority is binding on the principal with respect to persons having notice of the restriction (*b*).

A signature "per procuration" on a bill of exchange, promissory note, or cheque, operates as notice that the agent has but a limited authority to sign, and the principal is only bound by such signature if the agent in so signing was acting within the actual limits of his authority (*c*).

Illustrations.

1. A broker in possession of goods upon which he has a lien for advances, pledges the goods for valuable consideration to a person who has notice that in so pledging them the broker is exceeding his authority. The transaction is not protected by the Factors Act, and the pledgee acquires no right to retain the goods as against the principal, even to the extent of the broker's lien, the lien not being transferable by such an unauthorized act (*d*).

(*b*) *Collen* v. *Gardner*, 1856, 21 Beav. 540; *Howard* v. *Braithwaite*, 1812, 1 Ves. & B. 202, at p. 209, *Strauss* v. *Francis*, 1866, L. R. 1 Q. B. 379, 35 L. J. Q. B. 133; 12 Jur. N. S. 486, 14 L. T. 326; 14 W. R. 634; Illustrations 1 to 4.

(*c*) 45 & 46 Vict. c. 61 (Bills of Exchange Act, 1882), s. 25; *Alexander* v. *Mackenzie*, 1848, 6 C. B. 766, 18 L. J. C. P. 94, *Attwood* v. *Mannings*, 1827, 7 B. & C. 278, 1 M. & R. 66, *Stagg* v. *Elliott*, 1862, 12 C. B. N. S. 373; 31 L. J. C. P. 260, 9 Jur. N. S. 158; 6 L. T. 433. In *Smith* v. *M'Guire*, 1858, 3 H. & N. 554; 27 L. J. Ex. 465, 1 F. & F. 199, it was held that this principle did not apply to a charter-party signed "per procuration" by a general agent.

(*d*) *M'Combie* v. *Davies*, 1805, 7 East, 5; 3 Smith, 3; 8 R. R. 534; *Daubigny* v. *Duval*, 1794, 5 T. R. 604.

2. A. authorized his son to take delivery of a mare, provided that a certain warranty was given, and told the owner so. The son took away the mare without the warranty in question. Held, that the son's act did not amount to an acceptance of the mare, so as to bind the father (*e*).

3. A. paid money to a broker for a specific purpose. B., knowing that the money belonged to A., obtained it from the broker under pretence of a loan for a few days, and then claimed it for a debt due to him from the broker. Held, that B. was liable to repay the amount to A. (*f*). So, the transferee of a bank note has no title thereto if he takes it with notice that the transfer is fraudulent (*g*).

4. A. indorses a bill of exchange "pay B. or order for my use." B.'s bankers discount the bill and pay the proceeds to B.'s account. The bankers are liable to A. for the amount, because the restrictive indorsement operated as notice that the bill did not belong to B. (*h*). So, where A. gave bills to his agent indorsed "on account of A.," it was held that the agent could give no title to a pledgee, the indorsement operating as notice that he had no authority to pledge the bills (*i*).

Article 85.

HOLDING OUT ANOTHER AS AGENT.

Where a person, by words or conduct, represents or permits it to be represented that another person has authority to act on his behalf, he is bound by the acts of such other person with respect to any one dealing

---

(*e*) *Jordan* v. *Norton*, 1838, 4 M. & W. 155; 1 H. & H. 234.

(*f*) *Litt* v. *Martindale*, 1856, 18 C. B. 314.

(*g*) *Solomons* v. *Bank of England*, 1810, 13 East, 135; 12 R. R. 341.

(*h*) *Sigourney* v. *Lloyd*, *Lloyd* v. *Sigourney*, 1828, 8 B. & C. 622; 5 Bing. 525.

(*i*) *Truettell* v. *Barandon*, 1817, 1 Moore, 543; 8 Taunt. 100; 19 R. R. 472.

with him as an agent on the faith of any such representation, to the same extent as if he had the authority that he was represented to have (*j*).

The committee of management of a club are not, as such, deemed to be held out by the members of the club as having authority to pledge the personal credit of the members (*k*).

Illustrations.

1. The owner of certain goods permits A., who in the ordinary course of his business is accustomed to sell that class of goods, to have possession of the goods or of the documents of title thereto. A. sells the goods to a person who buys them in the belief that he has authority to sell. The owner is bound by the sale, independently of the Factors Acts, though he did not, in fact, authorize A. to sell the goods (*l*).

2. A. and B. permitted their names to appear on a programme as stewards of a fête, C.'s name appearing thereon as general manager. A. and B. took an active part in the conduct of the fête. Held, that they were liable on orders given by C. for tents, &c. (*m*).

3. A coachman in livery entered into a contract for the hire of horses, the person from whom he hired them giving credit to the master. The coachman had, in fact, agreed with the master to pay for the hire of the horses, but the person from whom they were hired had no notice of the agreement. Held, that the

---

(*j*) Illustrations 1 to 7. This is an instance of the principle of estoppel by conduct. See *Brazier* v. *Camp*, 1894, 9 R. 852, 63 L. J. Q. B. 257.

(*k*) *Cullen* v. *Queensberry*, 1781, 1 Br. P. C. 101, 1 Br. P. 396, H. L.; *Flemyng* v. *Hector*, 1836, 2 M. & W. 172, *Todd* v. *Emly*, 1841, 7 M. & W. 427. In the absence of evidence of authority, the committee alone are liable for goods supplied to a members' club.

(*l*) *Pickering* v. *Busk*, 1812, 15 East, 38, 13 R. R. 364, *Dyer* v. *Pearson*, 1824, 4 D. & R. 648, 3 B. & C. 38. See also, *Whitehead* v. *Tuckett*, 1812, 15 East, 400; 13 R. R. 509.

(*m*) *Pilot* v. *Craze*, 1888, 52 J. P. 311.

master was liable on the contract (*n*). So, a shipowner was held liable for the price of necessaries supplied upon the orders of the master, although the master was a lessee of the ship for a term, and had expressly agreed to do all the repairs, of which he had the sole benefit (*o*).

4. A wife gave orders for furniture to be supplied and work to be done at the house where she resided with her husband, the husband being present giving directions as to the work, &c. Held, that the husband was liable on the orders, although he had expressly forbidden his wife to pledge his credit, and it had been agreed between them that she should pay for the furniture and work, the plaintiff having had no notice of such prohibition or agreement (*p*).

5. A. occasionally employed B. to purchase goods from C., and duly ratified the purchases. Subsequently, B. purchased goods from C. for his own use, C. believing him to be buying them on behalf of A., and giving credit to A. Held, that it was a question for the jury whether A. had, by his conduct, held out B. as his agent to purchase the goods, and that if he had done so, he was liable to C. for the price (*q*). So, where a wife ordered goods in her husband's name, to be sent to the house of a third person, and the husband paid for the goods, that was held to be sufficient evidence to justify a jury in finding that she had authority to pledge his credit on a subsequent occasion for goods to be sent to the same house (*r*).

6. A. was in B.'s counting-house, apparently conducting B.'s business. Held, that a payment to A. on B.'s account operated

---

(*n*) *Rimell* v. *Sampayo*, 1824, 1 C. & P. 254; *Precious* v. *Abel*, 1795, 1 Esp. 350. See, however, *Maunder* v. *Conyers*, 1817, 2 Stark. 281.

(*o*) *Rich* v. *Coe*, 1777, Cowp. 636.

(*p*) *Jetley* v. *Hill*, 1884, 1 C. & E. 239.

(*q*) *Todd* v. *Robinson*, 1825, 1 R. & M. 217, *Gilman* v. *Robinson*, 1825, 1 R. & M. 226, *Trueman* v. *Loder*, 1840, 11 A. & E. 589, 3 P. & D. 267; *Dodsley* v. *Varley*, 1840, 4 P. & D. 448; 12 A. & E. 632; 5 Jur. 316. See *Llewellyn* v. *Winckworth*, 1845, 13 M. & W. 598; 14 L. J. Ex. 329; *Prescott* v. *Flynn*, 1832, 9 Bing. 19; 2 M. & Scott, 18.

(*r*) *Filmer* v. *Lynn*, 1835, 4 N. & M. 559; 1 H. & W. 59.

as a payment to B., although A. was not, in fact, employed by B. (*s*).

7. A., in good faith, deals with persons acting as directors of a company, believing them to be duly authorized. The company is bound by their acts as directors, within the scope of the articles of association, though they have not, in fact, been properly appointed (*t*).

8. The directors of a company hold out to the world that A. is the agent of the company for a particular purpose. The company is bound by A.'s acts, within the scope of such countenanced agency, done to the knowledge of the directors, though A. is not a duly appointed agent of the company (*u*).

Sect. 2.—*Rights and liabilities of the principal on contracts made by agent.*

Article 86.

MAY SUE OR BE SUED IN OWN NAME.

Every principal, whether disclosed or undisclosed, may sue or be sued in his own name on all contracts duly made on his behalf (*v*), and in respect of any money paid or received by his agent on his behalf (*w*).

Where an agent enters into a contract in his own name, parol evidence is admissible to show who is the real principal, in order to charge him or entitle him to

---

(*s*) *Barrett* v. *Deere*, 1828, Moo. & M. 200.

(*t*) *Mahony* v. *East Holyford Mining Co.*, 1875, L. R. 7 H. L. 869; 33 L. T. 383, H. L.

(*u*) *Wilson* v. *West Hartlepool Harbour, &c. Co.*, 1864, 34 Beav. 187, 11 L. T. 327, 13 W. R. 4.

(*v*) Illustrations 1 to 4, *Browning* v. *Provincial Insurance Co. of Canada*, 1873, L. R. 5 P. C. 263, 28 L. T. 853; 21 W. R. 587, P. C.

(*w*) Illustrations 5 and 6.

sue on the contract (*x*), provided that such evidence is not inconsistent with the terms of a written contract (*y*).

This article, so far as concerns undisclosed principals, does not apply to foreign principals, nor to deeds, bills of exchange, promissory notes, or cheques.

Illustrations.

1. A factor sells goods in his own name. The principal may intervene and sue for the price (*z*).

2. A wife, who carried on a business on behalf of her husband upon premises of which she was tenant and in respect of which she paid the rates, ordered goods for the business in her own name. Held, that the husband was liable for the price of the goods (*a*).

3. S., a solicitor, practised in the name of S. and C. C. was also a solicitor, but acted as clerk to S. Held, that S., being the real principal, was entitled to sue alone upon a contract made in the name of the firm (*b*).

4. A part-owner of a whaling vessel sold whale oil in his own name. Held, that the owners were entitled to sue jointly for the price, though the purchaser did not know that any person besides the seller was interested (*c*).

5. An agent entered into a contract in his own name for the purchase of property, and paid a deposit. Held, that on the

---

(*x*) *Morris* v. *Wilson*, 1859, 5 Jur. N. S. 168; *Calder* v. *Dobell*, 1871, L. R. 6 C. P. 486; 40 L. J. C. P. 224, 25 L. T. 129, *Wilson* v. *Hart*, 1817, 1 Moore, 45; 7 Taunt. 295.

(*y*) Illustration 7.

(*z*) *Sadler* v. *Leigh*, 1815, 4 Camp. 195; 2 Rose, 286.

(*a*) *Petty* v. *Anderson*, 1825, 3 Bing. 170; 10 Moore, 577; 2 C. & P. 38; *Smallpiece* v. *Dawes*, 1835, 7 C. & P. 40.

(*b*) *Spurr* v. *Cass*, *Cass* v. *Spurr*, 1870, L. R. 5 Q. B. 656, 39 L. J. Q. B. 249; 23 L. T. 409; *Kell* v. *Nainby*, 1829, 10 B. & C. 20; 5 M. & R. 76.

(*c*) *Skinner* v. *Stocks*, 1821, 4 B. & Ald. 437.

default of the vendor, the principal was entitled to sue in his own name for the return of the deposit (*d*).

6. A custom-house officer took exorbitant fees from a ship-master. Held, that the owner of the vessel had a right to sue in his own name to recover the amount paid in excess of the proper fees (*e*).

7. An agent executed a charter-party in his own name, and was described in the contract as the owner of the vessel. It was held that the principal was not entitled to give evidence to show that the agent contracted on his behalf, so as to enable him to maintain an action on the contract, because such evidence was contradictory to the statement that the agent was the owner of the vessel (*f*).

Article 87.

FOREIGN PRINCIPALS.

No foreign principal may sue or be sued on a contract made by his agent in England, unless it is proved that the agent was authorized to make the principal a contracting party, and it appears, either from the terms of the contract or from the surrounding circumstances, that the principal, and not the agent, was intended to be the contracting party (*g*).

(*d*) *Norfolk* v. *Worthy*, 1808, 1 Camp. 337, 10 R. R. 749.

(*e*) *Stevenson* v. *Mortimer*, 1778, Cowp. 805.

(*f*) *Humble* v. *Hunter*, 1848, 12 Q. B. 310, 17 L. J. Q. B. 350.

(*g*) *Die Elbinger Actien Gesellschaft* v. *Claye*, 1873, L. R. 8 Q. B. 313; 42 L. J. Q. B. 151, 28 L. T. 405, C. A., *Hutton* v. *Bullock*, 1874, 9 Q. B. D. 572; *Dramburg* v. *Pollitzer*, 1873, 28 L. T. 470, 21 W. R. 682, *Smyth* v. *Anderson*, 1849, 7 C. B. 21, 18 L. J. C. P. 109, 13 Jur. 211; *Paterson* v. *Gandasequi*, 1812, 15 East, 162, 2 Sm. L. C. 378, 13 R. R. 368.

Article 88.

DEEDS.

No principal may sue or be sued on any deed, even if it is expressed to be executed on his behalf, unless he is described as a party thereto and it is executed in his name (*h*).

This article is subject to the 46th section of the Conveyancing and Law of Property Act, 1881 (*i*), which provides that every assurance, instrument and thing executed and done by the donee of a power of attorney in and with his own name and signature and his own seal, by the authority of the donor of the power, shall be as effectual in law, to all intents, as if it had been executed or done by the donee of the power in the name and with the signature and seal of the donor.

Illustrations.

1. An agent entered into a contract by deed in his own name, the principal not being named therein. It was held that the principal was not liable to be sued on the contract (*j*).

2. A shipmaster executed a charter-party by deed in his own name "as agent for the owners." Held, that the owners were not entitled to sue for the freight, because they were not parties to the deed (*k*).

3. An attorney, who was authorized in writing to execute a lease, signed and sealed the lease in and with his own name and

---

(*h*) *Chesterfield and Mid Silkstone Colliery Co.* v. *Hawkins*, 1865, 3 H. & C. 677; 11 Jur. N. S. 468; *Southampton* v. *Brown*, 1827, 6 B. & C. 718; *Barford* v. *Stuckey*, 1823, 8 Moore, 88; 1 Bing. 225; Illustrations 1 to 3.

(*i*) 44 & 45 Vict. c. 41.

(*j*) *Re Pickering's claim*, 1871, L. R. 6 Ch. App. 525.

(*k*) *Schack* v. *Anthony*, 1813, 1 M. & S. 573.

seal. It was held that the principal was not entitled to sue on the covenants in the lease, though they were expressed to be made by the tenant with the landlord, because the deed was not executed in his name (*l*).

The Conveyancing Act, 1881, applies only to instruments executed in pursuance of a power of attorney, and, apparently, only where the donor of the power expressly gives the donee authority to act in his own name. How far the Act affects the principle that no person can sue or be sued on a deed except the parties thereto has not yet been judicially determined.

Article 89.

BILLS, NOTES AND CHEQUES.

The only persons liable on a bill of exchange, promissory note, or cheque, are those whose signatures appear thereon (*m*), and in determining whether a signature is that of the principal, or that of the agent by whose hand it is written, the construction most favourable to the validity of the instrument is adopted (*n*). And no person can be liable as acceptor of a bill of exchange except the person on whom it is drawn, unless it be accepted for honour (*o*). Hence—

(a) where a bill of exchange is drawn on the principal, the principal is deemed to be the acceptor, whether the acceptance is in his name or in that of the agent (*p*);

(*l*) *Berkeley* v. *Hardy*, 1826, 8 D. & R. 102, 5 B. & C. 355.

(*m*) 45 & 46 Vict. c. 61 (Bills of Exchange Act, 1882), sect. 23; *Ex p. Rayner, re Waud*, 1868, 17 W. R. 64.

(*n*) *Ibid.* sect. 26 (2).

(*o*) *Polhill* v. *Walter*, 1832, 3 B. & Ad. 114.

(*p*) Illustrations 1 to 3.

(b) where a bill of exchange is drawn on an agent, the principal is not liable as acceptor, even if it is accepted in his name and with his authority (*q*);

(c) where a signature is placed on a bill of exchange, promissory note, or cheque, otherwise than as that of the acceptor of a bill of exchange, the principal is liable only if his name is signed, or the signature is expressed to be made on his behalf (*r*).

Illustrations.

1. A bill of exchange was addressed to "William Bradwell." His wife wrote across it "Mary Bradwell." On the bill being presented to William Bradwell, he said that he knew about it and would pay it shortly. Held, that he was liable as acceptor, his promise to pay being sufficient evidence of authority or ratification (*s*).

2. A bill of exchange was addressed to "E. M. and others, trustees of Clarence Temperance Hall," and was accepted by E. M. in his own name. The jury found that E. M. had authority to accept on behalf of all the trustees. Held, that they were all liable as acceptors (*t*).

3. A bill of exchange was addressed to a company, and was accepted by authorized directors in their own names. Held, that the company were liable as acceptors (*u*).

4. A bill of exchange is addressed to A. B., and is accepted "A. B. for and on behalf of C. D." C. D. is not liable as

(*q*) Illustration 4.

(*r*) Illustrations 5 and 6.

(*s*) *Lindus* v. *Bradwell*, 1848, 5 C. B. 583; 17 L. J. C. P. 121; 12 Jur. 230.

(*t*) *Jenkins* v. *Morris*, 1847, 16 M. & W. 877.

(*u*) *Okell* v. *Charles*, 1876, 34 L. T. 822, C. A.

acceptor, even if A. B. was expressly authorized to accept the bill on his behalf (*v*).

5. A duly authorized agent draws or indorses a bill, or indorses a note or cheque, in his own name. The principal is not liable on the bill, note, or cheque (*w*). (A firm is not liable unless either the firm name appears, or the names of all the partners (*x*).)

6. A joint stock company was held liable on a promissory note, sealed with the common seal, in the following form:— "We, two directors of P. Society, by and on behalf of the said society, do hereby promise, &c. (Signed) A. B., C. D., directors" (*y*).

Article 90.

BROKERS' BOUGHT AND SOLD NOTES.

Where a broker contracts on behalf of both buyer and seller, an entry of the transaction in his book, signed by him, operates as a memorandum of the contract signed by both parties, for the purpose of satisfying the provisions of the 4th section of the Sale of Goods Act, 1893 (*z*); and a mistake in the bought and sold notes does not affect the validity of such a contract (*a*).

Where there is no such signed entry, signed bought and sold notes form a binding contract in writing, if they agree (*a*); but not if they materially differ (*a*).

(*v*) *Polhill* v. *Walter*, 1832, 3 B. & Ad. 114.

(*w*) *Ducarrey* v. *Gill*, 1830, M. & M. 450.

(*x*) *Re Adansonia Fibre Co., Miles' claim*, 1874, 9 Ch. Ap. 635; 43 L. J. Ch. 732; 31 L. T. 9, 22 W. R. 889; *Ex p. Buckley*, 1845, 14 M. & W. 469, 14 L. J. Ex. 341.

(*y*) *Aggs* v. *Nicholson*, 1856, 1 H. & N. 165.

(*z*) *Heyman* v. *Neale*, 1809, 2 Camp. 337, *Thompson* v. *Gardiner*, 1876, 1 C. P. D. 777, *Sivewright* v. *Archibold*, 1851, 20 L. J. Q. B. 529; 15 Jur. 947.

(*a*) *Sivewright* v. *Archibold*, *supra*; *Grant* v. *Fletcher*, 1826, 5 B. & C.

Article 91.

EFFECT OF PARTICULAR CUSTOMS OR USAGES.

Where an agent contracts in a particular market, the contract is deemed to be made subject to the rules and customs of that market (*b*). Provided, that the principal is not bound by any unreasonable rules or customs of the existence of which he has no knowledge (*c*). Provided also, that the right of the principal, whether disclosed or undisclosed, to sue in his own name on a contract made on his behalf, is not affected by the circumstance that it was made in a market by the rules of which the agent is personally liable on the contract, and the contract is regarded as that of the agent alone, even if such rules were known to the principal (*d*).

Illustrations.

1. A. authorizes a member of the Stock Exchange to purchase shares on his behalf. A. must indemnify the seller against any liability for calls on the shares subsequent to the contract of sale, though the transfer of the shares, by reason of the winding-up of the company, cannot be registered (*b*).

436; *Goom* v. *Aflalo*, 1826, 6 B. & C. 117; *Townend* v. *Drakeford*, 1843, 1 C. & K. 20. And see *McCaull* v. *Strauss*, 1883, 1 C. & E. 106.

(*b*) *Hodgkinson* v. *Kelly*, 1868, 37 L. J. Ch. 837; L. R. 6 Eq. 496; 16 W. R. 1078, *Nickalls* v. *Merry*, 1875, L. R. 7 H. L. 530; 45 L. J. Ch. 575, 23 W. R. 663, H. L.

(*c*) *Sweeting* v. *Pearce*, 1859, 7 C. B. N. S. 449; 29 L. J. C. P. 265; *Pearson* v. *Scott*, 1878, 38 L. T. N. S. 747, 9 Ch. Div. 198, 47 L. J. Ch. 705, 26 W. R. 796.

(*d*) *Langton* v. *Waite*, 1868, L. R. 6 Eq. 165, 37 L. J. Ch. 345; *Humphrey* v. *Lucas*, 1845, 2 C. & K. 152; *Lissett* v. *Reave*, 1742, 2 Atk. 394.

2. A broker contracts on the Stock Exchange for an undisclosed principal. The principal may sue in his own name on the contract, even if he was aware, at the time that he employed the broker, that by the rules of the exchange the broker is personally liable, and is regarded as the contracting party (*d*).

Article 92.

EFFECT ON RIGHT TO SUE THE PRINCIPAL, OF GIVING CREDIT TO OR OBTAINING JUDGMENT AGAINST THE AGENT.

Where an agent enters into a contract in such terms that he is personally liable thereon, and a judgment is obtained against him on the contract, the judgment, unless and until set aside, is a bar to any proceedings against the principal on the contract (*e*).

Where an agent enters into a contract in such terms that he is personally liable thereon, and the other contracting party, with a full knowledge who is the real principal, elects to give exclusive credit to the agent, he is irrevocably bound by his election, and cannot afterwards charge the principal on the contract (*f*). Where such party sues and recovers judgment against the agent on the contract, he is conclusively deemed to have elected to give exclusive credit to the agent (*g*). Where he has not sued the agent to judgment, the question whether he has elected to trust

(*d*) See note (*d*), *ante*.

(*e*) Illustrations 4 and 5.

(*f*) Illustration 3, *Smethurst* v. *Mitchell*, 1859, 1 El. & El. 623; 28 L. J. Q. B. 241; 5 Jur. N. S. 978, 7 W. R. 226, *Thornton* v. *Meux*, 1827, M. & M. 43.

(*g*) Illustration 6.

the agent exclusively is a question of fact for the jury (*h*).

Except as in this article provided, the liability of the principal, whether disclosed or undisclosed, upon a contract made on his behalf, is not affected by the circumstance that credit was given to the agent who made the contract (*i*).

Illustrations.

1. An agent buys goods in his own name, and the seller, not knowing that he is acting on behalf of a principal, or not knowing who the principal is, debits him with the price. The seller, on ascertaining who the principal is, may sue him for the price (*j*).

2. A broker buys goods in his own name, and does not mention the principal to the seller until after he (the broker) becomes insolvent. The principal is liable to the seller for the price, and has no right to set off a debt due to him from the broker (*k*).

3. An agent purchases goods, and the seller, knowing at the time of the contract who the principal is, elects to give exclusive credit to the agent. The seller cannot subsequently change his mind and charge the principal (*l*). So, a husband is not liable for the price of necessaries ordered by his wife if the jury find that exclusive credit was given to her (*m*).

(*h*) Illustrations 7 and 8.

(*i*) Illustrations 1, 2, 7 and 8; *Dunn* v. *Newton*, 1884, 1 C. & E. 278.

(*j*) *Thompson* v. *Davenport*, 1829, 9 B. & C. 78; 4 M. & R. 110; *Paterson* v. *Gandassequi*, 1812, 15 East, 62, 2 Sm. L. C. 378, 13 R. R. 368, *Smyth* v. *Anderson*, 1849, 7 C. B. 21, 18 L. J. C. P. 109; 13 Jur. 211, *Snee* v. *Prescott*, 1743, 1 Atk. 245, at p. 248.

(*k*) *Waring* v. *Favenck*, 1807, 1 Camp. 85; 10 R. R. 638.

(*l*) *Addison* v. *Gandassequi*, 1812, 4 Taunt. 574, 2 Sm. L. C. 387, 13 R. R. 689, *Paterson* v. *Gandassequi*, 1812, 15 East, 62, 2 Sm. L. C. 378; 13 R. R. 368.

(*m*) *Bentley* v. *Griffin*, 1814, 5 Taunt. 356; *Metcalfe* v. *Shaw*, 1814, 3 Camp. 22; 13 R. R. 740.

4. An agent contracts in his own name, and judgment is recovered against him on the contract. The judgment is a bar to an action against the principal on the contract (*n*).

5. An agent ordered goods in his own name, and a judgment was obtained against him for the price. The seller then commenced an action against the principal, who raised the defence of *res judicata*, and obtained judgment. Subsequently, the judgment against the agent was set aside, and the seller then appealed from the decision in favour of the principal. It was held, on the appeal, that the judgment having been set aside, the principal was liable (*o*).

6. An agent purchases goods in his own name. The seller, after discovering who the principal is, sues the agent to judgment. The seller is conclusively deemed to have elected to look to the agent alone, and cannot subsequently charge the principal (*p*).

7. A broker purchased cotton and gave the name of his principal, but inserted his own name, as buyer, in the sold note. The seller invoiced the cotton to the broker, and called upon him to accept and pay for it, threatening legal proceedings. Held, in an action by the seller against the principal, that these facts did not necessarily amount to an election to give exclusive credit to the broker, and that the question whether the seller had so elected was one of fact for the jury (*q*).

8. A., who was employed as a factor by both B. and C., sold some of B.'s goods to C. A. then became bankrupt, and B. filed an affidavit in the bankruptcy, alleging that A. was indebted to him for the price of certain goods sold on his behalf to C., for which A. had received payment by goods sold and

---

(*n*) *Priestley* v. *Fernie*, 1865, 3 H. & C. 977; 11 Jur. N. S. 813; 34 L. J. Ex. 172; 13 L. T. 208.

(*o*) *Partington* v. *Hawthorne*, 1888, 52 J. P. 807.

(*p*) *Priestley* v. *Fernie*, *supra*. See *MacClure* v. *Schemeil*, 1871, 20 W. R. 168.

(*q*) *Calder* v. *Dobell*, 1871, L. R. 6 C. P. 486; 40 L. J. C. P. 224; 25 L. T. 129; 19 W. R. 978, Ex. Ch.

delivered to him by C. Held, that B. was not estopped by the affidavit from suing C. for the price of the goods (*r*). No proceedings, short of suing the agent to judgment, are conclusive proof in point of law of an election to credit the agent exclusively; but such an act as proving for the debt against the agent's estate in bankruptcy after the principal becomes known is, of course, strong evidence for the jury of such an election (*s*).

Article 93.

HOW FAR RIGHT OF RECOURSE TO PRINCIPAL AFFECTED BY A SETTLEMENT BETWEEN PRINCIPAL AND AGENT.

Where a debt has been contracted through an agent, and the principal is induced by the words or conduct of the creditor to reasonably believe that the agent has paid the debt, or that the creditor has elected to look to the agent alone for payment, and in consequence of such belief pays or settles, or otherwise deals to his prejudice with the agent, the creditor is not permitted to deny, as between himself and the principal, that he has been paid, or has elected to give exclusive credit to the agent so as to discharge the principal (*t*); but mere delay by the creditor in enforcing payment, or in making application to the principal for the debt, is not sufficient inducement for this purpose, unless there are special circumstances

---

(*r*) *Morgan* v. *Couchman*, 1853, 14 C. B. 100; 2 C. L. R. 53; 23 L. J. C. P. 36.

(*s*) *Curtis* v. *Williamson*, 1874, L. R. 10 Q. B. 57; 44 L. J. Q. B. 27; 31 L. T. 678; 23 W. R. 236; *Taylor* v. *Sheppard*, 1835, 1 Y. & Coll. 271.

(*t*) Illustrations 1 and 2, *Horsfall* v. *Fauntleroy*, 1830, 10 B. & C. 755; *Macfarlane* v. *Giannacopulo*, 1858, 3 H. & N. 860.

rendering the delay misleading in the particular case (*u*).

Where an agent buys goods in his own name from a person who believes him to be buying on his own account, and whilst the seller continues to give exclusive credit to the agent, believing him to be the principal and not knowing of any other person in the transaction, the principal in good faith pays the agent for the goods, the principal is discharged from liability to the seller (*v*).

Except as in this article provided, the principal, whether disclosed or undisclosed, is not discharged, nor is the right of recourse to him affected, by the circumstance that he has paid or settled or otherwise dealt to his prejudice with the agent (*w*).

Illustrations.

1. A creditor takes a security from the agent of his debtor,

(*u*) Illustration 3, *Davison* v. *Donaldson*, 1882, 9 Q. B. D. 623; 4 Asp. M. C. 601; 47 L. T. 564, 31 W. R. 277, C. A. In this case the principal was held not to be discharged by a settlement with his agent, though the creditor made no application to the principal until three years after the debt was contracted, the agent having in the meantime become bankrupt. See, however, *Smethurst* v. *Mitchell*, 1859, 1 El. & El. 623; 28 L. J. Q. B. 241, 5 Jur. N. S. 978, 7 W. R. 226; *Fell* v. *Parkin*, 1882, 52 L. J. Q. B. 99, 47 L. T. 350.

(*v*) *Armstrong* v. *Stokes*, 1872, L. R. 7 Q. B. 598; 41 L. J. Q. B. 253; 26 L. T. 872, 21 W. R. 52, Q. B. This case must be treated as still being law, because it has not been definitely overruled. It is, however, of very doubtful authority, and certainly will not be in the least extended. See, per Brett, L. J., in *Irvine* v. *Watson*, cited below, note (*z*). The decision was expressly confined to the circumstances of the particular case, and was not founded on any general principle.

(*w*) Illustration 3, *Heald* v. *Kenworthy*, 1855, 10 Ex. 739, 24 L. J. Ex. 76, 1 Jur. N. S. 70, *Dent* v. *Dunn*, 1812, 3 Camp. 296, 13 R. R. 809; *Nelson* v. *Powell*, 1784, 3 Doug. 410.

and gives the agent a receipt for the debt. The principal deals to his detriment with the agent on the faith of the receipt. The principal is discharged from liability to the creditor (*x*).

2. Goods were sold, on the terms that they should be paid for in cash, to an agent who appeared to be buying on his own account. The seller omitted to enforce cash payment, and the principal, not knowing that the seller had not been paid, paid the agent for the goods. Held, that the principal was discharged (*y*).

3. A. employed a broker to buy oil. The broker bought from B., telling him that he was acting for a principal, the terms being that the oil should be paid for by "cash on or before delivery." B. delivered the oil without payment, and A., not knowing that B. had not been paid, in good faith paid the broker. The broker soon afterwards became insolvent, and B. sued A. for the price of the oil. It was proved that it was not the invariable custom in the oil trade to insist on prepayment in the case of a sale for "cash on or before delivery." Held, that, in the absence of such an invariable custom, the mere omission to insist on prepayment was not such conduct as would reasonably induce A. to believe that the broker had paid for the oil, and that, therefore, A. was liable to B. for the price (*z*).

Article 94.

RIGHT OF UNDISCLOSED PRINCIPAL TO SUE IN OWN NAME.

The right of an undisclosed principal to sue in his own name on a contract made on his behalf is not

---

(*x*) *Wyatt* v. *Hertford*, 1802, 3 East, 147.

(*y*) *MacClure* v. *Schemeil*, 1871, 20 W. R. 168; *Kymer* v. *Suwercropp*, 1807, 1 Camp. 109, 10 R. R. 646. See, however, Illustration 3.

(*z*) *Irvine* v. *Watson*, 1880, 5 Q. B. D. 102, 414; 49 L. J. Q. B. 239, 531; 42 L. T. 51, 800, C. A. See *Davison* v. *Donaldson*, 1882, 9 Q. B. D. 623; 4 Asp. M. C. 601, 47 L. T. 564, 31 W. R. 277, C. A. The principal must show that he was induced to settle with the agent by the conduct of the creditor, and that he was reasonably misled by such conduct. It is merely an instance of the principle of estoppel by conduct.

affected by the circumstance that the contract is to be partly performed by the agent, and, from the terms thereof, the consideration appears to move from the agent alone(*a*); or by the circumstance that the agent was acting under a *del credere* commission, and has accepted in favour of the principal bills of exchange for the amount due under the contract, the agent having become bankrupt before the maturity of the bills (*b*).

Article 95.

FRAUD, MISREPRESENTATIONS, OR KNOWLEDGE OF AGENT MAY BE SET UP IN AN ACTION BY THE PRINCIPAL.

Where a principal sues upon a contract made by his agent, the fraud, misrepresentation, non-disclosure, or knowledge of either the principal or the agent may be set up by way of defence in the same manner as the fraud, misrepresentation, non-disclosure, or knowledge of the principal might have been if he had himself made the contract.

Illustrations.

1. A person is induced by the fraudulent misrepresentations of the directors to contract to take shares in a company. The contract is voidable as against the company (*c*).

2. An agent who was employed to find a purchaser for certain

(*a*) *Phelps* v. *Prothero*, 1855, 16 C. B. 370, 24 L. J. C. P. 225; 1 Jur. N. S. 1170.

(*b*) *Hornby* v. *Lacy*, 1817, 6 M. & S. 166, 18 R. R. 345.

(*c*) See *Western Bank of Scotland* v. *Addie*, 1867, L. R. 1 H. L. (Sc.) 145, H. L.

property, misrepresented certain facts bearing on the value of the property. Specific performance was refused (*d*).

3. A., knowing that his sheep are diseased, employs an agent to sell them, and conceals their condition from him, intending him to sell them as sound. The agent, believing the sheep to be sound, so represents them to the purchaser. The contract is voidable, on the ground of the principal's fraud (*e*).

4. A. instructed B. to re-insure an overdue ship at a certain rate. B. was unable to obtain the rate mentioned, but received a quotation at a higher rate from C. B. then heard that the vessel was lost, and wired in A.'s name to C. to insure at the higher rate. Subsequent negotiations took place between A. and C., and ultimately C. re-insured the vessel at a higher rate than that originally quoted by him. The jury found that the insurance was effected through B.'s agency. Held, that A. could not recover on the policy, because B. had not disclosed to C. the fact that he had heard of the loss of the ship (*f*).

5. An agent of an assurance company negotiated for a contract of insurance with a man who had lost an eye. Held, that the knowledge of the agent as to the state of health of the assured must be deemed to be the knowledge of the company, and that the company were not entitled to avoid the policy on the ground that the assured had not disclosed the fact that he had lost an eye (*g*).

6. An agent sent notes to his principal by carrier, and they were lost in transit. The carrier had given notice to the principal that he would not be liable for the loss of notes, but had not given any such notice to the agent. An action being brought

---

(*d*) *Mullens* v. *Miller*, 1882, 22 Ch. Div. 194; 52 L. J. Ch. 380; 48 L. T. 103; 31 W. R. 559, C. A. But see *Cornfoot* v. *Fowke*, 1840, 6 M. & W. 358; 4 Jur. 919.

(*e*) *Ludgater* v. *Love*, 1881, 44 L. T. 694; 45 J. P. 600, C. A.; *Cornfoot* v. *Fowke, supra.*

(*f*) *Blackburn* v. *Haslam*, 1888, 21 Q. B. D. 144; 57 L. J. Q. B. 479; 59 L. T. 407, 36 W. R. 855.

(*g*) *Bawden* v. *L. E. & G. Assurance Co.*, (1892) 2 Q. B. 534, C. A. And see Article 96, Illustration 4.

by the principal in respect of the loss of the notes, it was held that the carrier was not liable (*h*).

7. A partner sold certain goods, and they were packed, to his knowledge, for the purpose of smuggling. Held, that the firm were not entitled to recover the price of the goods, though the other partners were not aware of the illegal nature of the transaction (*i*).

Article 96.

HOW FAR PRINCIPAL BOUND BY PAYMENT TO, OR SETTLEMENT WITH, OR SET OFF AGAINST AGENT.

Every person who, in dealing with an agent, is led by the conduct of the principal to believe, and does in fact believe, that he is dealing with the principal, is discharged from liability by payment to or settlement with the agent in any manner which would have operated as a discharge if the agent had been the principal (*j*), and is entitled, as against the principal, to set off a debt due from the agent personally (*k*); provided that he had not, at the time the payment or settlement was made, or the set off accrued, received notice that the agent was not in fact the principal (*l*).

Where a principal permits his agent to have the possession of goods, or of the documents of title there-

---

(*h*) *Mayhew* v. *Eames*, 1825, 3 B. & C. 601; 1 C. & P. 550.

(*i*) *Biggs* v. *Lawrence*, 1789, 3 T. R. 454; 1 R. R. 740.

(*j*) Illustration 1; *Curlewis* v. *Birkbeck*, 1863, 3 F. & F. 894. And see *Favenc* v. *Bennett*, 1809, 11 East, 36; 10 R. R. 425; *Blackburn* v. *Scholes*, 1810, 2 Camp. 343; 11 R. R. 723.

(*k*) Illustrations 2, 5 and 7.

(*l*) Illustrations 8 and 9; *Ex p. Dixon, re Henley*, 1876, 46 L. J. Bk. 20; 25 W. R. 105; 4 Ch. Div. 133, C. A.

to, he is deemed, for the purposes of this article, by his conduct to hold out the agent as the owner of the goods (*m*).

Where an agent contracts in his own name in respect of goods upon which he has a lien as against the principal, the right of the principal to sue on the contract is, while the claims of the agent are unsatisfied, subservient to that of the agent; and a payment to or settlement with the agent during that time, operates as a discharge, notwithstanding that the person making the payment or settlement has had notice from the principal or his trustee in bankruptcy not to pay or settle with the agent (*n*).

Except as in this article provided, the defendant has no right, in an action by the principal, to set off a debt due from the agent personally (*o*); and the principal is not bound by a payment to or settlement with the agent, unless such payment or settlement was made in the ordinary course of business, and in a manner actually or apparently authorized by him (*p*). A custom or usage of business whereby an agent may receive payment on his principal's behalf by way of set off or settlement of accounts is unreasonable, and is not binding on the principal unless he was aware of

---

(*m*) Illustration 2.

(*n*) Illustrations 10 and 11.

(*o*) Illustrations 3 to 9; *Young* v. *White*, 1844, 7 Beav. 506; 8 Jur. 654; 13 L. J. Ch. 419.

(*p*) Illustrations 12 to 14; *Campbell* v. *Hassell*, 1816, 1 Stark. 233; *Kaye* v. *Brett*, 1850, 5 Ex. 269; 19 L. J. Ex. 346; *Mann* v. *Forrester*, 1814, 4 Camp. 60; 15 R. R. 724.

its existence when he authorized the agent to receive the payment (*q*).

Illustrations.

1. A., the owner of certain goods, permits B. to hold himself out as the owner thereof. B. holds himself out as owner to C., and C., believing him to be the owner, receives the goods in part payment of a debt owing by B. C. is not liable to A. for the price of the goods (*r*). If an owner of goods permits his agent to sell them as principal, the buyer is discharged by payment to the agent in any way which would have operated as a discharge if the agent had been the true owner (*s*).

Right of Set off.

2. A factor sells goods in his own name, the buyer dealing with him as principal, and believing him to be selling his own goods. The buyer, in an action by the principal for the price of the goods, has a right to set off a debt due to him from the factor personally, provided that the debt was incurred before he had received notice that the goods did not belong to the factor (*t*).

3. A factor sells goods in his own name, the buyer knowing that he is selling them as factor, but not knowing who the principal is. The principal sues the buyer for the price. The buyer has no right to set off a debt due to him from the

---

(*q*) Illustration 15.

(*r*) *Ramozotti* v. *Bowring*, 1860, 7 C. B. N. S. 851; 29 L. J. C. P. 30; 6 Jur. N. S. 172.

(*s*) *Coates* v. *Lewes*, 1808, 1 Camp. 444; 10 R. R. 725.

(*t*) *Borries* v. *Imperial Ottoman Bank*, 1873, L. R. 9 C. P. 38; 43 L. J. C. P. 3, 29 L. T. 689, 22 W. R. 92, *Carr* v. *Hinchcliffe*, 1825, 7 D. & R. 42; 4 B. & C. 547, *Rabone* v. *Williams*, 1785, 7 T. R. 360; 4 R. R. 463; *Baring* v. *Corrie*, 1818, 2 B. & A. 137, 20 R. R. 383, *George* v. *Clagett*, 1797, 7 T. R. 359; 2 Esp. 557; 4 R. R. 462, *Ex p. Dixon*, 1876, 4 Ch. Div. 133; 46 L. J. Bk. 20; 25 W. R. 105.

factor (*u*). The circumstance that the factor sells under a *del credere* commission does not affect this rule (*v*).

4. A broker purchased goods on behalf of A. from a factor who sold them on behalf of B. The broker knew that the factor sold the goods on behalf of a principal, but A. thought that he was selling his own goods. B. sued A. for the price. Held, that A. was bound by the knowledge of his broker, and therefore had no right to set off a debt due to him from the factor (*w*).

5. A broker, who was intrusted by his principal with the possession of goods, sold them in his own name without disclosing the principal. The buyer knew that he sometimes sold goods in his own name, though acting as a broker, and sometimes sold goods of his own, and in this case had no particular belief one way or the other. Held, that the buyer was not entitled, in an action by the principal for the price, to set off a debt due from the broker personally (*x*). The right to set off, as against the principal, a debt due from the agent, is founded on the principle of estoppel, and to establish such a right the buyer must show that he was led by the conduct of the principal to believe and did in fact believe that the agent was acting as principal (*x*).

6. An agent, with the permission of the owner, sold goods as principal. The agent afterwards became bankrupt, and the principal sued the buyer for non-acceptance of the goods. Held, that the defendant was not entitled to set up, by way of defence, that there were mutual credits between the agent and himself

---

(*u*) *Semenza* v. *Brinsley*, 1865, 18 C. B. N. S. 467; 34 L. J. C. P. 161; 12 L. T. 265; 13 W. R. 634; *Moore* v. *Clementson*, 1809, 2 Camp. 22, 11 R. R. 653, *Fish* v. *Kempton*, 1849, 7 C. B. 687; 18 L. J. C. P. 206; 13 Jur. 750.

(*v*) *Hornby* v. *Lacy*, 1817, 6 M. & S. 166; 18 R. R. 345.

(*w*) *Dresser* v. *Norwood*, 1864, 17 C. B. N. S. 466; 34 L. J. C. P. 48; 10 Jur. N. S. 851; 12 W. R. 1030, Ex. Ch.

(*x*) *Cooke* v. *Eshelby*, 1887, 12 App. Cas. 271, 56 L. J. Q. B. 505, 56 L. T. 673, 35 W. R. 629, H. L., *Baring* v. *Corrie*, 1818, 2 B. & A. 137; 20 R. R. 383.

resulting in a balance in his favour, the mutual credits clause of the Bankruptcy Act applying only as between the bankrupt and his creditors (*y*). In order to constitute a right of set off as against the principal, each of the debts must be liquidated (*z*).

7. A. employed B. to collect general average contributions under an insurance policy. B. instructed a broker to collect the contributions, the broker believing him to be the principal. B. became bankrupt. In an action by A. against the broker for the contributions, as money received to his use, it was held that the defendant was entitled to set off a debt due from B. (*a*).

8. A., who acted as shipping agent for B., a merchant in Havannah, consigned in his own name to C. a cargo of tobacco. C., according to his instructions, insured the cargo for the benefit of all concerned, having had notice that there was a principal. The cargo was lost, and the insurance money was paid to C. after he had received notice that B. claimed it. Held, that C. was not entitled to set off, as against B., debts due to him from A. personally (*b*).

9. Goods were consigned to an agent for sale. The agent pledged the goods to certain brokers as security for a specific advance, and authorized them to sell. The brokers sold the goods, but before receiving the proceeds had notice that the principal was the owner, and that he claimed the proceeds. Held, that the principal was entitled to the balance of the proceeds after deducting the amount of the advance, and that the brokers were not entitled to set off such balance against a general account due to them from the agent (*c*). Otherwise, if they had received the proceeds in the *bonâ fide* belief that they

---

(*y*) *Turner* v. *Thomas*, 1871, L. R. 6 C. P. 610, 40 L. J. C. P. 271; 24 L. T. 879. See 46 & 47 Vict. c. 52, s. 38.

(*z*) *Luckie* v. *Bushby*, 1853, 13 C. B. 864, 1 C. L. R. 685, 22 L. J. C. P. 220, 17 Jur. 625.

(*a*) *Montagu* v. *Forwood*, (1893) 2 Q. B. 350; 69 L. T. 371; 42 W. R. 124; 9 T. L. R. 634, C. A.

(*b*) *Mildred* v. *Maspons*, 1883, 8 App. Cas. 874, 53 L. J. Q. B. 33, 49 L. T. 685, 32 W. R. 125, 5 Asp. M. C. 182, H. L.

(*c*) *Kaltenbach* v. *Lewis*, 1885, 10 App. Cas. 617, 55 L. J. Ch. 58, 53 L. T. 787, 34 W. R. 477, H. L.

belonged to the agent, and had credited the amount in the account with the agent before receiving notice of the principal's claim (*d*).

Where the agent has a lien.

10. A factor, who has a lien on certain goods for advances, sells the goods in his own name. The buyer, though he knew that the factor was acting as an agent, is discharged by a payment to him, even if the payment is by way of set-off (*e*), or is made out of the ordinary course of business (*e*), or after the bankruptcy of the principal and notice from the trustee in bankruptcy not to pay the factor (*f*).

11. A factor, who had a lien on certain goods in excess of their value, sold the goods to A., to whom he was indebted. The factor became bankrupt. A. gave credit for the price of the goods, and proved in the bankruptcy for the residue of his debt against the factor. Held, that this settlement was a good answer to an action by the principal against A. for the price (*g*).

Payment to or settlement with agent.

12. A power of attorney to sell certain stock was given through a country stockbroker to his London agent. The agent sold the stock, and settled with the country broker, who was not authorized to receive payment. The principal did not receive any part of the money. Held, that the principal was not bound by the settlement with the broker, and that the London agent was liable to him for the proceeds of the stock (*h*).

13. An auctioneer sold goods by auction, the conditions pro-

(*d*) *Ibid.*; *New Zealand and Australian Land Co.* v. *Watson*, 1881, 7 Q. B. D. 374; 50 L. J. Q. B. 433; 44 L. T. 675; 29 W. R. 694, C. A.

(*e*) *Warner* v. *M'Kay*, 1836, 1 M. & W. 591; 2 Gale, 86, Ex. Ch.

(*f*) *Drinkwater* v. *Goodwin*, 1775, Cowp. 251.

(*g*) *Hudson* v. *Granger*, 1821, 5 B. & A. 27.

(*h*) *Crossley* v. *Magniac*, (1893) 1 Ch. 594; 67 L. T. 798; 9 T. L. R. 126; 41 W. R. 598.

viding that the deposit should be paid to him at once, and the balance of the purchase-money on or before delivery. The purchaser duly paid the deposit, and on delivery of the goods gave the auctioneer a bill of exchange for the balance. Before the bill matured, the principal revoked the auctioneer's authority to receive payment, and gave notice of the revocation to the purchaser. Held, that the purchaser was not discharged by the payment to the auctioneer, it not being shown that he was authorized, or that it was customary, to take bills of exchange in payment (*i*). A payment to an agent who is known to be such must be in cash in order to bind the principal, unless he authorized the agent, or held him out as having authority to receive payment in some other form (*j*). But a custom in a particular business to receive payment by cheque is reasonable and binding (*k*).

14. An agent is authorized to sell certain goods and receive payment. He sells the goods, and the buyer, knowing that he is acting as an agent, pays him before the credit has expired, deducting discount. The agent does not pay over the money to the principal, and becomes bankrupt before payment is due under the terms of the contract of sale. The principal is not bound by the payment, unless it be shown that it is customary in the ordinary course of the particular business to make payments before they are due, or that the agent had authority to receive payment otherwise than in accordance with the terms of the contract (*l*).

(*i*) *Williams* v. *Evans*, 1866, L. R. 1 Q. B. 352; 35 L. J. Q. B. 111; 13 L. T. 753, 14 W. R. 330.

(*j*) *Sykes* v. *Giles*, 1839, 5 M. & W. 645; *Barker* v. *Greenwood*, 1836, 2 Y. & C. 414, 1 Jur. 541, 6 L. J. (N. S.) Ex. Eq. 54. And see *Papé* v. *Westacott*, (1894) 1 Q. B. 272, 63 L. J. Q. B. 222, 70 L. T. 18, 9 R. 55, C. A., where it was held that a payment by cheque to a house agent was not a good payment.

(*k*) *Bridges* v. *Garrett*, 1870, L. R. 5 C. P. 451, 39 L. J. C. P. 251; 22 L. T. (N. S.) 448, Ex. Ch. Such a custom must be proved.

(*l*) *Catterall* v. *Hindle*, 1867, L. R. 2 C. P. 368, Ex. Ch., *Heisch* v. *Carrington*, 1833, 5 C. & P. 471; *Breming* v. *Mackie*, 1862, 3 F. & F. 197.

15. An insurance broker is authorized to receive payment of moneys due under a policy. The underwriters are not discharged by a payment to the broker by way of set off or settlement of accounts, notwithstanding a usage at "Lloyds" permitting payment in such a manner, unless the principal is shown to have been aware of such usage (*m*). So, a custom of the Stock Exchange, whereby a member who has sold shares on the instructions of a country broker acting for an undisclosed principal, may set off against the proceeds a debt due from the country broker in respect of other transactions, is not binding on principals who are not shown to have been aware of the custom (*n*).

Sect. 3.—*Liability of the principal for torts of agent.*

Article 97.

PRINCIPAL LIABLE FOR ALL AGENT'S TORTS IN COURSE OF EMPLOYMENT ON HIS BEHALF.

Where loss or injury is caused to third persons, or a penalty is incurred (*o*), by any wrongful act or omission of an agent while acting on behalf of the prin-

---

(*m*) *Sweeting* v. *Pearce*, 1859, 7 C. B. N. S. 449; 29 L. J. C. P. 265; *Bartlett* v. *Pentland*, 1830, 10 B. & C. 760; *Todd* v. *Reid*, 1821, 4 B. & Ald. 210; *Stewart* v. *Aberdein*, 1838, 4 M. & W. 211, 1 H. & H. 284. And see *Hine* v. *SS. Ins. Syndicate*, 1895, 72 L. T. 79, 11 T. L. R. 224, as to payment by bill of exchange.

(*n*) *Blackburn* v. *Mason*, 4 R. 297; 68 L. T. 510; 9 T. L. R. 286, C. A.; *Pearson* v. *Scott*, 1878, 38 L. T. N. S. 747, 26 W. R. 796, 9 Ch. Div. 198; 47 L. J. Ch. 705, *Underwood* v. *Nicholls*, 1855, 17 C. B. 239; 25 L. J. C. P. 79.

(*o*) As to liability for penalties, see *A.-G.* v. *Siddon*, 1830, 1 C. & J. 220, 1 Tyr. 41, *A.-G.* v. *Riddle*, 1832, 2 C. & J. 493, 2 Tyr. 523, *Reg.* v. *Stephens*, 1865, L. R. 1 Q. B. 702, 14 L. T. 593; 14 W. R. 859, 7 B. & S. 710, *Miles* v. *M'Ilwraith*, 1883, 8 App. Cas. 120; 52 L. J. P. C. 17, 48 L. T. 689; 31 W. R. 591, P. C.

cipal (*p*), either in the ordinary course of his employment (*q*), or with the authority of the principal (*r*), the principal is liable therefor jointly and severally with the agent (*s*).

Illustrations.

1. A factor makes misrepresentations as to the quality of goods sold on his principal's behalf. The principal is liable in an action for deceit, even if he did not authorize the factor to make the misrepresentations, to the same extent as if he had made them himself (*t*).

2. An agent, while acting in the ordinary course of his employment on the principal's behalf, infringes a patent. The principal is liable for the infringement (*u*).

3. A bailiff wrongfully distrains chattels after having improperly refused a tender of the rent and expenses. The landlord for whom he is acting is liable for the wrongful distraint (*v*).

(*p*) See Article 99.

(*q*) See *Bartonshill Coal Co.* v. *McGuire, Same* v. *Reid*, 1858, 3 Macq. at p. 283, and p. 306, H. L. And see Illustrations, and Article 99.

(*r*) A husband is still liable for his wife's torts during coverture *Seroka* v. *Kattenberg*, 1886, 17 Q. B. D. 177.

(*s*) It is no defence that the act amounts to felony: *Osborn* v. *Gillett*, 1873, L. R. 8 Ex. 88, 28 L. T. 197, 21 W. R. 409. As to intentional wrongs, see Article 100.

(*t*) *Hern* v. *Nichols*, 1 Salk. 289.

(*u*) *Sykes* v. *Howarth*, 1879, 12 Ch. Div. 826, 48 L. J. Ch. 769, 41 L. T. 79. And see *Betts* v. *De Vitre*, 1868, L. R. 3 Ch. 429, 37 L. J. Ch. 325, 18 L. T. 165, 16 W. R. 529.

(*v*) *Hatch* v. *Hale*, 1850, 15 Q. B. 10; 19 L. J. Q. B. 289; 14 Jur. 459; *Hurry* v. *Rickman*, 1831, 1 M. & Rob. 126. And see *Gauntlett* v. *King*, 1857, 3 C. B. N. S. 59, *Freeman* v. *Rosher*, 1849, 13 Q. B. 780, 18 L. J. Q. B. 340, *Haselar* v. *Lemoyne*, 1858, 5 C. B. N. S. 530, 28 L. J. C. P. 103. The distinctions made in these cases between the actions of trespass and case are not of importance since the Judicature Act, 1873, the liability of the landlord now depends simply upon whether in doing the

4. A servant of an incorporated company, in the ordinary course of his employment on the company's behalf, wrongfully refuses to deliver up goods to the owner. The company are liable for the conversion (*w*). A corporation is liable for the wrongs of its agents to the same extent as an individual principal would be (*x*). The better opinion seems to be that this is so, even when malice in fact is an essential element in the wrong (*y*); but this cannot yet be considered as altogether free from doubt (*z*). Municipal and public authorities, though acting in the performance of a public duty, without reward or funds, are liable for the negligence, in the course of their employment, of agents employed by them (*a*).

5. A solicitor by an indorsement on the back of a writ of execution directing the sheriff to levy the goods of a judgment debtor, misled the sheriff by giving the address of the debtor's father, and the father's goods were wrongfully seized by the

---

wrongful act the bailiff is acting on his behalf, and in the ordinary course of his employment or with his authority.

(*w*) *Barnett* v. *Crystal Palace Co.*, 1861, 4 L. T. 403, *Taff Vale Rail. Co.* v. *Giles*, 1853, 2 El. & Bl. 822, 23 L. J. Q. B. 43, 18 Jur. 510, Ex. Ch.; *Yarborough* v. *Bank of England*, 1812, 16 East, 6, 14 R. R. 272.

(*x*) *Ranger* v. *G. W. Rail.*, 1854, 5 H. L. Cas. 72, H. L.; *Smith* v. *Birmingham Gas Co.*, 1834, 3 N. & M. 771, *Maund* v. *Monmouth Canal Co.*, 1842, 4 M. & G. 452, 5 Railw. Cas. 159, Car. & M. 606, 5 Scott, N. R. 457, 6 Jur. 932.

(*y*) See *Edwards* v. *Mid. Rail. Co.*, 1880, 6 Q. B. D. 287; 50 L. J. Q. B. 281; 43 L. T. 694, 29 W. R. 609, 45 J. P. 374: overruling, on this point, *Stevens* v. *Mid. Counties Rail. Co.*, 1854, 2 C. L. R. 1300, 10 Ex. 352; 23 L. J. Ex. 328, 18 Jur. 932.

(*z*) See per Chelmsford, L. C., in *Western Bank of Scotland* v. *Addie*, 1867, L. R. 1 H. L. Sc. 145, *Nevill* v. *Fine Arts and General Ins. Co.*, (1895) 2 Q. B. 156, 72 L. T. 525; 64 L. J. Q. B. 681, C. A.

(*a*) *Scott* v. *Manchester*, 1857, 2 H. & N. 204, 26 L. J. Ex. 406; 3 Jur. N. S. 590, Ex. Ch.; *Cowley* v. *Sunderland*, 1861, 6 H. & N. 565, 30 L. J. Ex. 127, 4 L. T. 120, *Mersey Docks Trustees* v. *Gibbs*, 1864, L. R. 1 H. L. 93, 12 Jur. N. S. 571, 14 L. T. 677, H. L., *Coe* v. *Wise*, 1866, L. R. 1 Q. B. 711, 37 L. J. Q. B. 262, 14 L. T. 891, 7 B. & S. 831; *Jones* v. *Bird*, 1822, 1 D. & R. 497, 5 B. & A. 837, *The Rhosina*, 1885, 10 P. Div. 131, 54 L. J. P. 72, 53 L. T. 30; 33 W. R. 794; 5 Asp. M. C. 460, C. A.

sheriff. Held, that the client was liable for the wrongful seizure, it being part of the solicitor's duty, in the ordinary course of his employment, to indorse the writ (*b*). Otherwise, where a solicitor, in issuing a writ, verbally directed the sheriff to seize particular goods which were not the debtor's property (*c*).

6. A. employed B., a solicitor, to sue for a debt. C., who was B.'s agent, issued execution after the debt had been paid to B., C. being ignorant of such payment. Held, that both A. and B. were liable for the trespass (*d*).

7. A carman was permitted by his employer to take an hour for dinner, but was not permitted to go home to dine, nor to leave his horse. He left his horse unattended, and went home to dinner. The horse bolted, and caused damage. Held, that the jury were justified in finding that the damage was caused by the negligence of the carman in the course of his employment, for which the employer would be liable (*e*). So, where a carman left a coal-shoot open in the highway, his employer was held liable for injury resulting therefrom (*f*). So, a shipowner is liable for damage caused by a collision in consequence of the negligence or unreasonable navigation of the master, subject to a statutory limitation on the liability, based on the tonnage of the vessel (*g*).

8. A. sent a barge under the management of his lighterman to be loaded at a wharf. The foreman at the wharf directed

---

(*b*) *Morris* v. *Salberg*, 1889, 22 Q. B. D. 614; 61 L. T. 283, C. A.; *Jarmain* v. *Hooper*, 1843, 1 D. & L. 769, 6 M. & G. 827, 8 Jur. 127.

(*c*) *Smith* v. *Keal*, 1882, 9 Q. B. D. 340, 47 L. T. 142, 31 W. R. 76, C. A.

(*d*) *Bates* v. *Pilling*, 1826, 6 B. & C. 38, 9 D. & R. 44.

(*e*) *Whatman* v. *Pearson*, 1868, L. R. 3 C. P. 422. Comp. with Illustrations 9 and 10 to Article 99.

(*f*) *Whiteley* v. *Pepper*, 1876, 2 Q. B. D. 276, 46 L. J. Q. B. 436, 36 L. T. 588, 25 W. R. 607.

(*g*) *The Thames*, 1805, 5 Rob. 345. See 57 & 58 Vict. c. 60. Liability for damage to cargo depends on the bill of lading. see *The Duero*, 1869, L. R. 2 Adm. 393; 38 L. J. Adm. 69.

the lighterman to move another barge out of his way, and the lighterman did so, causing damage to such other barge. Held, that A. was liable to make good the damage (*h*).

9. A master told his servant to lay rubbish near a neighbour's wall, but so as not to touch the wall. The rubbish ran against the wall. Held, that the master was liable for the trespass (*i*).

10. An inspector of a railway company gave a passenger into custody on a charge of refusing to give up his ticket or pay his fare, and thereby defrauding the company. Held, that the company, having power to arrest passengers committing such a fraud, were liable in an action for false imprisonment, the inspector being their representative at the station in question, and having made a mistake in arresting the plaintiff (*j*). So, where a tram conductor, who had authority to seize anyone seeking to avoid payment of his fare, gave a passenger into custody for tendering what the conductor thought was bad money, the company were held liable (*k*).

11. A porter, in the erroneous belief that a passenger was in the wrong train, violently pulled him out of the railway carriage, and the passenger was injured. It was the duty of the porter, as far as possible, to prevent passengers from going by wrong trains, but not to remove them from carriages. Held, that the jury were justified in finding that it was an act done by the porter in the course of his employment, for which the company would be liable. He simply did in an improper manner what he was employed to do (*l*).

(*h*) *Page* v. *Defries*, 1866, 7 B. & S. 137, overruling *Lamb* v. *Palk*, 1840, 9 C. & P. 629.

(*i*) *Gregory* v. *Piper*, 1829, 9 B. & C. 591; 4 M. & R. 500.

(*j*) *Moore* v. *Metropolitan Rail. Co.*, 1872, L. R. 8 Q. B. 36; 42 L. J. Q. B. 23, 27 L. T. 579, 21 W. R. 145; *Goff* v. *G. N. Rail.*, 1861, 3 El. & El. 672; 30 L. J. Q. B. 148, 3 L. T. 850. Comp. with Illustrations 6 and 7 to Article 99.

(*k*) *Furlong* v *South London Tramways Co.*, 1884, 48 J. P. 329, 1 C. & E. 316. Comp. with Illustration 5 to Article 99.

(*l*) *Bayley* v. *M. S. & L. Rail.*, 1873, L. R. 8 C. P. 148, 42 L. J. C. P.

12. A tram conductor negligently and brutally pushed a passenger off the tram because he refused to pay his fare. The company were held liable for the assault and injury (*m*). So, where a passenger who misconducted himself was carelessly and with unnecessary violence dragged from a tram by the conductor and thrown to the ground, the employer was held liable for the injury (*n*).

Article 98.

MONEY, ETC. MISAPPROPRIATED BY AGENT.

Where the money or property of a third person is received by an agent while acting within the scope of his apparent authority, or by the principal, and is misapplied by the agent, the principal is liable to make good the loss.

Illustrations.

1. A local manager, acting as agent for a bank, induced a lady to invest money in paying off a certain mortgage. The money was paid to him for that purpose, and he misappropriated it. Held, that he was acting within the scope of his apparent authority in receiving the money, which must therefore be deemed to have been received by the bank, and that the bank was liable to repay it (*o*).

78; 28 L. T. 366, Ex. Ch.; and see *Lowe* v. *G. N. Rail.*, 1893, 62 L. J. Q. B. 524; 5 R. 535.

(*m*) *Smith* v. *North Met. Tram. Co.*, 1891, 55 J. P. 630; 7 T. L. R. 459, C. A. See also *East. Counties Rail. Co.* v. *Broom*, 1851, 6 Ex. 314; 20 L. J. Ex. 196; 15 Jur. 297. The fact that the agent has been convicted and criminally punished for the assault does not affect the liability of the principal. *Dyer* v. *Munday*, (1895) 1 Q. B. 742, 64 L. J. Q. B. 448, 73 L. T. 12; 43 W. R. 657; 11 T. L. R. 282, C. A.

(*n*) *Seymour* v. *Greenwood*, 1861, 30 L. J. Ex. 327, 7 H. & N. 355, 9 W. R. 785, Ex. Ch.

(*o*) *Thompson* v. *Bell*, 1854, 10 Ex. 10, 2 C. L. R. 1213, 23 L. J. Ex.

2. An agent, acting apparently in the ordinary course of business, sent an account to A., representing that certain advances had been made on his account, and drew on him for the amount. It was within the scope of the agent's authority to make advances of that kind, but he had, in fact, misappropriated the money, and had not made the advances. A. accepted and paid the bill. Held, that the principal was liable to A. for the amount (*p*).

3. The directors of an unincorporated company held out the secretary as having authority to receive, as agent for the company, loans in excess of the company's borrowing powers. The secretary borrowed in excess of the company's powers, and appropriated the money to his own use. Held, that the directors were personally liable for the amount so borrowed in excess (*q*). (The company were not liable, because the act was *ultra vires*.)

4. A., the manager of a shop belonging to B., had for several years ordered goods in B.'s name from C., and B. had duly paid for them. A. absconded, called on C. and bought goods in B.'s name, and took them away. Held, that B. was liable for the price of the goods (*r*).

Article 99.

PRINCIPAL NOT LIABLE FOR WRONGS OUTSIDE COURSE OF EMPLOYMENT ON HIS BEHALF.

No principal is liable for any wrongful act or omission of his agent while acting, without the principal's authority, outside the ordinary course of his

321. See also *Melville* v. *Doidge*, 1848, 6 C. B. 450; 18 L. J. C. P. 7; 12 Jur. 922; *Mutual Aid, &c., Society, Ex p. James*, 1883, 49 L. T. 530.

(*p*) *Swire* v. *Francis*, 1877, 3 App. Cas. 106, 37 L. T. N. S. 554, P. C.

(*q*) *Chapleo* v. *Brunswick Building Society*, 1881, 6 Q. B. D. 696, 50 L. J. Q. B. 372, 44 L. T. 449, C. A.

(*r*) *Summers* v. *Solomon*, 1857, 26 L. J. Q. B. 301; 3 Jur. N. S. 962.

employment (*s*), or while acting otherwise than on the principal's behalf (*t*).

Illustrations.

1. A bailiff, who is employed to levy a distress for water rates, commits an unnecessary and unauthorized assault in levying the distress. His employer is not liable for the assault (*u*).

2. A solicitor, when issuing a writ of *fieri facias*, verbally directs the sheriff to seize particular goods, without the client's authority. The client is not liable for the wrongful seizure, because it is not in the ordinary course of a solicitor's employment to interfere with the sheriff in the performance of his duties (*v*).

3. The secretary of a company fraudulently, and without the knowledge of the directors, represented to A. that if he took certain shares he would be appointed solicitor to the company, and subsequently that he had been so appointed. A., on the faith of the representations, applied for the shares, and they were allotted to him in the usual way. Held, that A. was bound by the contract to take the shares, the representations being quite outside the scope of the secretary's employment. The duties of a secretary are *primâ facie* clerical and ministerial only, and it is not within the ordinary course of his employment to induce persons to take shares, nor to make any bargains or conditions as to taking shares (*w*).

4. A company declared dividends which were not warranted by its financial condition. A law agent (who was also a member) of the company mentioned the dividends to A. as proof of the

(*s*) Illustrations 1 to 8.

(*t*) Illustrations 8 to 11.

(*u*) *Richards* v. *West Middlesex Waterworks Co.*, 1885, 15 Q. B. D. 660, 54 L. J. Q. B. 551, 33 W R. 902, 49 J. P 631.

(*v*) *Smith* v. *Keal*, 1882, 9 Q. B. D. 340, 47 L. T. 142, 31 W. R. 76, C. A.

(*w*) *Newlands* v. *National Employers Accident Association*, 1885, 54 L. J. Q. B. 428; 53 L. T. 242, 49 J. P. 628, C. A.

flourishing condition of the company, and on the faith of his representations A. purchased shares. Held, that A. was bound by his contract to take the shares, it not being in the ordinary course of a law agent's employment to make representations as to the financial state of the company (*x*).

5. A tram conductor detained and gave into custody a passenger on a charge of having passed bad money, she having already paid her fare and received the change. Printed instructions were issued to the conductors not to give persons into custody without the authority of an inspector or timekeeper. Under the Tramways Act, the officers and servants of the company had authority to detain anyone defrauding the company of the fare. Held, that the Act must be construed as applying only to officers and servants appointed for the purpose, and that the company were not liable for the detention or wrongful imprisonment of the passenger (*y*).

6. A station-master detained a person for not having paid the fare for his horse, the railway company having no power to arrest in such cases. Held, that the company were not liable, because it was beyond their powers to authorize the detention (*z*).

7. A barman gave a person into custody for attempting to pass bad money, the bad money having been returned and good money paid. Held, that the employer was not liable (*a*). So, where a booking clerk gave a person into custody for attempting to steal from the till, after the attempt had ceased, the railway company were held not liable (*b*). The liability of a principal

---

(*x*) *Burnes* v. *Pennell*, 1849, 2 H. L. Cas. 497, H. L.

(*y*) *Charleston* v. *London Tram. Co.*, 1888, 36 W. R. 367. Comp. with Illustration 9 to Article 97.

(*z*) *Poulton* v. *L. & S. W. Rail. Co.*, 1867, L. R. 2 Q. B. 534; 36 L. J. Q. B. 294; 17 L. T. 11, 8 B. & S. 616. Comp. with Illustration 10 to Article 97.

(*a*) *Abraham* v. *Deakin*, (1891) 1 Q. B. 516; 60 L. J. Q. B. 238; 63 L. T. 690, 39 W. R. 183, 55 J. P. 212; 7 T. L. R. 117, C. A.

(*b*) *Allen* v. *L. & S. W. Rail.*, 1870, L. R. 6 Q. B. 65; 40 L. J. Q. B. 55, 23 L. T. 612, 19 W. R. 127. Compare with Illustration 10 to Article 97.

for false imprisonment in such cases depends upon whether it is within the ordinary course of the agent's employment to arrest persons or give them into custody on behalf of the principal, and the general rule is that an agent or servant has implied authority to do so only when such a course is necessary for the protection of his principal's or master's property (*c*).

8. A clerk, without the authority of his master, used his master's lavatory and carelessly left the tap running. Held, that the master was not liable for the damage done (*d*).

9. A carman, having finished work for the day, goes off on a journey of his own for his own purposes, and causes damage by his negligent driving. The employer is not liable (*e*).

10. A servant obtained permission to take out his master's horse and trap for purposes of his own, and proposed to bring something back with him on behalf of the master. Held, that the master was not liable for damage caused by the servant's negligence in the course of the drive (*f*).

11. A shipowner is not liable for the negligence of a compulsory pilot, because the pilot is not deemed to be acting as his agent. Otherwise, if the employment of a pilot is optional (*g*).

(*c*) *Edwards* v. *L. & N. W. Rail.*, 1870, L. R. 5 C. P. 445; 39 L. J. C. P. 241; 22 L. T. 656, 18 W. R. 834, *Bank of New South Wales* v. *Owston*, 1879, 4 App. Cas. 270, 48 L. J. P. C. 25, 40 L. T. 500, P. C.; *Walker* v. *S. E. Rail.*, 1870, L. R. 5 C. P. 640, 39 L. J. C. P. 346; 23 L. T. 14, 18 W. R. 1032, *Rowe* v. *London Pianoforte Co.*, 1876, 34 L. T. 450; *Roe* v. *Birkenhead, &c. Rail. Co.*, 1851, 7 Ex. 36, 6 Railw. Cas. 795, 21 L. J. Ex. 9; *Stevens* v. *Hinshelwood*, 1891, 55 J. P. 341, C. A.

(*d*) *Stevens* v. *Woodward*, 1881, 6 Q. B. D. 318; 50 L. J. Q. B. 231; 44 L. T. 153; 29 W. R. 506.

(*e*) *Storey* v. *Ashton*, 1869, L. R. 4 Q. B. 476; 38 L. J. Q. B. 223, 17 W. R. 727; 10 B. & S. 337, *Rayner* v. *Mitchell*, 1877, 2 C. P. D. 357, 25 W. R. 633, *Mitchell* v. *Crassweller*, 1853, 13 C. B. 237, 22 L. J. C. P. 100, 17 Jur. 716. Comp. Illustration 7 to Article 97.

(*f*) *Cormack* v. *Digby*, 1876, 9 Ir. R. C. L. 557, *Patten* v. *Rea*, 1857, 2 C. B. N. S. 606, 26 L. J. C. P 235.

(*g*) *Lucey* v. *Ingram*, 1840, 6 M. & W. 302, *The Maria*, 1839, 1 Rob. N. A. 95.

Article 100.

HOW FAR LIABLE FOR INTENTIONAL WRONGS BY AGENT.

Except as provided in Article 98, no principal is liable in excess of the value of the benefit (if any) acquired by him (*h*), for any fraud or other intentional wrong committed without his authority, unless it was committed on his behalf (*i*). But every principal is civilly liable for every fraud or other intentional wrong committed by his agent in the ordinary course of his employment, and for the benefit of the principal (*j*), though he did not authorize (*j*), and even if he had expressly forbidden it (*k*).

Illustrations.

1. The secretary of a company, for his own benefit, fraudulently gave untrue answers to inquiries as to the validity of certain debenture stock. The jury found that he was held out by the company as a person to answer such inquiries on their behalf. Held, that the company were not liable, because the fraud was committed by the secretary for his own private purposes, and not on behalf of the company (*l*).

(*h*) See *Ex p. Shoolbred*, 1880, 28 W. R. 339; *Western Bank of Scotland* v. *Addie*, 1867, L. R. 1 H. L. Sc. 145, H. L.

(*i*) Illustrations 1, 2, 4 and 5; *Lyons* v. *Martin*, 1838, 8 A. & E. 512; 3 N. & P. 509; *Weir* v. *Barnett*, 1878, 3 Ex. Div. 238; 47 L. J. Ex. 704; 38 L. T. 929; 26 W. R. 746, C. A.; *Williams* v. *Preston*, 1882, 20 Ch. Div. 672; 51 L. J. Ch. 927; 47 L. T. 265, 30 W. R. 555, C. A.; *M'Manus* v. *Crickett*, 1800, 1 East, 106; 5 R. R. 518; *Gordon* v. *Rolt*, 1849, 4 Ex. 365; 7 D. & L. 87; 18 L. J. Ex. 432.

(*j*) Illustrations 3 to 9; *Doe* d. *Willis* v. *Martin*, 1790, 4 T. R. 39; 2 R. R. 324; *Bowles* v. *Stewart*, 1803, 1 Sch. & Lef. 209.

(*k*) Illustration 6.

(*l*) *British Mutual Bank* v. *Charnwood Forest Rail.*, 1887, 18 Q. B. D.

2. A wharfinger's agent, who had authority to give receipts for goods actually received by him, fraudulently, and not for the wharfinger's benefit, gave a receipt for goods which he had not, in fact, received. Held, that the wharfinger was not liable, the fraud not being committed on his behalf or with his authority (*m*).

3. The servants of an omnibus company, in the course of their employment on behalf of the company, molest and interfere with a person in his use of the highway. The company are liable (*n*).

4. A servant wantonly, and not for the purpose of his master's business, strikes the horse of a third person. The master is not liable. Otherwise, if the servant had struck the horse in the course of his employment and for the master's supposed benefit (*o*).

5. An omnibus driver, intending to strike with his whip the driver of another bus, struck a passenger and injured him. Held, that the question whether the employer was liable or not depended on whether the act was done in private spite or in the supposed furtherance of the employer's interest (*p*).

6. An omnibus driver, in order to prevent a rival bus from passing him, drove recklessly and caused the rival bus to overturn. The driver had received printed instructions from his employers not to race with nor obstruct other buses. Held,

---

714; 56 L. J. Q. B. 449, 57 L. T. 833, 35 W. R. 590, 52 J. P. 150, C. A. Followed in *Thorne* v. *Heard*, (1895) A. C. 495, 64 L. J. Ch. 652, 11 T. L. R. 464, H. L. affirming (1894) 1 Ch. 599, 63 L. J. Ch. 356; 70 L. T. 541; 42 W. R. 274, C. A. *Shaw* v. *Port Philip Gold Mining Co.*, 1884, 13 Q. B. D. 103; 53 L. J. Q. B. 369, 50 L. T. 685, would seem to be no longer law.

(*m*) *Coleman* v. *Riches*, 1855, 3 Ch. R. 795, 24 L. J. C. P. 125, 1 Jur. N. S. 596.

(*n*) *Green* v. *L. G. O. Co.*, 1859, 7 C. B. N. S. 290, 29 L. J. C. P. 13; 6 Jur. N. S. 228, 1 L. T. 95; 8 W. R. 88.

(*o*) *Croft* v. *Alison*, 1821, 4 B. & A. 590, *Ellis* v. *Turner*, 1800, 8 T. R. 531, 5 R. R. 441.

(*p*) *Ward* v. *G. O. Co.*, 1873, 42 L. J. C. P. 265, 28 L. T. 850, Ex. Ch.

that the employers were liable, the wrongful act being done for their benefit and in the course of the servant's employment (*q*).

7. A wife, who managed a business on her husband's behalf, fraudulently misrepresented the quantity of business done to an intending purchaser, who subsequently bought the business on the faith of such misrepresentations. Held, that the husband was liable for the fraud (*r*).

8. An agent made fraudulent misrepresentations as to the quality of an article, and a person was thereby induced to purchase it from him for more than its value. Held, that the principal was liable in an action of deceit for the misrepresentations, though they were made without his authority or knowledge (*s*). So, fraudulent misrepresentations made by directors on behalf and for the benefit of a company, bind the company, though the shareholders be not aware either of the misrepresentations or of their falsehood (*t*).

9. It was the duty of an agent of a banking corporation to obtain the acceptance of bills in which the corporation was interested. He fraudulently, and without the knowledge of the directors, made a misrepresentation, whereby a person was misled and induced to accept a bill in which the corporation was interested. Held, that as the misrepresentation was made in the course of the agent's employment and for the benefit of the corporation, the corporation was liable in an action for deceit, though the agent was not authorized to make the misrepresentation (*u*). Whenever an agent, for the benefit of the prin-

---

(*q*) *Limpus* v. *L. G. O. Co.*, 1862, 1 H. & C. 526; 32 L. J. Ex. 34; 9 Jur. N. S. 333; 7 L. T. 641; 11 W. R. 149, Ex. Ch.

(*r*) *Taylor* v. *Green*, 1837, 8 C. & P. 316.

(*s*) *Udell* v. *Atherton*, 1861, 7 H. & N. 172; 30 L. J. Ex. 337; 7 Jur. N. S. 777; 4 L. T. 797.

(*t*) *National Exchange Co. of Glasgow* v. *Drew*, 1855, 2 Macq. 103, H. L.

(*u*) *Mackay* v. *Commercial Bank of New Brunswick*, 1874, L. R. 5 P. C. 394, 43 L. J. P. C. 31, 30 L. T. 180; 22 W. R. 473, P. C. See, however, *dicta* of Chelmsford, L. C., in *Western Bank of Scotland* v. *Addie*, 1867, 1 H. L. Sc. 145, to the effect that an action for deceit will not lie against a corporation.

cipal, commits a fraud or other wrong in the course of his employment, the principal is answerable (*v*).

Article 101.

HOW FAR LIABLE FOR MISREPRESENTATIONS BELIEVED BY AGENT TO BE TRUE.

Where a principal intentionally conceals from his agent circumstances material to the business for which the agent is employed, in order that the agent may make misrepresentations relating to such circumstances, and the agent in good faith makes any such misrepresentation believing it to be true, the principal is liable therefor to the same extent as if the agent had made it fraudulently, knowing it to be false. Whether a principal, in the absence of such an intentional concealment, is liable for a statement known by him to be false, but made without his knowledge or authority by an agent who believes it to be true, is a question upon which there is a conflict of authority, and which cannot be considered settled.

In *Cornfoot* v. *Fowke* (*w*), decided in 1840, in the Court of Exchequer, the circumstances were as follows:—An agent was employed to let a house, and on being asked by C. if there was

---

(*v*) *Barwick* v. *English Joint Stock Bank*, 1867, L. R. 2 Ex. 259, Ex. Ch.; *Swire* v. *Francis*, 1877, 3 App. Cas. 106. And see *Weir* v. *Barnett*, 1878, 3 Ex. Div. 238; 47 L. J. Ex. 704, 38 L. T. 929, 26 W. R. 746, C. A.

(*w*) 6 M. & W. 358; 4 Jur. 919. And see *Wilde* v. *Gibson*, 1848, 1 H. L. Cas. 605, 12 Jur. 527, H. L.; *Derry* v. *Peek*, 1891, 14 App. Cas. 337; 58 L. J. Ch. 864, 61 L. T. 265, 38 W. R. 33, 1 Meg. 292, H. L.

any objection to the house, said that there was not. On the faith of this representation, C. entered into an agreement for a lease. C. then discovered that the adjoining house was a brothel. In an action against C. for non-performance of the agreement, he pleaded fraud and misrepresentation. It appeared that the principal was aware of the objection to the house, but that the agent was not. Held, that the plea was bad, though it would have been otherwise if the principal had expressly authorized the agent to say that the nuisance did not exist, or had intentionally employed an ignorant agent in order that he might innocently make a false statement, believing it to be true. In *Fuller* v. *Wilson*, 1842 (*x*), an agent who was employed to sell a house described it as being free from taxes, and it was bought on the faith of that description. The principal knew that the house was not free from taxes, but the agent did not. The Court of Queen's Bench held that the principal was liable in an action for deceit, though it did not appear that he had authorized the agent to make any representation as to the taxes. This case, however, was reversed, on other grounds, on appeal. In *Ludgater* v. *Love*, 1881 (*y*), an agent who was employed to sell sheep represented them as being sound. The principal knew that the sheep had the rot and concealed that fact from the agent, intending him to represent them as sound. The Court of Appeal held that the principal was liable in an action for fraudulent misrepresentation, having intentionally employed an agent ignorant of the truth, in order that he might make a false statement. *Cornfoot* v. *Fowke* was doubted in this case, and was thought to have been decided on a mere point of pleading; but its authority has been strengthened by the judgments of the Lords in *Derry* v. *Peek* (*z*), and it would seem more satisfactory, if the principal ought to be liable in cases where neither he nor the agent is guilty of fraud, to base his liability on an

(*x*) 3 Q. B. 58; 2 G. & D. 460.

(*y*) 44 L. T. 694; 45 J. P. 600, C. A.

(*z*) 1891, 14 App. Cas. 337; 58 L. J. Ch. 864; 61 L. T. 265; 38 W. R. 33, 1 Meg. 292, H. L.

implied warranty that representations made by the agent in the course of his employment are true.

Article 102.

NOT LIABLE FOR MISREPRESENTATIONS BY AGENT AS TO CREDIT, ETC., OF THIRD PERSONS.

No action can be maintained against a principal in respect of any representation as to the character, conduct, credit, ability, trade or dealings of another person, to the intent that such other person may obtain credit (*a*), unless such representation is in writing, signed by the principal—the signature of an agent is not sufficient, even if expressly authorized by the principal (*b*).

Sect. 4.—*Admissions by and notice to agents.*

Article 103.

HOW FAR AGENT'S ADMISSIONS EVIDENCE AGAINST THE PRINCIPAL.

An admission or representation by an agent is evidence against the principal—

(a) where it is made with his authority; or

(b) where it concerns a matter upon which the agent is employed on his behalf at the time that the admission or representation is made,

(*a*) "May obtain credit, money or goods upon (*sic*), unless, &c."

(*b*) Lord Tenterden's Act (9 Geo. IV. c. 14), s. 6, *Swift* v. *Jewesbury*, 1874, L. R. 9 Q. B. 301; 30 L. T. 31, 43 L. J. Q. B. 56; 22 W. R. 319, Ex. Ch.; *Williams* v. *Mason*, 1873, 28 L. T. 232, 21 W. R. 386.

and is made in the ordinary course of that employment (*c*); or

(c) where it concerns a matter respecting which the person to whom the admission or representation is made was expressly referred by the principal to the agent for information (*d*);

provided, that a report made by an agent to his principal cannot be used as evidence against the principal by third persons (*e*).

No principal is bound by any unauthorized admission or representation concerning any matter upon which the agent who makes it is not employed on his behalf at the time that it is made (*f*), or which is not made in the ordinary course of the agent's employment (*g*), unless he expressly refers to the agent for information on the particular matter (*d*).

(*c*) Illustrations 1 to 6; *Standage* v. *Creighton*, 1832, 5 C. & P. 406; *Meux's Exors'. case*, 1852, 2 De G. M. & G. 522. As to statements in bills of lading signed by the master, see *M'Lean* v. *Fleming*, 1871, 2 H. L. Sc. App. 128, 25 L. T. 317, H. L., *Howard* v. *Tucker*, 1831, 1 B. & Ad. 712, *The Prosperino Palasso*, 1872, 29 L. T. 622; 2 Asp. 158, *The Ida*, 1875, 32 L. T. 541, P. C.

(*d*) Illustration 7.

(*e*) Illustrations 9 and 10, *Rayner* v. *Pearson*, 1812, 4 Taunt. 662; *Kahl* v. *Jahnsen*, 1812, 4 Taunt. 565. See, however, *The Solway*, 1885, 10 P. D. 137, 54 L. J. P. 83; 53 L. T. 680, 34 W. R. 232, 5 Asp. M. C. 482.

(*f*) Illustrations 2 to 6, *Fairlie* v. *Hastings*, 1803, 10 Ves. 123; *Betham* v. *Benson*, 1818, Gow, 45; *Peto* v. *Hague*, 1804, 5 Esp. 134; *Allen* v. *Denstone*, 1839, 8 C. & P. 760.

(*g*) Illustration 8, *Schumack* v. *Lock*, 1825, 10 Moore, 39; *Garth* v. *Howard*, 1832, 1 M. & Scott, 628; 8 Bing. 451, 5 C. & P. 346, *Whitehouse* v. *Abberley*, 1845, 1 C. & K. 642, *Olding* v. *Smith*, 1852, 16 Jur. 497.

Illustrations.

1. A parcel sent by railway was lost in transit. The station master, in the ordinary course of his duty, made a statement to the police as to the absconding of a porter. Held, that the statement was admissible in evidence as an admission by the railway company (*h*).

2. In an action against a railway company for not delivering certain cattle within a reasonable time, it appeared that a servant of the company, a week after the alleged cause of action arose, in answer to the question why he had not sent on the cattle, said that he had forgotten them. Held, that this admission was not admissible in evidence against the company, because it concerned a bygone transaction (*i*).

3. An agent, who was employed to buy certain goods, acknowledged having received them. Held, that the acknowledgment was evidence of a delivery to the principal (*j*).

4. An agent is employed to pay workmen for work done. A promise by him to pay is an admission which can be used against the principal as evidence that the money is due, and if the promise be in writing and signed by the agent, it interrupts the operation in the principal's favour of the Statute of Limitations (*k*).

5. A wife carries on a business on her husband's behalf, and purchases all the goods required for such business. An admission by her as to the state of accounts between her husband and the persons supplying the goods is evidence against the husband (*l*), and a written and signed promise by her to pay interrupts the operation of the Statute of Limitations (*k*). So, a

---

(*h*) *Kirkstall Brewery* v. *Furness Rail.*, 1874, L. R. 9 Q. B. 468, 43 L. J. Q. B. 142; 30 L. T. 783, 22 W. R. 876. See also *Ruddy* v. *Mid. G. W. Rail.*, 1880, 8 L. R. Ir. 224.

(*i*) *G. W. Rail.* v. *Willis*, 1865, 18 C. B. N. S. 748, 34 L. J. C. P. 195.

(*j*) *Biggs* v. *Lawrence*, 1789, 3 T. R. 454; 1 R. R. 740.

(*k*) *Burt* v. *Palmer*, 1804, 5 Esp. 145, *Palethorp* v. *Furnish*, 1796, 2 Esp. 511, n.; 9 Geo. IV. c. 14, s. 6, 19 & 20 Vict. c. 97, s. 13.

(*l*) *Anderson* v. *Sanderson*, 1817, 2 Stark. 204, Holt, 591; 19 R. R. 703.

part payment by an agent, in the course of his employment, of a debt owing by the principal, interrupts the operation of the Statute of Limitations (*m*).

6. A solicitor is retained to conduct an action. Statements made by him in the conduct and for the purposes of the action are evidence against the client (*n*). But statements made by him in casual conversation, and not in the course and for the purposes of the action, are not (*o*). So, statements made by a solicitor for the purposes of one action cannot be used as evidence in another action which the solicitor is conducting on behalf of the same client (*p*).

7. A. refers B. to C., for information concerning a particular matter. Statements made by C. to B. respecting such matter are evidence against A. (*q*).

8. The secretary of a tramway company represented that certain money was due from the company. Held, that the company were not estopped by such representation from saying that the money was not due, because it was not within the scope of the secretary's employment to make any such representation (*r*).

9. The chairman of a company makes a statement at a meeting of shareholders. The statement cannot be used by third persons as evidence against the company (*s*).

10. An agent writes letters to his principal containing an account of transactions performed on his behalf. The letters

---

(*m*) See note (*k*), *ante*, p. 262.

(*n*) *Marshall* v. *Cliff*, 1815, 4 Camp. 133.

(*o*) *Petch* v. *Lyon*, 1846, 9 Q. B. 147; 15 L. J. Q. B. 393; *Parkins* v. *Hawkshaw*, 1814, 2 Stark. 239, 19 R. R. 711; *Wilson* v. *Turner*, 1808, 1 Taunt. 398, 9 R. R. 797; *Young* v. *Wright*, 1807, 1 Camp. 140.

(*p*) *Blackstone* v. *Wilson*, 1857, 26 L. J. Ex. 229.

(*q*) *Williams* v. *Innes*, 1808, 1 Camp. 364, 10 R. R. 702; *Hood* v. *Reeve*, 1828, 3 C. & P. 532; *Burt* v. *Palmer*, 1804, 5 Esp. 145.

(*r*) *Barnett* v. *South London Tram. Co.*, 1887, 18 Q. B. D. 815, 56 L. J. Q. B. 452; 57 L. T. 436, 35 W. R. 640, C. A.

(*s*) *Re Devala Provident, &c. Co., Ex p. Abbott*, 1883, 22 Ch. Div. 593, 52 L. J. Ch. 434; 48 L. T. 259, 31 W. R. 425.

cannot be used by third persons as evidence against the principal (*s*).

Article 104.

DOCTRINE OF CONSTRUCTIVE NOTICE.

Where any circumstance, material to the business upon which an agent is employed, comes to his knowledge in the course of such employment, and is of such a nature that it is his duty to communicate it to his principal, the principal is deemed to have notice thereof (*t*), unless there is a strong probability in the particular case that the agent will conceal such circumstance from the knowledge of the principal (*u*); but notice to an agent, otherwise than in the course of his employment on the principal's behalf (*v*), or of circumstances which are not material to the business for which he is employed (*w*), does not operate as notice to the principal.

Illustrations.

1. An agent of an assurance company negotiated a contract of insurance with a man who had lost an eye. Held, that the company must be deemed to have had notice that the assured had lost an eye, and that they could not avoid the contract on the ground of non-disclosure by him of that fact (*x*).

(*s*) *Langhorn* v. *Allnutt*, 1812, 4 Taunt. 511, 13 R. R. 663, Ex. Ch.

(*t*) Illustrations 1 to 3, *Graves* v. *Legg*, 1857, 2 H. & N. 210, 26 L. J. Ex. 316, 3 Jur. N. S. 519, Ex. Ch., *Gosling's case*, 1829, 3 Sim. 301.

(*u*) Illustrations 4 and 5.

(*v*) Illustration 6.

(*w*) Illustrations 7 to 10.

(*x*) *Bawden* v. *London, Edinburgh, &c. Assurance Co.*, (1892) 2 Q. B. 534, C. A.

2. A broker bought goods from a factor, knowing him to be selling on behalf of a principal. Held, that the principal for whom the broker acted must be deemed to have had notice that the factor was not selling his own goods (*y*).

3. A solicitor induced a client to advance money on mortgage, and afterwards induced another client to advance money on the same land. Held, that the last-mentioned client must be deemed to have had notice of the prior mortgage (*z*).

4. A solicitor, in the course of a transaction on his client's behalf, became a party to a fraud. Held, that that did not operate as constructive notice to the client of the fraud, because no person would be likely to disclose his own fraud (*a*). So, where the directors of a company took part in a misfeasance, it was held that their knowledge did not operate as notice to the company of the misfeasance (*b*). But it is not sufficient merely to show that the agent had an interest in concealing the facts from the principal, if it was his duty to communicate them; the principal must show that there was a strong probability that he would conceal them (*c*). Where a solicitor told a person who gave him notice that he intended to conceal the knowledge from his client, it was held that the notice to the solicitor did not operate as notice to the client (*d*).

5. A solicitor mortgaged certain property, and himself drew the mortgage deed, the mortgagee employing no other solicitor. Held, that the mortgagor was not the agent of the mortgagee

---

(*y*) *Dresser* v. *Norwood*, 1864, 17 C. B. N. S. 466; 34 L. J. C. P. 48; 10 Jur. N. S. 851, 12 W. R. 1030, Ex. Ch.

(*z*) *Rolland* v. *Hart*, 1871, L. R. 6 Ch. 678, 40 L. J. Ch. 701; 25 L. T. N. S. 191, Ch. App. And see *Le Neve* v. *Le Neve*, 1747, Ambl. 436.

(*a*) *Cave* v. *Cave*, 1880, 15 Ch. Div. 639; 49 L. J. Ch. 505; 42 L. T. 730, 28 W. R. 798.

(*b*) *Re Fitzroy Bessemer Steel Co.*, 1844, 50 L. T. 144; 32 W. R. 475.

(*c*) *Thompson* v. *Cartwright*, 1863, 33 Beav. 178; *Rolland* v. *Hart*, *ante*, note (*z*), *Bradley* v. *Riches*, 1878, 9 Ch. Div. 189; 47 L. J. Ch. 811, 38 L. T. N. S. 810.

(*d*) *Sharpe* v. *Foy*, 1868, 17 W. R. 65, Ch. App.

so as to affect him with constructive notice of incumbrances of which the mortgagor had knowledge (*e*).

6. The secretary of a company, in his private capacity, and when he was not transacting the business of the company, casually acquired knowledge of certain facts concerning the company's business. Held, that that did not operate as notice to the company of such facts (*f*).

7. A solicitor who was employed to transfer a mortgage knew that there were incumbrances on the property subsequent to such mortgage. Held, that his knowledge did not operate as constructive notice of the incumbrances to the transferee, because the incumbrances were not material to the transfer, for which alone the solicitor was employed (*g*). As a general rule, in order that the principal may be deemed to have constructive notice of facts coming to the knowledge of his agent, the facts must come to the agent's knowledge in the course of the transaction with respect to which the question of notice arises (*h*), or, at all events, must be fresh in his memory at the time of such transaction (*i*).

8. Directors of a banking company, who had no voice in the management of the accounts, acquired a knowledge of certain circumstances relating to the accounts. Held, that that did not operate as notice of such circumstances to the company (*j*).

9. An underwriter sought to avoid a policy on the ground of the non-disclosure of a material fact. The fact had been disclosed to his solicitor, but had not been communicated to him. Held, that he was not bound by the disclosure to his solicitor, it

---

(*e*) *Espin* v. *Pemberton*, 1859, 3 De G. & J. 547.

(*f*) *Société Générale de Paris* v. *Tramways Union Co.*, 1884, 14 Q. B. D. 424, 54 L. J. Q. B. 177, 52 L. T. 912, C. A.

(*g*) *Wyllie* v. *Pollen*, 1863, 32 L. J. Ch. 782; 11 W. R. 1081, 3 De G. J. & S. 596, 9 L. T. N. S. 71.

(*h*) *Hiern* v. *Mill*, 1806, 13 Ves. 120, 9 R. R. 149, *Wyllie* v. *Pollen*, *supra*.

(*i*) *Fuller* v. *Bennett*, 1843, 2 Hare, 394, 12 L. J. (N. S.) Ch. 355, 7 Jur. 1056; *Hargreaves* v. *Rothwell*, 1836, 1 Keen, 154, 5 L. J. (N. S.) Ch. 118.

(*j*) *Powles* v. *Page*, 1846, 3 C. B. 16.

not being in the ordinary course of a solicitor's employment to receive mercantile notices as to mercantile transactions (*k*).

10. A broker was employed to effect an insurance, but did not effect it. Subsequently, another broker effected a policy in respect of the same risk, on behalf of the same principal. It was sought to avoid the policy on the ground of the non-disclosure of a material fact which had come to the knowledge of the first-mentioned broker in the course of his employment, but which he had not communicated to the principal, and which was not known, either to the principal or to the broker who effected the policy. Held, that the policy was valid (*l*).

Constructive notice to Purchasers for Value.

The third section of the Conveyancing Act, 1882 (*m*), provides that a purchaser of property for valuable consideration shall not be prejudicially affected by notice of any instrument, fact, or thing, unless it is within his own knowledge, or would have come to his knowledge if such inquiries and inspections had been made as ought reasonably to have been made by him; or in the same transaction with respect to which a question of notice to the purchaser arises, it has come to the knowledge of his counsel, as such (*n*), or of his solicitor, or other agent, as such (*n*), or would have come to the knowledge of his solicitor, or other agent, as such, if such inquiries and inspections had been made as ought reasonably to have been made by the solicitor or other agent.

(*k*) *Tate* v. *Hyslop*, 1885, 15 Q. B. D. 368; 54 L. J. Q. B. 592; 53 L. T. 581, C. A.

(*l*) *Blackburn* v. *Vigors*, 1887, 12 App. Cas. 531; 57 L. J. Q. B. 114; 57 L. T. 730, 36 W. R. 449; 6 Asp. M. C. 216, H. L.

(*m*) 45 & 46 Vict. c. 39.

(*n*) *I.e.*, as *his* agent, see *Re Cousin's Trusts*, 1886, 31 Ch. Div. 671; 55 L. J. Ch. 662; 54 L. T. 376, 34 W. R. 393.

Article 105.

RIGHTS OF PRINCIPAL WHERE AGENT BRIBED.

Where an agent is induced by bribery to depart from his duty to his principal, the person who bribed the agent is liable, jointly and severally with the agent, to the principal for any loss incurred by him in consequence of the breach of duty, without taking into account the amount of the bribe, or any part thereof that may have been recovered by the principal from the agent as money received to his use (*o*).

Every contract made by an agent under the influence of bribery, or (to the knowledge of the other contracting party), in violation of his duty to his principal, is voidable by the principal (*p*).

Illustrations.

1. An agent contracted, on behalf of a corporation, for a supply of coals, the persons with whom he contracted making him an allowance of 1*s*. per ton, and charging 1*s*. per ton more than the market price, to enable them to make the allowance. The corporation, on discovering the bribery, sued the persons who supplied the coals for the amount so overcharged. Held, that the defendants were liable, and that the fact that the agent had deposited with the corporation the amount of the

---

(*o*) Illustration 1. And see *East India Co.* v. *Henchman*, 1791, 1 Ves. jun. 289.

(*p*) Illustrations 2 and 3, *Panama Telegraph Co.* v. *India Rubber, &c. Co.*, 1875, L. R. 10 Ch. 515, 45 L. J. Ch. 121, 32 L. T. 517, 23 W. R. 583, *Odessa Tramways Co.* v. *Mendel*, 1877, 8 Ch. Div. 235, 47 L. J. Ch. 505; 38 L. T. 731; 26 W. R. 887, C. A.

bribe, and the corporation had agreed to allow him what was recovered from the defendants, constituted no defence (*q*).

2. A person who dealt with an agent gave him a gratuity in order to influence him, generally, in favour of the giver. The agent was, in fact, so influenced in making a contract with the giver on the principal's behalf. Held, that the contract was voidable by the principal, although the gratuity was not given in direct relation to the particular contract (*r*).

3. A broker who was employed to sell certain property sold it, ostensibly to A., really to A. and himself. Both A. and the broker became insolvent, the goods still being in the broker's possession. Held, that the contract was voidable, and that the principal was entitled to recover the goods as against the broker's trustee in bankruptcy (*s*).

(*q*) *Mayor of Salford* v. *Lever*, (1891) 1 Q. B. 168; 60 L. J. Q. B. 39; 63 L. T. 658, C. A.

(*r*) *Smith* v. *Sorby*, 1875, 3 Q. B. D. 552, n.

(*s*) *Ex p. Huth, re Pemberton*, 1840, Mont. & Ch. 667; 4 Dea. 294. See Article 60 as to the right of the principal to recover goods on an agent's bankruptcy.

CHAPTER X.

Relations between Agents and Third Persons.

Sect. 1.—*Liabilities of agents in respect of contracts made by them.*

Article 106.

PUBLIC AGENTS NOT LIABLE ON CONTRACTS MADE AS SUCH.

No public officer is liable to be sued on any contract entered into by him on behalf of a department of state (*a*), or to be sued in respect of any sums which, as a public officer, it is his duty to pay to individuals (*b*); but a public officer is personally liable where he expressly pledges his personal credit (*c*), or where he contracts otherwise than as an agent of the government (*c*).

This article applies also to agents of foreign states (*d*).

(*a*) Illustrations 1 to 3, *Palmer* v. *Hutchinson*, 1881, 6 App. Cas. 619, 50 L. J. P. C. 62, 45 L. T. 180, P. C.; *Prosser* v. *Allen*, 1819, Gow, 117, *Whitfield* v. *Le Despencer*, 1778, Cowp. 754, *Lane* v. *Cotton*, 12 Mod. 488.

(*b*) Illustration 4, *Gidley* v. *Palmerston*, 1822, 3 Brod. & B. 275.

(*c*) Illustrations 5 and 6.

(*d*) *Twycross* v. *Dreyfus*, 1877, 5 Ch. Div. 605; 46 L. J. Ch. 510, 36 L. T. 752, C. A.

Illustrations.

1. The Secretary of State for War enters into a contract on behalf of the War Department. He is not liable to be sued on the contract (*e*). Probably, this rule applies even where the contract is under seal, provided that it is expressed to be made on behalf of the government (*f*). The only remedy in such cases is a petition of right.

2. A colonial governor orders goods. The goods are supplied and debited to the government. The governor is not liable on the contract (*g*).

3. Orders were given for forage to be supplied to a troop, by a clerk who was appointed by the captain of the troop. Held, that the captain was not liable for the price of the forage (*h*).

4. The Secretary for War was sued by a retired clerk of the War Office for his retired allowance. Held, that the action would not lie, even if the defendant was shown to have received the money applicable to such allowance (*i*). So, where booty was granted by the Queen to the Secretary of State for India in Council, in trust to distribute it to those who were found to be entitled thereto, it was held that he was not liable to account as a trustee to persons who were entitled to the booty (*k*).

5. A naval commander, when employing a cook, undertook to pay him a certain sum per annum in addition to the government pay. Held, that the commander was personally liable to pay such additional sum, he having contracted personally, and not as an agent for the government (*l*).

(*e*) *O'Grady* v. *Cardwell*, 1873, 21 W. R. 340, Ir.

(*f*) *Unwin* v. *Wolseley*, 1787, 1 T. R. 674. See *contra: Cunningham* v. *Collier*, 1785, 4 Doug. 233.

(*g*) *Macbeath* v. *Haldimund*, 1786, 1 T. R. 172; 1 R. R. 177.

(*h*) *Rice* v. *Chute*, 1801, 1 East, 579.

(*i*) *Gidley* v. *Palmerston*, 1822, 3 Brod. & B. 275.

(*k*) *Kinloch* v. *Sec. of State for India in Council*, 1882, 7 App. Cas. 619; 51 L. J. Ch. 885; 47 L. T. 133, 30 W. R. 845, H. L.

(*l*) *Clutterbuck* v. *Coffin*, 1842, 3 M. & G. 842, 4 Scott, N. R. 509; Car. & M. 273, 11 L. J. C. P. 65; 6 Jur. 131.

6. A clerk of a county court gave orders for the fitting up, &c., of the court-house. Held, that it was properly left to the jury to say whether he had contracted personally, and that, if he had, he was personally liable on the contract (*m*).

Article 107.

AGENT LIABLE IF HE CONTRACTS PERSONALLY, BUT NOT IF HE CONTRACTS MERELY AS AN AGENT.

Every agent who contracts personally, though on behalf of his principal, is personally liable, and may be sued in his own name, on the contract, whether the principal is named therein, or is known to the other contracting party, or not (*n*). But no agent is personally liable on any contract made by him merely in his capacity of an agent, even if he makes it fraudulently, knowing that he has not authority to do so (*o*).

The question whether an agent who has entered into a contract on behalf of his principal is to be deemed to have contracted personally, and if so, the extent of his liability on the contract (*p*), depends on the intention of the parties as shown by the nature and terms of the particular contract, and the circumstances under which it was made (*q*).

(*m*) *Auty* v. *Hutchinson*, 1848, 6 C. B. 266; 17 L. J. C. P. 304; 12 Jur. 962.

(*n*) Illustrations 1 to 9, *Reid* v. *Dreaper*, 1861, 6 H. & N. 813; 30 L. J. Ex. 268, *Turrell* v. *Collet*, 1795, 1 Esp. 320, *Iveson* v. *Conington*, 1823, 1 B. & C. 160; 2 D. & R. 307; *Watson* v. *Murrel*, 1824, 1 C. & P. 307. In these cases, either the principal or the agent may be sued.

(*o*) Illustrations 5, 10 and 11. He may be liable on an implied warranty of authority, see *post*, Article 115.

(*p*) Illustrations 7 and 12.

(*q*) Illustrations 1 to 9, and see Articles 108 to 112.

Where an agent contracts in England on behalf of a foreign principal, he is presumed to contract personally, unless a contrary intention appears from the terms of the contract, or from the surrounding circumstances (*r*).

Illustrations.

1. A. acted as the London agent of C. & Co., who were paper manufacturers in Vienna. B., by letter, ordered paper from A., who in his own name acknowledged the letter, and promised to supply the paper in certain quantities at certain times. A portion of the paper was delivered, and on B. complaining to A. respecting the non-delivery of the remainder, A. stated that it was the default of C. & Co. B. then wrote to C. & Co. telling them of the position of affairs, and the excuses made by A. Subsequently B. sued A. for breach of contract. Held, that A., having contracted personally, was liable, and that B.'s letter to C. & Co. did not amount to an election by B. to substitute C. & Co. for A. as the contracting parties. Some weight was attached to the circumstance that the principals were foreigners (*s*).

2. A solicitor in his own name contracted to buy certain freehold property. Held, that he was personally liable, although he was, in fact, acting on behalf of a client (*t*). So, where a solicitor bought property at a sale by auction, he was held personally liable for the deposit, though he openly declared that he was bidding in trust for a client (*u*).

(*r*) *Hutton* v. *Bullock*, 1874, 9 Q. B. D. 572, *Dramburg* v. *Pollitzer*, 1873, 28 L. T. 470; 21 W. R. 682; *Die Elbinger Actien Gesellschaft* v. *Claye*, 1873, L. R. 8 Q. B. 313; 42 L. J. Q. B. 151; 28 L. T. 405; *Reynolds* v. *Peapes*, 1890, 6 T. L. R. 49; *Peterson* v. *Ayre*, 1853, 13 C. B. 353; *Houghton* v. *Matthews*, 1803, 3 B. & P. 490; 7 R. R. 815. See Article 110, for rules of construction, where the contract is in writing.

(*s*) *Dramburg* v. *Pollitzer*, *supra*.

(*t*) *Saxon* v. *Blake*, 1861, 29 Beav. 438.

(*u*) *Hobhouse* v. *Hamilton*, 1826, 1 Hog. 401.

3. An agent signed in his own name, without mentioning his principal, an undertaking to accept shares in a company, and the shares were allotted to him. Subsequently, the principal took a larger number of shares, in satisfaction, as the agent said, of his undertaking. Held, that the agent, having personally accepted the shares, was liable as a contributory (*x*).

4. An agent buys goods at a sale by auction, and gives his own name, which is entered as that of the buyer. He is personally liable, unless it be clearly proved that he did not intend to bind himself, and that the auctioneer knew that (*y*).

5. An agent verbally orders goods on behalf of his principal. He is personally liable, unless the seller knows that he is merely contracting as an agent (*z*). But he is not liable if he orders the goods in the principal's name, and credit is given to the principal, or if he tells the seller that he does not intend to be personally responsible (*a*).

6. A broker sent a contract note in his own name, and afterwards a corrected one in the name of the principal, the buyer receiving both notes together. Held, that it was a question for the jury whether he intentionally sent the first contract note in his own name, or sent it merely by mistake, and that if he sent it intentionally, he could not, having contracted personally, afterwards discharge himself by setting up the agency, even if he was known to be a broker when he made the contract (*b*).

Auctioneers.

7. Where an auctioneer sells for an undisclosed principal, he is deemed to contract personally, and is liable in damages for

---

(*x*) *Ex p. Bird*, 1864, 10 Jur. N. S. 138; 33 L. J. Bky. 49, 12 W. R. 321; 9 L. T. N. S. 669.

(*y*) *Williamson* v. *Barton*, 1862, 7 H. & N. 899, 31 L. J. Ex. 170; 8 Jur. N. S. 341, 5 L. T. 800.

(*z*) *Seaber* v. *Hawkes*, 1831, 5 M. & P. 549.

(*a*) *Ex p. Hartop*, 1806, 12 Ves. 352, *Johnson* v. *Ogilby*, 1734, 3 P. Wms. 277, *Owen* v. *Gooch*, 1797, 2 Esp. 567.

(*b*) *Magee* v. *Atkinson*, 1837, 2 M. & W. 440.

non-performance, even if he subsequently offers to name the principal (*c*). The character and extent of his contract with the purchaser in such a case depends on the conditions of sale, the nature of the subject-matter, and the other surrounding circumstances. Thus, in the case of a sale of standing corn with straw, to be removed at the purchaser's expense, it was held that the auctioneer contracted to give proper authority to enter and carry away the corn and straw, and undertook that he was in fact authorized to sell, but that he did not warrant the title (*d*).

8. An auctioneer sold goods on behalf of a disclosed principal, the conditions of sale providing that the lots should be cleared within three days, and that if from any cause the auctioneer was unable to deliver, &c., the purchaser should accept compensation. Held, that the auctioneer, being in possession of the goods, and having contracted to duly deliver, was personally liable to the purchaser for non-delivery (*e*).

Where a sale by auction is advertised as being "without reserve," the auctioneer impliedly contracts to accept the offer of the highest *bonâ fide* bidder, and is liable to him in damages for breach of such implied contract if he accepts a bid from the vendor (*f*). But an advertisement to the effect that certain goods will be sold on certain days does not amount to a contract to so sell them, so as to entitle a person who acts on the advertisement to recover damages for loss of time or expenses if the goods are not put up (*g*).

(*c*) *Franklyn* v. *Lamond*, 1847, 4 C. B. 637; 16 L. J. C. P. 221; 11 Jur. 780; *Hanson* v. *Roberdeau*, 1792, 1 Peake, 163.

(*d*) *Wood* v. *Baxter*, 1883, 49 L. T. 45. See, however, as to the warranty of title, Sale of Goods Act, 1893 (56 & 57 Vict. c. 71), s. 12.

(*e*) *Woolfe* v. *Horne*, 1877, 2 Q. B. D. 355; 46 L. J. Q. B. 534; 36 L. T. 705; 25 W. R. 728; *Williams* v. *Millington*, 1788, 1 H. Bl. 81, 2 R. R. 724.

(*f*) *Warlow* v. *Harrison*, 1858, 1 El. & El. 309; 29 L. J. Q. B. 14; 6 Jur. N. S. 66, Ex. Ch.

(*g*) *Harris* v. *Nickerson*, 1873, L. R. 8 Q. B. 286; 42 L. J. Q. B. 171;

9. *Shipmasters.*—A shipmaster is personally liable to the seamen for their wages (*h*).

Not liable if he contracts merely as an agent.

10. A solicitor is *primâ facie* not personally liable for the expenses of witnesses retained or subpœnaed by him (*i*). Nor is he personally liable for sheriff's fees merely because, in the course of his duty, he lodges a writ at the sheriff's office for execution (*k*). In such matters, he is deemed to act merely as the agent of his client, unless he expressly pledges his personal credit (*i*).

11. A. professes to contract as an agent for B., the terms of the contract being such as to exclude any supposition of an intention by A. to be personally liable. A. is not liable on the contract, even if he made it fraudulently, knowing that he had no authority from B. (*l*), unless he is shown to be the real principal (*m*); but he may be liable for breach of an implied warranty that he had B.'s authority to make the contract (*n*).

Liability may be expressly limited.

12. Where an agent contracts personally, his liability under the contract may be expressly restricted to certain events. Thus,

---

28 L. T. 410, 21 W. R. 635, *Mainprice* v. *Westley*, 1865, 6 B. & S. 420; 34 L. J. Q. B. 229; 13 L. T. 560, 14 W. R. 9.

(*h*) *The Salacia*, 1863, 32 L. J. Adm. 41; 9 Jur. N. S. 27; 7 L. T. 440; 11 W. R. 189. As to his liability for repairs, &c. ordered by him, see *Essery* v. *Cobb*, 1832, 5 C. & P. 358.

(*i*) *Robins* v. *Bridge*, 1837, 3 M. & W. 114, 6 D. P. C. 140; M. & H. 357, *Lee* v. *Everest*, 1857, 2 H. & N. 285, 26 L. J. Ex. 334.

(*k*) *Royle* v. *Busby*, 1880, 6 Q. B. D. 171, 50 L. J. Q. B. 196, 43 L. T. 717, 29 W. R. 315, C. A.

(*l*) *Lewis* v. *Nicholson*, 1852, 18 Q. B. 503, 21 L. J. Q. B. 311, 16 Jur. 1041; *Jenkins* v. *Hutchinson*, 1849, 13 Q. B. 744, 18 L. J. Q. B. 274; 13 Jur. 763.

(*m*) See Article 113.

(*n*) See Article 115.

where a clause in a charter-party provided that the liability of the agent as to all matters—as well before as after the shipping of the cargo—should cease as soon as the cargo was shipped, it was held that he was not personally liable for demurrage at the port of discharge (*o*).

Article 108.

LIABILITY ON CONTRACTS UNDER SEAL.

Where an agent is a party to a deed and executes it in his own name, he is personally liable thereon, even if he is described in the deed as acting for and on behalf of a named principal.

Illustrations.

1. A., on behalf of B., contracted by deed to purchase certain houses, and covenanted that he (A.) would pay 800*l.* for them. The houses were destroyed. Held, that A. was personally liable to pay the 800*l.*, although he had no effects in his hands belonging to B. (*p*). If A. covenants under his own hand and seal for the act of B., A. is personally liable, though he describe himself as covenanting for and on behalf of B. (*q*).

2. The directors of a company contracted by deed to purchase a mine, the price to be paid in twelve months out of moneys raised by the company, with a proviso that if the directors should not by that time have received sufficient deposits from shareholders, &c. to enable them to pay, they should be allowed a further six months for payment. And the directors covenanted that they would, "out of the said payments so to be made by

(*o*) *Oglesby* v. *Yglesias*, 1858, El. Bl. & El. 930; 27 L. J. Q. B. 356, Ex. Ch. And see *Milvan* v. *Perez*, 1861, 3 El. & El. 495, 30 L. J. Q. B. 90; 3 L. T. 736; 9 W. R. 269, *Christofferson* v. *Hansen*, 1872, L. R. 7 Q. B. 509, 41 L. J. Q. B. 217, 26 L. T. 547, 20 W. R. 626.

(*p*) *Cass* v. *Rudele*, 1692, 2 Vern. 280.

(*q*) *Appleton* v. *Binks*, 1804, 5 East, 148, 1 Smith, 361; 7 R. R. 672.

subscribers or shareholders in the said company," pay, according to the terms specified and subject to the said proviso. Held, that they were personally liable for the price, at the end of the eighteen months (*r*).

Article 109.

LIABILITY ON BILLS OF EXCHANGE, PROMISSORY NOTES AND CHEQUES.

No agent is personally liable on any bill of exchange, promissory note, or cheque, unless his name appears thereon (*s*).

(a) Where a bill of exchange is drawn on an agent in his own name and is signed by him, he is personally liable as acceptor, even if he adds words to the signature, indicating that he signs for and on behalf of a principal, or as an agent (*t*).

(b) Where a bill of exchange is drawn on a principal, the agent is not liable as acceptor, even if he signs his own name, without qualification (*u*).

(c) Where an agent signs a bill of exchange, promissory note, or cheque otherwise than as acceptor of a bill of exchange, he is personally liable, unless he qualifies the signature by adding words thereto, indicating that

(*r*) *Hancock* v. *Hudson*, 1827, 12 Moore, 504; 4 Bing. 269.

(*s*) 45 & 46 Vict. c. 61 (Bills of Exchange Act, 1882), s. 23; *Wilson* v. *Barthrop*, 1837, 2 M. & W. 863, M. & H. 81; 1 Jur. 949.

(*t*) Illustrations 1 and 2, 45 & 46 Vict. c. 61, s. 26 (2); *Herald* v. *Connah*, 1876, 34 L. T. 885, *Thomas* v. *Bishop*, 1743, 2 Str. 955.

(*u*) Illustration 3; 45 & 46 Vict. c. 61, s. 26 (2), *Polhill* v. *Walter*, 1832, 3 B. & Ad. 114.

he signs for and on behalf of a principal, or as an agent. If he so qualifies the signature, he is not personally liable (x).

The mere addition to the name or signature of an agent on a bill of exchange, promissory note, or cheque, of words describing him as an agent, does not exempt him from personal liability on the instrument, whether the principal is named therein or not (y).

Illustrations.

Liability as acceptor.

1. A bill was drawn on W. Charles, who wrote across it "Accepted, for the Company; W. Charles, purser." Held, that W. Charles was personally liable as acceptor (z).

2. A bill was directed to "Messrs. J. and S., joint managers of R. M. M. A. Association," and was accepted "J. J., W. S., as joint managers of R. M. M. A. Association." Held, that J. J. and W. S. were personally liable as acceptors, because, though they were described as agents, the bill was drawn on them personally (a). So, where a bill was directed "A. B., purser, W. D. Mining Company," and was accepted "A. B., *per proc.* W. D. Mining Company," A. B. was held personally liable as acceptor (b).

3. A bill is directed to a company, and is accepted by the directors in their own names, without qualification. The directors are not liable as acceptors (c).

(x) Illustrations 4 to 9; 45 & 46 Vict. c. 61, s. 26 (1); *Ex p. Buckley*, 1845, 14 M. & W. 469; 14 L. J. Ex. 341.

(y) Illustrations 2, 5 to 7; 45 & 46 Vict. c. 61, s. 26 (1).

(z) *Mare* v. *Charles*, 1856, 5 El. & Bl. 978; 25 L. J. Q. B. 119; 2 Jur. N. S. 234.

(a) *Jones* v. *Jackson*, 1870, 22 L. T. 828.

(b) *Nichols* v. *Diamond*, 1853, 9 Ex. 154; 23 L. J. Ex. 1.

(c) *Okell* v. *Charles*, 1876, 34 L. T. 822, C. A.

Liability as drawer or indorser.

4. An agent draws a bill in his own name. He is personally liable as drawer, even to a holder who knows that he is merely an agent, unless words are added to the signature, indicating that he signs merely as an agent (*d*).

5. An agent is under an obligation, as such, to indorse a bill. He may indorse it in such terms as to negative personal liability (*e*), but merely describing himself as an agent for a named principal is not sufficient for that purpose (*e*).

Promissory notes.

6. The trustees of a building society were held personally liable on a promissory note in the following terms: "On demand, we promise to pay A. B. £200 for the S. G. Provident Building Society"; (signed) "C. D., E. F., G. H., trustees, I. J., secretary" (*f*).

7. Directors have been held personally liable on promissory notes in the following forms:—

(a) "We, directors of A. B. Company, Limited, do promise to pay J. D., &c."; sealed and signed by four directors without qualification (*g*).

(b) "We, directors of A. B. Company, for ourselves and other shareholders of the company, jointly and severally promise to pay, &c., on account of the company"; signed without qualification (*h*).

(c) "We jointly and severally promise, &c., for and on

(*d*) *Leadbitter* v. *Farrow*, 1816, 5 M. & S. 345; 17 R. R. 345; *Sowerby* v. *Butcher*, 1834, 2 C. & M. 368; 4 Tyr. 320.

(*e*) 45 & 46 Vict. c. 61, s. 26 (1) and (5).

(*f*) *Allan* v. *Miller*, 1870, 22 L. T. 825. And see *Price* v. *Taylor*, 1860, 5 H. & N. 540, 29 L. J. Ex. 331, 2 L. T. 221, 8 W. R. 419.

(*g*) *Dutton* v. *Marsh*, 1871, L. R. 6 Q. B. 361, 40 L. J. Q. B. 175, 24 L. T. 470, 19 W. R. 754.

(*h*) *Penkivil* v. *Connell*, 1850, 5 Ex. 381, 19 L. J. Ex. 305.

behalf of, &c." Jointly and severally is equivalent to jointly and personally (*i*).

(d) "We jointly promise to pay J. F., &c."; signed by directors without qualification (*k*).

8. The secretary of a company signed a note in the following form:—"I promise to pay, &c."; (signed) "For M. T. and W. Railway Company, J. S., secretary." Held, that he was not personally liable (*l*).

9. A note in the following form was signed by directors, and sealed with the common seal of the society:—"We, two directors of A. B. Society, by and on behalf of the said society, do hereby promise, &c."; (signed) "C. D., E. F., directors." Held, that C. D. and E. F. were not personally liable (*m*).

Article 110.

OTHER WRITTEN CONTRACTS.

The question whether the agent is to be deemed to have contracted personally, in the case of a contract in writing other than a bill of exchange, promissory note, or cheque, depends upon the intention of the parties, as appearing from the terms of the written agreement as a whole, the construction whereof is a matter of law for the Court (*n*)—

(a) if the contract is signed by the agent in his own name without qualification, he is deemed to have contracted personally, unless a con-

---

(*i*) *Healey* v. *Storey*, 1848, 3 Ex. 3; 18 L. J. Ex. 8; *Bottomley* v. *Fisher*, 1862, 1 H. & C. 211; 31 L. J. Ex. 417; 8 Jur. N. S. 895.

(*k*) *Fox* v. *Frith*, 1842, 10 M. & W. 131.

(*l*) *Alexander* v. *Sizer*, 1869, L. R. 4 Ex. 102; 38 L. J. Ex. 59; 20 L. T. 38.

(*m*) *Aggs* v. *Nicholson*, 1856, 1 H. & N. 165.

(*n*) Illustrations 1 to 3; *Spittle* v. *Lavender*, 1821, 5 Moo. 270; 2 B. & B. 452.

trary intention clearly appears from other portions of the document (*o*);

(b) if the agent adds words to his signature, indicating that he signs as an agent, or for or on behalf of a principal, he is not deemed to have contracted personally, unless it appears from other portions of the document that, notwithstanding such qualified signature, he intended to bind himself (*p*);

(c) the mere fact that the agent is described as an agent, whether in the signature or in the body of the contract, and whether the principal is named or not, raises no presumption that the agent did not intend to contract personally (*q*).

This article extends to cases where the principal is a foreigner (*r*).

(*o*) Illustrations 4 to 7; *Dutton* v. *Marsh*, 1871, L. R. 6 Q. B. 361; 40 L. J. Q. B. 175, 24 L. T. 470, 19 W. R. 754, *Hick* v. *Tweedy*, 1890, 63 L. T. 765, 6 Asp. M. C. 599, *Hough* v. *Manzanos*, 1879, 4 Ex. Div. 104; 48 L. J. Ex. 398, 27 W. R. 536, *Cooke* v. *Wilson*, 1856, 1 C. B. N. S. 153; 26 L. J. C. P. 15, 2 Jur. N. S. 1094, *Paice* v. *Walker*, 1870, L. R. 5 Ex. 173, 39 L. J. Ex. 109, 22 L. T. 547. See, however, *Spittle* v. *Lavender*, 1821, 5 Moo. 270; 2 B. & B. 452.

(*p*) Illustrations 8 to 10, *Green* v. *Hopke*, 1856, 18 C. B. 549; 25 L. J. C. P. 297, 2 Jur. N. S. 1049; *Mahony* v. *Kekule*, 1854, 14 C. B. 390, 23 L. J. C. P. 54; 18 Jur. 313; *Hahn* v. *North German Pitwood Co.*, 1892, 8 T. L. R. 557.

(*q*) Illustration 4. *Paice* v. *Walker*, 1870, L. R. 5 Ex. 173, 39 L. J. Ex. 109; 22 L. T. 547; 18 W. R. 789; *Hutcheson* v. *Eaton*, 1884, 13 Q. B. D. 861, 51 L. T. 846, C. A.

(*r*) *Gadd* v. *Houghton*, 1876, 1 Ex. Div. 357, 46 L. J. Ex. 71; 35 L. T. 222, 24 W. R. 975, C. A.; *Ogden* v. *Hall*, 1879, 40 L. T. 751, *Glover* v. *Langford*, 1892, 8 T. L. R. 628, *Hahn* v. *North German Pitwood Co.*, 1892, 8 T. L. R. 557; *Green* v. *Hopke*, 1856, 18 C. B. 549, 25 L. J. C. P. 297; 2 Jur. N. S. 1049; *Reynolds* v. *Peapes*, 1890, 6 T. L. R. 49.

Illustrations.

1. An agent entered into a written agreement to grant a lease of certain premises. He was described in the agreement as making it on behalf of the principal, but in a subsequent portion of the document it was provided that he (the agent) would execute the lease. Held, that the agent was personally liable for a breach of the agreement, though the premises belonged to the principal (*s*).

2. The directors of a company signed a contract in the following terms:—"We, the undersigned, three of the directors, agree to repay 500*l.* advanced by A. to the company," and at the same time assigned to A., as security, certain property belonging to the company. Held, that the directors were personally liable (*t*). But where an agent signed a contract in the following form—"I undertake, on behalf of A. (the principal), to pay, &c.," it was held that he was not personally liable (*u*).

3. A broker sent a contract note in the following terms:—"Messrs. S.—I have this day sold by your order and for your account to my principals, &c., one per cent. brokerage"; (signed) "W. A. B." Held, that W. A. B. was not personally liable in an action for goods sold (*x*).

4. A charter-party was expressed to be made between A. B. and C. D., agent for E. F. and Son, and was signed by C. D., without qualification. Held, that C. D. was personally liable, though the principals were named, there being nothing in the terms of the contract clearly inconsistent with an intention to contract personally (*y*).

(*s*) *Norton* v. *Herron*, 1825, 1 C. & P. 648; R. & M. 229. And see *Tanner* v. *Christian*, 1855, 4 El. & Bl. 591, 24 L. J. Q. B. 91; 1 Jur. N. S. 519.

(*t*) *McCollin* v. *Gilpin*, 1881, 6 Q. B. D. 516, 44 L. T. 914, C. A.

(*u*) *Downman* v. *Williams*, 1845, 7 Q. B. 103; 14 L. J. Q. B. 226; 9 Jur. 454, Ex. Ch.

(*x*) *Southwell* v. *Bowditch*, 1876, 1 C. P. D. 374; 45 L. J. C. P. 630; 35 L. T. 196, 24 W. R. 838, C. A.

(*y*) *Parker* v. *Winlow*, 1857, 7 El. & Bl. 942; 27 L. J. Q. B. 49; 4 Jur. N. S. 84.

5. An agent was described in a contract as "consignee and agent on behalf of Mr. M., of L.," and it was stated that "the said parties agreed," &c., the contract being signed by the agent in his own name without qualification. Held, that the agent was personally liable (*z*).

6. An agent signed, without qualification, a contract in the following form:—"Sold A. B. 200 quarters wheat (as agent for C. F. & Co., Dantzig)." Held, that the words, "as agent for C. F. & Co., Dantzig," in the body of the contract, did not clearly show that the agent did not intend to contract personally; and that, as he had signed it without qualification, he was personally liable (*a*). This was a unanimous decision of the Court of Exchequer; but it was disapproved by James, L. J., and Mellish, L. J., in *Gadd* v. *Houghton* (cited below), on the ground that the words "as agent" were sufficient to show that there was no intention to contract personally.

7. A contract in the following terms—"We have this day sold to you, on account of J. M. & Co., Valencia, &c.," was signed by the agents in their own names without qualification. Held, that the agents were not personally liable, though the principal was a foreigner, the words "on account of" clearly showing that there was no intention to contract personally (*b*). So, where an agent was described as contracting "on behalf of A. B., Roanne," it was held that he was not liable, though he signed the contract in his own name without qualification (*c*).

8. A contract is signed "for A. B., of L., C. Bros., as agents." C. Bros. are not liable, unless it clearly appears from the body of the contract that they intended to bind themselves (*d*).

(*z*) *Kennedy* v. *Gouveia*, 1823, 3 D. & R. 503.

(*a*) *Paice* v. *Walker*, 1870, L. R. 5 Ex. 173, 39 L. J. Ex. 109, 22 L. T. 547, 18 W. R. 789.

(*b*) *Gadd* v. *Houghton*, 1876, 1 Ex. Div. 357, 46 L. J. Ex. 71, 35 L. T. 222; 24 W. R. 975, C. A.

(*c*) *Ogden* v. *Hall*, 1879, 40 L. T. 751.

(*d*) *Deslandes* v. *Gregory*, 1860, 30 L. J. Q. B. 36; 6 Jur. N. S. 651, 8 W. R. 585, Ex. Ch.

9. A charter-party was signed "A. B., by authority of and as agent for P., of L.," but A. B. appeared in the body of the agreement as the principal. Held, that A. B. was personally liable, because, notwithstanding the qualified signature, he appeared from the agreement to have intended to contract personally (*e*).

10. An agent signed a contract—"P. P. A., J. A. & Co., A. B." The contract contained a clause, providing that A. B. should guarantee moneys due from his principal to the other contracting party. Parol evidence was admitted to show that A. B. intended to sign, not only as an agent, but also as a surety. Held, by the Court of Appeal, that such evidence was rightly admitted, and that he must be taken to have signed in both capacities (*f*).

Article 111.

ADMISSIBILITY OF PAROL EVIDENCE OF INTENTION.

Where an agent appears, from the terms of a written agreement entered into by him, to have contracted personally, parol evidence is not admissible to show that, in fact, he merely contracted as an agent, and was not intended to be personally liable on the contract, because such evidence would be contradictory to the written agreement (*g*); but he may, by way of equitable defence, prove a verbal agreement that, in consideration of his being merely an agent, he should not be personally liable on the contract, because it

---

(*e*) *Lennard* v. *Robinson*, 1855, 5 El. & Bl. 125; 24 L. J. Q. B. 275; 1 Jur. N. S. 853.

(*f*) *Young* v. *Schuler*, 1883, 11 Q. B. D. 651; 49 L. T. 546, C. A.

(*g*) *Higgins* v. *Senior*, 1841, 8 M. & W. 834; *Holding* v. *Elliott*, 1860, 5 H. & N. 117, 29 L. J. Ex. 134; 8 W. R. 192, *Jones* v. *Littledale*, 1837, 1 N. & P. 677; 6 A. & E. 486.

would be inequitable in such a case to take advantage of his having contracted personally (*h*).

Where an agent appears, from the terms of a written agreement, to have contracted merely as an agent, parol evidence is admissible to show that, by a custom or usage in the particular business, an agent so contracting is liable on the contract, either absolutely or conditionally; provided that such custom or usage is not inconsistent with nor repugnant to the express terms of the written agreement (*i*).

Illustrations.

1. An agent signed a charter-party expressly "as agent for principals," the principals being undisclosed. It was held that, though it plainly appeared that he did not intend to contract as principal, it might, nevertheless, be proved that, by a general custom, an agent so signing was, in the ordinary course of trade, personally liable on the contract in the event of his not disclosing the principals within a reasonable time, such a custom not being inconsistent with the terms of the contract (*k*).

2. A broker entered into a contract in the following terms:— "Sold by A. to Messrs. B., for and on account of owner, 100 bales of hops." An action was brought against A. for not delivering hops according to sample. Evidence of a custom in the hop trade, whereby a broker who does not disclose his principal at the time of the contract is personally liable, was admitted, and the broker was held liable on the contract (*l*).

(*h*) *Wake* v. *Harrop*, 1862, 1 H. & C. 202, 31 L. J. Ex. 451; 8 Jur. N. S. 845; 7 L. T. 96, 10 W. R. 626, Ex. Ch. affirming 6 H. & N. 768, 30 L. J. Ex. 273. And see *Kidson* v. *Dilworth*, 1818, 5 Price, 564; 19 R. R. 656.

(*i*) Illustrations 1 to 4.

(*k*) *Hutchinson* v. *Tatham*, 1873. L. R. 8 C. P. 482; 42 L. J. C. P. 260; 29 L. T. 103; 22 W. R. 18.

(*l*) *Pike* v. *Ongley*, 1887, 18 Q. B. D. 708; 56 L. J. Q. B. 373; 35 W. R.

3. A. and B., who were brokers, contracted in the following terms:—"We have this day sold for your account to our principal, &c." (signed), "A. and B., brokers." Some of the goods were accepted by the principal, whose name was declared by A. and B. before delivery, and an action was subsequently brought against A. and B. for not accepting the residue. Held, that they were personally liable, it being proved that by a custom in the particular trade, the broker was personally liable for his principal's default unless the name of the principal was inserted in the written contract (*m*). So, by the usage of the London dry goods market, where a broker buys goods for an undisclosed principal, he is personally liable for the price (*n*).

4. Brokers entered, as such, into a contract, which contained a clause providing that they should act as arbitrators in the event of any dispute between the parties. Held, that evidence of a custom rendering them personally liable on the contract was inadmissible, because the custom was inconsistent with the clause appointing them arbitrators (*o*).

Article 112.

VERBAL CONTRACTS.

Where an agent enters into a contract which is not reduced to writing, the question whether he contracted personally or merely as an agent, is a question of fact

---

534; *Dale* v. *Humfrey*, 1858, El. Bl. & El. 1004; 27 L. J. Q. B. 390; 5 Jur. N. S. 191, Ex. Ch.

(*m*) *Fleet* v. *Murton*, (fruit trade and colonial market), 1871, L. R. 7 Q. B. 126; 41 L. J. Q. B. 49; 26 L. T. 181; 20 W. R. 97. Similar custom in the rice trade. *Baemeister* v. *Fenton*, 1883, 1 C. & E. 121.

(*n*) *Imperial Bank* v. *L. & St. Katharine's Docks Co.*, 1876, 5 Ch. Div. 195; 46 L. J. Ch. 335, 36 L. T. 233.

(*o*) *Barrow* v. *Dyster*, 1884, 13 Q. B. D. 635; 51 L. T. 573; 33 W. R. 199.

for the jury, depending upon the intention of the parties (*p*).

Illustrations.

1. Brokers sell goods by auction, and invoice them in their own names as sellers. It is a question for the jury whether the invoice was intended to be the contract. If so, the brokers are personally liable. If the invoice was not intended to be the contract, it is a question for the jury whether the brokers intended to contract personally (*q*).

2. An estate agent contracted to sell land, and gave a receipt in his own name for the deposit. It was left to the jury to say whether he contracted personally (*r*). So, where an agent bought goods at an auction, and gave his own name as buyer, it was left to the jury to say whether he contracted personally (*s*).

Article 113.

LIABLE IF SHOWN TO BE THE REAL PRINCIPAL.

Where a person professes to contract as an agent, whether in writing or verbally, and it is shown that he is, in fact, the principal, and was acting on his own behalf, he is personally liable on the contract (*t*).

(*p*) See *Magee* v. *Atkinson*, 1837, 2 M. & W. 440; *Seaber* v. *Hawkes*, 1831, 5 M. & P. 549; *Ex p. Hartop*, 1806, 12 Ves. 352, *Johnson* v. *Ogilby*, 1734, 3 P. Wms. 277; *Owen* v. *Gooch*, 1797, 2 Esp. 567.

(*q*) *Jones* v. *Littledale*, 1837, 1 N. & P. 677, 6 A. & E. 486, *Holding* v. *Elliott*, 1860, 5 H. & N. 117, 29 L. J. Ex. 134, 8 W. R. 192.

(*r*) *Long* v. *Millar*, 1879, 4 C. P. Div. 450, 48 L. J. C. P. 596, 41 L. T. 306, 27 W. R. 720, C. A.

(*s*) *Williamson* v. *Barton*, 1862, 7 H. & N. 899, 31 L. J. Ex. 170, 8 Jur. N. S. 341, 5 L. T. 800.

(*t*) *Carr* v. *Jackson*, 1852, 21 L. J. Ex. 137, *Jenkins* v. *Hutchinson*, 1849, 13 Q. B. 744, 18 L. J. Q. B. 274, 13 Jur. 763, *Railton* v. *Hodgson*, 1812, 15 East, 67; 13 R. R. 373, *Adams* v. *Hall*, 1877, 37 L. T. 70.

Article 114.

LIABILITY WHEN NO PRINCIPAL IN EXISTENCE.

Where a person professes to contract as an agent, and there is no other person in existence who is, or who can, by ratification or otherwise, become liable on the contract, the person so professing to contract as an agent is personally liable thereon (*u*).

Illustration.

A. enters into a contract on behalf of a company in the course of formation and not yet incorporated. A. is personally liable on the contract, even if he expresses himself as contracting on behalf of the future company, and parol evidence is not admissible to show that he did not intend to contract personally (*u*). This principle applies only where there is no one in existence (except the persons contracting) who can become liable on the contract, and is, therefore, practically confined to contracts made by promoters of companies. To what extent a person professing to contract on behalf of a principal who is non-existent, has a right to sue on the contract, is not clear (*x*).

Article 115.

IMPLIED WARRANTY OF AUTHORITY.

Where any person, by words or conduct, represents that he has authority to act on behalf of another, and

---

(*u*) *Kelner* v. *Baxter*, 1866, L. R. 2 C. P. 174; 36 L. J. C. P. 94, 15 L. T. 213; 15 W. R. 278. A company cannot ratify a contract made before its incorporation.

(*x*) See *Hollman* v. *Pullin*, 1884, 1 C. & E. 254.

a third person is induced by any such representation to act in a manner in which he would not have acted but for such representation, the first-mentioned person is deemed to warrant that the representation is true, and is liable for any loss caused to such third person by a breach of such implied warranty, even if he acted in good faith, under a mistaken belief that he had the authority he represented himself to have (*y*). Where any such representation is made fraudulently, the person injured thereby may elect to sue, either in contract for the breach of warranty or in tort for the deceit, at his option (*z*).

Every person who professes to contract as an agent is deemed to represent that he is, in fact, duly authorized to make the contract (*a*), except where he acts in good faith, in the belief that he is so authorized, and the other contracting party has a full knowledge of all the facts upon which such belief is founded, and of all the circumstances known to the first-mentioned person which are relevant to the existence of the supposed authority (*b*).

(*y*) Illustrations 1 to 7; *Firbank* v. *Humphreys*, 1886, 18 Q. B. D. 60; 56 L. J. Q. B. 57, 56 L. T. 36, 35 W. R. 92, C. A., *Oxenham* v. *Smythe*, 1861, 6 H. & N. 690, 31 L. J. Ex. 110, *Cherry* v. *Colonial Bank of Australasia*, 1869, 17 W. R. 1031; 38 L. J. P. C. 49, 21 L. T. 356, P. C.

(*z*) *Randell* v. *Trimen*, 1856, 18 C. B. 786, 25 L. J. C. P. 307.

(*a*) *Collen* v. *Wright*, 1857, 7 El. & Bl. 301, 8 El. & Bl. 647, 26 L. J. Q. B. 147, 27 L. J. Q. B. 215, 3 Jur. N. S. 363, 4 Jur. N. S. 357, Ex. Ch. followed by the House of Lords in *Stuart* v. *Haigh*, 1893, 9 T. L. R. 488. See Illustrations 2, and 5 to 7.

(*b*) Illustration 8. This seems to be the *ratio decidendi* of *Smout* v. *Ilbery*, 1842, 10 M. & W. 1.

This article does not extend to a representation made in good faith with regard to a mere question of law, in which no representation of fact is involved (*c*).

Illustrations.

1. The directors of a company represented to the company's bankers that A. had been appointed manager and had authority to draw cheques on the company's account, the account, to the knowledge of the directors, being already overdrawn. A. further overdrew the account, the directors having, in fact, no authority to overdraw. Held, that the directors were liable to the bankers for breach of an implied warranty that they had the company's authority to overdraw the account (*d*).

2. A. lent 70*l*. to a building society, and received a certificate of the deposit, signed by two directors. The society had no borrowing powers. Held, that the directors were personally liable to A. on an implied warranty that they had authority to borrow on behalf of the society (*e*).

3. The directors of a company issued a certificate for debenture stock, which A. agreed to accept in lieu of cash due to him from the company, all the debenture stock that the company had power to issue having already been issued. Held, that the directors were liable to A. on an implied warranty that they had authority to issue valid debenture stock, although they had acted in good faith, not knowing that all the stock had been issued (*f*). So, where directors of a company issued a debenture

---

(*c*) *Beattie* v. *Ebury*, 1874, 41 L. J. Ch. 804; L. R. 7 Ch. 777: affirmed L. R. 7 H. L. 102; 44 L. J. Ch. 20; 30 L. T. 581, 22 W. R. 897, H. L.; *Eaglesfield* v. *Londonderry*, 1876, 38 L. T. 303; 26 W. R. 540, H. L.: affirming 4 Ch. Div. 693, C. A., *West London Commercial Bank* v. *Kitson*, 1884, 13 Q. B. D. 360, 53 L. J. Q. B. 345, 50 L. T. 656; 32 W. R. 757, C. A.

(*d*) *Cherry* v. *Colonial Bank of Australasia*, 1869, 17 W. R. 1031, 38 L. J. P. C. 49; 21 L. T. 356, P. C.

(*e*) *Richardson* v. *Williamson*, 1871, L. R. 6 Q. B. 276; 40 L. J. Q. B. 145.

(*f*) *Firbank* v. *Humphreys*, 1886, 18 Q. B. D. 60, 56 L. J. Q. B. 57;

bond, which was duly sealed and sent to A., who had paid for it, it was held that the directors thereby impliedly warranted that they had authority to issue a debenture which should be valid and binding on the company, the company having, in fact, already fully exercised their borrowing powers (*g*).

4. The directors of an unincorporated company held out the secretary as having authority to borrow in excess of the amount prescribed by the rules of the company. The secretary borrowed in excess of such amount, and misappropriated the money. Held, that the directors were personally liable to the lenders on an implied warranty of authority, though they had not acted fraudulently (*h*).

5. A. acts as broker for both buyer and seller. He impliedly warrants to each that he is duly authorized to act on behalf of the other (*i*).

6. A bill of exchange was presented for acceptance at the office of the drawee. The drawee was absent, and A., who lived on the premises, being assured that the bill was perfectly regular, in good faith accepted it on the drawee's behalf, believing that the acceptance would be sanctioned by the drawee. The holder (an indorsee) sued the drawee on the bill, and was nonsuited. Held, that A. was liable to him on an implied warranty that he had authority to accept the bill on the drawee's behalf (*k*).

7. The directors of a company accepted a bill drawn on the company, but told the drawer that they had no power to accept bills on the company's behalf, and that they merely did it in recognition of the company's debt, and on the express understanding that the bill should not be negotiated. Held, that the

---

56 L. T. 36; 35 W. R. 92, C. A. Comp. *Elkington* v. *Hurter*, (1892) 2 Ch. 452, 61 L. J. Ch. 514, 66 L. T. 764.

(*g*) *Weeks* v. *Propert*, 1873, L. R. 8 C. P. 427, 42 L. J. C. P. 129; 21 W. R. 676.

(*h*) *Chapleo* v. *Brunswick Building Society*, 1881, 6 Q. B. D. 696; 50 L. J. Q. B. 372; 44 L. T. 449, 29 W. R. 529, C. A.

(*i*) *Hughes* v. *Graeme*, 1864, 33 L. J. Q. B. 335; 12 W. R. 857.

(*k*) *Polhill* v. *Walter*, 1832, 3 B. & Ad. 114.

directors were liable to an indorsee for value, who had no notice of the circumstances, on an implied warranty that they had authority to accept the bill on behalf of the company (*l*).

8. A widow, after the death of her husband, but before she had received information of his death, ordered necessaries from a tradesman who had previously supplied goods to her on the credit of the husband and been paid for them by him, the husband, to the knowledge of the tradesman, being resident abroad. Held, that the widow was not liable on an implied warranty of authority, the circumstances being equally within the knowledge of both parties, and she not having omitted to state any fact known to her affecting the continuance of the authority that she originally had (*m*).

9. Where a solicitor without authority prosecutes or defends an action, the action will in general be dismissed on the motion of the defendant, or the defence struck out on the motion of the plaintiff, and the solicitor so acting without authority be ordered to pay all the costs occasioned thereby (*n*).

Article 116.

MEASURE OF DAMAGES FOR BREACH OF WARRANTY OF AUTHORITY.

The measure of damages for breach of an express or implied warranty of authority is the loss directly re-

---

(*l*) *West London Commercial Bank* v. *Kitson*, 1884, 13 Q. B. D. 360; 53 L. J. Q. B. 345, 50 L. T. 656, 32 W. R. 757, C. A.

(*m*) *Smout* v. *Ilbery*, 1842, 10 M. & W. 1. Nor are the husband's representatives liable in such a case, see Article 134, Illustration 3.

(*n*) *Hubbard* v. *Phillips*, 1845, 2 D. & L. 707, 13 M. & W. 703, 14 L. J. Ex. 103, *Nurse* v. *Durnford*, 1879, 13 Ch. Div. 764, 49 L. J. Ch. 229, 41 L. T. 611, 28 W. R. 145; *Schjott* v. *Schjott*, 1881, 45 L. T. 333, C. A. See, however, *Hammond* v. *Thorpe*, 1834, 1 C. M. & R. 64, 4 Tyr. 838; *Thomas* v. *Finlayson*, 1871, 19 W. R. 255.

sulting as a natural or probable consequence of the breach of warranty (*o*).

Where a contract is repudiated by the person on whose behalf it was made, on the ground that it was made without his authority, such loss is *primâ facie* the amount that would have been recoverable as against him if he had duly authorized and refused to perform the contract, together with the costs (if any) incurred by an action against him on the contract (*p*). Where the contract would not have been enforceable at law, as against the principal, even if he had duly authorized it, because the formalities required by law were not observed, the equitable doctrine of part performance does not apply so as to give a remedy in equity for damages in respect of the breach of warranty of authority (*q*).

Illustrations.

1. The directors of a company represent that they have authority to issue debenture stock, and A. is induced to accept such stock in lieu of cash, in payment of a debt owing to him by the company. The measure of damages for breach of the implied warranty of authority is the amount that would have been recoverable by A. as against the company if the stock had been valid (*r*).

(*o*) Illustrations 1 to 8.

(*p*) Illustrations 3, and 6 to 8.

(*q*) Illustration 9. Nor is there any remedy at law in such a case, because, the contract not being enforceable at law, there is no legal damage from the breach of warranty.

(*r*) *Firbank* v. *Humphreys*, 1886, 18 Q. B. D. 60; 56 L. J. Q. B. 57; 56 L. T. 36, 35 W. R. 92, C. A.; *Weeks* v. *Propert*, 1873, L. R. 8 C. P. 427; 42 L. J. C. P. 129; 21 W. R. 676.

2. Directors of a building society represent that they have authority to borrow money on behalf of the society, and A. is induced to lend 70*l.* The society being solvent, the measure of damages for breach of the implied warranty of authority, is 70*l.*, with interest at the rate agreed upon (*s*).

3. A. contracted, on behalf of B., to buy a ship. A. was not authorized, and B. repudiated the contract. The seller having resold the ship at a lower price, it was held that the measure of damages recoverable against A. was the difference between the contract price and the price at which the vessel was resold (*t*).

4. A. instructed B. to apply for shares in a certain company. B. by mistake applied for shares in another company, and they were duly allotted to A. The last-mentioned company was ordered to be wound up, and A.'s name was removed from the list of contributories on the ground that he had not authorized the application for shares. Held, that, A. being solvent and the shares unsaleable, the liquidator of the company was entitled to recover from B. the full amount payable on the shares (*u*).

5. A. brought an action against a company in the United States, and recovered judgment for 1,000*l.* An agent of the company in good faith represented that he had authority to settle for 300*l.*, and A. agreed to accept that sum. The agent was, in fact, not authorized to settle. Held, that, the judgment against the company being, under the circumstances, unenforceable, A. was entitled to recover 300*l.* from the agent for the breach of the implied warranty of authority (*x*).

Costs of action against principal.

6. A. bought goods, professedly on behalf of B. The seller brought an action for the price against B., which was dismissed

---

(*s*) *Richardson* v. *Williamson*, 1871, L. R. 6 Q. B. 276; 40 L. J. Q. B. 145.

(*t*) *Simons* v. *Patchett*, 1857, 7 El. & Bl. 568; 26 L. J. Q. B. 195, 3 Jur. N. S. 742. See also *Mitchell* v. *Kahl*, 1862, 2 F. & F. 709.

(*u*) *Re National Coffee Palace Co., Ex p. Panmure*, 1883, 24 Ch. Div. 367, 50 L. T. 38, 32 W. R. 326; 53 L. J. Ch. 57, C. A.

(*x*) *Meek* v. *Wendt*, 1889, 21 Q. B. D. 126; 59 L. T. 558.

with costs, on the ground that A. was not authorized by B. Held, that the seller was entitled to recover from A. the price of the goods, and also the costs incurred in the action against B. (*y*).

7. A. professed to sell property on behalf of B. Held, that A., not being authorized to sell, was liable to the buyer for the costs of a suit for specific performance against B., as well as for the value of the contract (*z*). But where an agent without authority verbally contracted to grant a lease for seven years, and the lessee entered into possession and defended an action of ejectment brought by the owner of the property, it was held that the lessee was not entitled to recover from the agent the costs of such action, as damages for the breach of warranty of authority, because he could not have successfully defended an action of ejectment, even if the agent had been duly authorized to grant the lease (*a*).

8. *Loss must be a natural or probable consequence of the breach.*—A. contracted to sell an estate to B., and sent him an abstract of title, representing that he had the authority of the owners to sell. The owners repudiated the contract and sold the estate at a higher price to C. B. sued the owners until they had all sworn that A. was not authorized to sell, and was then non-suited. In an action by B. against A., it was held that the measure of damages for the breach of warranty of authority was—(1) the costs of investigating the title; (2) the costs of the action up to the non-suit; and (3) the difference between the contract and market prices of the estate, the price at which it was resold to C. being *primâ facie* evidence of the market price; but that the loss on a re-sale of horses, which were bought to stock the land before the investigation of the title and without

(*y*) *Randell* v. *Trimen*, 1856, 18 C. B. 786, 25 L. J. C. P. 307.

(*z*) *Hughes* v. *Greame*, 1864, 33 L. J. Q. B. 335, 12 W. R. 857, *Collen* v. *Wright*, 1857, 8 El. & Bl. 647; 27 L. J. Q. B. 215, 4 Jur. N. S. 357, Ex. Ch.

(*a*) *Pow* v. *Davis*, 1861, 1 B. & S. 220; 30 L. J. Q. B. 257, 7 Jur. N. S. 1010, 4 L. T. 399, 9 W. R. 611. Such a lease must be by deed (8 & 9 Vict. c. 106, s. 3), and every contract for a lease must be in writing (Statute of Frauds, sect. 4).

notice to A., was too remote a consequence of the breach of warranty and was not recoverable, it not appearing that the purchase of stock was distinctly contemplated by the parties when the contract was made (*b*). So, where an agent without authority granted a lease, and the lessee agreed to sell his interest, it was held that damages and costs recovered against the lessee for breach of such agreement to sell could not be recovered by him in an action against the agent for breach of warranty of authority, because such damages and costs were not a natural or probable consequence of the breach of warranty; but that the lessee was entitled to recover the value of the lease, and the costs of a suit for specific performance against the principal (*c*).

9. *No remedy on doctrine of part performance.*—A. verbally contracted, without authority, to sell real estate to B. Held, that B. had no remedy in equity against A. for the breach of warranty of authority, on the ground of part performance (*d*).

Sect. 2.—*Liabilities of agents in respect of moneys received by them.*

Article 117.

MONEY PAID BY THIRD PERSONS.

Where money is paid to an agent for the use of his principal, and the agent in good faith pays it over, or otherwise deals to his detriment with the principal by reason of the payment, the agent is discharged from liability to the person making the payment, in respect of the money so paid (*e*).

(*b*) *Godwin* v. *Francis*, 1870, L. R. 5 C. P. 295, 39 L. J. C. P. 121; 22 L. T. 338.

(*c*) *Spedding* v. *Nevell*, 1869, L. R. 4 C. P. 212; 38 L. J. C. P. 133.

(*d*) *Warr* v. *Jones*, 1876, 24 W. R. 695. See, also, *Sainsbury* v. *Jones*, 1840, 4 Jur. 499; 2 Beav. 462. Nor is there any remedy at law in such a case, in consequence of the provisions of the 4th section of the Statute of Frauds.

(*e*) Illustrations 1 to 3; *Cary* v. *Webster*, 1731, 1 Str. 480.

But every agent is personally liable—

(a) to account for money deposited with him as a stakeholder; and if he wrongfully refuses to pay it over, to pay interest thereon from the date of such refusal (*f*);

(b) to repay money paid to him for the use of his principal, under a mistake of fact, or for a consideration which fails; provided that such money is reclaimed before he has actually paid it over, or dealt to his detriment with the principal on the faith of the payment (*g*);

(c) to repay money obtained by him wrongfully (*h*), or by duress (*i*), or paid to him under protest, in order to obtain goods or documents improperly withheld by him from the person making the payment (*k*), even if he has paid over the money to the principal.

Illustrations.

Not liable if paid over in good faith.

1. An insurance agent received money from an underwriter in respect of a voidable policy, and settled with the principal for the amount, amongst other matters, without notice of the

(*f*) Illustration 4.

(*g*) Illustration 5, *Cary* v. *Webster*, 1731, 1 Str. 480, and see *Gurney* v. *Womersley*, 1854, 4 El. & Bl. 133, 24 L. J. Q. B. 146, 1 Jur. N. S. 328.

(*h*) Illustrations 6 and 7; *Townson* v. *Wilson*, 1808, 1 Camp. 396.

(*i*) Illustration 8. This does not apply where the duress does not proceed from the agent, and he has paid over the money without notice that it was paid under duress. *Owen* v. *Cronk*, (1895) 1 Q. B. 265; 64 L. J. Q. B. 288.

(*k*) Illustration 9.

underwriter's intention to dispute the policy, and without fraud. Held, that the agent was not liable to repay the amount to the underwriter, who had paid it to him under a mistake of fact (*l*).

2. A bill of exchange was indorsed, without the holder's authority, to A. The acceptor paid A.'s agent for collection, who handed the money over to A. without notice of any defect in A.'s title. The acceptor was compelled to pay over again to the payee whose authority was wrongfully assumed. Held, that A.'s agent for collection was not personally liable to refund the amount to the acceptor (*m*).

3. The solicitor of the vendor at a sale by auction received a deposit, which he paid over to the vendor. Held, that the purchaser could not maintain an action against the solicitor for the return of the deposit (*n*).

4. *Liability of stakeholder.*—The auctioneer at a sale by auction receives a deposit, and pays it over to the vendor. He is personally liable to refund the amount on the default of the vendor, because it was his duty to hold it as a stakeholder until the completion or rescission of the contract (*o*). But he is not liable to pay interest, however long he may have held the deposit, until it has been demanded, and he has improperly refused to pay it over to the person entitled (*p*)—at all events, unless he is shown to have received interest on the money (*q*).

5. *Liable if not paid over.*—A. bought goods from B., a broker, and by mistake paid him too much. B. gave his principal, who

---

(*l*) *Holland* v. *Russell*, 1863, 4 B. & S. 14; 32 L. J. Q. B. 297; 8 L. T. 468, Ex. Ch.; *Shand* v. *Grant*, 1863, 15 C. B. N. S. 324; 9 L. T. 390.

(*m*) *East India Co.* v. *Tritton*, 1824, 5 D. & R. 214; 3 B. & C. 280.

(*n*) *Ellis* v. *Goulton*, (1893) 1 Q. B. 350, 62 L. J. Q. B. 232, 9 T. L. R. 223, *Bamford* v. *Shuttleworth*, 1840, 11 A. & E. 926.

(*o*) *Edwards* v. *Hodding*, 1814, 1 Marsh, 377, 5 Taunt. 815; 15 R. R. 662, *Burrough* v. *Skinner*, 1770, 5 Burr. 2639, *Gray* v. *Gutteridge*, 1827, 3 C. & P. 40.

(*p*) *Lee* v. *Munn*, 1817, 1 Moore, 481; 8 Taunt. 45; 19 R. R. 452; *Gaby* v. *Driver*, 1828, 2 Y. & J. 549.

(*q*) *Curling* v. *Shuttleworth*, 1829, 6 Bing. 121, at p. 134.

was largely indebted to him, credit for the amount received. Held, that B. was liable to repay to A. the amount paid in excess, on the ground (1) that B. virtually dealt as principal with A., and (2) that the mistake accrued to B.'s personal benefit (*r*). Where there is no actual change of circumstances to the detriment of the agent in consequence of the payment, merely crediting the principal with the amount is not sufficient to discharge the agent from liability to repay money paid to him under a mistake of fact (*s*).

Payment over no defence if obtained wrongfully.

6. Pending a bankruptcy petition, and with notice of the act of bankruptcy, a solicitor, as the agent of the petitioning creditor, received from the debtor various sums of money in consideration of the adjournment of the petition, and paid such sums over to his principal. Held, that the solicitor was personally liable to repay the amount to the trustee in bankruptcy, notwithstanding the payment over, because the money was obtained wrongfully (*t*).

7. An agent who acts for an executor *de son tort*, with the knowledge that his principal is not the proper executor, is liable to account for assets collected by him, even if he has paid them over to the principal. Payment over is no defence in the case of wrongdoers (*u*).

8. A sheriff issued a warrant of distress against A. The bailiff levied the debt on the goods of B., and, under terror of the illegal distress, B. paid the debt. Held, that the bailiff was personally liable to repay B., though he had paid the amount over to the sheriff (*x*).

(*r*) *Newall* v. *Tomlinson*, 1871, L. R. 6 C. P. 405, 25 L. T. 382.

(*s*) *Buller* v. *Harrison*, 1777, Cowp. 565, *Cox* v. *Prentice*, 1815, 3 M. & S. 344; 16 R. R. 288.

(*t*) *Ex p. Edwards, re Chapman*, 1884, 13 Q. B. D. 747, 51 L. T. 881, 33 W. R. 268, C. A.

(*u*) *Sharland* v. *Mildow*, 1846, 5 Hare, 469, 15 L. J. Ch. 434, 10 Jur. 771.

(*x*) *Snowdon* v. *Davis*, 1808, 1 Taunt. 359.

9. An agent demands more money than is due and wrongfully withholds documents from A., who pays him the amount demanded, under protest, in order to recover the documents. The agent is personally liable to A. in respect of the amount overpaid, even if he has paid the money over to the principal (*y*).

Article 118.

MONEY RECEIVED TO USE OF THIRD PERSONS.

Where an agent is authorized to pay to a third person money existing or accruing in his hands on the principal's behalf, and he expressly or impliedly contracts with such third person to pay him, or to receive or hold the money on his behalf, or to his use, he is personally liable to such third person for the amount when received, even if he has had fresh instructions from the principal not to pay such third person (*z*). But no agent is liable to third persons in respect of money in his hands that he has been authorized to pay them, unless he has entered into such an express or implied contract (*a*).

(*y*) *Smith* v. *Sleap*, 1844, 12 M. & W. 585; *Oates* v. *Hudson*, 1851, 6 Ex. 346, 20 L. J. Ex. 284.

(*z*) Illustrations 1 to 3, *Griffin* v. *Weatherby*, 1868, L. R. 3 Q. B. 753; 37 L. J. Q. B. 280; 18 L. T. 881; 9 B. & S. 726, 17 W. R. 8; *Hodgson* v. *Anderson*, 1842, 3 B. & C. 842; *Webb* v. *Smith*, 1885, 30 Ch. Div. 192; 55 L. J. Ch. 343, 53 L. T. 737, C. A.

(*a*) Illustrations 4 to 6, *Heath* v. *Chilton*, 1844, 12 M. & W. 632; 13 L. J. Ex. 225; *Gibson* v. *Minet*, 1824, 9 Moore, 31, 2 Bing. 7; 1 C. & P. 247; R. & M. 68.

Illustrations.

1. A principal gives his agent authority to pay money to A., a third person. The agent promises A. that he will pay him when the amount is ascertained. The agent is liable to A. for the amount when it is ascertained, though in the meantime the principal has become bankrupt (*b*), or has countermanded his authority (*c*).

2. A principal writes a letter authorizing his agent to pay to A. the amounts of certain acceptances, as they become due, out of the proceeds of certain assignments. The agent assents. Before the acceptances fall due, the principal becomes bankrupt, and the agent pays the proceeds of the assignments to the trustee in bankruptcy. The agent is personally liable to A. for the amounts of the acceptances as they become due (*d*).

3. A bill drawn on an agent is made payable out of a particular fund, and the agent promises to pay the holder when he receives money for the principal. The agent is liable to the holder, if he subsequently receives the money (*e*).

4. An agent is authorized to pay a certain debt out of moneys in his hands. He is not liable to the creditor, unless he contracts to pay him, or to hold the money to his use (*f*), and a mere statement of an intention to pay him does not necessarily amount to such a contract (*g*).

5. An agent receives money for the express purpose of taking up a bill two days after its maturity. On tendering the money, he finds that the holders have sent back the bill, protested for non-acceptance, to their indorsers. He then receives fresh instructions not to pay. He is not liable to the holders of the

---

(*b*) *Crowfoot* v. *Gurney*, 1832, 9 Bing. 372; 2 M. & Scott, 473.

(*c*) *Robertson* v. *Fauntleroy*, 1823, 8 Moore, 10.

(*d*) *Walker* v. *Rostron*, 1842, 9 M. & W. 411.

(*e*) *Stevens* v. *Hill*, 1805, 5 Esp. 247.

(*f*) *Howell* v. *Batt*, 1833, 2 N. & M. 381, 5 B. & Ad. 504.

(*g*) *Malcolm* v. *Scott*, 1850, 5 Ex. 601, *Williams* v. *Everett*, 1811, 14 East, 582, 13 R. R. 315.

bill, not having agreed to hold the money to their use (*h*). So, where an agent, who was authorized to pay money to a third person, offered to pay on a condition to which such third person would not agree, it was held that that was not a sufficient agreement to render him liable to such third person (*i*).

6. An agent of an executor wrote to a legatee, stating and offering to remit the amount of his legacy, and subsequently remitted the amount, after deducting certain expenses. Held, that the agent had not contracted with the legatee, and was not liable to an action at his instance for the amount so deducted (*j*).

Sect. 3.—*Rights of agents against third persons.*

Article 119.

RIGHT OF AGENT TO SUE IN OWN NAME ON CONTRACTS MADE BY HIM.

An agent may sue in his own name on contracts made by him on behalf of his principal—

(a) where he has contracted personally (*k*);

(b) where, as in the case of factors and auctioneers, he has a special property in, or a lien upon, the subject-matter of the contract, or has a beneficial interest in the completion thereof (*l*);

(*h*) *Stewart* v. *Fry*, 1817, 1 Moore, 74; 7 Taunt. 339.

(*i*) *Baron* v. *Husband*, 1838, 4 B. & Ad. 611.

(*j*) *Barlow* v. *Browne*, 1846, 16 M. & W. 126, 16 L. J. Ex. 63.

(*k*) Illustrations 1 and 2. See Articles 107 to 112, as to when an agent is deemed to contract personally.

(*l*) Illustration 3. *Snee* v. *Prescott*, 1743, 1 Atk. 248; *Fisher* v. *Marsh*,

(c) in the case of insurance brokers, who may sue in their own names on all policies effected by them (*m*).

Where a person who enters into a contract professedly as an agent is in fact the real principal, he may sue on the contract—

if it has been partly performed by the other contracting party with the knowledge that he is the real principal (*n*); and

(probably) in all cases where the identity of the contracting party is not a material element in the making of the contract, provided that he gives notice to the other contracting party, before action, that he is the real principal (*o*).

Except as in this article provided, no agent can maintain an action in his own name on any contract made

---

1865, 6 B. & S. 411, 34 L. J. Q. B. 177, 11 Jur. N. S. 795; 12 L. T. 604; 13 W. R. 834; *Dickinson* v. *Naul*, 1833, 4 B. & Ad. 638, *Fairlie* v. *Fenton*, 1870, L. R. 5 Ex. 169; 39 L. J. Ex. 107, 22 L. T. 373; 18 W. R. 700.

(*m*) *Provincial Insurance Co. of Canada* v. *Leduc*, 1874, L. R. 6 P. C. 224, 43 L. J. P. C. 49, 31 L. T. 142; 22 W. R. 929, P. C., *Sunderland Marine Insurance Co.* v. *Kearney*, 1851, 16 Q. B. 939; *Oom* v. *Bruce*, 1810, 12 East, 225; 11 R. R. 367, *Fairlie* v. *Fenton*, 1870, L. R. 5 Ex. 169, 39 L. J. Ex. 107, 22 L. T. 373, 18 W. R. 700. As to the right of an insurance broker, on the bankruptcy of an underwriter, to set off losses on policies effected by him, against premiums due from him, see *Lee* v. *Bullen*, 1858, 27 L. J. Q. B. 161, 8 El. & Bl. 692, 4 Jur. N. S. 557.

(*n*) Illustration 4.

(*o*) Illustrations 4 to 6. *Bickerton* v. *Burrell*, 1816, 5 M. & S. 383. See, however, *Hollman* v. *Pullin*, 1884, 1 C. & E. 254.

by him, as such (*p*), whether the principal be disclosed or undisclosed (*p*), and whether the agent was acting under a *del credere* commission or not (*q*).

Illustrations.

May sue if he contracts personally.

1. A contract was made in the following form:—"It is mutually agreed between J. & R. W., of the one part, and S. J. C., on behalf of G. & M. Rail. Co., of the other part, &c." (signed) "J. & R. W., S. J. C." Held, that S. J. C. was entitled to sue in his own name for breach of the contract, he having contracted personally (*r*).

2. A broker contracted in writing in his own name to purchase goods, the seller being told that there was a principal. The broker then, under a general authority from the principal, contracted to resell the goods. On hearing of the last-mentioned contract, the principal refused to have anything to do with the goods, and the broker acquiesced. The seller then refused to deliver the goods. Held, that the broker, having contracted personally, had a right to recover damages for the non-delivery, and that the principal's renunciation of the contract did not affect that right (*s*).

3. *Special property in the goods.*—An auctioneer sells goods at the house of the owner, and they are known to be the owner's property. The auctioneer may, nevertheless, sue in his own name for the price (*t*).

4. *Where really principal.*—A., professedly as agent for a named principal, contracted in writing to sell certain goods.

(*p*) Illustrations 7 to 9, *Sargent* v. *Morris*, 1820, 3 B. & Ald. 277; 22 R. R. 382.

(*q*) *Bramble* v. *Spiller*, 1870, 21 L. T. 672; 18 W. R. 316.

(*r*) *Cooke* v. *Wilson*, 1856, 1 C. B. N. S. 153, 26 L. J. C. P. 15; 2 Jur. N. S. 1094.

(*s*) *Short* v. *Spackman*, 1831, 2 B. & Ad. 962.

(*t*) *Williams* v. *Millington*, 1788, 1 H. Bl. 81, 2 R. R. 724.

The buyer, with notice that A. was the real principal, accepted and paid for part of the goods. Held, that A. might sue for the non-acceptance of the residue (*u*). Otherwise, if the skill or solvency of the supposed principal had formed an ingredient in the contract (*u*).

5. A. signed a charter-party "as agent for the freighter," a clause being inserted therein, limiting A.'s liability to certain events, in view of his being an agent. A. was himself the freighter. Held, that he might sue on the contract (the clause limiting his liability would be inoperative). Otherwise, if the other contracting party had relied on his character as agent, and would not have contracted with him had he known him to be the principal. The freighter, whoever he might have been, would have had a right to sue (*v*).

6. A broker signed a contract note, professedly as agent for an undisclosed principal. He was, in fact, acting on his own behalf, but the other contracting party was not aware of that. Held, that he could not sue on the contract, because there was no memorandum thereof to satisfy the 17th section of the Statute of Frauds. Some of the judges in this case laid down that he had no right to sue because no contract had been made with him (*w*).

Brokers, in general, cannot sue.

7. A broker sent a contract note in the following form :—"I have this day sold you, on account of B., &c." (signed) "A. B., broker." Held, that the broker had no right of action in his own name against the buyer for refusing to accept the goods (*x*). So, where a broker sent a contract note as follows,—"Mr. L., I

(*u*) *Rayner* v. *Grote*, 1846, 15 M. & W. 359, 16 L. J. Ex. 79.

(*v*) *Smalz* v. *Avery*, 1851, 20 L. J. Q. B. 228, 15 Jur. 291, 16 Q. B. 655. See, however, illustration 6.

(*w*) *Sharman* v. *Brandt*, 1871, L. R. 6 Q. B. 720, 40 L. J. Q. B. 312; 19 W. R. 936, Ex. Ch.

(*x*) *Fairlie* v. *Fenton*, 1870, L. R. 5 Ex. 169, 39 L. J. Ex. 107, 22 L. T. 373, 18 W. R. 700.

have this day bought in my own name for your account, of A. K. T., &c." (signed) "A. B., broker,"—it was held that he had no right to sue L. for the price (*y*). Where a broker enters into a contract as such, he has no right of action in his own name on the contract, except in the case of an insurance broker, or where he has a beneficial interest in the completion of the contract; a broker thus differs from a factor or auctioneer, who has a right to sue by reason of his special property in the goods (*z*).

8. By an agreement in writing, in consideration of the letting of certain tolls by commissioners, A. undertook to pay the rent to the treasurer of the commissioners. Held, that the treasurer had no right to sue in his own name for the rent, the contract being made in the names of the principals (*a*).

9. On a sale of land by a corporation, the mayor signed a contract "on behalf of himself and the rest of the burgesses and commonalty of the borough." The conditions provided that the corporation should convey, and a deposit be paid to the mayor. Held, that the mayor could not sue in his own name for breach of the contract (*b*).

Article 120.

EFFECT OF INTERVENTION OF OR SETTLEMENT WITH THE PRINCIPAL.

Except as in this article provided, the right of an agent to sue on a contract made on behalf of his principal ceases on the intervention of the principal; and a settlement with or set-off against the principal may be set up by way of defence to an action by the agent (*c*).

(*y*) *Fawkes* v. *Lamb*, 1862, 31 L. J. Q. B. 98; 8 Jur. N. S. 385.

(*z*) *Fairlie* v. *Fenton*, *supra*, p. 306.

(*a*) *Pigott* v. *Thompson*, 1802, 3 B. & P. 147.

(*b*) *Bowen* v. *Morris*, 1810, 2 Taunt. 374, Ex. Ch.

(*c*) *Sadler* v. *Leigh*, 1815, 4 Camp. 195; 2 Rose, 286. And see *Dickinson* v. *Naul*, 1833, 4 B. & Ad. 638.

Provided that, where the agent has, as against the principal, a right of lien on the subject-matter of the contract, the right of the agent to sue on the contract has priority, during the existence of his claim, to that of the principal (*c*); and a settlement with or set-off against the principal cannot be set up by way of defence to an action by the agent where such settlement or set-off would operate to the prejudice of the agent's claim, unless the defendant was led by the terms or conditions of the contract, or by the conduct of the agent, to believe that the agent acquiesced in a settlement with the principal (*d*).

Illustrations.

1. A factor sells, in his own name, goods on which he has a lien for advances. While the advances are unpaid, the factor's right to sue the purchaser and compel payment has priority to that of the principal or his trustee in bankruptcy (*e*).

2. A broker sells, in his own name, goods on which he has made advances. The buyer has no right, in an action by the broker for the price, to set off a debt due to him from the principal (*f*).

3. An auctioneer sued for the price of goods sold and delivered. The defendant pleaded that the plaintiff acted as an auctioneer, and that the defendant had paid the principal for the goods before action. Held, that the plea was bad, because the auctioneer would have had, as against the principal, a lien on

(*c*) Illustration 1.

(*d*) Illustrations 2 to 5. And see *Tagart* v. *Marcus*, 1888, 36 W. R. 469.

(*e*) *Drinkwater* v. *Goodwin*, 1775, Cowp. 251.

(*f*) *Atkyns* v. *Amber*, 1796, 2 Esp. 493.

the proceeds for charges, &c. (*g*). The defendant should have shown that, either by the conditions of sale or by facts accruing subsequently, payment to the principal was permitted in discharge of the plaintiff's claim (*g*).

4. An auctioneer, on behalf of A., sold goods to B. A. was indebted to B., and there was an agreement between them before the sale that the price of any goods bought by B. should be set off against the debt, but the auctioneer had no notice of the agreement. The auctioneer permitted B. to take away the goods, thinking that he was going to pay for them, B. thinking that he was taking them in pursuance of his agreement with A. The auctioneer paid A. on account, and after receiving notice of the agreement between A. and B., paid him the balance of the proceeds of the sale, such balance exceeding the amount of B.'s purchases. The auctioneer subsequently sued B. for the price of the goods. Held, that, the auctioneer's charges having been paid before action, and he having had notice of the agreement between A. and B. at the time of his payment to A. (exceeding the amount for which he was suing B.), the settlement between A. and B. constituted a good defence (*h*). Here, the auctioneer was not really prejudiced by the settlement with the principal.

5. Goods belonging to A. and B. were sold by auction at A.'s house, and were described in the catalogue as A.'s property. C. bought some of the goods and settled with A., the auctioneer having permitted him to take away the goods without giving him notice not to pay A. D. also bought goods and was similarly permitted to take them away. The auctioneer brought actions against C. and D. Held, that the settlement between C. and A. was a good defence (*i*), and that D. was entitled to set off a debt due to him from A. (*j*).

(*g*) *Robinson* v. *Rutter*, 1855, 4 El. & Bl. 954; 24 L. J. Q. B. 250; 1 Jur. N. S. 823.

(*h*) *Grice* v. *Kenrick*, 1870, L. R. 5 Q. B. 340; 39 L. J. Q. B. 175, 22 L. T. 743; 18 W. R. 1155.

(*i*) *Coppin* v. *Walker*, 1816, 2 Marsh. 497, 7 Taunt. 237, 17 R. R. 505.

(*j*) *Coppin* v. *Craig*, 1816, 2 Marsh. 501; 7 Taunt. 243; 17 R. R. 508.

Article 121.

DEFENCES AVAILABLE WHERE AGENT SUES IN OWN NAME.

Where an agent sues in his own name on a contract made on behalf of his principal, any statements which he has himself made, as well as the statements of the principal on whose behalf he is acting, may be used in evidence against him (*k*); and the defendant may avail himself of any defence, including that of set-off, which would have been available against the plaintiff if he had been suing on a contract made on his own behalf, even if the defence would not have been available in an action by the principal on the contract (*l*).

Illustration.

A broker sues on a policy effected in his own name. Payment of the loss by settlement of accounts with the broker, or by way of set-off, is a good defence, though it would not have been a valid payment as between the insurer and the assured (*l*).

Article 122.

RIGHT OF AGENT TO SUE FOR MONEY PAID BY MISTAKE, ETC.

Where an agent pays money on his principal's behalf under a mistake of fact, or for a consideration

---

See also *Holmes* v. *Tutton*, 1855, 5 El. & Bl. 65; 24 L. J. Q. B. 346; 1 Jur. N. S. 975.

(*k*) *Smith* v. *Lyon*, 1813, 3 Camp. 465; 14 R. R. 810, *Bauerman* v. *Radenius*, 1798, 7 T. R. 663, 2 Esp. 653, *Welstead* v. *Levy*, 1831, 1 M. & Rob. 138.

(*l*) *Gibson* v. *Winter*, 1833, 5 B. & Ad. 96, 2 N. & M. 737.

which fails, or in consequence of the fraudulent misrepresentations of the payee, he may sue in his own name for its recovery (*m*).

Article 123.

NO RIGHT OF ACTION FOR PROMISED BRIBES.

No action will lie by an agent for the recovery of property or money promised him by way of a bribe, whether he was, in fact, induced thereby to depart from his duty, or not (*n*).

Sect. 4.—*Liabilities of agents in respect of torts committed on principal's behalf.*

Article 124.

AGENT PERSONALLY LIABLE FOR ALL WRONGS COMMITTED BY HIM.

Where loss or injury is caused to third persons, or any penalty is incurred, by any wrongful act or omission of an agent while acting on behalf of the principal, the agent is personally liable therefor, whether he is acting with the authority of the principal or not (unless the principal can justify the wrong (*o*)),

(*m*) *Stevenson* v. *Mortimer*, 1778, Cowp. 805; *Holt* v. *Ely*, 1853, 1 E. & B. 795, 17 Jur. 892. In such a case, either the principal or the agent may sue.

(*n*) *Harrington* v. *Victoria Dock Co.*, 1878, 3 Q. B. D. 549; 47 L. J. Q. B. 594; 39 L. T. 120; 26 W. R. 740.

(*o*) See Illustration 6.

to the same extent as if he were acting on his own behalf (*p*).

Provided, that no public officer is liable for loss or injury caused to a member of any foreign state by any act authorized or ratified by the government (*q*).

Illustrations.

1. An agent signed a distress warrant, and after the warrant was issued, but before it was executed, refused a tender of the rent. Held, that the agent was personally liable for the illegal distress (*r*).

2. The manager of a bank signed a letter, as such, falsely and fraudulently representing that the credit of a certain person was good. Held, that the manager was personally liable in an action for deceit (*s*). All persons directly concerned in the commission of a fraud are personally liable, though acting on behalf of others (*t*). But, in the absence of fraud, an agent is not personally liable for misrepresentations made by him on behalf of the principal (*u*).

(*p*) *Hugh* v. *Abergavenny*, 1874, 23 W. R. 40, *Sharland* v. *Mildow*, 1846, 5 Hare, 469, 15 L. J. Ch. 434, 10 Jur. 771, *Merryweather* v. *Nixan*, 1800, 8 T. R. 186, *Stevens* v. *Midland Counties Rail. Co.*, 1854, 10 Ex. 352, 2 C. L. R. 1300, 23 L. J. Ex. 328, 18 Jur. 932 (malicious prosecution); *Nobel's Explosives Co.* v. *Jones*, 1882, 8 App. Cas. 5, 52 L. J. Ch. 339, 31 W. R. 388, 48 L. T. 490, H. L. (infringement of patent). The principal may be liable jointly and severally with the agent. See Article 97.

(*q*) *Buron* v. *Denman*, 1848, 2 Ex. 167.

(*r*) *Bennett* v. *Bayes*, 1860, 5 H. & N. 391, 29 L. J. Ex. 224, 8 W. R. 320.

(*s*) *Swift* v. *Jewesbury*, 1874, L. R. 9 Q. B. 301, 43 L. J. Q. B. 56, 30 L. T. 31, 22 W. R. 319.

(*t*) *Cullen* v. *Thompson*, 1862, 4 Macq. H. L. Cas. 424, 9 Jur. N. S. 85, 6 L. T. 870, *Bulkeley* v. *Dunbar*, 1792, 1 Anstr. 37.

(*u*) *Eaglesfield* v. *Londonderry*, 1876, 38 L. T. 303, 26 W. R. 540, H. L.

3. A solicitor who was employed in the sale of an estate concealed an incumbrance from the purchaser. Held, that he was personally liable (*v*). So, where an agent assists in the commission of a breach of trust, he is personally liable therefor (*w*).

4. The directors of a company improperly pay dividends out of capital. They are personally liable to the creditors of the company (*x*).

5. An agent converts the goods of a third person to his principal's use. He is liable to the true owner for their value, even if he acted in good faith, in the belief that his principal was the owner of the goods (*y*).

6. *Act justified by principal.*—An agent, on behalf of his principal, but without the principal's authority, distrains the goods of a third person. The principal ratifies the distress, which is justifiable at his instance. The agent ceases to be liable, his act being justified by the ratification (*z*).

7. *Distinction between trespass and case.*—A solicitor, being retained to sue for a debt, by mistake and without malice takes all the proceedings to judgment and execution against another person of the same name as the debtor; or, having obtained judgment against the debtor, by mistake and without malice issues execution against another person of the same name. The solicitor is not liable for the wrongful seizure, unless he directed the sheriff to seize the goods of the wrong person (*a*). But where a solicitor directs the seizure of particular goods, he is

---

(*v*) *Arnot* v. *Biscoe*, 1748, 1 Ves. 95.

(*w*) *A.-G.* v. *Corporation of Leicester*, 1844, 7 Beav. 176.

(*x*) *Salisbury* v. *Metropolitan Rail. Co.*, 1870, 22 L. T. 839; 18 W. R. 484.

(*y*) *Perkins* v. *Smith*, 1752, 1 Wils. 328; *Cranch* v. *White*, 1835, 1 Scott, 314, 1 Bing. N. C. 414, 1 Hodges, 61, *Stevens* v. *Elwall*, 1815, 4 M. & S. 259; *Wilson* v. *Anderton*, 1830, 1 B. & Ad. 450; *Hardacre* v. *Stewart*, 1804; 5 Esp. 103. And see cases cited under Article 125.

(*z*) *Hull* v. *Pickersgill*, 1 Brod. & B. 282, 3 Moore, 612, 21 R. R. 598. And see *Anderson* v. *Watson*, 1827, 3 C. & P 314.

(*a*) *Davies* v. *Jenkins*, 1843, 1 D. & L. 321; 11 M. & W. 745, 12 L. J. Ex. 386, 7 Jur. 801.

personally liable if the seizure turns out to be a wrongful one (*b*). So, where a solicitor directed the execution of a warrant for arrest, he was held liable in an action for false imprisonment, the warrant being bad (*c*). This distinction is founded on the difference between the old actions of trespass and case. Trespass would not lie unless the injury was a direct consequence of the act of the defendant, but malice was unnecessary. Case would lie for indirect injuries, but malice was essential. The distinction is still important, for, although actions are not now classified under particular heads and forms, the Judicature Acts have not created any new causes of action.

Article 125.

CONVERSION BY INNOCENT AGENT.

Where an agent has the possession or control of goods, and—

(a) sells and delivers, or otherwise assumes to transfer the possession and property in the goods, without the authority of the true owner (*d*); or

(b) refuses without qualification to deliver up possession of the goods to the true owner on demand (*e*); or

(c) transfers the possession of the goods to his principal or any other person except the true owner, with notice of the claim of the true owner (*f*)—

he is guilty of a conversion of the goods, and is liable

(*b*) *Rowles* v. *Senior*, 1846, 8 Q. B. 677, *Davies* v. *Jenkins*, *ante*, note (*a*).
(*c*) *Green* v. *Elgie*, 1843, 5 Q. B. 99, D. & M. 199, 14 L. J. Q. B. 162.
(*d*) Illustrations 1 to 4.
(*e*) Illustration 7.
(*f*) Illustration 5.

to the true owner for their value, even if he obtained possession from the apparent owner of the goods, and acted in good faith on the authority of such apparent owner (*g*). Provided, that this does not apply to acts done in good faith, and without notice of the claim of the true owner, on the authority of a mercantile agent, or of a buyer or seller of the goods, in possession of the goods or of the documents of title thereto with the consent of the true owner, within the meaning of the Factors Act, 1889 (*h*).

But an agent is not guilty of conversion who, in good faith, merely—

(a) contracts on behalf of his principal to sell goods of which he has neither possession nor control (*i*); or

(b) by the authority of the apparent owner, and without notice of the claim of the true owner, deals with the possession without assuming to deal with the property in the goods (*j*); or

(c) refuses in such reasonably qualified terms to deliver up to the true owner goods in his possession by the authority of the apparent owner that the refusal does not amount to a repudiation of the title of the true owner (*k*).

(*g*) Illustrations 1 to 5.

(*h*) See *Shenstone* v. *Hilton*, (1894) 2 Q. B. 452; 10 R. 390; 63 L. J. Q. B. 584; 71 L. T. 339. See the Factors Act set out in the Appendix.

(*i*) *Turner* v. *Hockey*, 1887, 56 L. J. Q. B. 301; *Barker* v. *Furlong*, (1891) 2 Ch. 172, 60 L. J. Ch. 368; 64 L. T. 411, 39 W. R. 621, C. A.; *Cochrane* v. *Rymill*, 1879, 40 L. T. 744; 27 W. R. 776, C. A.

(*j*) Illustration 6.

(*k*) Illustration 7.

Illustrations.

1. An auctioneer was instructed to sell by auction furniture which the possessor and apparent owner had assigned by bill of sale to a third person. The auctioneer, who had no notice of the assignment, sold the furniture at the residence of the assignor, and, in the ordinary course of business, delivered it to the purchasers. Held, that the auctioneer was liable to the assignee for the value of the furniture (*l*).

2. A. obtained certain goods by fraud. B., a broker, bought the goods in his own name from A., thinking that they would suit C., a customer of his. B., having sold the goods to C. at the same price at which he had bought them from A., merely charging the usual commission, took delivery and conveyed the goods to the railway station, whence they were conveyed to C. The jury found that B. bought the goods merely as an agent, in the ordinary course of his business. Held, that B. was liable to the true owner for the value of the goods (*m*). Anyone who, however innocently, obtains possession of the goods of a person who has been fraudulently deprived of them, and disposes of them, whether for his own benefit or that of any other person, is guilty of a conversion, and it is no answer to say that he was acting on the authority of another person who himself had no authority to dispose of them (*m*).

3. A. hired certain cabs from B., and obtained advances thereon from an auctioneer. The auctioneer, on A.'s instructions, and without notice of B.'s title, in good faith sold the cabs, and after deducting the advances and his expenses, paid the proceeds to A. Held, that the auctioneer was liable to B. for the value of the cabs, having had control of them, and having

(*l*) *Consolidated Co.* v. *Curtis*, (1892) 1 Q. B. 495, 61 L. J. Q. B. 325, 40 W. R. 426, 56 J. P. 565, C. A., *Barker* v. *Furlong*, (1891) 2 Ch. 172, 60 L. J. Ch. 368, 64 L. T. 411, C. A.

(*m*) *Hollins* v *Fowler*, 1872, L. R. 7 Q. B. 616, 41 L. J. Q. B. 277, 27 L. T. 168, 20 W. R. 868. affirmed, L. R. 7 H. L. 757, 44 L. J. Q. B. 169, 33 L. T. 73, H. L.

sold them in such a way as to pass the property therein (*n*). Otherwise, if he had not had possession or control of the cabs, and had merely contracted to sell, without delivering them (*n*).

4. An insurance broker effected a policy on behalf of A. A. became bankrupt, and after the adjudication instructed the broker to collect money due under the policy and pay it to him. The broker, without notice of the bankruptcy, collected the money and paid it to A. Held, that the broker was liable to the trustee in bankruptcy for the amount (*o*).

5. A husband intrusted separate property of his wife's to an auctioneer for sale. The auctioneer received notice of the wife's claim, and subsequently sold a portion of the property, and permitted the husband to remove the remainder. Held, that the auctioneer was liable to the wife for the value of the property removed by the husband, as well as of that which had been sold (*p*).

6. A. held a bill of sale over horses in the possession of B. B. took the horses to C.'s repository for sale by auction, and they were entered in the catalogue for sale. Before the sale took place B. sold the horses by private contract in C.'s yard. The price was paid to C., who deducted his commission and charges, and handed the balance to B., and the horses, on B.'s instructions, were delivered by C. to the purchaser. Held, that C., having merely delivered the horses according to B.'s orders, and not having himself sold or otherwise assumed to deal with the property in them, was not guilty of a conversion (*q*).

7. An agent in possession of goods by the authority of his principal, on demand by the true owner refuses to deliver them up without an order from the principal, or requires a reasonable

---

(*n*) *Cochrane* v. *Rymill*, 1879, 40 L. T. 744; 27 W. R. 776, C. A.; *Barker* v. *Furlong*, *ante*, note (*l*).

(*o*) *McEntire* v. *Potter*, 1889, 22 Q. B. D. 440. And see *Pearson* v. *Graham*, 1837, 6 A. & E. 899; 2 Nev. & P. 636.

(*p*) *Davis* v. *Artingstall*, 1880, 49 L. J. Ch. 609; 42 L. T. 507; 29 W. R. 137.

(*q*) *National Mercantile Bank* v. *Rymill*, 1881, 44 L. T. 767, C. A.

time to ascertain whether the person demanding the goods is the true owner. Such a qualified refusal is not a conversion. Otherwise, where the refusal is absolute, or amounts to a setting-up of the principal's title to the goods (*r*).

Article 126.

AGENTS NOT LIABLE FOR TORTS OF CO-AGENTS OR SUB-AGENTS.

No agent is liable to any third person for loss or injury caused by the wrongful act or omission of a co-agent or sub-agent, unless he authorized, induced, or participated in such wrongful act or omission (*s*).

(*r*) *Alexander* v. *Southey*, 1821, 5 B. & Ald. 247; *Lee* v. *Bayes and Robinson*, 1856, 18 C. B. 599, 25 L. J. C. P. 249, 2 Jur. N. S. 1093.

(*s*) *Cargill* v. *Bower*, 1878, 10 Ch. Div. 502, 47 L. J. Ch. 649; 38 L. T. 779; 26 W. R. 716; *Bear* v. *Stevenson*, 1874, 30 L. T. 177, P. C.; *Weir* v. *Barnett*, 1878, 3 Ex. Div. 238; 47 L. J. Ex. 704; 38 L. T. 929; 26 W. R. 746, C. A.; *Stone* v. *Cartwright*, 1795, 6 T. R. 411; 3 R. R. 220.

CHAPTER XI.

Determination of Agency.

Article 127.

DETERMINATION BY EFFLUXION OF TIME, ETC.

The authority of an agent is determined—

(a) if given for a particular transaction, by the completion of that transaction (*a*);

(b) if given for a fixed period, by the expiration of that period (*b*);

(c) by the destruction of the subject-matter of the agency (*c*).

Illustrations.

1. A broker is employed to sell goods. Immediately the contract of sale is completed, he is *functus officio*, and cannot subsequently alter the terms of the contract without fresh authority from the principal (*d*).

2. A solicitor is retained to conduct an action. In the absence of express agreement to the contrary, his authority to act for the client ceases at the judgment (*e*).

(*a*) Illustrations 1 to 4.

(*b*) See Illustration 5.

(*c*) *Rhodes* v. *Forwood*, 1876, 1 App. Cas. 256; 47 L. J. Ex. 396; 34 L. T. 890; 24 W. R. 1078, H. L.

(*d*) *Blackburn* v. *Scholes*, 1810, 2 Camp. 343; 11 R. R. 723.

(*e*) *Macbeath* v. *Ellis*, 1828, 4 Bing. 578; *Butler* v. *Knight*, 1867, L. R. 2 Ex. 109; 36 L. J. Ex. 66; 15 L. T. 621; 15 W. R. 407.

3. An auctioneer is authorized to sell property. His authority ceases when the sale is completed (*f*).

4. A house agent was employed to let or sell a house. Having let the house, he negotiated for a sale, and subsequently found a purchaser. Held, that he had no authority to sell after having let the house, and that he was not entitled to commission on the sale (*g*).

5. A broker is authorized to sell goods. It may be shown that by the custom of the particular trade such an authority expires with the expiration of the day on which it is given (*h*).

Article 128.

HOW AGENT'S AUTHORITY MAY BE DETERMINED.

Subject to the provisions of Articles 129 to 135, the authority of an agent is determined—

(a) by the death, lunacy, unsoundness of mind, or bankruptcy of either principal or agent (*i*);

(b) by notice of revocation by the principal (*k*);

(c) by renunciation by the agent (*k*).

Article 129.

WHEN AUTHORITY IRREVOCABLE.

Where an authority is given by deed, or for valuable consideration (*l*), for the purpose of effectuating any

---

(*f*) *Seton* v. *Slade*, 1802, 7 Ves. 276, 6 R. R. 124.

(*g*) *Gillow* v. *Aberdare*, 1893, 9 T. L. R. 12.

(*h*) *Dickinson* v. *Lilwall*, 1815, 4 Camp. 279, 1 Stark. 128.

(*i*) See Articles 131 and 132. As to bankruptcy of agent, see, however, *M'Call* v. *Australian Meat Co.*, 1870, 19 W. R. 188.

(*k*) See Article 133.

(*l*) See Illustrations 1 and 3.

security (*m*), or of protecting or securing any interest of the agent (*n*), it is irrevocable during the subsistence of such security or interest (*o*). But an authority is not irrevocable merely because the agent has an interest in the exercise of it, or has a special property in, or lien for advances upon, the subject-matter thereof, the authority not being given expressly for the purpose of securing such interest or advances (*p*).

Where an agent is employed to do an act involving personal liability, and is given authority to discharge such liability on behalf of the principal, the authority becomes irrevocable so soon as the liability is incurred by the agent (*q*).

Where an agent is authorized to pay money on behalf of the principal to a third person, the authority becomes irrevocable so soon as the agent has entered into a binding contract to pay or hold the money to or to the use of such third person (*r*).

(*m*) *Walsh* v. *Whitcomb*, 1797, 2 Esp. 565, *Smart* v. *Sandars*, 1848, 5 C. B. 895, 17 L. J. C. P. 258, 12 Jur. 751.

(*n*) Illustrations 1 to 6, *Alley* v. *Hotson*, 1815, 4 Camp. 325.

(*o*) See *Chinnock* v. *Sainsbury*, 1860, 30 L. J. Ch. 409; 6 Jur. N. S. 1318; 9 W. R. 7; 3 L. T. N. S. 258.

(*p*) Illustrations 2 to 5.

(*q*) Illustration 7, *Read* v. *Anderson*, 1884, 13 Q. B. D. 779, 53 L. J. Q. B. 532; 51 L. T. 55; 49 J. P. 4; 32 W. R. 950, C. A., *Thacker* v. *Hardy*, 1878, 4 Q. B. D. 685; 48 L. J. Q. B. 289, 39 L. T. 595, 27 W. R. 158, C. A. The importance of this principle is much diminished by the Gaming Act, 1892. See Article 69.

(*r*) Illustration 8, *Robertson* v. *Fauntleroy*, 1823, 8 Moore, 10, *Metcalfe* v. *Clough*, 1828, 2 M. & R. 178; *Fisher* v. *Miller*, 1823, 7 Moore, 527; 1 Bing. 150, *Griffin* v. *Weatherby*, 1868, L. R. 3 Q. B. 753, 37 L. J. Q. B. 280, 18 L. T. 881, 9 B. & S. 726, *Hodgson* v. *Anderson*, 3 B. & C. 842.

Where an agent has a right to sue on a contract made on behalf of the principal, and would be entitled to a lien, as against the principal, on any sum recovered in respect of such contract, the authority of the agent to sue and give a discharge for the sum due under the contract is irrevocable during the subsistence of the claim in respect of which he would be entitled to the lien (*s*).

An authority expressed by this article to be irrevocable is not determined by the death (*t*), lunacy, unsoundness of mind, or bankruptcy (*u*) of the principal, and cannot be revoked by him without the consent of the agent.

Illustrations.

Authority coupled with an interest.

1. A., being indebted to B., gives him a power of attorney to sell certain land and discharge his debt out of the purchase-money. The power is irrevocable (*v*).

2. Goods are consigned to a factor for sale, with a certain limit as to price. The factor makes advances to the principal, in consideration of his giving him authority to sell at the market price and retain the advances. The authority is irrevocable (*w*).

(*s*) Illustration 9.

(*t*) See, however, *Watson* v. *King*, 1815, 1 Stark. 121; 4 Camp. 272, where it was held that a power of attorney, though coupled with an interest, was revoked by the death of the donor.

(*u*) Illustrations 8 and 9; *Raleigh* v. *Atkinson*, 1840, 6 M. & W. 676; *Yates* v. *Hoppe*, 1850, 9 C. B. 541; 19 L. J. C. P. 180; 14 Jur. 372; *Crowfoot* v. *Gurney*, 1832, 9 Bing. 372, 2 M. & Scott, 473.

(*v*) *Gaussen* v. *Morton*, 1830, 10 B. & C. 731.

(*w*) *Raleigh* v. *Atkinson*, 1840, 6 M. & W. 676.

3. Goods are consigned to a factor for sale, and he makes advances to the principal on the credit thereof. Subsequently, the principal gives him authority to sell at the market price and retain the advances out of the proceeds. The authority is revocable, not being given for valuable consideration (*x*).

4. Goods are consigned to a factor for sale. He makes advances, in consideration of an agreement by the principal that his authority to sell shall be irrevocable. The authority is irrevocable (*y*). It is a question for the jury whether such an agreement was made, and it may be inferred by them from the circumstances (*z*). In the absence of such an agreement for valuable consideration, the authority of a factor to sell does not become irrevocable by the failure of the principal to duly repay advances made on the security of the goods (*y*).

5. An auctioneer was authorized to sell goods, and after he had incurred expenses in respect thereof, the principal revoked his authority. Held, that the authority of the auctioneer was not irrevocable by reason of his special property in the goods and his lien thereon for advances, and that he was liable to the principal in trespass for going to the premises to sell the goods after notice of the revocation (*a*).

6. The drawer of an accommodation bill, shortly before the bill was due, gave the acceptor money to pay it, and became bankrupt before the maturity of the bill. Held, that the authority to pay the bill, being given in performance of an implied contract of indemnity, was irrevocable, and that the acceptor was not liable to refund the amount to the trustee in bankruptcy of the drawer (*b*).

7. *Liability incurred by agent in pursuance of authority.*—A.

(*x*) *Raleigh* v. *Atkinson*, 1840, 6 M. & W. 676.

(*y*) *Smart* v. *Sandars*, 1848, 5 C. B. 895; 17 L. J. C. P. 258; 12 Jur. 751; *De Comas* v. *Prost*, 1865, 3 Moo. P. C. C. (N. S.) 158; 11 Jur. N. S. 417; 12 L. T. 682; 13 W. R. 595, P. C.

(*z*) *De Comas* v. *Prost*, *ante*, note (*y*).

(*a*) *Taplin* v. *Florence*, 1851, 10 C. B. 744.

(*b*) *Yates* v. *Hoppe*, 1850, 9 C. B. 541; 19 L. J. C. P. 180; 14 Jur. 372.

employs B. to make a bet on his behalf, and authorizes him to pay the bet if he loses it, out of moneys in his hands belonging to A. The authority becomes irrevocable as soon as the bet is made, provided that B. would incur loss in his business or suffer actual damage in the event of the bet not being paid (*c*).

8. An agent is authorized to pay to B. the proceeds of a sale of certain goods. The agent assents and promises B. that he will pay him. The authority is irrevocable, and is not revoked by the principal's bankruptcy (*d*).

9. *Authority to sue cannot be revoked to prejudice of agent's lien.*—A factor sells goods on behalf of a principal, who afterwards becomes bankrupt. At the time of the bankruptcy, the principal is indebted to the factor in respect of advances. The factor may, as against the principal's trustee in bankruptcy, compel the purchaser to pay the price to him, and may set off the amount of the advances; and his authority to give the purchaser a discharge for the price cannot be revoked by the principal, or by his trustee in bankruptcy (*e*).

Article 130.

POWERS OF ATTORNEY IRREVOCABLE IN FAVOUR OF PURCHASERS FOR VALUE (*f*).

Where a power of attorney, created by an instrument executed after December 31st, 1882, and given for valuable consideration, is, in the instrument creating

(*c*) Submitted, on the authority of *Read* v. *Anderson*, 1884, 13 Q. B. D. 779; 53 L. J. Q. B. 532, 51 L. T. 55, 49 J. P. 4, 32 W. R. 950, C. A. The principle of this decision would seem to still hold good, though the effect of its application is altered by the Gaming Act, 1892 (55 Vict. c. 9). See Article 69.

(*d*) *Crowfoot* v. *Gurney*, 1832, 9 Bing. 372, 2 M. & Scott, 473, *Walker* v. *Rostron*, 1842, 9 M. & W. 411.

(*e*) *Drinkwater* v. *Goodwin*, 1775, Cowp. 251, *Robson* v. *Kemp*, 1802, 4 Esp. 233. See also *Hudson* v. *Granger*, 1821, 5 B. & A. 27.

(*f*) 45 & 46 Vict. c. 39 (Conveyancing Act, 1882), ss. 8 and 9.

it, expressed to be irrevocable, or, whether given for valuable consideration or not, is, in the instrument creating it, expressed to be irrevocable for a fixed time therein specified, not exceeding one year from the date of the instrument, then, in favour of a purchaser for valuable consideration—

(a) the power is not revoked at any time, or during the time fixed (as the case may be), either by anything done by the donor of the power without the concurrence of the donee, or by the death, lunacy, unsoundness of mind, or bankruptcy of the donor;

(b) any act done by the donee, in pursuance of the power, at any time, or during the time fixed (as the case may be), is as valid as if anything done by the donor without his concurrence, or the death, lunacy, unsoundness of mind, or bankruptcy of the donor, had not been done or happened;

(c) neither the donee, nor the purchaser, is at any time prejudicially affected by notice of anything done by the donor without the concurrence of the donee, or of the death, lunacy, unsoundness of mind, or bankruptcy of the donor, at any time, or during the time fixed (as the case may be) (*g*).

(*g*) 45 & 46 Vict. c. 39 (Conveyancing Act, 1882), ss. 8 and 9.

Article 131.

REVOCATION OF AUTHORITY BY DEATH OR INSANITY.

Except as provided in Articles 129 and 130, the authority of every agent, whether conferred by deed or not, is determined by the death (*h*), lunacy, or unsoundness of mind (*i*) of either the principal or the agent.

Illustrations.

1. A. undertakes to pay B. 100*l*. if B. succeeds in selling a picture at a certain price—"no sale, no pay." B. endeavours to sell the picture, and after A.'s death succeeds in doing so. The representatives of A.'s estate are not bound by the contract of sale (*k*), but they may ratify it if they think fit (*l*). Even if the representatives ratify the sale, they are not liable to pay B. the 100*l*. unless they ratify his contract with A., but they are liable to pay him a reasonable sum for the services performed (*m*).

2. A. is appointed agent to a firm, for a fixed period. The agency is determined by the death of any one of the partners before the expiration of that period (*n*).

(*h*) Illustrations 1 and 2, *Shipman* v. *Thompson*, 1738, Willes, 104, n.; *Farrow* v. *Wilson*, 1869, L. R. 4 C. P. 744, 38 L. J. C. P. 326, *Whitehead* v. *Lord*, 1852, 7 Ex. 691, 21 L. J. Ex. 239.

(*i*) See *Drew* v. *Nunn*, 1879, 4 Q. B. D. 661; 48 L. J. Q. B. 591; 40 L. T. 671; 27 W. R. 810, C. A. As to third persons dealing with the agent, without notice of the insanity, see Article 134, Illustration 2.

(*k*) *Blades* v. *Free*, 1829, 9 B. & C. 167, 4 M. & R. 282.

(*l*) *Foster* v. *Bate*, 1844, 12 M. & W. 226, 1 D. & L. 400, 13 L. J. Ex. 88, 7 Jur. 1093.

(*m*) *Campanari* v. *Woodburn*, 1854, 15 C. B. 400; 3 C. L. R. 140; 24 L. J. C. P. 13; 1 Jur. N. S. 17.

(*n*) *Tasker* v. *Shepherd*, 1861, 6 H. & N. 575, 30 L. J. Ex. 207, 4 L. T. 19; 9 W. R. 476.

Article 132.

REVOCATION OF AUTHORITY BY BANKRUPTCY OF PRINCIPAL.

Except as provided in Articles 129 and 130, the authority of every agent, whether conferred by deed or not (*o*), other than an authority to do a merely formal act in completion of a transaction already binding on the principal (*p*), is revoked by the first act of bankruptcy committed by the principal within the three months next preceding the date of the presentation of a bankruptcy petition upon which the principal is afterwards adjudicated bankrupt (*q*). Provided always, that—

(a) where the authority is given in the course, and for the protection, of mutual dealings between the principal and the agent (*r*), it is not revoked by the bankruptcy of the principal, until either the agent has notice of an available (*s*) act of bankruptcy, or the receiving order is made (*r*);

(b) every payment or act (*t*) made to or by, or done

(*o*) *Markwick* v. *Hardingham*, 1880, 15 Ch. Div. 339; 43 L. T. 647; 29 W. R. 361, C. A.; *Ex p. Snowball, re Douglas*, 1872, L. R. 7 Ch. 534; 41 L. J. Bky. 49; 26 L. T. 894; 20 W. R. 786, Ch. App.

(*p*) Illustration 2.

(*q*) 46 & 47 Vict. c. 52 (Bankruptcy Act, 1883), s. 43. See Illustration 1.

(*r*) Illustration 3.

(*s*) *I. e.*, an act of bankruptcy, committed within the three months next preceding the presentation of the petition whereon the receiving order is made. 46 & 47 Vict. c. 53, ss. 6 and 168.

(*t*) "Payment or delivery to, or payment, conveyance, assignment, contract, dealing, or transaction by or with the agent."

by the agent before the date of the receiving order, is as valid, with respect to persons dealing with him for valuable consideration without notice of any available (*u*) act of bankruptcy by the principal, as if the agent's authority had not been revoked by the bankruptcy of the principal (*v*).

Illustrations.

1. An agent, acting under a general authority, sold and delivered goods belonging to his principal, after the principal had committed an act of bankruptcy. Held, that the agent was liable in trover, for the value of the goods, to the assignees in bankruptcy, though he had not at the time of the sale had notice of the act of bankruptcy (*x*).

2. *Merely formal act.*—An agent was by power of attorney given authority to execute an indorsement of sale on the register of a ship when she returned home. Held, that the power was not revoked by the bankruptcy of the donor, the act being merely a formal one, which the principal, though a bankrupt, might have been compelled to do (*y*).

3. *Authority given in protection of mutual dealings.*—An agent is authorized to receive the purchase-money of an estate and place it to the credit of the principal in an account of mutual dealings between the principal and agent. The agent receives the money after an act of bankruptcy by the principal, but before the date of the receiving order, without notice of the act of bankruptcy. The money becomes an item in the account

---

(*u*) See note (*s*), *ante*, p. 327.

(*v*) 46 & 47 Vict. c. 52, s. 49.

(*x*) *Pearson* v. *Graham*, 1837, 6 A. & E. 899; 2 Nev. & P. 636. See also *McEntire* v. *Potter*, 1889, 22 Q. B. D. 440, *Kynaston* v. *Crouch*, 1845, 14 M. & W. 266, 14 L. J. Ex. 324, 9 Jur. 584.

(*y*) *Dixon* v. *Ewart*, 1817, Buck. 94, 3 Mer. 327.

between the principal and agent, and may be set off by the agent as against the trustee in bankruptcy (z).

Acts done before date of receiving order.

4. After an act of bankruptcy, but before the date of the receiving order, property of the bankrupt is conveyed to a purchaser for valuable consideration, in pursuance of a power of attorney given by the bankrupt, the purchaser acting in good faith, without notice of the act of bankruptcy. The purchaser has a good title as against the trustee in bankruptcy (*a*).

5. An agent, on behalf of his principal, enters into a contract after an act of bankruptcy by the principal, but before the date of the receiving order, the other contracting party having had no notice of any act of bankruptcy by the principal. The contract is as valid against the trustee in bankruptcy as it would have been against the principal if he had not become bankrupt (*b*).

Article 133.

DETERMINATION OF AUTHORITY BY NOTICE OF REVOCATION OR RENUNCIATION.

Except as provided in Articles 129 and 130, the authority of an agent, whether conferred by deed or not (*c*), is determined by the principal giving the

---

(*z*) *Elliott* v. *Turquand*, 1881, 7 App. Cas. 79; 51 L. J. P. C. 1; 45 L. T. 771; 30 W. R. 477, P. C., as qualified by 46 & 47 Vict. c. 52, s. 38. See also *Palmer* v. *Day*, 1895, 11 T. L. R. 565.

(*a*) *Ex p. Snowball, re Douglas*, 1872, L. R. 7 Ch. 534; 41 L. J. Bky. 49, 26 L. T. N. S. 894; 20 W. R. 786, Ch. App., as qualified by 46 & 47 Vict. c. 52, s. 49.

(*b*) *Ex p. MacDonnell*, 1819, Buck. 399, as qualified by 46 & 47 Vict. c. 52, s. 49.

(*c*) Illustration 1; *Bromley* v. *Holland*, 1802, 7 Ves. 28.

agent notice of revocation at any time before the authority has been completely exercised (*d*), or by the agent giving the principal notice of renunciation; but without prejudice to any claim for damages that the principal or agent may have against the other for breach of the contract of employment (*e*).

Where an authority is given by two or more principals jointly, it is determined by notice of revocation being given to the agent by any one of the principals (*f*).

Illustrations.

1. An indenture of lease provided that an agent therein named should have authority to receive the rent on behalf of the lessor, and that his receipt should be a sufficient discharge, during the term thereby granted. Held, that the lessor might revoke the authority during the term, the agent having no interest in the rent (*g*). An authority, though given by deed, may be revoked by a verbal notice of revocation (*h*).

2. An auctioneer is authorized to sell certain goods by auction. His authority may be revoked by the principal at any time before the goods are knocked down to a purchaser (*i*). So, where a broker is authorized to buy or sell goods, the authority may be revoked at any time before the contract of purchase or sale is completed, and where writing is necessary, even after he has verbally contracted to buy or sell the goods (*k*). So, where a

(*d*) Illustrations 2 to 6; *Freeman* v. *Fairlie*, 1838, 8 L. J. (N. S.) Ch. 44; *Bromley* v. *Holland*, 1802, 7 Ves. 28.

(*e*) See Articles 41, 54, and 64.

(*f*) *Bristow* v. *Taylor*, 1817, 2 Stark. 50, 19 R. R. 675.

(*g*) *Venning* v. *Bray*, 1862, 2 B. & S. 502, 31 L. J. Q. B. 181; 8 Jur. N. S. 1039; 6 L. T. 327.

(*h*) *The Margaret Mitchell*, 1858, Swabey, 382.

(*i*) *Warlow* v. *Harrison*, 1859, 1 El. & El. 309; 29 L. J. Q. B. 14; 6 Jur. N. S. 66, Ex. Ch.; *Manser* v. *Back*, 1848, 6 Hare, 443.

(*k*) *Farmer* v. *Robinson*, 1805, 2 Camp. 338, n.

broker is authorized to effect an insurance policy, the authority may be revoked even after he has signed the slip (*l*).

3. An agent undertakes to endeavour to sell a picture, it being agreed that he shall receive remuneration only in the event of a sale. His authority may be revoked after endeavours by him to sell the picture (*m*).

4. Money is deposited with A., to be applied for the use of the poor. The authority may be countermanded at any time before the application of the money, and the money be recovered by the principal from A. (*n*).

5. Money is deposited with a stakeholder, to be paid to the winner of a wager. The authority of the stakeholder may be revoked at any time before he has actually paid over the money to the winner, and if he pays it over after notice of revocation, he is personally liable to the depositor for the amount (*o*). So, where authority is given to pay money in respect of an illegal transaction, the authority may be revoked at any time before the money has been paid over, even if it has been credited in account (*p*).

6. A. authorizes his banker to hold 20*l*. at the disposal of B. The authority of the banker may be countermanded, provided that he has not paid the money to B., nor contracted with him to hold it on his behalf (*q*).

(*l*) *Warwick* v. *Slade*, 1811, 3 Camp. 127; 13 R. R. 772.

(*m*) *Campanari* v. *Woodburn*, 1854, 15 C. B. 400; 3 C. L. R. 140; 24 L. J. C. P. 13; 1 Jur. N. S. 17.

(*n*) *Taylor* v. *Lendey*, 1807, 9 East, 49.

(*o*) *Hampden* v. *Walsh*, 1876, 1 Q. B. D. 189; 45 L. J. Q. B. 238; 33 L. T. 852; 24 W. R. 607; *Diggle* v. *Higgs*, 1877, 2 Ex. Div. 422; 46 L. J. Ex. 721; 37 L. T. 27, C. A.; *Trimble* v. *Hill*, 1879, 5 App. Cas. 342; 49 L. J. P. C. 49; 42 L. T. 103; 28 W. R. 479, P. C.; *Gatty* v. *Field*, 1846, 9 Q. B. 431, 25 L. J. Q. B. 408; 10 Jur. 980. These cases are not affected by the Gaming Act, 1892. See *O'Sullivan* v. *Thomas*, (1895) 1 Q. B. 698; 64 L. J. Q. B. 398, 72 L. T. 285; 43 W. R. 269; 11 T. L. R. 225.

(*p*) *Edgar* v. *Fowler*, 1803, 3 East, 222; 7 R. R. 433.

(*q*) *Gibson* v. *Minet*, 1824, 9 Moore, 31; 2 Bing. 7; 1 C. & P. 247; R. & M. 68.

Article 134.

WHEN NOTICE OF REVOCATION TO THIRD PERSONS NECESSARY.

Where a principal, by words or conduct, represents that an agent is authorized to act on his behalf, he is bound by the acts of the agent, notwithstanding the revocation of the authority otherwise than by the death (*r*) or bankruptcy (*s*) of the principal, to the same extent as if the authority had not been revoked, with respect to third persons dealing with the agent on the faith of any such representation, without notice of the revocation of his authority (*t*).

Illustrations.

1. A. authorizes B. to purchase goods on his credit, and holds him out to C. as his agent for that purpose. C. supplies goods to B., on A.'s credit, after revocation by A. of B.'s authority to act on his behalf, C. having had no notice of such revocation. A. is liable to C. for the price of the goods, even if B. was contracting on his own behalf, and did not intend to bind A. (*u*). Where a person holds out another as his agent, the person to whom that other is so held out is justified in dealing with him

---

(*r*) See Illustration 3.

(*s*) See Article 132, as to revocation by bankruptcy.

(*t*) Illustrations 1 and 2, *Pole* v. *Leask*, 1862, 33 L. J. Ch. 155; 9 Jur. N. S. 829, 8 L. T. 645, H. L., *Scarf* v. *Jardine*, 1882, 7 App. Cas. at p. 349, H. L., *Nickson* v. *Brohan*, 1718, 10 Mod. 110, *Curlewis* v. *Birkbeck*, 1863, 3 F. & F. 894, —— v. *Harrison*, 12 Mod. 346, *Ryan* v. *Sams*, 1848, 12 Q. B. 460, 17 L. J. Q. B. 271, 12 Jur. 745.

(*u*) *Trueman* v. *Loder*, 1840, 11 A. & E. 589, 3 P. & D. 267.

as such, until he receives notice that the authority has been revoked (*x*).

2. A husband holds out his wife as having authority to pledge his credit, and subsequently becomes insane. A tradesman, on the faith of such holding out, supplies goods to the orders of the wife, without notice of the husband's insanity. The husband is liable for the price of the goods (*y*).

3. A widow ordered necessaries from a tradesman to whom she had been held out by her deceased husband as having authority to pledge his credit, the tradesman having had no notice of his death. Held, that the estate of the husband was not liable for the price of the goods (*z*).

Article 135.

PROTECTION OF AGENT ACTING UNDER POWER OF ATTORNEY WITHOUT NOTICE OF REVOCATION.

Where a person makes or does any payment or act in good faith, in pursuance of a power of attorney, he is not liable in respect of the payment or act by reason that before the payment or act the donor of the power had died or become lunatic, of unsound mind, or bankrupt, or had revoked the power, if the fact of death, lunacy, unsoundness of mind, bankruptcy, or revocation was not at the time of the payment or act known to the person making or doing the same. But

---

(*x*) *Staveley* v. *Uzielli*, 1860, 2 F. & F. 30; *Ex p. Bright*, 1832, 2 Dea. & Ch. 8; *Aste* v. *Montague*, 1858, 1 F. & F. 264; *Dodsley* v. *Varley*, 1840, 4 P. & D. 448, 12 A. & E. 632, 5 Jur. 316.

(*y*) *Drew* v. *Nunn*, 1879, 4 Q. B. D. 661; 48 L. J. Q. B. 591; 40 L. T. 671; 27 W. R. 810, C. A.

(*z*) *Blades* v. *Free*, 1829, 9 B. & C. 167, 4 M. & R. 282.

this does not affect any right against the payee, of any person interested in any money so paid; and that person has the like remedy against the payee as he would have had against the payer if the payment had not been made by him (*a*).

(*a*) 44 & 45 Vict. c. 41 (Conveyancing Act, 1881), s. 47.

APPENDIX.

FACTORS ACT, 1889.

(52 & 53 Vict. c. 45.)

ARRANGEMENT OF SECTIONS.

Preliminary.

Section.

1. Definitions.

Dispositions by Mercantile Agents.

2. Powers of mercantile agent with respect to disposition of goods.
3. Effect of pledges of documents of title.
4. Pledge for antecedent debt.
5. Rights acquired by exchange of goods or documents.
6. Agreements through clerks, &c.
7. Provisions as to consignors and consignees.

Dispositions by Sellers and Buyers of Goods.

8. Disposition by seller remaining in possession.
9. Disposition by buyer obtaining possession.
10. Effect of transfer of documents on vendor's lien or right of stoppage in transitu.

Supplemental.

11. Mode of transferring documents.
12. Saving for rights of true owner.
13. Saving for common law powers of agent.
14. Repeal.
15. Commencement.
16. Extent of Act.
17. Short title.

Schedule.

FACTORS ACT, 1889.

52 & 53 Vict. c. 45.

An Act to amend and consolidate the Factors Acts.

[26th August 1889.]

Be it enacted by the Queen's most Excellent Majesty, by and with the advice and consent of the Lords Spiritual and Temporal and Commons, in this present Parliament assembled, and by the authority of the same, as follows.

Preliminary.

Definitions.

1. For the purposes of this Act—

(1.) The expression "mercantile agent" shall mean a mercantile agent having in the customary course of his business as such agent authority either to sell goods, or to consign goods for the purpose of sale, or to buy goods, or to raise money on the security of goods

(2.) A person shall be deemed to be in possession of goods or of the documents of title to goods, where the goods or documents are in his actual custody or are held by any other person subject to his control or for him or on his behalf·

(3.) The expression "goods" shall include wares and merchandise

(4.) The expression "document of title" shall include any bill of lading, dock warrant, warehouse-keeper's certificate, and warrant or order for the delivery of goods, and any other document used in the ordinary course of business as proof of the possession or control of goods, or authorising or purporting to authorise, either by endorsement or by delivery, the possessor of the document to transfer or receive goods thereby represented.

(5.) The expression "pledge" shall include any contract pledging, or giving a lien or security on, goods, whether in consideration of an original advance or of any further or continuing advance or of any pecuniary liability

(6.) The expression "person" shall include any body of persons corporate or unincorporate.

Dispositions by Mercantile Agents.

Powers of mercantile agent with

2.—(1.) Where a mercantile agent is, with the consent of the owner, in possession of goods or of the documents of title to goods, any sale, pledge, or other disposition of the goods, made by him when acting in the ordinary course of business of a mercantile agent, shall, subject to the provisions of this Act, be as valid as if he were expressly authorised by the owner of the goods to make the same; provided that the person taking under the disposition acts in good faith, and has not at the time of the disposition notice that the person making the disposition has not authority to make the same.

respect to disposition of goods.

(2.) Where a mercantile agent has, with the consent of the owner, been in possession of goods or of the documents of title to goods, any sale, pledge, or other disposition, which would have been valid if the consent had continued, shall be valid notwithstanding the determination of the consent: provided that the person taking under the disposition has not at the time thereof notice that the consent has been determined.

(3.) Where a mercantile agent has obtained possession of any documents of title to goods by reason of his being or having been, with the consent of the owner, in possession of the goods represented thereby, or of any other documents of title to the goods, his possession of the first-mentioned documents shall, for the purposes of this Act, be deemed to be with the consent of the owner.

(4.) For the purposes of this Act the consent of the owner shall be presumed in the absence of evidence to the contrary.

Effect of pledges of documents of title.

3. A pledge of the documents of title to goods shall be deemed to be a pledge of the goods.

Pledge for antecedent debt.

4. Where a mercantile agent pledges goods as security for a debt or liability due from the pledgor to the pledgee before the time of the pledge, the pledgee shall acquire no further right to the goods than could have been enforced by the pledgor at the time of the pledge.

Rights acquired by exchange of goods or documents.

5. The consideration necessary for the validity of a sale, pledge, or other disposition, of goods, in pursuance of this Act, may be either a payment in cash, or the delivery or transfer of other goods, or of a document of title to goods, or of a negotiable security, or any other valuable consideration; but where goods are pledged by a mercantile agent in consideration of the delivery or transfer of other goods, or of a document of title to goods, or of a negotiable security, the pledgee shall acquire no right or interest in the goods so pledged in excess of the value of the goods, documents, or security when so delivered or transferred in exchange.

Agreements through clerks, &c.

6. For the purposes of this Act an agreement made with a mercantile agent through a clerk or other person authorised in the ordinary course of business to make contracts of sale or pledge on his behalf shall be deemed to be an agreement with the agent.

Provisions as to consignors and consignees.

7.—(1.) Where the owner of goods has given possession of the goods to another person for the purpose of consignment or sale, or has shipped the goods in the name of another person, and the consignee of the goods has not had notice that such person is not the owner of the goods, the consignee shall, in respect of advances made to or for the use of such person, have the same lien on the goods as if such person were the owner of the goods, and may transfer any such lien to another person.

(2.) Nothing in this section shall limit or affect the validity of any sale, pledge, or disposition, by a mercantile agent.

Dispositions by Sellers and Buyers of Goods.

Disposition by seller remaining in possession.

8. Where a person, having sold goods, continues, or is, in possession of the goods or of the documents of title to the goods, the delivery or transfer by that person, or by a mercantile agent acting for him, of the goods or documents of title under any sale, pledge, or other disposition thereof, or under any agreement for sale, pledge, or other disposition thereof, to any person receiving the same in good faith and without notice of the previous sale, shall have the same effect as if the person making the delivery or transfer were expressly authorised by the owner of the goods to make the same.

Disposition by buyer obtaining possession.

9. Where a person, having bought or agreed to buy goods (a), obtains with the consent of the seller possession of the goods or the documents of title to the goods, the delivery or transfer, by that person or by a mercantile agent acting for him, of the goods or documents of title, under any sale, pledge, or other disposition thereof, or under any agreement for sale, pledge, or other disposition thereof, to any person receiving the same in good faith and without notice of any lien or other right of the original seller in respect of the goods, shall have the same effect as if the person making the delivery or transfer were a mercantile agent in possession of the goods or documents of title with the consent of the owner.

Effect of transfer of documents on vendor's lien or right of stoppage in transitu.

10. Where a document of title to goods has been lawfully transferred to a person as a buyer or owner of the goods, and that person transfers the document to a person who takes the document in good faith and for valuable consideration, the last-mentioned transfer shall have the same effect for defeating any vendor's lien or right of stoppage in transitu as the transfer of a bill of lading has for defeating the right of stoppage in transitu.

(a) See *Helby* v. *Matthews*, (1895) A. C. 471, 64 L. J. Q. B. 465, 72 L. T. 841, 43 W. R. 561, 11 T. L. R. 446, H. L.

Supplemental.

11. For the purposes of this Act, the transfer of a document may be by endorsement, or, where the document is by custom or by its express terms transferable by delivery, or makes the goods deliverable to the bearer, then by delivery. Mode of transferring documents.

12.—(1.) Nothing in this Act shall authorise an agent to exceed or depart from his authority as between himself and his principal, or exempt him from any liability, civil or criminal, for so doing. Saving for rights of true owner.

(2.) Nothing in this Act shall prevent the owner of goods from recovering the goods from an agent or his trustee in bankruptcy at any time before the sale or pledge thereof, or shall prevent the owner of goods pledged by an agent from having the right to redeem the goods at any time before the sale thereof, on satisfying the claim for which the goods were pledged, and paying to the agent, if by him required, any money in respect of which the agent would by law be entitled to retain the goods or the documents of title thereto, or any of them, by way of lien as against the owner, or from recovering from any person with whom the goods have been pledged any balance of money remaining in his hands as the produce of the sale of the goods after deducting the amount of his lien.

(3.) Nothing in this Act shall prevent the owner of goods sold by an agent from recovering from the buyer the price agreed to be paid for the same, or any part of that price, subject to any right of set off on the part of the buyer against the agent.

13. The provisions of this Act shall be construed in amplification and not in derogation of the powers exerciseable by an agent independently of this Act. Saving for common law powers of agent.

14. The enactments mentioned in the schedule to this Act are hereby repealed as from the commencement of this Act, but this repeal shall not affect any right acquired or liability incurred before the commencement of this Act under any enactment hereby repealed. Repeal.

15. This Act shall commence and come into operation on the first day of January one thousand eight hundred and ninety. Commencement.

16. This Act shall not extend to Scotland. Extent of Act.

17. This Act may be cited as the Factors Act, 1889. Short title.

[SCHEDULE.

SCHEDULE.

Section 14.

ENACTMENTS REPEALED.

Session and Chapter.	Title.	Extent of Repeal.
4 Geo. 4, c. 83.	An Act for the better protection of the property of merchants and others who may hereafter enter into contracts or agreements in relation to goods, wares, or merchandises entrusted to factors or agents.	The whole Act.
6 Geo. 4, c. 94.	An Act to alter and amend an Act for the better protection of the property of merchants and others who may hereafter enter into contracts or agreements in relation to goods, wares, or merchandise entrusted to factors or agents.	The whole Act.
5 & 6 Vict. c. 39.	An Act to amend the law relating to advances bonâ fide made to agents entrusted with goods.	The whole Act.
40 & 41 Vict. c. 39.	An Act to amend the Factors Acts	The whole Act.

INDEX.

ACCEPTANCE,
of offer may be ratified after notice of withdrawal, 39, 41.
of bill of exchange: *see* BILL OF EXCHANGE.

ACCOUNT,
when agent liable to, in equity, 111—114.
where agency of fiduciary character, 112, 113.
where accounts are complicated or intricate, 112, 113.
illegality of transaction not necessarily a bar to an action for, 112.
when principal liable to, in equity, 203.
every agent must, to his own principal, 85, 96—99, 101, 102: *but see* INTERPLEAD.
solicitor's town agent not liable to, to client, 86, 87.
sub-agent *primâ facie* not liable to, to principal, 83—86.
agent must, for all secret profits and benefits, 84, 103, 105, 114—120: *and see* SECRET PROFITS.
for money received under void or illegal contract, 96, 98.
for bribes, 139, 140.
duty of directors to, for secret profits, 105, 117—119: *and see* DIRECTORS.
agent, when bound to, to third persons, 301—303.
right of stockbroker to close, 70, 175.
payment by agent of principal's money into his own, 93, 130, 146, 190, 213.
how far Statute of Limitations a defence to an action for, 114.
damages for breach of duty cannot be passed in taking, 113.

ACCOUNTS,
duty of agent to preserve and be ready with, 92, 111.
effect of agent failing to keep, 92, 167.
though settled, may be reopened in cases of fraud, 112, 113.

ACKNOWLEDGMENT OF DEBT,
by agent, when principal bound by, 262, 263.
by wife, when husband bound by, 26, 263.
if signed by agent, interrupts Statute of Limitations, 26, 262, 263.

ACT OF BANKRUPTCY: *see* BANKRUPTCY.

ACT OF STATE: *see* PUBLIC AGENT.

ACTS, how far principal bound by agent's, 205 *et seq*: *see* PRINCIPAL.

ADMISSIBILITY: *see* EVIDENCE.

ADMISSIONS,
by agent, when evidence against the principal, 260—263.
when made in ordinary course of employment, 260, 262.
when expressly referred to for information, 261, 263.
not when made outside course of employment, 261—263.
not when they concern bygone transactions, 262.
reports by agent to principal cannot be used as, by third persons, 261, 263.
by directors to shareholders are not evidence against the company as, 263.
by solicitor, when evidence against client, 263.
of either principal or agent may be used where agent sues in own name, 310.

ADULTERY, effect of, on implied authority of wife, 24, 25.

ADVANCES,
lien of agent for *see* LIEN.
to apparent owner of goods, 217.
failure to repay, does not render authority irrevocable, 322, 323.

ADVERSE CLAIMS,
when agent may set up, against principal, 99—102.
right of agent to interplead in case of, 201—203 *see* INTERPLEAD.

ADVERSE POSSESSION *see* TITLE, PRESCRIPTION.

AGENCY,
cannot impose obligation to commit a wrong, 7, 8.
how it arises, 10.
may be express or implied, 10 *et seq.*
requires assent of principal and agent, 10.
by estoppel *see* ESTOPPEL, HOLDING OUT.
by ratification, 34—49 *see* RATIFICATION.
contract of, is of a fiduciary character, 102 *et seq.* *see* DUTIES OF AGENT.
determination of *see* DETERMINATION, REVOCATION.

AGENT *and see* COMMISSION AGENT; ESTATE AGENT, HOUSE AGENT, PUBLIC AGENT, PATENT AGENT; BROKER, FACTOR, AUCTIONEER, MERCANTILE AGENT, STOCKBROKER, INSURANCE AGENT, INSURANCE BROKER.
acts of, are deemed to be acts of the principal, 6, 100.
acts of, how far binding on principal, 205 *et seq.* *see* PRINCIPAL.
appointment of, 29—33 *see* APPOINTMENT OF AGENTS.
for what purposes, 7.
attachment of, 142.
acknowledgment of debt by, 26 · *see* ACKNOWLEDGMENT OF DEBT.
authority of, 50 *et seq.* *see* AUTHORITY; IMPLIED AUTHORITY.
admissions by, 260—263 · *see* ADMISSIONS.
bankruptcy of: *see* BANKRUPTCY.
bribery of *see* BRIBERY.
breach of duty by · *see* BREACH OF DUTY.
capacity to act as, 5, 6.
contracts made by, no implied authority to cancel, 65, 70.
criminal liability of, for fraudulent breach of duty, 143 note (*h*).
contracts made by, liability of principal on *see* PRINCIPAL.
conversion by, 314 *et seq.*. *see* CONVERSION.

AGENT—*continued.*
definition of an, 1, 3.
definitions of, and distinctions between, general and special, 1.
del credere see DEL CREDERE AGENT.
delegation of authority by, 80—83 *see* DELEGATION.
duties of, 88 *et seq.* *see* DUTIES OF AGENT.
estoppel of *see* ESTOPPEL.
general, distinction between special and, 1.
gratuitous. *see* GRATUITOUS UNDERTAKING.
holding out person as *see* HOLDING OUT.
interpleader by, 201—203 *see* INTERPLEAD.
jus tertii, when he may set up, against principal, 96—102 *see* ESTOPPEL.

liability of, to principal, 126 *et seq.*
to account in equity, 111—114 *see* ACCOUNT.
to account for all secret profits and benefits: *see* SECRET PROFITS.
in case of bribery *see* BRIBERY.
for negligence and breach of duty: *see* NEGLIGENCE; BREACH OF DUTY.
to pay interest, 105, 141, 142 *see* INTEREST.
criminal, for fraudulent breach of duty, 143 note (*h*).
for breach of duty, and money received, by sub-agent, 143, 144.
for failure of banker, 93, 130.
for want of skill. *see* NEGLIGENCE.
for disobeying instructions, 130, 131, 139.
for taking cheque or bill of exchange in lieu of cash without authority, 131.
for exceeding authority, effect of ratification on, 48.
for exceeding authority, not affected by Factors Act, 216.
for breach of contract of agency depends on capacity of agent, 5.
in respect of contracts made on principal's behalf, 126, 127.
when he acts under *del credere* commission, 126.
on bills of exchange signed without qualification, 127, 128.

liability of, to third persons,
(1) *in respect of contracts made by him,* 270 *et seq.*
public agents not liable on contracts made as such, 270, 271 *see* PUBLIC AGENT.
liable where he contracts personally, whether principal disclosed or not, 272—275.
not liable on contracts made merely in his capacity as agent, even if guilty of fraud, 272, 274, 276.
depends on intention as appearing from nature and terms of the contract and the surrounding circumstances, 272—276.
primâ facie liable if principal a foreigner, 273.
but this is a rebuttable presumption, 282, 284.
on deeds when executed in own name, 277.
on bills of exchange, promissory notes, and cheques, 128, 278—281 *see* BILL OF EXCHANGE, NEGOTIABLE INSTRUMENTS; NOTES.
on contracts in writing depends on intention as appearing from the terms of the contract, 281—285.
construction is a matter of law for the Court, 281.
if signed in own name without qualification, *primâ facie* liable, 281, 283, 284.
if signed "as agent," *primâ facie* not liable, 282, 284, 285.

AGENT—*continued.*

liability of, to third persons—*continued.*

on contracts in writing—*continued.*

may be liable though described as an agent for a named principal, 282, 283.

admissibility of parol evidence of intention, 285—287 *see* EVIDENCE.

may be liable by special custom if not inconsistent with the written contract, 286, 287.

liable on verbal contracts, unless known to be acting as an agent, 274.

intention in case of verbal contract is a question of fact, 287, 288.

liability may be conditional or limited to certain events, 276, 277.

person contracting professedly as agent is liable if shown to be the principal, 288.

personally liable if he contracts on behalf of a future company, 289.

implied warranty of authority, 289 *et seq.* *see* WARRANTY OF AUTHORITY.

(2) *in respect of moneys received by him*, 297 *et seq.* *see* MONEY.

(3) *in respect of wrongs committed on principal's behalf*, 311 *et seq.*: *see* WRONGS.

not liable for torts of co-agents or sub-agents, 318.

liabilities incurred by, right of indemnity against *see* INDEMNITY.

lien of, 180 *et seq.* · *see* LIEN.

money paid by mistake to and by *see* MONEY.

misappropriation by, liability of principal for, 250, 251 *see* WRONGS.

necessity, of, 10.

notice to, 264—267 · *see* NOTICE.

payment to *see* PAYMENT.

possession of, is deemed to be possession of principal, 99—101.

part payment by, interrupts the Statute of Limitations, 262, 263.

promise to pay by, interrupts the Statute of Limitations, 262, 263.

purchase of land by, in own name, 31, 106.

rights of, against principal, 149 *et seq.*

of remuneration, 149—168 *see* REMUNERATION.

to damages for breach of contract of agency, 159—163 *see* REMUNERATION.

of re-imbursement and indemnity, 169—179 *see* RE-IMBURSEMENT, INDEMNITY.

of lien, 180—200 · *see* LIEN.

of stoppage *in transitu*, 200.

of interpleader, 201—203 : *see* INTERPLEAD.

rights of, against third persons, 303 *et seq.*

to sue in own name for money paid by mistake, &c., 310.

to sue in own name on contracts, 303—307.

where he contracts personally, 303, 305.

where he has a special property or lien, 303, 305.

where he has a beneficial interest, 308, 309.

in the case of insurance brokers, 304.

otherwise, cannot sue in own name, even if acting under *del credere* commission, 305—307

right to sue in own name is subject to intervention of principal, except where the agent has a lien, 307

AGENT—*continued.*

rights of, against third persons—*continued.*

where agent has a lien his right to sue has priority, 239, 243, 308, 322, 324.

settlement with or set-off against principal, how far binding on agent, 307—309.

statements made by principal may be used against agent, 310.

right of person contracting as agent to sue if really principal, 304—306.

special, distinction between general and, 1.

settlement with, how far principal bound by · *see* PAYMENT.

set-off against, how far principal bound by · *see* SET-OFF.

torts committed by · *see* WRONGS.

warranty of authority by, 289 *et seq.* · *see* WARRANTY OF AUTHORITY.

wrongs by · *see* WRONGS.

AGENT FOR PURCHASE · *see* PURCHASE, AGENT FOR.

AGENT FOR SALE · *see* SALE, AGENT FOR.

AGREEMENT between principal and agent does not affect third persons unless they have notice of it, 206, 220, 221.

ALTERATION of cheque without authority, 178.

AMBIGUOUS

instructions or authority, 53, 54.

contract, parol evidence is admitted to explain, 149.

APPARENT AUTHORITY,

governs principal's liability with respect to persons having no notice of actual limits, 17, 53, 54, 205—208, 220, 250, 251.

this rule applies where principal undisclosed, 207.

of mercantile agent, 213—217, 335 *et seq.* *see* FACTORS ACT.

APPLICATION for shares, liability of agent in respect of unauthorized, 295.

APPOINTMENT OF AGENTS, 29 *et seq.*

by deed, when necessary, 29, 30.

may be verbal, though authorized to execute written contract, 30.

verbal, to purchase land, 30, 31.

by corporations, 31—33 : *see* CORPORATION.

for fixed term, 161, 162.

informal, 222.

APPROPRIATION,

of goods or chattels in possession of agent, for specific purpose, 186, 323, 324.

of money in hands of agent to use of third persons, 302, 324.

ARBITRATION,

implied authority of solicitor to refer to, 63, 73.

insurance broker to refer to, 64.

ARBITRATOR,

cannot delegate his authority, 82.

effect of appointment of agent as, 287.

not liable for negligence, as such, 95.

ARREST,
when agent has implied authority to, 61, 62, 254.
to protect principal's property, but not to punish a wrong-doer, 61, 62, 253, 254.
by manager of bank, 61.
by servants of railway and tramway companies, 62, 249, 253.
by agent, liability of principal for, 249, 253, 254.

ASSAULT,
by agent, liability of principal for, 249, 250, 252, 256.
not affected by criminal punishment of agent, 250 note (*m*).
by servant of railway or tramway company, liability of company for, 249, 250.

ASSURANCE: *see* INSURANCE.

ATTACHMENT of agent for default in payment of money, 142, 143 note (*p*).

ATTORNEY, married woman may appoint an, 5 *and see* POWER OF ATTORNEY, SOLICITOR.

AUCTION,
auctioneer and clerk are implied agents of purchaser at a sale by, 11.
purchaser at a sale by, is personally liable for deposit, though acting as an agent, 273.

AUCTIONEER,
definition of, 2.
has implied authority to sign contract for highest bidder, 11, 71.
no implied authority to sign for purchaser by private contract, 11.
signature of, binds both vendor and purchaser, 6, 71, 83.
declarations by, how far binding on principal, 211.
must not take a bill of exchange in payment without express authority, 52, 71, 131, 244.
but may take a cheque in payment of deposit, 90.
must not buy for himself, 104, 123.
but may sell his own goods without disclosing the fact, 104.
implied authority of, 71, 72.
not to sell by private contract, even if sale by auction abortive, 64, 72.
not to delegate his authority, 82, 122.
not to rescind a sale, nor to warrant goods sold, 71.
not to deal, after sale, with the terms on which a title shall be made, 72.
duties of, 122, 123.
to accept highest *bonâ fide* bid, at a sale without reserve, notwithstanding express instructions to contrary, 90, 123, 131.
to sell for ready money, 90, 122.
to see that the deposit is duly paid, 122, 132.
to hold the deposit as stakeholder until completion, 123, 299.
not to deliver goods sold, without payment, 123.
not liable to pay interest on deposit unless he wrongfully refuses to pay over, 142, 299.
liable to attachment for default in payment of proceeds, 143 note (*p*).
right of, to set up the title of third persons against principal, 102.
right of, to interplead, 202.

AUCTIONEER—*continued.*
remuneration of, contract to pay usual commission implied, 151.
commission on sale resulting indirectly from his acts, 154.
after authority withdrawn, 155.
no commission on unauthorized sale by private contract, 167.
where sale nugatory in consequence of negligence, 168.
right of, to indemnity against liabilities incurred, 170, 177: *see* INDEMNITY.
may sue in own name for price of goods sold, 305, 308, 309.
right of purchaser to set off debt due from principal, 308, 309.
how far bound by a settlement with principal, 308, 309.
personally liable if principal undisclosed, 274, 275.
for non-delivery if he has possession, 275.
if he accepts a bid from vendor at a sale without reserve, 275.
liability of, for innocent conversion, 177, 316, 317.
not liable in damages for not putting up property advertised for sale, 275.
authority of, ceases as soon as the sale is completed, 320.
may be revoked any time before the goods are knocked down, 330.
does not become irrevocable by incurring expense, 323.

AUTHORITY, 50 *et seq.*: *see also* IMPLIED AUTHORITY, DELEGATION, REVOCATION.
distinction between joint and several, 8, 9.
may be express or implied, 50: *see* IMPLIED AUTHORITY.
of necessity, 22.
how conferred, 50.
to execute a deed must be given by deed, 29: *see* APPOINTMENT OF AGENTS.
otherwise may be given verbally, 31.
to subscribe memorandum of association may be verbal, 31.
is necessarily confined to powers of principal, 50.
construction of, where given by deed, 54—56: *see* POWER OF ATTORNEY.
where given by parol, 56.
where given in ambiguous terms, 53, 54.
where given in general terms, 51, 52.
must be executed in usual way and ordinary course of business, 51.
must be strictly pursued, 88, 89, 129.
to "sell stock or shares", "to receive and pay debts", "to settle affairs," 51.
to contract gives authority to sign to satisfy the Statute of Frauds, 57.
to discount a bill gives authority to warrant, but not to indorse it, 58.
to find a purchaser, 58, 91.
to sell, when it includes authority to warrant, 58.
to sell an estate does not give authority to receive the purchase-money, 59.
to make contracts does not imply authority to cancel them, 65, 70.
to sell by auction does not authorize a sale by private contract, 64.
to receive payment, 51, 52. *see* PAYMENT.
to deal with money illegally, 97, 331.
to pay money to third persons, when revocable, 321, 323, 324, 331.
to bind principal by negotiable instruments. *see* BILL OF EXCHANGE, NEGOTIABLE INSTRUMENTS.
of directors and agents of unincorporated companies, 61.
of shipmaster depends on law of the flag, 74. *see* SHIPMASTER.

AUTHORITY—*continued.*
ostensible, governs as between principal and third persons: *see* PRINCIPAL, FACTORS ACT.
as between principal and agent is not affected by Factors Act, 216.
liability of agent to third persons for exceeding, 289 *et seq.* *see* WARRANTY OF AUTHORITY.
when irrevocable, 320—325 *see* REVOCATION.

BAILIFF,
implied authority of, 63.
liability of landlord for illegal distress by, 246.
employer not liable for unnecessary assault by, 252.
personally liable to repay money paid to him under terror of illegal distress, 300.

BANKER,
relations between customers and, 98, 113.
liability of, for negligence, 131, 133, 134.
for loss of securities deposited at bank for safe keeping, 134.
for money received by his agent, 143.
for misappropriation by manager, 250.
for discounting bills restrictively indorsed, 219.
has a general lien by custom, 181.
general lien of, does not extend to securities left for safe custody, 185, 186.
nor to chattels mortgaged to him for a specific advance, 185, 187
nor to property deposited with him for special purpose inconsistent therewith, 186, 187.
on negotiable instruments not affected by equities between the customer and third persons, 190, 213.
payment of altered cheque by, 178.
liability of agent for failure of, 93, 130.

BANKRUPTCY *see also* MUTUAL DEALINGS.
of agent,
right of principal to follow money and goods on, 104, 144—148.
this right is subject to the agent's lien, 239, 243.
and to the reputed ownership clause, 145, 147, 148.
right of principal to sue for debts due to agent on, 146, 236, 241.
to recover sums paid to the trustee in bankruptcy, 146.
to follow proceeds of money or property misapplied, 145, 147, 148.
estoppel of trustee in bankruptcy by agent's misrepresentations, 147, 148.
generally revokes his authority, 320.

of principal,
effect of, on right of agent to commission, 154.
on agent's lien, 182, 183, 189, 190.
on agent's right to sue for proceeds of goods sold, &c., 239, 243, 308.
right of agent to set off losses, &c. against the trustee in bankruptcy, 127, 171, 190.
right of stockbroker to close account on, 174.

BANKRUPTCY—*continued.*
of principal—*continued.*
liability of agent who deals with principal's money or property after, 317, 328.
revocation of agent's authority by, 327—329.
when authority not revoked by, 320—325: *see* REVOCATION.
authority to do a merely formal act, 328.
authority given in course of mutual dealings, 327, 328.
acts done before date of receiving order, 328, 329.
of sub-agent, liability of agent to principal for, 143.
principal cannot commit act of, by act of agent done without his knowledge or authority, 211.

BANKRUPTCY ACT, 1883,
reputed ownership clause of, 145, 147, 148.
mutual credits clause of: *see* MUTUAL DEALINGS.
effect of, as to revocation of agent's authority, 327, 328, 329.

BARRISTER: *see* COUNSEL.

BARTER, factor no implied authority to, 69, 121.

BENEFIT,
agent must make full disclosure when he takes any personal, 108: *see* DISCLOSURE.
received without knowledge and consent of principal, agent must account for, 114—120: *see* SECRET PROFITS.
solicitor is not permitted to acquire any, beyond his legal remuneration, 111.
remuneration may be payable though principal acquires no, 156—159, 166—168.

BETS: *see* GAMING CONTRACTS.

BILL OF EXCHANGE: *see also* NEGOTIABLE INSTRUMENTS.
payment to agent by: *see* PAYMENT.
auctioneer no implied authority to take, in lieu of cash, 52, 71, 131.
implied authority to bind principal by, 51, 55, 56, 60, 82, 206, 211.
agent employed to discount, has implied authority to warrant, 58.
accepted by agent, lien of agent for amount of, 182, 183: *see* LIEN.
appropriation of funds in hands of agent to meet, 186, 323.
signed by agent without qualification, liability of agent to principal on, 127, 128.
no one liable on, unless his name appears, 226, 278.
signatures on, are construed in manner most favourable to validity, 226, 278.
liability as acceptor depends on name of drawee, 226, 227, 278, 279.
as drawer or indorser depends on form of signature, 227, 228, 280, 281.
of principal as acceptor, 206, 226, 227.
effect of signature "per procuration," 218.
personal liability of agent to third persons on, 278—280.
as acceptor, 278, 279.
where signed as drawer or indorser without qualification, 128, 278—280.
words describing him as agent do not exempt him, 279.
where signed without authority, 292.

BILL BROKER,
implied authority to warrant bills for discounting, 57.
custom of, to give general guarantee to bank, 171.
right of, to indemnity in respect of such a guarantee, 171.
no implied authority to indorse in principal's name, 58.

BILL OF LADING,
signature of shipmaster on, how far binding on owners, 79, 80.
statements in, how far evidence against owners, 261 note (*c*).
is a document of title for the purposes of the Factors Act, 213 note (*m*).

BONDS,
given by shipmaster, validity of, depends on law of the flag, 75.
implied authority of shipmaster to give bottomry and respondentia, 77.

BONUS: *see* BRIBERY.

BORROW *see* LOAN.
directors of unincorporated companies no implied authority to, 61.
implied authority of shipmaster to, 76, 77

BORROWING POWERS, liability of directors who exceed, 291, 292, 295.

BOTTOMRY BOND,
validity of, depends on law of flag, 75.
implied authority of shipmaster to give, 77.

BOUGHT NOTE *see* BROKER, NOTES.

BREACH,
of contract of agency, liability of principal for, 159—163 *see* REMUNERATION.
voluntary winding-up may operate as a, 162, 163.
of trust, agent assisting in commission of, personally liable, 313.
of warranty of authority *see* WARRANTY OF AUTHORITY.
of contract with third persons, right to sue, and liability, of agent for · *see* AGENT.

BREACH OF DUTY *see* NEGLIGENCE.
liability of agent to principal for, 94, 128—139.
disobedience to instructions, 130, 131.
other breaches of duty, 130—132, 138.
for accepting bribe, 139, 140 *see* BRIBERY.
counsel not liable for, 128.
measure of damages for, 137—139 *see* MEASURE OF DAMAGES.
damage must be a reasonable or probable consequence, 133.
must be legal damage, 133.
nominal damages, though no actual loss, 134.
agent will not be permitted to take advantage of a, 137
effect of a, on right of agent to remuneration, 166, 167, 168.
on right to indemnity and reimbursement, 176, 179.
criminal liability of agent for fraudulent, 143 note (*p*).
liability of agent for, is not affected by the Factors Act, 216.
by sub-agent, liability of agent for, 143, 144.

BRIBERY,
of agent, rights of principal against agent and briber, 139, 140, 268.
agent liable to pay interest on amounts received by way of, 142.
Statute of Limitations runs from when principal becomes aware of the bribery, 140.
principal cannot follow proceeds of money received by way of, 140.
justifies dismissal without notice, 140.
contract made under influence of, is voidable by principal, 268, 269.
agent cannot sue for money promised by way of, 311.

BROKER: *see* STOCKBROKER, BILL BROKER, INSURANCE BROKER; SHIP-BROKER.
definition of, 2.
distinction between factor and, 2.
signature of, in book or on bought and sold notes binds both parties, 6, 69, 228.

implied authority of, 69, 70.
to act on rules and usages of market if reasonable, 66, 67, 70, 172—175.
custom to buy in own name without notice to principal is reasonable, 67.
custom giving him interest in conflict with his duty is unreasonable, 67, 106.
custom to deal as principal without notice is unreasonable, 67, 106.
custom to make one contract for several principals unreasonable, 67, 70.
custom to receive payment by way of set-off unreasonable, 53, 68.
to receive payment when principal undisclosed, 70.
not to cancel nor vary the terms of contracts made by him, 65, 70, 319.
not to receive payment by way of set-off, 70, 122.
not to delegate his authority, even if acting under *del credere* commission, 71, 82.

duties of, 90, 94, 121, 122.
to act according to usage where reasonable, 90, 131.
to make separate contracts for each principal, 121.
to make an estimate of the value of goods intrusted to him for sale, 131.
to comply with statutory provisions in making contracts, 121.
not to deal as principal without full disclosure, 104, 105, 122, 269.
to account for all secret profits, 116.

liability of,
for negligence and breach of duty, 95, 131.
on bill signed without qualification, 128.
for innocent conversion, 316.
on contracts made on principal's behalf,
where he contracts personally, 274, 288.
by special custom where principal undisclosed, 286, 287.
not liable if appointed arbitrator, 287.
primâ facie, not liable where he contracts as a broker, 283.

BROKER—*continued.*
right of, to remuneration, 152, 153, 162 *see* REMUNERATION.
cannot recover unless duly licensed, or in respect of any illegal transaction, 164, 165, 176.
omission to send contract note does not render contract illegal, 165.
right to damages where prevented earning commission, 162.
right of, to set off debt due from agent employing him, as against the principal, 84, 85, 242.
to set off amount due from principal, as against principal's trustee in bankruptcy, 171.
right of, to indemnity against liabilities incurred as such, 172—175.
general lien of, 181, 186, 218 *see* LIEN.
cannot sue on contracts made as broker, 204, 306, 307 · *but see* INSURANCE BROKER.
may sue in own name where he contracts personally, 305.
or if he has a lien on the subject-matter of the contract, 308.
intrusted with the possession of goods or documents of title · *see* FACTORS ACT.
payment to, does not necessarily discharge principal, 233—235.
knowledge of, when it operates as notice to principal, 241, 265, 267.
is *functus officio* as soon as contract completed, 319.
authority of, may be revoked any time before contract completed, 330.
implied warranty of authority by, 292.

BURDEN OF PROOF, of good faith, &c., in transactions between agent and principal, lies on the agent, 107, 108.

CAPACITY,
to act as agent, infants, married women, &c. have, 5, 6.
to appoint an agent co-extensive with capacity to act on own behalf, 4.
of corporation to appoint an agent, 4.

CARGO *see* SHIPMASTER.
hypothecation or sale of, by shipmaster, 75, 77—79.
lien of shipmaster on, for freight and general average, 197.
liability of shipowners for damage to, 248 note (*g*).

CARRIER is not, as such, an agent of the consignee, 102.

CERTIFICATE, warehouse keeper's, is a document of title for purposes of the Factors Act, 213 note (*m*).

CHARTER PARTY,
implied authority of shipmaster to enter into a, 75.
commission for obtaining a, 152, 153, 165.
executed by agent in own name, right of principal to sue on, 224, 225.
liability of agent on, 283, 285.
may be restricted to certain events, 276, 277, 306.
executed by principal professedly as an agent, right to sue on, 306.

CHEQUE: *see* NEGOTIABLE INSTRUMENTS.
payment to agent by, 51, 90, 131, 244 *see* PAYMENT.
custom to take, in lieu of cash, is reasonable, 244.
in absence of special custom agent who takes, in lieu of cash, is personally responsible, 131, 244.
fraudulently altered and paid by banker in good faith, 178.

CHILD, a, has no implied authority to pledge parent's credit, 28.

CLAIMS OF THIRD PERSONS,
agent cannot in general set up, against principal, 96—102.
when agent may interplead in respect of, 201—203 *see* INTERPLEAD.

CLIENT: *see* SOLICITOR, COUNSEL.

CLUB, members of, are not, as such, liable on orders of committee, 220.

CO-AGENTS,
must, in general, act jointly, 8, 9 *see* JOINT AUTHORITY.
distinction between joint and several authority, 8, 9.
not liable to third persons for wrongs of each other, 318.

COHABITATION as man and wife, authority implied from, 27.

COLLECTOR of rents, no implied authority to receive notice to quit, 60.

COMMISSION *see* REMUNERATION.

COMMISSION AGENT,
employed to make bets must pay over winnings, but cannot recover losses, 64, 98, 176.
not liable for neglecting to bet, 133.
who buys goods as such cannot sue principal as for goods sold or for non-acceptance, 204.
no implied authority to pledge credit of foreign principal, 65.

COMPANIES. *see* DIRECTORS; RAILWAY COMPANY; TRAMWAY COMPANY.
ratification by, 36, 37, 41, 44, 45, 47. *see* RATIFICATION.
cannot ratify acts which are *ultra vires*, 36.
contracts made before incorporation, 37.
mining, powers of directors of, 56, 61.
unincorporated, powers of directors and agents of, 61.
insurance: *see* INSURANCE AGENT.
are bound by acts of *de facto* directors, though not duly appointed, 222.
how far liable for misrepresentations of directors, secretary, or agents, 211, 252, 253, 255, 257.
not liable for fraud of secretary committed for his own purposes, 255.
liability of, for wrongs by their agents, 247, 249, 250, 253, 256 *see* WRONGS.
not estopped from denying representations of secretary, 263.
liability of, on bills of exchange and promissory notes, 209, 227, 228.
shareholders in, are personally liable as contributories, though agents, 224.
lien on books of, 189.
right of agents to prove for prospective commission in winding-up of, 162, 163.

COMPLETION of transaction not necessary to entitle agent to commission, 153—155 *see* REMUNERATION.

COMPROMISE,
implied authority of solicitors and counsel to, 63, 72—74.
entered into contrary to client's instructions, 90, 130, 206.

CONCEALMENT *see* DISCLOSURE; KNOWLEDGE.
of incumbrance by solicitor, solicitor personally liable for, 313.

CONDITIONS of sale, auctioneer no implied authority to vary, 72.

CONDUCT *see* ESTOPPEL, HOLDING OUT.

CONFIDENCE, powers involving, cannot be delegated, 81, 82.

CONFIDENTIAL COMMUNICATIONS, duty of solicitors to keep secret all, 124.

CONFLICT between interest and duty, agent must not enter into transactions in which there is a, unless the principal, after full disclosure, consents, 102—106 *see* DISCLOSURE.

CONSIDERATION
for deed, implied authority of solicitor to receive, on production of the deed containing a receipt, 73.
failure of, agent may repay money paid to him on, 97.

CONSIGNEE,
carrier may dispute title of, 102.
lien of, 182, 183, 186, 217.
right of set-off against consignor of, 242.

CONSTRUCTION,
of powers of attorney, 54—56 · *see* POWER OF ATTORNEY.
of authority not given by deed, 56.
of authority given in general terms, 51, 52.
of authority given in ambiguous terms, 53, 54.
of written contracts made by agent, 281—285.

CONSTRUCTIVE NOTICE, doctrine of, 264—267 · *see* NOTICE.

CONTRACT · *see* STATUTE OF FRAUDS, SALE OF GOODS ACT.
of agent is deemed to be the contract of the principal, 6.
agent who makes a, has no implied authority, as such, to vary or cancel it, 65, 70, 71.
ratification of, after notice of withdrawal, 39, 41.
after refusal to recognize, 40 *see* RATIFICATION.
in writing may be ratified verbally or by conduct, 44.
cannot be varied or contradicted by parol evidence, 224, 285, 286 *see* EVIDENCE.
made by house or estate agent not binding on principal unless expressly authorized, 65, 210.
between principal and agent, duty of full disclosure, 107—110. *see* DISCLOSURE.
made by agent, rights and liabilities of principal on, 222 *et seq.*: *see* PRINCIPAL.
effect of fraud, non-disclosure. &c. of agent, 211, 236—238, 252.
rights and liabilities of agent on, 270 *et seq.*, *see* AGENT.
made on behalf of the government, agent not liable on, 270, 271: *see* PUBLIC AGENT.
remedy is a petition of right, 271.
under seal. *see* DEED.
made by agent without authority, 289—297 · *see* WARRANTY OF AUTHORITY.
in violation of duty, when voidable by principal, 103—105: *and see* BRIBERY.

CONTRACT NOTE: *see* NOTES.

CONVERSION OF GOODS OR CHATTELS,
by agent, what amounts to a, 314—318.
agent liable for, though he acts in good faith and without notice on the authority of the possessor and apparent owner, 313—318.
except in cases within the Factors Act, 315.
right of indemnity from principal, 177.
liability of principal for, 247.
by auctioneer, 316, 317.
of property of bankrupt, 317, 328.
mere ministerial dealing with the goods without notice is not a, 315, 317.

CONVEYANCE of principal's property after an act of bankruptcy, 329.

CONVEYANCING ACTS (1881 and 1882),
married woman may appoint an attorney, 5, 73.
donee of power of attorney may execute deeds, &c. in own name, 91, 225, 226.
protection of agent acting under power of attorney without notice of revocation, 333.
constructive notice to purchasers for value, 267.
powers of attorney may be made irrevocable in favour of purchasers for value, 324, 325.

CO-PRINCIPALS,
agent must account to, jointly, 98.
are jointly liable for agent's remuneration, 48.
must sue jointly on contracts made on their behalf, 223.
agency is determined by death of any one of several, 326.
may be revoked by notice from any one of several, 330.

CORPORATION,
cannot appoint an agent to do any act which is *ultra vires*, 4, 50.
appointment of agent by, when it must be under the common seal, 31—33.
ratification by, 36, 47: *see* RATIFICATION.
is bound by the acts of *de facto* agents, though not formally appointed, 33.
liability of, for wrongful acts of agents, 247, 253, 256.
quære, whether liable for malicious wrongs, 247.
mayor cannot sue in own name on a contract made with a municipal, 307.
liability of, for fraudulent misrepresentations by agent, 257.

COUNSEL,
implied authority of, 63, 72.
have no right of action for fees, 74, 150.
are not liable for negligence or breach of duty, 128.
duty of, where they have a personal interest in deeds drafted by them, 125 note (*y*).

COVENANTS: *see* DEED.

CREDIT: *see* EXCLUSIVE CREDIT.
implied authority of agent to pledge principal's, 65, 208, 211, 220.
of wife to pledge husband's. *see* MARRIED WOMAN.
factors and brokers have implied authority to sell on reasonable, 66, 69, 70.
auctioneers and stockbrokers have no implied authority to sell on, 51, 71, 122, 210.
in account is equivalent to payment as between bankers, 98.
given to agent, how far right of recourse to principal affected by, 230—233 *see* PRINCIPAL, ELECTION.

CRIMINAL LIABILITY of agent for fraudulent dealings with principal's property, 143 note (*p*), 216.

CROWN, servants of the: *see* PUBLIC AGENT.

CUSTOM,
of particular business, agent has implied authority to act on, unless it is illegal or unreasonable, or inconsistent with his express instructions, 65—68, 70, 80, 83.
duty of agents to act in accordance with, 89, 90, 129, 131.
of particular business, when binding on principal, 65—68, 229.
not bound by unreasonable, unless aware of it, 52, 53, 66, 172—175, 229, 245.
unreasonable, is binding on principal if known to him, 66, 172, 174.
of the Stock Exchange, 66—68, 173—175 *see* STOCK EXCHANGE.
at Lloyds' to pay brokers by way of set-off is unreasonable, 52, 68, 245.
which changes the intrinsic character of the contract of agency is unreasonable, 66—68, 106.
giving agent an interest in conflict with his duty is unreasonable, 67, 68, 106.
for broker to make one contract for several principals (except a stockbroker, 170), or to deal as principal without notice is unreasonable, 67, 68, 106.
for stockbrokers to ignore Leeman's Act is unreasonable, 121, 175.
for shipmasters to trade on their own account is illegal, 122.
for agents to receive payment by way of set-off or settlement of accounts is unreasonable, 52, 53, 68, 239, 245.
for agents to receive payment by cheque is reasonable, 52, 90, 244.
for broker to contract in own name without notice to principal is reasonable, 67.
authority to delegate may be implied from, 80, 83.
contract by principal to pay remuneration may be implied from, 149—152.
for auctioneers to sell by private contract without express authority inadmissible, 64.
for agents contracting as such for undisclosed principals to be personally liable, admissible, if not inconsistent with express contract, 286, 287.
right of agent to indemnity against liabilities incurred in accordance with, 171—175.
evidence of, when admissible to explain or add to written contract, 150, 151.
to claim commission on transaction which is not a proximate result of the agency is invalid, 153, 154.

DAMAGES: *see* MEASURE OF DAMAGES.
for negligence, &c., cannot be passed in taking an account, 113.
nominal, for breach of duty, where no actual loss, 134.
too remote, 133, 296, 297.
agent entitled to, if wrongfully prevented earning his commission, 159—163 *see* REMUNERATION.
incurred by agent in executing his authority, right of agent to reimbursement of, 171.

DEATH,
of principal, when authority revoked by, 320—326: *see* REVOCATION.
liability of agent who continues to act after, 100, 293.
agent no right to damages when agency determined by, 161.
remuneration for acts done by agent after, 167, 326.
stockbroker is justified in closing account on, 174.
acts done by agent after revocation by, do not bind the executors, 326, 333.
does not affect agent's lien, 183.
of a partner determines a contract of agency with the firm, 326.

DEBENTURES, liability of directors for issuing, without authority, 291, 292, 294.

DEBT,
tender of, to apparently authorized agent operates as a tender to principal, 207.
acknowledgment of, by agent, when principal bound by, 262, 263.
part payment of, by agent, interrupts the Statute of Limitations, 263.
owing by principal, purchase of, by agent, 115.

DECEIT · *see* FRAUD, MISREPRESENTATION.

DECLARATIONS,
by auctioneer, principal not bound by, if inconsistent with conditions, 71, 211.
by agent, estoppel of principal by, 208, 211, 263.
by agent, how far evidence against principal, 260—263: *see* ADMISSIONS.
by principal, when evidence against agent, 310.

DEED,
authority to execute a, must be conferred by deed, 29.
but may be revoked verbally, 330.
ratification of a, must (probably) be by deed, 44.
construction of authority given by *see* POWER OF ATTORNEY.
implied authority of solicitor to receive consideration for, 73.
agent may execute, in own name, 91, 225.
agent who executes, in own name is personally liable, 271, 277.
rights and liabilities of principal on, when executed in agent's name, 225, 226.

DEFAULT: *see* REMUNERATION; REIMBURSEMENT; INDEMNITY.

DEFAULTER: *see* STOCKBROKER.

DEFENCES,
to action by principal on contract made by agent, 236—245: *see* PRINCIPAL.
to action by agent on contract made as such, 307—310. *see* AGENT.

DEFINITIONS, 1 *et seq.*
of agent, general agent, special agent, 1.
of factor, broker; auctioneer; mercantile agent, 2, 336.
of *del credere* agent, 2, 3.
of possessory lien, particular lien, general lien, 180.
of goods, for the purposes of the Factors Act, 213 note (*k*), 336.
of mercantile agent, for the purposes of the Factors Act, 2, 336.
of document of title, for the purposes of the Factors Act, 213 note (*m*), 336.
of pledge, for the purposes of the Factors Act, 336.

DEL CREDERE AGENT,
definition of, 2.
is, in effect, a surety, 3, 126, 127.
may be appointed verbally, 3.
distinction between vendee and, 3.
no implied authority, as such, to delegate, 69, 71.
right of, to sue third persons on contracts made as such, 305.
right of, to indemnity against losses, 169.

DEL CREDERE COMMISSION, 3.
may be inferred from a course of conduct, 3.
does not affect principal's right to sue in own name, 236.

DELAY in applying to principal for debt contracted by agent, effect of, 233, 234, 235.

DELEGATION of authority, 80 *et seq.*: *see* SUB-AGENT.
by agent not permitted without authority of principal, 80—83.
when authority to delegate is implied, 80—83.
from usage if not inconsistent with instructions, 80, 83.
when principal knows a substitute will be appointed, 81, 83
from the conduct of the parties, 81, 83.
in cases of unforeseen emergency, 81.
when nature of authority necessitates its execution by a deputy, 81.
when the act is purely ministerial, 81, 82.
of discretionary or confidential powers not permitted, 7, 81, 82.
by auctioneers, factors, brokers, directors, &c., *primâ facie* not permitted, 82.
by solicitors, 83.
acquiescence of principal in appointment of sub-agent, 83.

DELIVERY OF GOODS,
by auctioneer without payment, liability of auctioneer, 72, 123.
by agent, contrary to instructions, liability of agent, 138.
by broker, otherwise than in accordance with the contract, 122, 131.

DELIVERY ORDER,
is a document of title, for purposes of the Factors Act, 213 note (*m*).
estoppel of wharfinger who accepts a, 101.

DEPOSIT,
liability of auctioneer who neglects to obtain payment of, 122, 132.
auctioneer may accept a cheque in payment of, 90.
ought to be retained by auctioneer as stakeholder, 123.
if vendor's solicitor receives a, he ought to pay it over to vendor, 125, 299.

DEPOSIT—*continued.*
liability of auctioneer to pay interest on, 142, 299.
right of auctioneer to interplead respecting, 202.
purchaser at sale by auction is liable for the, though acting as agent, 273.
paid by agent, right of principal to sue for recovery of, 223, 224.
of money with stakeholder, liability of stakeholder to account for, 298, 299.

DEPUTY *see* DELEGATION, SUB-AGENT.

DETERMINATION OF AGENCY, 319 *et seq.* *see* REVOCATION.
right of agent to commission on business resulting after, 153, 156.
for fixed term, right of agent to recover damages on, 161.
by effluxion of time, &c., 319, 320.
by death or bankruptcy of principal, 320—329 *see* BANKRUPTCY, DEATH.
by notice, 329—331 *see* REVOCATION.

DIFFERENCES,
paid by stockbroker, right of broker to recover from principal, 170, 178, 179.
plea of "gaming and wagering" to action by broker for, 98, 176, 177.
right of stockbroker to close account on failure by principal to pay, 70, 175.

DILIGENCE. *see* DUTIES OF AGENT, NEGLIGENCE.

DIRECTORS *see* COMPANIES.
duty of, to account for all secret profits and benefits, 105, 117—119, 140.
to make full disclosure whenever they have a personal interest in a transaction with the company, 103, 105.
who receive qualification shares or other gifts from promoters must account to the company for highest value, with interest, 118, 119.
de facto, dealings with, by third persons, 222.
of unincorporated companies, no implied authority to borrow money or accept bills, 56, 61.
liability of, on contracts made on behalf of the company, 283.
on bills of exchange and promissory notes signed by them 279—281.
on deeds executed in own name, 277.
acting in excess of their authority, 291, 292.
borrowing in excess of borrowing powers, 251, 291, 292, 295.
issuing invalid debentures, 291, 294.
for negligence, 133.
paying dividends out of capital, 313.
must make full disclosure if they contract with the company, 108, 109.
fraudulent misrepresentations by, liability of the company for, 257.
effect of, on contract with the company, 236.
cannot delegate their authority, 82.
acts of, how far binding on company, 209.
notice to, when constructive notice to company, 265, 266.

DISBURSEMENTS *see* REIMBURSEMENT.
maritime lien of shipmaster for, 197.

DISCLOSURE *see* DUTIES of AGENT; KNOWLEDGE.
duty of agent to make a full, whenever he deals with the principal or acquires any personal benefit in course of the agency, 67, 84, 102—110, 125.
burden of proof as to, lies on the agent, 107.

DISCRETION,
powers involving, must be exercised in person, 7, 81, 82.
agent acting in good faith in a matter of, is not liable to principal for the consequences, 129.

DISMISSAL OF AGENT,
bribery justifies, without notice, 140.
right to commission on transactions resulting after, 156.
right of agent to damages for wrongful, 159—163.
voluntary winding-up of company may operate as a wrongful, 162, 163.

DISOBEDIENCE to instructions, liability of agent for, 130, 131.

DISPOSITIONS of goods by mercantile agents, 213—217, 335 *et seq.* *see* FACTORS ACT.

DISTRESS, wrongful, by agent, 246, 300, 312, 313.

DIVORCE proceedings, implied authority of wife to pledge husband's credit for costs of, 22, 23.

DOCK WARRANT is a document of title, for purposes of Factors Act, 213 note (*m*).

DOCUMENT OF TITLE: *see* FACTORS ACT.
definition of, for purposes of Factors Act, 213 note (*m*), 336.
pledge of a, is deemed to be a pledge of the goods, 215, 216, 337.

DURESS, money obtained by, personal liability of agent to repay, 298, 300, 301.

DUTIES OF AGENT, 88 *et seq.*. *see* BREACH OF DUTY, NEGLIGENCE.
to perform undertaking, unless gratuitous, 88.
to act in person, unless authorized to delegate, 88 *see* DELEGATION.
to obey instructions, unless illegal, 88—90, 186, 187.
to act according to usage, 89, 90.
to act in good faith solely for benefit of principal, 89, 115.
to strictly pursue his authority, 88, 89, 178.
to disregard illegal instructions, 90.
not to accept cheques or bills in payment, unless customary to do so, 90.
to execute deeds in the name of the principal, 91.
to keep principal's money and property separate, 91, 92, 120.
to preserve and be ready with correct accounts, 92, 111, 120.
to produce documents relating to the principal's affairs, 92.
to pay over, on request, money received to principal's use, 92, 96—98 *see* MONEY.
though received under a void or illegal contract, 96, 98.
to act as a trustee if permitted to retain money for investment, 92.

DUTIES OF AGENT—*continued.*
to exercise due skill, care and diligence, 93—96 · *see* NEGLIGENCE.
if a paid agent, such skill, &c. as is usual or necessary in the ordinary course of his employment, 93—96, 168.
if a gratuitous agent, such skill as he possesses, or has held himself out to possess, and such care and diligence as he would exhibit in his own concerns, 93, 96.
to take reasonable care of principal's property and money, 94, 96, 121.
not to set up the title of third persons, 96—102 · *see* ESTOPPEL. *See, however*, INTERPLEAD.
to repay money obtained wrongfully or paid by mistake, 96, 97.
Arising from the fiduciary character of the relationship, 102 *et seq.*
to make a full and fair disclosure, where he enters into any transaction in which he has a personal interest, 102—106, 108.
and not to enter into any such transaction unless principal consents, 102—106.
to make a full disclosure, where he acquires any personal benefit, 107.
where he contracts with the principal or his representatives, to deal at arm's length, and fully disclose everything known respecting the subject-matter, 107—110.
to account for all secret profits and benefits, 84, 103, 105, 114—120: *see* SECRET PROFITS.
to account in a court of equity, 111—114: *see* ACCOUNT.
not to use his influence to obtain gifts from principal, 111: *see* GIFT.
Special duties
of auctioneers, 90, 122, 123, 168.
of brokers, 90, 94, 121, 122.
of directors, 103, 117—119.
of estate agents, 90, 94.
of factors, 120.
of house agents, 90, 94.
of insurance brokers, 94, 97.
of patent agents, 95.
of solicitors, 89, 108—110, 123—125.
of stockbrokers, 90, 95.
of valuers, 95.

ELECTION,
to give exclusive credit to agent, 26, 27, 230—233.
cannot charge principal after, 26, 27, 230—233.
suing agent to judgment is conclusive proof of an, 230, 232.
question of fact for jury where agent not sued to judgment, 231—233.
must be founded on full knowledge, 231.

ESTATE AGENT,
no implied authority to enter into binding contracts on principal's behalf, 65, 210.
duty of, to submit all offers to principal, 65, 91.
to examine takings, if employed to buy a business, 94.
liability of, for taking cheque in lieu of cash, 131, 244 note (*j*).
on contract made in own name, 288.
has a right to commission on sale resulting from his introduction, even if he does not complete the sale, 154, 155. *see* REMUNERATION.

ESTOPPEL,
of agent, after acting as such, 10.
who misleads principal by signing bills without qualification, 127, 128.
from disputing principal's title, 96—102 *but see* INTERPLEAD.
of wharfinger, 101.
by holding out. *see* HOLDING OUT.
by negligence, 178, 179.
of trustee in bankruptcy, by representations of bankrupt, 147.
of principal, by representations of agent, 208, 263.
of creditor who, by his conduct, induces principal to settle with agent, 233—235.
of principal who permits agent to appear as principal, 238—245.

EVIDENCE,
what sufficient, of ratification, 42, 43, 45, 46, 227.
of custom, when admissible to vary or explain written contract, 149, 150, 152, 286, 287.
not admissible if inconsistent with the terms of the contract, 287.
admissible to charge principal, but not to discharge agent, where agent contracts personally, 222—224, 285.
to explain ambiguity in written contract, 285.
of separate verbal agreement may be given, 285.

EXCLUSIVE CREDIT· *see* ELECTION.
to agent, effect on liability of principal of giving, 26, 27, 230—235.

EXECUTION OF AUTHORITY, agent has implied authority to do what is necessary for or ordinarily incidental to, 57 *et seq.* *see* IMPLIED AUTHORITY.

EXECUTOR,
de son tort, liability of agent of, 300.
agent of, not liable to account to legatees, 303.
may ratify act done by agent of testator after death, 326.
not liable for necessaries supplied to testator's widow, 333.

EXPENSES INCURRED BY AGENT,
right of agent to reimbursement of, 169—179: *see* REIMBURSEMENT.
right to set off, in action by principal, 169, 171.
agent's authority does not become irrevocable by reason of, 323.

FACTOR,
definition of, 2.
distinction between broker and, 2, 307.
implied authority of, 68, 69.
to sell in own name on reasonable credit, and to receive payment, 68, 69.
not to barter or pledge, even to meet bills accepted by him, 69, 121.
not to delegate his authority, 69, 82, 120.

FACTOR—*continued.*
general lien of, 181—190, 243, 324 · *see* LIEN.
confined to goods acquired by him as factor, 184, 187.
may be excluded by special agreement, 185, 186.
does not extend to goods intrusted for special purposes inconsistent with, 187.
confined to debts and liabilities incurred as factor, 182, 183, 184.
effect of principal's bankruptcy on, 189, 190.
duties of, 120, 121.
dispositions of goods by · *see* FACTORS ACT.
right of, to sue in own name on contracts made on principal's behalf, 223, 307.
has priority to right of principal to sue, where factor has a lien, 243, 308, 322, 324.
right of purchaser to set off debt due from, in action by principal for price, 240, 241.
liability of principal for misrepresentations by, 246.
right of principal to goods and debts on bankruptcy of, 146, 147.
when authority of, irrevocable, 322—324: *see* REVOCATION.

FACTORS ACT (1889), 213—217 · *and see* 335 *et seq.*
definition of mercantile agent, 2, 336.
of document of title, 213 note (*m*), 336.
dispositions by, or in pursuance of authority given by, mercantile agent in possession of goods or documents of title with consent of owner, 213—217, 315.
applies only to dispositions in course of business of mercantile agent, 215, 217.
only protects persons taking in good faith and without notice, 214, 215.
pledge for antecedent debt, 214, 216.
in consideration of other goods or securities, 215.
of documents of title deemed to be a pledge of the goods, 215, 216.
does not affect agent's liability for exceeding authority, 216.
principal may sue for price of or redeem goods sold or pledged, 216.
lien of consignee for advances to apparent owner of goods, 217.

FALSE IMPRISONMENT by agent or servant, liability of principal or master for, 249, 253, 254.

FEES. *see* COUNSEL; REMUNERATION.

FI. FA., WRIT OF,
solicitor has implied authority to issue and indorse, 73.
but not to direct sheriff to seize particular goods, 74, 252.
liability of solicitor for wrongful seizure under, 313, 314.
of execution creditor for wrongful seizure under, 247, 248, 252.

FIDUCIARY RELATION · *see* DISCLOSURE, SECRET PROFITS.
duties arising from the, between principal and agent, 102 *et seq*: *see* DUTIES OF AGENT.
transactions violating the, principal may repudiate, or may adopt and claim an account of the profit made by the agent, 103—105, 119, 120.

FIXED TERM, appointment of agent for, does not necessarily oblige the principal to continue the business, 161—163.

FOLLOWING money and property wrongfully dealt with by agent, 144—148, 212, 213, 219, 269 *see* FACTORS ACT.

FOREIGN PRINCIPAL,
agent no implied authority to pledge credit of, 65.
primâ facie, cannot sue or be sued on contracts made by agent in England, 224.
agent of, is *primâ facie* presumed to contract personally, 273, 282, 284.

FORGERY, a, cannot be ratified, 35.

FRAUD,
of either principal or agent renders contract voidable against principal, 97, 98, 236, 237, 259.
of agent, liability of principal for, 246, 250—252, 255—257 *see* WRONGS.
of secretary, liability of company for, 252.
of wife, liability of husband for, 257.
of sub-agent, liability of agent to principal for, 144.
settled accounts will be reopened in cases of, 112, 113.
Statute of Limitations is no defence in cases of, 112, 114.

FRAUDS, STATUTE OF: *see* STATUTE OF FRAUDS.

FRAUDULENT dealings by agent,
with principal's money or property, right of principal to follow proceeds, on agent's bankruptcy, 145—148.
with negotiable securities, when principal bound by, 212, 213, 219.
with goods in possession of mercantile agent, 213—217 · *see* FACTORS ACT.
criminal liability of agent for, 143 note (*p*), 216.

FUNCTUS OFFICIO, 72, 74, 319.

FUTURE COMPANY, agent personally liable on contracts made for, 289.

GAMING ACT, 1892..64, 321 (*q*), 324 (*c*), 331 (*o*).
does not affect liability of agent to pay over winnings received, 98.
precludes agent from recovering losses or remuneration in respect of any gaming or wagering contract, 98, 165, 176, 177.

GAMING CONTRACTS,
are void, but not illegal, 98, 133, 165, 177.
agent cannot recover indemnity or remuneration in respect of, 164, 165, 176—178.
agent is bound to pay over winnings received under, 98.
but is not liable for neglecting to make, 133.
authority to pay money in respect of, when revocable, 324, 331.
the question whether particular transactions are, is a question for the jury, 165, 178.

GENERAL AGENT,
definition of, 1.
distinction between special and, 1.
implied authority of, 59 *et seq.* *see* IMPLIED AUTHORITY.

GENERAL MANAGER of railway company, implied authority of, 60.

GENERAL WORDS in power of attorney are restricted to the objects of the power, 54, 55.

GIFT,
by principal to agent, validity of, 107, 110, 111.
by client to solicitor, during subsistence of relationship, void, 111, 125.
by promoters to directors and officers of company, 117—119 *see* DIRECTORS, SECRET PROFITS.

GOOD FAITH *see* DISCLOSURE, DUTIES OF AGENT.
meaning of, for purposes of Factors Act, 215.
for purposes of Bills of Exchange Act, 212.

GOODS,
intrusted to agent, agent must not set up *jus tertii* to, 99, 102: *but see* INTERPLEAD.
in possession of agent, must be returned to principal on agent's bankruptcy, 104, 145—147, 269.
sale of, by agent intrusted with possession, 220.
dispositions of, by mercantile agents, 213—217 *see* FACTORS ACT.
lien of consignee for advances on, to apparent owner, 217.
right of principal to follow, 144—148, 219, 269.
wrongful pledge of, does not transfer agent's lien, 218.
conversion of, by innocent agent, 314—318 *see* CONVERSION.

GOVERNMENT, agent of the. *see* PUBLIC AGENT.

GRATUITOUS UNDERTAKING,
agent is not bound to perform, 88.
liability of agent for negligence in performance of, 93, 96, 129, 134.
for breach of duty, 93, 130.
to account for secret profits, 116.

HOLDING OUT, 12, 13, 15, 219 *et seq.*
by conduct, 220—222.
a wife as housekeeper, 16, 17.
a person as having authority, effect of, 208, 219—222, 251.
a person as agent, after revocation of authority, 332, 333.
by corporations and companies, 33, 222.
an agent as the owner of goods, 217.
an agent as the principal, 238—243. *see* SET-OFF, PAYMENT.
secretary as having authority to borrow in excess of powers, liability of directors, 251.

HORSE DEALER,
bound by a warranty given by his agent on sale of a horse, 58, 206.
has implied authority to warrant a horse intrusted to him for sale, 64.

HOUSE AGENT. *see* ESTATE AGENT.
claim of, to commission, 154 *see* REMUNERATION.
duty of, to inquire as to solvency of tenants, 94.
must not take a cheque in lieu of cash, 131, 244 note (*j*).

HUSBAND, liability of, on wife's contracts, 13 *et seq.* *see* MARRIED WOMAN.

HYPOTHECATION of ship or cargo by master, 75, 77.

ILLEGAL,
instructions, agent should disregard, 90, 131.
transaction, agent must pay over money received in respect of an, 96, 98, 112.
agent not liable for negligence in respect of an, 134.
agent cannot claim indemnity or remuneration in respect of any apparently, 164, 165, 175—177.
insurance, broker cannot recover premiums on an, 176.
purpose, authority to expend money for an, 97.

IMPLIED AUTHORITY, 11, 12, 50, 57 *et seq.*
of agent, to do what is necessary for or incidental to execution of his express authority, 57, 58, 81.
to discharge liabilities incurred on principal's behalf, 64.
to delegate his authority *see* DELEGATION.
cannot exceed powers of principal, 50.
not to do anything outside ordinary scope of employment, 59—63.
where employed in course of his business or profession, 62 *et seq.*
to give a warranty · *see* WARRANTY.
to sign for the purpose of the Statute of Frauds, &c., 11, 57, 71, 83.
to arrest offenders, or give them into custody, 61, 62, 253, 254 · *see* ARREST.
to act on rules and customs of particular markets, 65—68, 70 · *see* CUSTOM.
of agent for sale, 58, 59, 64—66, 91 · *see* SALE, AGENT FOR.
of general agent, to do everything incidental to ordinary course of employment, or necessary for proper performance of duties, 59 *et seq.*
of auctioneer, 11, 64, 71, 72 : *see* AUCTIONEER.
of broker, 65, 66, 69—71 *see* BROKER.
of bailiff employed to distrain for rent, 63, 252.
of counsel, 63, 72.
of directors of unincorporated companies, 61.
of estate agent, 65, 91, 110.
of factor, 68, 69, 120, 121 *see* FACTOR.
of insurance broker, 52, 64, 65, 70 : *see* INSURANCE BROKER.
of manager, 59, 60, 61.
of married woman to pledge her husband's credit: *see* MARRIED WOMAN.
of partners, 10 note (*l*).
of rent collector, 60.
of shipmaster, 75—80 · *see* SHIPMASTER.
of solicitor, 63—65, 73, 74 *see* SOLICITOR.
of servants of railway companies, 61, 62.
of steward, 60.
of stockbroker · *see* STOCKBROKER.
of traveller for the sale of goods, 60.

IMPLIED WARRANTY OF AUTHORITY · *see* WARRANTY OF AUTHORITY.

INCUMBRANCE,
where notice of, to solicitor is notice to client, 265—267.
liability of solicitor for wrongful concealment of, 313.

INDEMNITY, right of agent to, 169 *et seq.*: *see* REIMBURSEMENT.
against all losses and liabilities properly incurred in execution of authority, 169—171.
liabilities incurred under rules or customs of market, 171—175: *see* STOCKBROKER.
not if the custom unreasonable, unless principal aware of it, 175.
where authority revoked after partial execution, 170, 177.
not in respect of any apparently illegal act or transaction, 8, 175—177.
nor of any gaming or wagering transaction, 98, 176, 177.
nor of any unauthorized act or transaction, 176, 178.
unless ratified, 46, 48, 49.
nor of losses incurred by own breach of duty, negligence, or insolvency, 176, 179.

INDORSEMENT: *see* BILL OF EXCHANGE; NEGOTIABLE INSTRUMENTS.
restrictive, effect of, 219.

INFANT,
may act and contract as an agent, 5, 6.
may appoint an agent to act for him, 4.
cannot appoint an attorney to make a feoffment on his behalf, 4.
married woman though an, may appoint an attorney, 5.
has no implied authority to pledge parent's credit, 28.

INFRINGEMENT OF PATENT by agent, 246, 312 note (*p*).

INJUNCTION restraining solicitor from acting for opponent of former client, 124.

INJURY: *see* WRONGS.

INSANITY of principal or agent, revocation of authority by, 320—326, 333.

INSOLVENCY: *see* STOPPAGE IN TRANSITU.
of principal, right of stockbroker to close account on, 174.
of agent, no right of indemnity against losses caused by, 176, 179.

INSTRUCTIONS,
duty of agent to obey principal's, 54, 88—90, 123, 186, 187.
unless illegal, 90, 123, 131.
liability of agent for disobedience to, 130.
not to take less than certain price at sale without reserve, illegal, 123, 131.
when ambiguous, 53, 54.
third persons are not affected by special, unless they have notice, 206, 207, 221.

INSURANCE AGENT: *see* INSURANCE BROKER.
no implied authority to receive overdue premiums or to grant policies, 60, 61, 210.
estoppel of company by representations of, 208.
knowledge of, when constructive notice to company, 237, 264.

INSURANCE BROKER,
acts for underwriters as well as for assured, 6, 99.
implied authority of, 64, 70.
no implied authority to cancel policies effected by him, 65.
duty of, to use due diligence and insert all usual clauses in policies, 94, 95, 132.
settlement with, by way of set-off, when binding on principal, 52, 68, 70, 245, 310.
liability of, for negligence, 94, 95, 132, 138.
to underwriter for premiums, 99, 126.
right of set-off as against bankrupt underwriter, 126.
as against principal of person employing him, 192, 242.
right of, to sue in own name for premiums, 204.
cannot recover premiums in respect of illegal or unauthorized insurance, 176, 178.
right of, to set up *jus tertii* against assured or underwriter, 97, 99, 202.
general lien of, 181, 186, 192, 242.
how lost, 200.
lien of, where person employing him is an agent, 192, 193.
non-disclosure of material facts by, 132, 237, 267.
authority of, to effect a policy may be revoked after slip signed, 178, 331.
underwriter not bound if limit exceeded by, 210.

INSURANCE POLICY *see* INSURANCE BROKER.
ratification of, 38, 40, 48.
is voidable if material facts concealed by either party, 236, 237.
local agent no implied authority to grant, 61, 210.
not binding until subscribed by underwriters, 178.

INSURE, duty of agent to, and liability for not doing so, 89, 121, 130, 138.

INTEREST,
agent must pay, if he wrongfully refuses to pay over money, 93, 141, 142.
on secret profits and bribes, 104, 105, 119, 139, 140, 142.
where he applies principal's money to own use, 141, 142.
in all cases of fraud and wilful concealment, 142.
stakeholder is not liable to pay, 142, 298, 299.
authority coupled with an, when irrevocable, 321—323.
agent must make full disclosure where he has a personal, 102—106, 108.

INTERPLEAD,
right of agent to, in respect of chattels in his possession, 201—203.
as against own principal, if no notice of adverse claim, 201, 202.
agent cannot, if he claims a lien as against particular claimant, 202, 203.
right of auctioneer, wharfinger, or insurance broker to, 202.

INTERPRETATION *see* CONSTRUCTION.

INTRODUCTION. *see* REMUNERATION.

INTRUSTING agent with possession of goods or documents of title, 220: *see* Factors Act.

INVESTMENT, agent permitted to retain money for, is a trustee, 92, 141, 142.

IRREVOCABLE AUTHORITY, 320—325: *see* Revocation.

JOINT AGENTS. *see* Co-Agents.

JOINT AUTHORITY,
distinction between several and, 8, 9.
in private agencies, all must join in the exercise of a, 8, 9.
in public agencies, execution by a majority is a good execution of a, 8, 9.

JOINT PRINCIPALS: *see* Co-Principals.

JUDGMENT against agent on contract made on behalf of principal, effect of, 230, 232.

JUS TERTII, agent must not set up, 96—102: *but see* Interplead.

KNOWLEDGE,
acquired by agent as such, agent must not make use of for own benefit, 115.
must be fully disclosed by agent where he deals with the principal or his representatives, 107—110.
acquired by solicitor as such, duty of solicitor to keep secret, 124, 131.
of agent or solicitor may operate as constructive notice to principal or client, 237, 241, 264—267 *see* Notice.
of either principal or agent may be set up in an action on a contract by agent, 236—238.

LACHES,
by principal in repudiating transaction with agent, 107, 110.
by creditor in making application to principal for debt, 233—235.

LAND, agent who purchases, as such, in own name is a trustee, 30, 31.

LANDLORD, liability of, for wrongful distress by bailiff, 246.

LEEMAN'S ACT (30 Vict. c. 29),
duty of stockbrokers to comply with provisions of, 121, 174.
custom of Stock Exchange to disregard, is unreasonable, 121, 175.
liability of stockbroker for neglecting to observe, 138.

LIABILITIES,
of agents to their principals, 126 *et seq.*: *see* Agent.
of principal to third persons—
on agent's contracts, 222 *et seq.* see Principal.
for agent's wrongs, 245 *et seq.* see Wrongs.
of agents to third persons, 270 *et seq.* *see* Agent, Wrongs.
of principal to agent, 149 *et seq.* *see* Agent.
incurred by agent, right of agent to indemnity against: *see* Indemnity.

LIEN, 180 *et seq.*
definitions and distinction between general and particular, 180.
possessory, of agent, 180 *et seq.*
on money and chattels in his possession belonging to principal, 180—188.
confined to property acquired in capacity in which lien claimed, 181, 184, 185.
none on property obtained wrongfully, 181, 182, 184.
or for special purpose inconsistent with lien, 181, 186, 187, 200.
excluded by express agreement inconsistent therewith, 181, 185.
effect of death or bankruptcy of principal, 182, 183, 189, 190.
not excluded by express contract unless inconsistent therewith, 185, 186, 190.
on proceeds of goods sold on principal's behalf, 183, 190, 308, 309.
confined to rights of principal, except on money and negotiable securities, 188, 189.
not affected by subsequent acts or bankruptcy of principal, 188, 190.
on negotiable securities is not affected by rights of third persons if acquired by agent in good faith and without notice, 188, 190, 191.
does not attach on trust funds, &c., 189.
how extinguished, 198—200.
not affected by Statute of Limitations, 199.
cannot be transferred by wrongful act, 218.
attaches only for debts and liabilities incurred in course of the agency, 182—184.
and in the same capacity in which the lien claimed, 184.
general, exists only by express agreement or special custom, 181.
factors, brokers, solicitors, bankers and wharfingers have a, by custom, 181.
does not attach on chattels left merely for safe custody, 185, 186.
of sub-agents, 86, 191, 192.
of consignee, 182, 183, 186, 217.
possessory, of solicitors, 184, 185, 187—189, 193.
charging, of solicitors, 193—197 *see* SOLICITOR.
of shipmaster, 197—199: *see* SHIPMASTER.
of banker, 185—187, 190: *see* BANKER.
of insurance broker, 186, 192, 200.
of factor, 181—187, 189, 190 *see* FACTOR.
right of agent to sue in own name where he has a, 239, 243, 303, 305, 308, 309, 324.
when authority irrevocable by reason of, 321, 323, 324.

LIMITATIONS, STATUTE OF *see* STATUTE OF LIMITATIONS.

LLOYDS': *see* CUSTOM.

LOAN,
commission for procuring, 154, 156, 157, 167: *see* REMUNERATION.
payable as soon as person found who is able and willing to lend, 157.
to secretary or directors in excess of borrowing powers, 251, 291, 292, 295.
to shipmaster, 76, 77.
to directors of unincorporated companies, 61.

LOSSES: *see* STOCKBROKER, GAMING CONTRACTS.
implied authority of insurance broker to adjust, 64, 70.
right of insurance broker to set off, against premiums, 127.
incurred by own negligence, default, or insolvency, no indemnity in respect of, 179.

LUNACY,
of husband does not increase wife's implied authority, 13.
revocation of authority by principal's, 320—326, 333.

MANAGER,
of estate, implied authority of, 59.
of public-house, implied authority of, 60, 210.
of mine, implied authority of, 61.
of business, implied authority of, 60, 206, 207.
of bank, no implied authority to arrest a supposed offender, 61.
liability of banker for misappropriation by, 250.

MARINE INSURANCE: *see* INSURANCE BROKER; UNDERWRITERS.

MARITIME LIEN, 197, 198: *see* SHIPMASTER.

MARRIED WOMAN,
capacity of, to appoint or act as an agent, 5.
implied authority of, to pledge husband's credit, 13 *et seq.*
husband not liable unless credit given to him, 13, 16, 26, 27, 231.
where she carries on separate trade, 13.
authority is confined to necessaries, 13—15, 17.
not increased by lunacy of husband, 13.
no implied authority where she has an adequate allowance, 14, 19, 20.
where living with husband, presumption of authority, 14—16.
how presumption rebutted, 14, 15.
no authority to borrow money, even for necessaries, 14.
effect of forbidding her to pledge his credit, 14—17, 221.
does not extend to articles of luxury, 15, 19.
if she acts as housekeeper, husband may be liable though he makes her an adequate allowance, 16, 17.
where living apart from husband, *primâ facie* no authority, 17, 18.
when separated by mutual consent, with fixed allowance, 18—20.
without any fixed allowance, 19—21.
when living apart without husband's consent, 21.
in consequence of husband's misconduct, 21—24.
costs of proceedings for divorce, &c., 22, 23.
loans to wife for necessaries, maintenance of children, &c., 22.
authority of necessity, irrevocable, 22.
what degree of misconduct justifies separation, 24.
effect of adultery by wife, 24, 25.
connivance or condonation of husband, 25.
implied authority of, to acknowledge debts for necessaries, 26, 262.
if acknowledgment in writing, &c., it interrupts Statute of Limitations, 26, 262.

MAXIMS,
"*omnis ratihabitio retrotrahitur et mandato priori æquiparatur*," 41.
"*delegatus non potest delegare*," 81.

MEASURE OF DAMAGES,
for breach of duty or negligence of agent, 137—139.
for neglecting to insure, 130, 138.
for purchasing goods of inferior quality, 137, 138.
for omitting to disclose material fact, 138.
for delivering goods without payment, contrary to instructions, 139.
for wrongful dealing with principal's property, 139.
for wrongfully preventing agent earning commission, 160, 162.
for breach of warranty of authority, 293—297 *see* WARRANTY OF AUTHORITY.

MEMORANDUM: *see* STATUTE OF FRAUDS, SALE OF GOODS ACT.

MEMORANDUM OF ASSOCIATION, authority to subscribe may be verbal, 31.

MERCANTILE AGENT, definition of, 2: *see* FACTORS ACT.

MINING COMPANY, powers of directors and officers of, 56, 61.

MINISTERIAL ACT, agent may appoint a sub-agent to do a, 81, 82.

MISAPPLICATION of money or property of principal, right of principal to follow proceeds, 145—148.

MISAPPROPRIATION,
by agent, liability of principal for, 208, 211, 221, 250, 251.
by sub-agent, liability of agent to principal for, 144.

MISCONDUCT, agent not entitled to remuneration in cases of wilful, 166.

MISDESCRIPTION by agent for sale, liability of principal for, 259.

MISREPRESENTATION,
by agent, how far principal liable for, 246, 252, 253, 257: *see* WRONGS.
liability of agent for, 312.
as to the credit or character of a third person, 260, 312.
as to his authority, 289 *et seq.* *see* WARRANTY OF AUTHORITY.
as to a mere matter of law, 291.
innocent, by agent, liability of principal for, 258, 259.
conflict of authority on this point, 259.
by secretary of company, liability of company for, 211, 252.
by either principal or agent may be set up in an action on a contract made by agent, 236, 237, 252, 259.

MISTAKE OF FACT,
money paid to agent under a, agent may repay, 96, 99.
liability of agent in respect of, 297—300.
money paid by agent under a, agent may sue in own name for, 310.

MIXING,
by agent of principal's money or property with his own, 145—148.
charge of principal on the mixed fund or property, or proceeds, 145, 147, 148.
right of principal to have mixed fund, &c. marshalled, 146, 148.

MONEY: *see* ACCOUNT; PAYMENT.
authority to receive payment of: *see* PAYMENT.
received by agent to principal's use—
duty of agent to pay over or account for, on request, 92, 96—98, 121.
even if received under a void or illegal contract, 97, 98.
agent discharged if he pays over in good faith, 297—299.
if obtained wrongfully or by duress, agent personally liable to repay, 97, 298, 300, 301.
agent must repay, if paid to him by mistake and not paid over, 97—99, 298, 300.
agent ought not to pay into his own account, 91, 93, 146, 148.
money received by way of a bribe is deemed to be, 139, 140.
right of principal to follow, 140, 145—148, 213, 219.
money raised by wrongful pledge may be treated as, 99.
duty of agent to take reasonable care of, 93, 96.
liability of agent to attachment for default in payment of, 142, 143 note (*p*).
received by agent to use of third persons, liability of agent to account to third persons for, 301—303.
paid by agent under a mistake of fact, agent may sue in own name for recovery of, 310.
on principal's behalf, principal may sue for recovery of, 222—224.
received by sub-agent, liability of agent for, 143, 144.
deposited with agent as stakeholder, agent personally liable to account for, 298, 299.
received by agent when acting within apparent authority is deemed to be received by principal, 250, 251.
authority to pay, to third persons, when revocable, 321—324, 331.
to use, for illegal purpose, when revocable, 97, 331.

MORTGAGE by client to solicitor, duty of good faith, right to costs, &c., 109.

MUTUAL DEALINGS,
between underwriter and broker, right of set-off, 127.
between agent and third persons, no right to set up against principal, 241, 242.
authority given in course of, not revoked by act of bankruptcy until notice, 327, 328.

NECESSARIES,
implied authority of wife to pledge husband's credit for: *see* MARRIED WOMAN.
child no implied authority to pledge parent's credit for, 27.
supplied to widow without notice of husband's death, 293, 333.
what are, is a question of fact, 15, 19.

NECESSITY, authority of, 22.

NEGLIGENCE. *see* DUTIES OF AGENT.
liability of agent to principal for, 94—97, 128—139.
what is actionable, in the case of a paid agent, 130.
an unpaid agent, 96, 129, 134, 135.
only liable for legal damage proximately caused by, 133, 134.
when authorized to do an imprudent act, 129, 133.
when he follows usage of business, 94, 95, 129, 131, 132.

NEGLIGENCE—*continued.*
liability of agent to principal for—*continued.*
when he strictly follows instructions, 129.
in matters of pure discretion, 129, 132.
agent to purchase business not examining takings, 94.
agent for sale (broker) selling below value, 131.
auctioneer permitting purchaser to go away without paying deposit, 132.
not liable when acting as arbitrator, 95.
liability of insurance broker for, 94, 95, 132, 138.
solicitor for, 135, 136, 138 *see* SOLICITOR.
counsel not liable for, 128.
of sub-agent, liability of agent for, 143, 144.
of agent, liability of principal to third persons for, 247—250, 254, 256: *see* WRONGS.
effect of, on right of agent to remuneration and indemnity, 166—168, 176, 179.
measure of damages for, 137—139 *see* MEASURE OF DAMAGES.
damages for, cannot be passed in taking an account, 113.
does not affect the title of persons taking negotiable securities, 212.

NEGOTIABLE INSTRUMENTS *see* BILL OF EXCHANGE, NOTES.
authority to bind principal by, 51, 55, 56, 60, 61, 82, 206, 211.
effect of signature "per procuration," 218.
directors can only bind company by, when necessary or usual in ordinary course of the business, 210.
dealings by agent with, how far principal bound by, 212, 213, 219.
effect of restrictive indorsement, 219.
lien of agent on, not affected by rights of third persons, unless agent has notice, 188, 190, 191.
signed by agent, liability of principal on, 210, 226—228: *see* BILL OF EXCHANGE.
personal liability of agent on, 278—281, 283 *see* BILL OF EXCHANGE.
construction of signature of agent on, 226.

NON-DISCLOSURE of material facts by principal or agent, 236, 237.

NOTES,
contract, omission by stockbroker to send, does not preclude him from recovering commission, 165.
for sale of banking shares should contain the numbers of the shares or name of the proprietor, 174.
broker's bought and sold, form a binding contract if they agree, 228.
promissory, signature is essential to liability on, 226—228, 280, 281.
signed by directors, liability of company on, 210.
directors on, 280, 281.
agent, liability of agent on, 278—281, 283.

NOTICE,
to agent, of facts material to and in course of employment, operates as notice to principal, 237, 241, 264, 265.
except where there is a strong probability that agent will conceal, 264, 265.
of facts not material to, or not in course of employment, is not notice to principal, 264, 266.
when notice to purchaser for value, 267.
must generally be in course of same transaction to bind principal, 266, 267.

NOTICE—*continued.*
to directors, when notice to the company, 265, 266.
to solicitor of incumbrances, when notice to client, 265—267.
that agent is exceeding his authority, 218, 219.
of revocation, when necessary, to third persons, 16, 17, 328, 329, 332, 333.
acts done in pursuance of power of attorney without, 333.
to quit, ratification of, 40, 46.
to rent collector or manager of estate, 59, 60.

OFFICERS, PUBLIC: *see* PUBLIC AGENT.

OVERDRAFT, general lien of banker for: *see* BANKER.

PARAMOUNT TITLE. *see* ESTOPPEL; INTERPLEAD.

PARENT, liability of, for necessaries ordered by children, 28.

PAROL EVIDENCE: *see* EVIDENCE.

PART PAYMENT by agent interrupts Statute of Limitations, 263.

PART PERFORMANCE, no damages for breach of warranty of authority on ground of, 294, 297.

PARTIAL EXECUTION of authority by agent, 155, 160, 162, 163, 331.

PARTNERS, implied agency of, 10 note (*l*), 211.

PATENT, infringement of, by agent, liability of principal for, 246.

PATENT AGENT, duty of, to know the practice relating to issue of patents, 95.

PAYMENT,
by third persons to agent, when principal bound by, 238—245.
ought to be in cash, 68, 90, 131, 244.
by cheque, when principal bound by, 51, 90, 131, 244.
by bill of exchange, when principal bound by, 52, 71, 131, 208, 244, 245 note (*m*).
by way of set-off, not binding on principal, 52, 68, 70, 85, 239, 243, 245.
unless agent held out as principal, 238, 240.
custom to receive, by way of set-off, unreasonable, 68, 245.
before expiration of credit, when principal bound by, 51, 70, 244.
by delivery of other goods, 60.
of premiums after expiration of time for payment, 60, 239.
where he is held out as principal, 238—240.
where he has a lien as against the principal, 239, 243.
when acting within apparent scope of authority operates as a payment to the principal, 250, 251.
by third persons to principal, how far a defence to action by agent in own name, 307—309.
by principal to agent, how far binding on third persons, 192, 233—235.
by agent in pursuance of power of attorney after revocation, 333, 334.
to person apparently authorized to receive payment, 221, 222.
implied authority to receive, 60, 63, 69, 70, 73, 74.

PENALTIES incurred by agent, liability of principal for, 245 note (*o*).

PER PROCURATION, effect of signature, 218, 218 note (*c*).

PERSONAL LIABILITY OF AGENT *see* AGENT.

PILOT, liability of shipowner for negligence of, 254.

PLEDGE,
- what words in a power of attorney give authority to, 56.
- factors and other agents for sale have no implied authority to, 64, 69, 121.
- authority to discount gives no power to, 71.
- wrongful, by factor, principal may adopt if he pleases, 99.
- of negotiable instruments, binding if pledgee takes in good faith, 212, 219.
- by mercantile agent in possession of goods or documents of title, 213—217 *see* FACTORS ACT.
- definition of, for purposes of Factors Act, 214 note (*n*).
- of jewellery to pawnbroker not protected by Factors Act, 217.
- wrongful, by agent does not transfer agent's lien, 218.

POLICY *see* INSURANCE POLICY.

POSSESSION,
- of property by agent as such, is deemed to be possession by principal, 99—101.
  - principal may acquire prescriptive title by, 100, 101.
- right of agent to interplead in respect of chattels in his, 201—203.
- of goods or documents of title by mercantile agent, 213—217 *see* FACTORS ACT.
- sale of goods by agent permitted to have, 220.
- settlement with and set-off against agent permitted to have, 239, 240.

POWER OF ATTORNEY,
- construction of general words in, 54, 55.
- operative part of, is controlled by the recitals, 54.
- is construed as including all medium powers necessary for effective execution, 55.
- execution of deed in pursuance of a, 91, 225, 226.
- may be irrevocable in favour of purchasers for value, 324, 325 *see* REVOCATION.
- revocation of *see* REVOCATION, BANKRUPTCY.
- may be revoked verbally, 330.
- acts done in pursuance of, after revocation, 333.

PREMIUMS *see* INSURANCE AGENT; INSURANCE BROKER.

PRESCRIPTION, possession by agent, as such, is deemed to be possession by the principal for purposes of, 99—101.

PRINCIPAL · *see* UNDISCLOSED PRINCIPAL.
- bankruptcy of *see* BANKRUPTCY.
- constructive notice to, 264—267 *see* NOTICE.
- estoppel of · *see* ESTOPPEL, HOLDING OUT.
- foreign *see* FOREIGN PRINCIPAL.
- **liability of, to agent,** 149 *et seq.*
  - for remuneration, 149—168. *see* REMUNERATION.
  - for breach of the contract of agency, 159—163: *see* REMUNERATION.
  - for expenses and liabilities incurred by agent, 169—179 *see* REIMBURSEMENT; INDEMNITY.

PRINCIPAL—*continued.*

liability of, to agent—*continued.*
to account in equity, 203.
on contracts made by agent on his behalf, 204.

RELATIONS OF, WITH THIRD PERSONS, 205 *et seq.*

how far bound by acts of agent, 205 *et seq.* *see* ADMISSIONS, REPRESENTATIONS.
all acts in course of employment and within scope of apparent authority, 17. 53, 54, 205—209, 220—222.
notwithstanding express instructions or private arrangement with respect to persons having no notice, 206, 207, 220, 221.
not bound by acts not done in course of employment, 209.
or beyond scope of actual and apparent authority, 209—211.
or done by agent for his own purposes, 209.
or in excess of actual authority, with respect to persons with notice, 17, 218, 219.
dealings by agent with money and negotiable securities, 212, 213.
dispositions protected by the Factors Act, 213—217 *see* FACTORS ACT.

liability of, to third persons—
on contracts made by agent on his behalf, 222 *et seq.*
may be sued in own name, whether disclosed or undisclosed, except where he is a foreigner, 222—224.
parol evidence admissible to charge him, where undisclosed, 222—224.
effect of special rules or customs, 229 *see* CUSTOMS.
how far liability affected by credit being given to agent, 230—232.
judgment being obtained against agent, 230, 232.
not liable if other contracting party elects to give exclusive credit to agent, 230—232 *see* ELECTION.
liability not affected by state of accounts between himself and agent, 231.
not discharged by settling with his agent unless reasonably induced to do so by conduct of creditor, 233—235.
effect of delay in applying to principal for the debt, 233—235.
on deeds executed by agent on his behalf, 225, 226.
on bills, notes and cheques, 226—228 *see* BILL OF EXCHANGE; NEGOTIABLE INSTRUMENTS.
for agent's wrongs, 245 *et seq.* *see* WRONGS.
for penalties incurred by agent, 245 note (*o*).
for misapplication by agent of money or property, 250, 251.

rights of, against third persons,
on contracts made by agent on his behalf, 222 *et seq.*
to sue in own name, whether disclosed or undisclosed, except where he is a foreigner, 222—224.
effect of particular rules or customs, 229, 230.
where contract to be partly performed by agent, 236.
effect of agent accepting bills for amount due under the contract, 236.
defences available where principal sues, 236—245.
defendant may set up fraud, &c., of either principal or agent, 236—238, 258, 259.
how far principal bound by payment to, or settlement with, or set-off against, the agent, 238—245 *see* PAYMENT; SET-OFF.
to sue in own name in respect of money paid on his behalf, 222—224.
on deeds executed on his behalf, 225—226.

PRINCIPAL—*continued.*

rights of, against agent, 88 *et seq.*, 126 *et seq.* · *see* Duties of Agent, Agent.

right of, to follow money and property as against the agent's trustee in bankruptcy and creditors, 144—148.

PRIVATE CONTRACT, auctioneer no implied authority to sell by, 64, 72.

PRIVATE INSTRUCTIONS do not bind third persons who have no notice of them, 206, 207, 221.

PRIVITY OF CONTRACT,

when there is, between principal and sub-agent, 83—87.

none between client and town agent, 86.

PROCEEDS,

of goods sold on principal's behalf, lien of agent on, 183, 190: *see* Lien.

of money or property of principal, right of principal to follow, 144—148, 213.

PROFITS: *see* Secret Profits.

PROMISE TO PAY by agent, when binding on principal, 26, 262, 263.

PROMISSORY NOTES · *see* Notes.

PROMOTERS,

company cannot ratify contracts made by, before incorporation, 37

are personally liable on contracts made on behalf of future company, 289.

are not permitted to make secret profits in dealing with the company, 117 note (*o*).

gifts by, to directors or officers must be accounted for to the company, 117—119.

PROOF, BURDEN OF · *see* Burden of Proof.

PROPERTY,

of principal, ought to be kept separate by agent, 91, 120.

rights of principal where agent mixes with his own, 92, 145, 148.

agent, whether paid or not, must take reasonable care of, 93, 96, 121, 134.

in possession of agent is deemed, as evidence and for acquisition of title, to be in possession of principal, 99—101.

agent must not purchase, without full disclosure, 108, 109.

liability of agent for dealing with, after act of bankruptcy by principal, 317, 328.

criminal liability of agent for fraudulent dealing with, 143 note (*p*).

lien of agent on, 180—200 · *see* Lien.

agent who purchases, as such, in own name, is a trustee, 106.

received by way of a bribe is received to principal's use, 139, 140.

of bankrupt, conveyance of, before receiving order, 329.

PROSPECTIVE COMMISSION, right of agent to prove in voluntary winding-up for, 162, 163.

PROTEST, liability of agent to repay money paid to him under, 301.

PUBLIC AGENT,
is not liable to be sued on contracts made on behalf of the government or of a foreign state, 270, 271.
or for money due from him as a public agent, 270, 271.
is liable if he expressly pledges his personal credit, 270—272.
is not liable to a member of any foreign state for any act authorized or ratified by the Crown, 35, 47, 312.

PUBLIC AUTHORITIES are liable for negligence of their agents in the execution of public works, 247: *see* WRONGS.

PUBLIC-HOUSE, implied authority of manager of, 60, 210.

PURCHASE, AGENT FOR: *and see* AGENT; DUTIES OF AGENT; CUSTOM.
must not sell his own goods to principal without full disclosure, 67, 103—106, 116.
must make a full disclosure if he acquires any benefit from the transaction, 103—105.
of business, duty of, to examine takings, 94.
liability of, to account for any secret profit, 116: *but see* 119, 120.
who buys and takes a conveyance in own name is a trustee for principal, 30, 31, 106.
must not accept gifts from the vendor, 140.
cannot sue principal as for goods sold or for non-acceptance, 204.
liability of principal for misappropriation by, 208, 211, 221.
of smuggled goods, or of shares in illegal company, no right of indemnity. 176, 177.

PURCHASE-MONEY, receipt of, by solicitor or agent for sale of estate, 59, 73, 74.

PURCHASER FOR VALUE,
constructive notice to, 267.
of property, after act of bankruptcy by vendor, 328, 329.
power of attorney may be irrevocable in favour of, 324, 325.

QUANTUM MERUIT *see* REMUNERATION.
right of agent to a, 150, 160, 163, 167.
cannot recover a, when there is an express contract or custom inconsistent therewith, 151, 152.

RAILWAY COMPANY,
implied authority of general manager of, 60.
servants of, 61, 62.
liability of, for false imprisonment and assaults by servants, 249, 253.
how far bound by admissions by servants, 262.

RATIFICATION,
doctrine of, 34 *et seq.*
is equivalent to previous authority, 34, 41, 47.
by the government, effect of, 35, 47.
applies to torts as well as contracts and other acts, 35, 43, 47.
cannot ratify an act void in its inception, *e.g.*, a forgery, 35.
by corporations and companies, 36, 37, 41, 44, 47.
cannot ratify an act which is *ultra vires*, 36.
or a contract made before incorporation, 37.
by directors, when binding, 44, 45.
who may ratify, 37, 38.
only the person on whose behalf the act was done, 37.
where unascertained at the time of the act, 37, 38, 100.

RATIFICATION—*continued.*
insurance policy may be ratified after loss of the property, 38, 40, 48.
of contract, after notice of withdrawal of offer, 39, 41.
after refusal to recognize it, 40.
of act *primâ facie* wrongful, 39, 41, 47, 313.
cannot operate to divest rights *in rem* vested in third persons, 39, 40, 47, 49.
conditions necessary for, 41—43.
must be founded on full knowledge, 41—43.
may be express or implied, 43.
what is sufficient evidence of, 42, 43, 45, 46, 227
may be implied from mere acquiescence, 43, 45, 46.
adoption of part of a transaction operates as a ratification of the whole, 44, 45.
of written contract may be verbal or by conduct, 44.
of a deed must be under seal (probably), 44.
by husband of wife's contracts, 46.
effect of, 46—49.
gives no new authority, 47.
discharges agent from liability for exceeding authority, 48.
renders principal liable for commission, indemnity, &c., 48, 49.

RECEIPT,
of money by agent when acting within apparent scope of authority is a receipt by the principal, 250, 251.
given by an agent fraudulently for goods not received, principal not bound by, 256.

RECEIVING ORDER: *see* BANKRUPTCY.

REFUSAL,
by principal to complete transaction, right of agent to damages for, 159—163.
by agent to deliver up goods to true owner may amount to a conversion, 314, 315, 317, 318.

REGISTERED OWNER of ship not necessarily liable on master's contracts, 75.

REGULATIONS of Stock Exchange *see* STOCKBROKER, CUSTOM.

REIMBURSEMENT, 169 *et seq.* *see* INDEMNITY.
implied contract to reimburse agent all expenses properly incurred in execution of his authority, 169—171.
of costs incurred in bringing or defending actions, 171.
of expenses incurred under special rules and customs, 172.
agent not entitled to, in respect of any apparently illegal transaction, 175—177
of any gaming or wagering transaction, 176, 177.
of any unauthorized act or transaction, 176, 178.
agent not entitled to, of any expenses incurred in consequence of his own insolvency, breach of duty, or default, 168, 176, 179.

REMOTE, damages too, 133, 134, 296, 297.

REMUNERATION, 149 *et seq.* *see* QUANTUM MERUIT.
right of agent to, is founded on an express or implied contract, 149—152.
where express contract for, no contract inconsistent therewith will be implied, 149, 151, 152.

REMUNERATION—*continued.*
ambiguity in express contract may be explained by custom, 149.
or provisions which are not inconsistent may be added, 150, 152.
where no express contract, the right to and amount of, depends on usage, 119, 150—152, 159.
when a contract to pay, will be implied, 151.
may be payable though the transaction goes off, 152, 156—159.
commission is only payable on business resulting directly from the agency, 152—156.
may be payable though the agent is not acting at the time of the completion of the transaction, 153—155.
what is sufficient connection between the introduction and the transaction, 154, 155.
may be payable on business resulting wholly after employment ceased, 153, 156.
when payable, 157—159.
may be payable though the principal acquire no benefit, 156—159.
of auctioneer, 151, 154, 155, 167, 168 · *see* AUCTIONEER.
of house and estate agents, 153—155.
of shipbroker, 152, 153, 165 : *see* SHIPBROKER.
of sub-agent, 85, 86.
for procuring loan, 154, 156, 157, 167.
of solicitor *see* SOLICITOR.
on transactions after death of principal, 167, 326.
principal liable in damages if he wrongfully prevents agent from earning, 159—163.
measure of damages for, 160, 162.
voluntary winding-up may operate as a wrongful dismissal, 162, 163.
right of agent to, when authority revoked after partial execution, 160, 162, 163.
agent cannot recover, unless legally qualified, 164, 165.
in respect of any obviously illegal, or any gaming or wagering transaction, 164, 165.
or in respect of any unauthorized transaction, unless ratified, 46, 48, 49, 166, 167
or in respect of any transaction in violation of the fiduciary character of the relationship, even if adopted, 166, 167.
effect of misconduct or negligence on right of, 166—168.

RENT COLLECTOR has no implied authority to receive a notice to quit, 60.

REPAIRS,
implied authority of shipmaster to pledge owner's credit for, 76.
to hypothecate ship or cargo for, 77.
to sell part of cargo for, 78, 79.

REPORT by agent to principal cannot be used as evidence against the principal by third persons, 261, 263.

REPRESENTATIONS. *see* ADMISSIONS; MISREPRESENTATIONS; HOLDING OUT.
by agent, estoppel of principal by, 208, 263.
by secretary, how far binding on company, 211, 263.
by auctioneer, how far binding on principal, 211.

REPUTED OWNER. *see* BANKRUPTCY.

RES JUDICATA, defence of, by principal, where judgment against agent, 230, 232.

RESERVE, sale without, auctioneer must accept highest *bonâ fide* bid at a, 90, 123.

RESPONDENTIA
bond, validity of, depends on law of flag, 75.
implied authority of shipmaster to give, 77.

RESTRICTIVE INDORSEMENT, effect of, 219.

REVOCATION of authority, 320 *et seq.*
when irrevocable, 320—324.
where given to effectuate a security, 320.
where coupled with an interest, 321—323.
where agent incurs personal liability, 321, 324.
powers of attorney, in favour of purchasers for value, 324, 325.
authority to pay money to third person, when revocable, 321, 323, 324, 331.
in respect of illegal transaction, when revocable, 97, 331.
to the winner of a wager, when revocable, 324, 331.
after partial execution, 170, 178, 330, 331.
right of agent to remuneration in case of, 155, 160, 163.
of agency for fixed term, right of agent to damages on, 161, 162.
where the agent has a lien or special property, 321—324.
by death or insanity, 167, 326, 333.
by bankruptcy of principal, 327—329 · *see* BANKRUPTCY.
acts done before date of receiving order, 328, 329.
by notice, 329—331.
authority by deed may be revoked by verbal notice, 330.
rights of third persons dealing with agent without notice of, 328, 329, 332, 333.
protection of agent acting in pursuance of power of attorney without notice of, 333.
right of agent to commission on business resulting after, 153, 155, 156, 167.

RIGHTS,
of agent against principal, 149 *et seq.* · *see* AGENT.
of principal against agent, 88 *et seq.*, 126 *et seq.* · *see* AGENT, DUTIES OF AGENT.
of agent against third persons, 303 *et seq.* · see AGENT.
of third persons against agent, 270 *et seq.* *see* AGENT.
of principal against third persons, 222 *et seq.* *see* PRINCIPAL.
of third persons against principal, 222 *et seq.* · *see* PRINCIPAL.

RULES of particular markets, how far binding: *see* STOCKBROKER; CUSTOM.

SAFE CUSTODY,
agent has no general lien on property left in his hands merely for, 185, 186.
liability of banker for loss of securities deposited for, 134.

SALARY: *see* REMUNERATION.

SALE, AGENT FOR: *see* FACTOR; BROKER; ESTATE AGENT.
of estate, no implied authority as such to receive purchase-money, 59.
implied authority of, 58, 64, 71.
to sell on credit, 51, 66, 69—71, 210.
to receive payment, 60, 69, 70.
not to barter or pledge, 64, 69.
warranty given by, 51, 58, 64, 66, 69, 71, 206: *see* WARRANTY.
must not buy himself, without full disclosure, 84, 104, 116, 123.
custom for, to buy himself, without notice to principal, is illegal, 68, 84, 106.
by auction: *see* AUCTIONEER.
must make a full disclosure where he takes any interest in the transaction, 105.
must not sell to a company in which he is a shareholder, without full disclosure, 105.
must account for all secret profits, 84, 116, 117.
misrepresentation or misdescription by, liability of principal for, 237, 246, 257, 259.
on *del credere* commission · *see* DEL CREDERE AGENT.
right of, to commission *see* REMUNERATION.
liability of, for delivering without payment, 131.
in possession of the goods or documents of title, 213—217, 220: *see* FACTORS ACT.

SALE OF GOODS ACT (1893), section 4: *see* STATUTE OF FRAUDS.
one contracting party cannot sign for the other so as to satisfy the, 5.
auctioneer or broker has implied authority to sign contract for both parties so as to satisfy the, 6, 11, 69, 71, 228.
authority to make a contract implies authority to sign so as to satisfy the, 57
authority to sign so as to satisfy the, may be given verbally, 30, 44.
verbal ratification of signature is sufficient to satisfy the, 34, 44.

SALVAGE AGREEMENTS, implied authority of shipmaster to make, 76.

SCRIP, fraudulent pledge of, by broker, 212.

SEAL, instrument under: *see* DEED, POWER OF ATTORNEY.

SECRET PROFITS,
what are, 115, 117, 119, 120.
acquired in course of agency, duty of agent to account for, 84, 103, 105, 114—120.
even if acting gratuitously, 116.
must account for highest value, 117—119.
liability of agent to pay interest on, 104, 119, 142.
duty of solicitor to account for, 104.
duty of directors and officers of companies to account for, 117—119.
duty of promoters of companies to account for, 117 note (*o*).

SECRETARY OF COMPANY,
must account to company for all secret profits and benefits acquired as such, 117.
liability of company for fraud by, 252, 255.
how far company bound by representations of, 211, 263.
liability of directors for money lent to, in excess of borrowing powers, 292.
not personally liable on promissory note signed as such, 281.
knowledge acquired by, privately, does not operate as notice to company, 266.

SECRETARY OF STATE, not liable personally on contracts made on behalf of the Crown, 271.

SECURITIES: see NEGOTIABLE INSTRUMENTS.
in hands of agent, right of principal to, on bankruptcy of agent, 145—147 see BANKRUPTCY.
deposited with banker, lien of banker on, 185, 186 see LIEN.

SECURITY, authority given by way of, is irrevocable, 320.

SEIZURE, WRONGFUL: see SHERIFF.

SERVICES, when a contract to pay for, will be implied, 149—152: see QUANTUM MERUIT, REMUNERATION.

SET-OFF,
by third person, as against principal, of debt due from agent, 238—243.
where agent held out as and believed to be the principal, 192, 238, 240, 242.
where agent permitted to have possession of goods or documents of title, 239, 240.
in the case of factors, 240, 241.
right of, is founded on the principle of estoppel, 241.
no right of, unless the agent was in fact believed to be the principal, 240—242.
by sub-agent, as against principal, of debt due from agent, 85, 192, 242.
by third person, as against agent, of debt due from principal, 307—309.
as against agent suing in own name, of debt due from him, 310.
by undisclosed principal, against third person, of debt due from agent, 231.
by agent against trustee in bankruptcy of principal, 171, 187, 190, 323.
by insurance broker against trustee in bankruptcy of underwriter, 126.
debts must be liquidated to constitute a right of, 241.
payment to agent by way of, does not bind principal. see PAYMENT.

SETTLED ACCOUNTS of agent will be reopened in cases of fraud, 112, 113.

SETTLEMENT. see PAYMENT.

SHAREHOLDER, though an agent, is liable as a contributory, 274.

SHARES, liability of agent who applies for, without authority, 295.

SHERIFF,
execution creditor cannot ratify acts of, as such, 37.
wrongful seizure by, liability of execution creditor for, 74, 247, 248, 252.
liability of solicitor for, 313, 314.

SHIPBROKER, right of, to commission, 152, 153, 165.

SHIPMASTER,
implied authority of, 74—80.
extent of, is governed by the law of the flag, 74.
to do what is necessary for prosecution of the voyage, 75.

SHIPMASTER—*continued.*
implied authority of—*continued.*
to contract for conveyance of merchandise, 75.
to enter into charter-party for owners, 75.
to make towage and salvage agreements, when necessary, 76.
to pledge owners' credit for necessary repairs and stores, 76.
when to borrow money on owners' credit, 76, 77.
when to give bottomry bonds, 77
when to give *respondentia* bonds, 77.
to sell the ship, in cases of urgent necessity, 78.
to sell a portion of cargo, if absolutely necessary for repairs, 78, 79.
no implied authority,
to sell the entire cargo, in any case, 78, 79.
to vary any contract made by the owners, 79.
to make any contract outside the scope of the voyage, 79.
to pledge the credit of any owner except his own principals, 75.
duty of, to give his whole time and account to owners for all profits made in course of employment, 116, 122.
liability of, for repairs and for seamen's wages, 276, 276 note (*h*).
negligence of, liability of owners for, 248, 248 note (*q*).
maritime lien of, for wages, disbursements, &c., 197.
priority of, 198.
surrender of, 199.
how enforced, 198.
possessory lien of, on cargo for freight and general average, 197.
signature of, on bill of lading, how far binding on owners, 79, 80.
validity of bottomry and *respondentia* bonds given by, depends on law of flag, 75.

SHIPOWNERS *see* SHIPMASTER.
not liable for negligence of compulsory pilot, 254.
not liable on master's contracts unless privy to his appointment, 75.
cannot sue on charter-party by deed in master's name, 225.
agreement between master and, does not affect liability of, for necessaries supplied without notice of the agreement, 221.

SIGNATURE *see* SALE OF GOODS ACT, STATUTE OF FRAUDS; TENTERDEN'S ACT.
is essential to liability on a bill, note, or cheque, 226 *see* BILL OF EXCHANGE, NEGOTIABLE INSTRUMENTS.
"per procuration," effect of, 218.
by agent without qualification, *primâ facie* personally liable, 127, 128, 281, 283, 284.

SKILL,
duty of agent to exercise due, 93—96.
paid agent is bound to exercise such, as is necessary for proper performance of his duties, 130, 168.
gratuitous agent is bound to exercise such, as he has, or has held himself out as having, 96, 129, 134.
liability of agent for want of, 128 *et seq.*: *see* NEGLIGENCE.

SOLE AGENT, meaning of, 161 note (*a*).

SOLICITOR,
implied authority of, 63—65, 73, 74.
to receive payment, 63, 73, 74.
to compromise action, or refer to arbitration, 63, 73, 74.
to abandon claims of client, 73.

SOLICITOR—*continued.*
implied authority of—*continued.*
to receive consideration for deed on its production receipted, 73.
to enter into undertaking, 73.
not to sign memorandum to satisfy Statute of Frauds, 64, 65, 74.
not to direct sheriff to seize particular goods, 74, 248, 252.
not to take special journeys or institute proceedings, 74.
duties of, 89, 123—125 *see* DUTIES OF AGENT.
to make full disclosure where he takes a personal interest, 103.
to insert all the usual clauses in deeds drafted by him in which he has an interest, 109, 125.
to account for all secret profits, 104.
to obey client's instructions notwithstanding counsel's advice to contrary, 89, 123.
to make a full disclosure and pay an adequate price if he purchases property of or contracts with a client, 104, 108, 110, 125.
not to accept any gift or remuneration from client beyond his legal costs, 111, 125.
to give his clients the benefit of his personal judgment and superintendence, 123.
to check useless litigation especially as between husband and wife, 124.
to keep secret all confidential communications and knowledge of client's affairs, 124.
not to act for opponent of his client or former client, 124.
to give reasonable notice when he intends to abandon a cause, and not to abandon it without reasonable ground, 125.
if he receives a deposit at a sale by auction, to pay it over to client on demand, 125, 299.
liability of,
for breach of duty, 130—132.
for negligence, 135, 136, 138.
not liable for a mere error of judgment or bad advice, 135.
ignorance of the rules of practice or procedure, 123, 136, 168.
to attachment for default in payment of money received as such, 143 note (*p*).
for negligence of town agent, 143.
on contracts made on behalf of client, 273, 276.
for expenses of witnesses, sheriff's fees, &c., 276.
for bringing or defending an action without authority, 293.
to repay money obtained wrongfully, though paid over to client, 300.
for concealing an incumbrance, 313.
for wrongful seizure by sheriff, 313, 314.
for money received by London agent, 87.
costs of,
in case of solicitor-mortgagee, 110.
not recoverable unless certificate in force, 164.
where he abandons action without reasonable cause, 167.
effect of breach of duty or negligence on right to recover, 167, 168, 179.
lien of,
general possessory lien by custom, 181, 185.
on books, &c. of joint stock companies, 189.
is restricted to the rights of the client, 189.
how extinguished, 199.

SOLICITOR—*continued.*
lien of—*continued.*
is confined to claims made by him as a solicitor, 184.
does not extend to client's original will, 185.
on property and money intrusted to him for specific purpose, 187, 188.
as between London agent and client of country solicitor, 86, 193.
charging lien of,
on property recovered or preserved through his instrumentality, 193—196.
only applies to proceedings in a court of justice, 194.
priority of, over garnishee order, 195.
attaches on property received by way of compromise, &c., 194.
is restricted to the rights of the client in the property, 195, 196.
agreements and conveyances intended to defeat, are void, 193, 196.
not entitled to, in respect of costs barred by Statute of Limitations, 194.
town agent has no right to, as such, 197.
admissions by, how far evidence against client, 263.
appointment of, by corporation should be under seal, 32, 33.
compromise by, client is bound by, though contrary to instructions, 206.
knowledge of, how far constructive notice to client, 265—267: *see* NOTICE.
London agent of, relations between client and, 86, 87.
negligence of, liability of client for, 247, 248.
notice to, how far constructive notice to client, 265—267: *see* NOTICE.
statements by, how far evidence against client, 263.
tender to, of debt for which he is instructed to sue, operates as a tender to client, 207.
town agent of, relations between client and, 86, 87.

SPECIAL AGENT,
definition of, and distinction between general and, 1.
implied authority of a, 57, 58.

SPECIFIC PURPOSE,
right of principal to follow money intrusted to agent for a, 144—148.
lien of agent on money or property intrusted to him for a, 181, 186, 187.
appropriation of money in hands of agent for a, 302.

SPECULATION: *see* STOCK EXCHANGE, STOCKBROKER, GAMING CONTRACTS.

STAKEHOLDER,
duty of auctioneer to hold deposit as a, 123.
liability of agent to account for and pay interest on money received as a, 142, 298, 299.
revocation of authority of a, 331.

STATE, officers of: *see* PUBLIC AGENT.

STATEMENTS by agent, how far evidence against principal, 260—263: *see* ADMISSIONS.

STATION MASTER, implied authority of, 61: *see* RAILWAY COMPANY.

STATUTE OF FRAUDS (29 Car. II. c. 3), 296, 297, 306.
signature to satisfy the 4th or 17th section of, must be that of a person expressly or impliedly authorized to sign a memorandum of the contract, 74, 82, 83.
auctioneer and his clerk have implied authority to sign for purchaser at sale by auction, 11, 71, 83.
authority to make a contract implies authority to sign for purposes of the, 57.
solicitor authorized to send a draft contract has no implied authority to sign for purposes of the, 64, 65, 74.
a party to a contract cannot sign as agent of another party for purposes of the, 5, 6, 12.
authority to sign for purposes of the, may be given verbally, 30.
signature for the purposes of the, may be ratified verbally or by conduct, 34, 44.
signature of broker or auctioneer binds both parties for purposes of the, 6, 11, 71, 83.
contract to sell on a *del credere* commission is not within the 4th section of, 3.
right of agent who purchases land in own name to plead the 7th section, 30, 31.

STATUTE OF LIMITATIONS,
acknowledgment in writing, or part payment by agent, of debt owing by principal interrupts the operation of the, 26, 262, 263.
does not run in favour of an agent in possession of land as such, 99—101.
right of agent to plead the, in an action by principal, 114, 140.
does not affect agent's lien, except a solicitor's charging lien, 194, 199.

STATUTES,
29 Car. II. c. 3 (Statute of Frauds) *see* STATUTE OF FRAUDS.
9 Geo. IV c. 14 (Lord Tenterden's Act) *see* TENTERDEN'S ACT.
8 & 9 Vict. c. 106 (Real Property Amendment), 30, 296.
8 & 9 Vict. c. 109 (Gaming and Wagering), 98, 164, 165.
17 & 18 Vict. c. 104 (Merchant Shipping), 197.
18 & 19 Vict. c. 111 (Bills of Lading), 79, 80.
19 & 20 Vict. c. 97 (Mercantile Law Amendment), 8, 26, 262.
23 & 24 Vict. c. 126 (Common Law Procedure), 201.
23 & 24 Vict. c. 127 (Solicitors' Charging Lien), 194.
24 & 25 Vict. c. 96 (Larceny Act), 143.
30 Vict. c. 29 (Leeman's Act) *see* LEEMAN'S ACT.
32 & 33 Vict. c. 62 (Debtors Act), 143.
44 & 45 Vict. c. 41 (Conveyancing Act, 1881): *see* CONVEYANCING ACTS.
45 & 46 Vict. c. 39 (Conveyancing Act, 1882): *see* CONVEYANCING ACTS.
c. 61 (Bills of Exchange), 212, 218, 226, 278—280.
c. 75 (Married Women's Property), 13.
46 & 47 Vict. c. 52 (Bankruptcy Act) *see* BANKRUPTCY ACT, 1883.
51 & 52 Vict. c. 59 (Trustee Act, 1888), 14.
52 & 53 Vict. c. 45 (Factors Act) *see* FACTORS ACT.
c. 46 (Merchant Shipping), 197.
53 & 54 Vict. c. 39 (Partnership), 10.
55 Vict. c. 9 (Gaming) *see* GAMING ACT, 1892.
56 & 57 Vict. c. 53 (Trustee Act, 1893), 7, 73.
c. 71 (Sale of Goods) *see* SALE OF GOODS ACT.
57 & 58 Vict. c. 60 (Merchant Shipping), 197
58 & 59 Vict. c. 25 (Mortgagees' Legal Costs), 110.

STEWARD, a, has no implied authority, as such, to grant leases, 60.

STOCK EXCHANGE: *see* STOCKBROKER; CUSTOM.
rules and customs of, how far binding on principal, 66, 67, 170, 173—175, 229, 230.
custom for broker to buy from or sell to himself without notice to principal is unreasonable, 68, 103, 106.
custom for brokers to settle by way of set-off is unreasonable, 52, 68, 245.
custom to ignore Leeman's Act is unreasonable, 121, 175.
usage of the, does not affect the right of an undisclosed principal to sue in his own name, 230.
speculation, question for the jury whether gaming or wagering transactions, 165, 178.

STOCKBROKER *see* STOCK EXCHANGE, CUSTOM.
has implied authority to act on reasonable usages and customs of the market in which he deals, 66, 67, 70.
to close the principal's account on his failure to duly pay differences, or on his death or insolvency, 70, 174, 175.
no implied authority to sell on credit, 51, 71, 90, 210.
or to receive payment by way of set-off, 52, 68.
duties of, 90, 121, 122.
to comply with statutory provisions in making contracts, 121, 175.
to send contract note to his principal, 165.
omission to send note does not make the contract illegal, 165.
not to buy his own shares nor sell to himself, without full disclosure, 68, 103, 106.
to account for all profits acquired in course of agency, 116.
general lien of, 181, 190.
right of, to indemnity against losses and liabilities incurred under reasonable rules and customs of the Stock Exchange, 170, 173—175.
though he does not make separate contracts for each principal, 170.
no right of indemnity against losses paid without authority, 178.
or losses caused by his own default or insolvency, 179.
or in respect of wagering transactions, 165, 176, 177.
liability of, for not complying with Leeman's Act, 138.
fraudulent pledge of scrip by, 212.

STOPPAGE IN TRANSITU,
unauthorized, by agent cannot be ratified after arrival of the goods, 40.
agent who renders himself personally liable has a right of, 200.
agent's possessory lien cannot be revived by, 200.

SUB-AGENT. *see* DELEGATION.
is generally answerable only to his own employer, 83—85, 138.
may be privity of contract between principal and, if appointed with his consent and knowledge, 83, 84.
right of, to commission or remuneration from principal, 49, 85, 86.
ratification by principal of the acts of, 49.
acts of, are not binding on principal unless appointed with his express or implied authority, 84.
liability of, to account for secret profits, 84.
set-off as against principal, right of, 85, 192, 242.
lien of, as against principal, 86, 191, 192.
money received and wrongs committed by, liability of agent for, 143, 144, 318.

SUBSTITUTE: *see* DELEGATION, SUB-AGENT.

TENDER to agent, when deemed to be a tender to principal, 63, 207.

TENTERDEN'S ACT, signature of an agent does not satisfy, even if expressly ratified, 8, 260, 262 note (*k*).

THIRD PERSONS,
- rights of, against agent, 270 *et seq.* · *see* AGENT.
- liabilities of, to agent, 303 *et seq.*. *see* AGENT.
- rights of, against principal, 222 *et seq.* · *see* PRINCIPAL.
- liabilities of, to principal, 222 *et seq.* · *see* PRINCIPAL.
- are entitled to act on apparent scope of agent's authority if they have no notice of actual authority, 17, 53, 54, 205—208, 220—222, 250, 251.
- are not affected by private instructions given to agent, or by arrangements between principal and agent, unless they have notice thereof, 206, 207, 220, 221.
- dealing with a person on the faith of his being held out as an agent are in the same position as if he were duly authorized, 219—223.
- dealing with mercantile agent in possession of goods or documents of title, 213—217. *see* FACTORS ACT.
- agent must not set up rights of, against principal, 96—102: *but see* INTERPLEAD.
- effect of ratification on the rights of · *see* RATIFICATION.
- misrepresentations by agent as to character of, principal not liable for, 260.
- liability of agent to, in respect of money received to their use, 301—303.
- dealing with agent without notice of revocation of authority, 328, 329, 332, 333.

TITLE,
- possession by agent, as such, is deemed to be possession by principal as evidence of, 99—101.
- principal may acquire a prescriptive, by means of agent's possession, though the agent be the true owner, 99—101.
- of principal, when agent is permitted to dispute, 96—102: *see* INTERPLEAD.

TORTS: *see* WRONGS.

TOWAGE, implied authority of shipmaster to make agreements as to, 75.

TRAMWAY COMPANY,
- how far bound by secretary's representations, 211, 263.
- liability of, for assaults and false imprisonment by servants, 249, 250, 253.

TRANSITU, STOPPAGE IN: *see* STOPPAGE IN TRANSITU.

TRAVELLER for sale of goods, implied authority of, to receive payment, 60.

TRESPASS,
- by agent, liability of principal for, 247—249, 252.
  - of agent for, 314.
- distinction between "case" and, 246 note (*v*), 313, 314.

TROVER: *see* CONVERSION.

TRUSTEE,
right of, to act through an agent, 7 note (*u*).
agent of, cannot purchase the trust property, 104, 108.
has no lien on the trust property, 189.
who assists in a breach of trust is personally liable, 313.
agent who purchases land as such, and takes a conveyance in own name, is a, 30, 31, 106.
agent permitted to retain money for investment is a, 92.

TURF COMMISSION AGENT,
must pay over winnings though he cannot sue for losses, 98, 176.
is not liable for neglecting to make bets, 133.

ULTRA VIRES,
a corporation or company cannot authorize or ratify any act which is, 4, 36, 50, 253.
personal liability of directors for acts which are, 291, 292.

UNAUTHORIZED ACTS · *see* FACTORS ACT; WRONGS.
principal may be bound by, if within scope of apparent authority, 205—208, 220—222.
are not binding on principal with respect to persons with notice, 218, 219.
ratification of: *see* RATIFICATION.
agent not entitled to remuneration, reimbursement, or indemnity, in respect of, unless ratified, 166, 167, 176, 178, 179.
liability of agent to third persons in respect of: *see* WARRANTY OF AUTHORITY.

UNDERTAKING,
agent is bound to perform an, for valuable consideration, but not a gratuitous, 88.
agent is entitled to remuneration as soon as he has substantially performed his, 156—159.

UNDERWRITERS: *see* INSURANCE BROKER.
settlement with broker by way of set-off does not discharge, 52, 68, 245.
not bound, if broker underwrites in excess of his limit, 210, 211.
broker personally liable to, for premiums, 99, 126.
right of broker to set-off losses against premiums on bankruptcy of, 126.

UNDISCLOSED PRINCIPAL: *see* PRINCIPAL.
is bound by all acts within scope of agent's apparent authority, 207.
rights and liabilities of, on contracts made by agent, 222 *et seq.*
may sue or be sued in own name, except in the case of foreigners, and on bills, notes, and cheques, 222—228, 236.
effect on liability of, of giving credit to agent, 230—233. *see* ELECTION.
of obtaining judgment against agent, 230, 232.
of state of accounts between self and agent, 231.
of payment to or settlement with agent, 233—235.
right of, to sue in own name, how far affected by special customs, 229, 230.
may sue in own name for return of money paid by agent on his behalf, 224.
defences available against, when suing on agent's contract, 236—245.

UNDISCLOSED PRINCIPAL—*continued.*
how far bound by settlement with, or set-off against, agent, 238—245 *see* PAYMENT, SET-OFF.
broker who sells for, has implied authority to receive payment, 70.
auctioneer who sells for, is personally liable on the contract, 274, 275.
agent who contracts for, may be personally liable by special custom, 286, 287 *see* AGENT.

UNDUE INFLUENCE · *see* DUTIES OF AGENT.

UNINCORPORATED COMPANIES, powers of directors and agents of, 61.

UNPAID AGENT. *see* GRATUITOUS UNDERTAKING.

USAGE: *see* CUSTOM.

VALIDITY,
of transactions between principal and agent, 107—110.
of gifts by principal to agent and solicitor to client, 107, 110, 111.
of bonds given by shipmaster depends on the law of the flag, 75.

VALUABLE CONSIDERATION · *see* PURCHASER FOR VALUE.
dealings by agent with negotiable instruments for, 212, 213.
authority given for, when irrevocable, 321—325.

VOID OR VOIDABLE CONTRACT, agent must pay over money received under a, 96—98.

VOLUNTARY WINDING-UP of company may operate as a wrongful dismissal, 162, 163.

WAGER *see* GAMING CONTRACTS.
authority to pay money to winner of, when revocable, 324, 331.

WAGES, maritime lien of shipmaster for, 197—199 · *see* REMUNERATION.

WARRANTY,
given by agent for sale, when principal bound by, 58, 64, 66, 69, 206.
must be given at the time of the sale, 51.
auctioneer has no implied authority to give a, 71.
agent merely to deliver goods has no implied authority to give a, 58.
agent employed to discount a bill has implied authority to give a, 58, 71.

WARRANTY OF AUTHORITY, 289 *et seq.*
implied whenever a person represents that he has authority to act as an agent, 289—293.
by person assuming to contract as an agent, 290—293.
does not extend to an innocent misrepresentation as to a mere question of law, 291.
by directors borrowing in excess of borrowing powers, 291, 292.
by person signing a bill of exchange as an agent, 292, 293.
liable for breach of, though acting in good faith, 290—292.
effect of ratification on liability for breach of, 48.
measure of damages for breach of, 293—297.
where contract repudiated as unauthorized, 294—296.
costs of action against principal, 295—297
where the contract would not have been enforceable at law even if authorized, 294, 297.
where shares applied for without authority, 295.
loss must be a reasonable or probable consequence of the breach, 296, 297.

WHARFINGER,
estoppel of, from disputing title of the person in whose name he holds goods, 101.
interpleader by, when adverse claims are made, 202, 203.
has a general lien by custom, 181.

WIDOW, necessaries supplied to, without notice of husband's death, 293, 333.

WIFE,
implied authority of, to pledge husband's credit: *see* MARRIED WOMAN.
liability of husband for fraudulent misrepresentations by, 257.
for torts of, during coverture, 246 note (*r*).

WINDING-UP,
voluntary, may operate as a wrongful dismissal, 162, 163.
effect of, on lien upon property of the company, 183, 189, 190.

WINNINGS, liability of turf commission agent to pay over, is not affected by Gaming Act, 98.

WITHOUT RESERVE, SALE, auctioneer must accept highest *bonâ fide* bid at a, 90.

WRITING,
not necessary for *del credere* commission, 3.
not necessary for appointment of agent to sign written contract, 30, 44.
acknowledgment of debt must be in, to interrupt Statute of Limitations, 26, 262.
parol evidence, when admissible to vary or explain contract in, 224, 285—287.
construction of contracts made by agent in, 281—285.

WRONGFUL ACT: *see* WRONGS.
is not justified by agency, 7, 8.
agent cannot claim indemnity or reimbursement in respect of a, 8, 175—177.
agent is personally liable to repay money obtained by a, 96, 298, 300, 301.
lien cannot be acquired or transferred by a, 181, 184, 218.
ratification of, 39, 41, 43, 47, 313.
agent is not permitted to take advantage of his own, 139.

WRONGFUL DISMISSAL: *see* DISMISSAL.

WRONGS: *see* WRONGFUL ACT.
by agent, liability of principal to third persons for, 245 *et seq.*
where committed in ordinary course of employment on his behalf or with his authority, 245—250.
no defence that the wrong is a felony, 246 note (*s*).
not liable if outside ordinary course of employment and unauthorized, 251—254.
nor when agent not acting on his behalf, 252, 254.
how far liable for fraud and other intentional wrongs, 255—258.
only if committed on his behalf and for his benefit, 255—258.

WRONGS—*continued.*

by agent, liability of principal to third persons for—*contd.*

fraud, 250—252, 255—257.

misrepresentation, 246, 252, 253, 257—260.

negligence, 247—250, 254, 256.

trespass, 247—249, 252.

assault, 249, 250, 252, 256.

criminal punishment of agent does not affect liability of principal, 250 note (*m*).

arrest and false imprisonment, 249, 253, 254.

wrongful distress, 246.

conversion, 247

infringement of patent, 246.

misappropriation of money or property, 250, 251.

liability of corporations and companies for, 247, 256, 257

where the act is *ultra vires*, 253.

malicious wrongs, 247.

liability of railway and tramway companies for assault and false imprisonment by servants, 249, 250, 253.

liability of agent to third persons for, 311 *et seq.*

personally liable, whether authorized or not, 311—314.

for conversion, where acting in good faith, 314—318 *see* CONVERSION.

distinction between "trespass" and "case," 313, 314.

acts authorized or ratified by the government, 312.

by co-agent or sub-agent, agent not liable to third persons for, 318.

C. F. ROWORTH, PRINTER, GREAT NEW STREET, FETTER LANE.